RETRAINING COGNITION

Techniques and Applications

Rick Parenté, PhD
Professor of Psychology
Towson State University
Towson, Maryland

Adjunct Associate Professor of Physiology
University of Maryland–Dental School
Baltimore, Maryland

Neuropsychological Consultant
Maryland Rehabilitation Center
Baltimore, Maryland

Douglas Herrmann, PhD
Professor and Chairperson
Psychology Department
Indiana State University
Terre Haute, Indiana

AN ASPEN PUBLICATION®
Aspen Publishers, Inc.
Gaithersburg, Maryland
1996

Library of Congress Cataloging-in-Publication Data

Parenté, Rick.
Retraining cognition: techniques and applications/
Rick Parenté, Douglas Herrmann.
p. cm.
Includes bibliographical references and index.
ISBN 0-8342-0764-8
1. Brain damage—Patients—Rehabilitation.
2. Cerebrovascular disease—Patients—Rehabilitation.
3. Cognition disorders—Patients—Rehabilitation.
I. Herrmann, Douglas J. II. Title.
RC387.5.P364   1996
616.8'043—dc20
96-12260
CIP

Editorial Resources: Jane Colilla

Library of Congress Catalog Card Number: 96-12260
ISBN: 0-8342-0764-8

Printed in the United States of America

1   2   3   4   5

Table of Contents

Acknowledgments

I would like to dedicate my contributions to this book to my parents, Fred and Julie Parenté, for their constant support over the years. I am especially indebted to my wife, Janet; my sister, Pam; my daughter, Alexis; and my son, Josh; for their support, inspiration, and encouragement.

Special thanks go to Dr. Jim McTamney for literally thousands of hours of supervised experience in clinical neuropsychology; to Dr. Craig Johnson for his exceptionally valuable coursework in neuropsychological theory; to Malcolm Bernstein for his insights regarding the real-world applications of these principles; to Drs. Henry Ellis and R. Reed Hunt for their singularly cogent explanations of cognitive theory; to Mary Stapleton for her brilliant insights and creative application of these principles with clients at the Maryland Rehabilitation Center; to Paul and Pam Mazmanian for their excellent conferences; and to Jeff Kreutzer for his eloquent summaries of cognitive rehabilitation literature.

—Rick Parenté

I am grateful to Donna, Mandy, and Zachary Herrmann for their support while I wrote this book, and to my friends Barbara Schwartz and Steve Deutsch for expanding my understanding of the many issues addressed in this book.

—Douglas Herrmann

Chapter 1

Overview of Cognitive Rehabilitation

What we call cognition is a complex collection of mental skills that includes attention, perception, comprehension, learning, remembering, problem solving, reasoning, and so forth. These mental attributes allow us to understand our world and to function within it. After a brain injury, a person typically loses one or more of these skills. Cognitive rehabilitation is the art and science of restoring these mental processes after injury to the brain.

The past two decades have witnessed a virtual revolution in the development of cognitive rehabilitation techniques and applications (Boake, 1991). This book summarizes many of these techniques as well as their theoretical underpinnings in cognitive psychology, neuropsychology, and speech/language therapy (Ellis & Hunt, 1993; Luria, 1963, 1980; Miller, 1980).

The history of cognitive rehabilitation therapy (CRT) is both old and new (Boake, 1991). World Wars I and II led to considerable development of methods of rehabilitation of all kinds. However, in the 1970s and 1980s, the field of CRT experienced the greatest change. This revolution was stimulated first because rehabilitation researchers and therapists became interested in cognitive psychology, which had gone through a period of rapid growth in the 1960s (Barsalou, 1992; Eysenck, 1993; Matlin, 1994; Newell,

1990). Also, certain distinguished figures such as Alexander Luria (1963, 1980) advanced a number of important ideas about neurocognition and the treatment of cognitive impairments. Subsequently, several researchers investigated the effects of a variety of new rehabilitation techniques on cognitive impairment (Gianutsos, 1991; Gianutsos & Grynbaum, 1982; Miller, 1980, 1984). Since the mid-1980s, the effectiveness of cognitive rehabilitation has been repeatedly evaluated, and several reviews have documented its efficacy (Butler & Namerow, 1988; Gianutsos, 1991; Glisky & Schacter, 1989; Godfrey & Knight, 1987; Gordon & Hibbard, 1991; Gouvier, 1987; Hayden, 1986; Parenté & Anderson-Parenté, 1991; Prigatano & Fordyce, 1987; Seron & Deloche, 1989; Sohlberg & Mateer, 1989; Wehman et al., 1989; Wood & Fussey, 1990). Each of these reviews attests to the success of one or more methods of cognitive rehabilitation.

TYPES OF CRT

CRT can include training the client in specific skills, educating the client about his or her condition, altering the client's environment, educating caregivers, family, and friends to assist the client better, and offering the client various lifestyle suggestions. It can be done individually or in groups. Specific areas of CRT are discussed below and noted in Exhibit 1–1.

Stimulation Therapy

Stimulation therapy is perhaps the oldest method of CRT. Harrell, Parenté, Bellingrath, and Lisicia (1992) have referred to this type of treatment as *direct retraining*. It is based on the assumption that one can improve cognitive functions by stimulating the cognitive system. The therapy usually includes paper-and-pencil exercises and, more recently, computer training that requires one or more mental skills. Presumably, by using these skills, clients will improve their cognition, and the improvement will transfer to their activities of daily living. We do not discuss stimulation therapy in detail because there is little research evidence to support its efficacy. However, the reader is referred to Craine and Gudeman (1981) for a thorough review.

Process Training

Process training is similar to stimulation therapy, although it focuses on specific areas of cognition. Bracy (1986) developed a process approach to CRT that emphasizes assessment and

---

Exhibit 1–1 Types of Cognitive Rehabilitation Therapy

- Stimulation therapy
- Process training
- Attention-concentration training
- Strategy training
- Domain-specific training
- Nutrient and drug treatment
- Use of external aids
- Enhancement of physical and emotional health and social functioning
- Stimulus-response conditioning
- Cognitive cycle technique
- Tissue replacement

treatment of specific cognitive defects. It is assumed that any complex process can be broken down into a limited number of specific complex behaviors. Parenté, Anderson-Parenté, and Shaw (1989) and McClur, Browning, Vantrease, & Bittle (1994) discussed techniques for training iconic memory. These techniques are discussed in detail in Chapter 8. In general, process training methods are all designed to improve specific aspects of cognition, and there is some evidence that improving these cognitive skills can facilitate performance on other cognitive tasks.

Attention-Concentration Training

This type of training is designed to improve clients' ability to focus their attention, maintain vigilance, resist distraction, and perform mental manipulations quickly and efficiently. It is one of the most widely researched areas of CRT, and there are commercially available training programs available with proven efficacy (Sohlberg & Mateer, 1987). This type of training is discussed in detail in Chapters 3 and 9. It is also an especially important area of rehabilitation because it precedes many of the other types of higher cognitive training that we discuss in Chapters 14 through 18.

Strategy Training

This method of CRT involves teaching the client mental sets that are applicable in a variety of different contexts. For example, the therapist may teach the client to use a certain strategy for solving problems, mnemonics to remember important information, or social strategies for carrying on conversations. These methods are discussed in Chapters 11 through 19.

Domain-Specific Training

These techniques emphasize training the client with simulated life experiences or within a specific functional domain. For example, the use of computer simulation to train data entry skills has been described by Schacter and Glisky

(1986). The theory that underlies domain-specific training is discussed in Chapter 6.

Nutrient and Drug Treatment

Various substances can affect cognition by correcting some chemical imbalance. For example, memory deficits secondary to long-term alcohol abuse can often be arrested with thiamine treatments. This type of CRT is relatively new, although the results are promising. We summarize most of the available research on cognitive-enhancing nutrients and drugs in Chapter 22.

External Aids

This type of treatment is based on the assumption that certain cognitive deficits are best treated by providing external aids that obviate the problem rather than retrain the defective process. For example, training clients to use a tape recorder can improve their functional memory immediately but may not have any effect on the underlying physiological cause of the deficit. Nevertheless, the tape recorder does rectify much of what clients experience as a memory deficit. Prosthetic device training is an especially effective and efficacious method of treatment. We therefore discuss it in detail in Chapter 25. Other external aids are memory cues provided by the client's living environment or by the client's family or friends.

Enhancement of Physical and Emotional Health and Social Functioning

Although CRT procedures like those discussed above may be the most direct approach to improving cognitive problems, other, more indirect approaches that focus on the client's lifestyle may also be effective (Herrmann & Parenté, 1994). For example, teaching the client to reduce stress or adhere to better sleeping and eating habits can improve cognitive function. Even the teaching of certain social skills (e.g., social cover-up skills, conversational ploys) can give some clients more control over everyday living situations so that they can make better use of their reduced cognitive functioning.

Stimulus-Response Conditioning

This approach to rehabilitation involves identifying potentially rewarding or punishing states, then either providing or withholding these in order to effect some desired change (Wolpe, 1973). Conditioning occurs most rapidly when the behavior is broken down into smaller parts that can be trained separately. Once the client has learned the parts, the behaviors can be shaped into a complex behavioral repertoire.

Cognitive Cycle Technique

Gross and Shutz (1986) proposed the following five-step process for training complex executive skills such as problem solving and decision making:

- *Step 1: Self-Identification of Goals.* The person identifies exactly what he or she wants to achieve in any situation.
- *Step 2: Conditional Thinking.* The person learns to generate options, ideas, or behaviors that may produce the goals identified in Step 1.
- *Step 3: Planning.* The person generates a plan of action that stems from Step 2. He or she learns that goals are obtained by following a specific behavioral action plan.
- *Step 4: Feedback Assessment.* The person evaluates the outcome of the action plan.
- *Step 5: Cognitive Cycling.* If the person does not achieve the goal, then he or she cycles through the entire process once again until the goal is achieved.

The cognitive cycle technique requires a certain amount of executive skill, such as the ability to anticipate behavioral consequences and to evaluate the results of behavior to determine if the goal was achieved. The person must also be able to initiate and self-monitor his or her behavior. Consequently, the cognitive cycle model may be most appropriate only for clients who are in the later stages of recovery.

Tissue Replacement

One of the most exciting areas of research in cognitive rehabilitation concerns the physical replacement of damaged brain tissue. This idea is not new, but until recently, there has been no clear model of treatment. As described by Kolb and Whishaw (1990), the process begins by dissecting tissues from the fetal brain that contain undeveloped embryonic cells. These tissues are treated to remove other tissues, such as blood vessels and glia. The treated tissue is next injected directly into the brain at the damage site. The embryonic cells then can travel through the nervous system and establish appropriate connections that are behaviorally functional (Dunnett, Low, Iversen, Stenevi, & Bjorklund, 1982; Zimmer, 1981).

ISSUES IN THE DEVELOPMENT OF CRT

Along with neurologists and psychiatrists, cognitive rehabilitation therapists and theorists have identified many of the subsystems of cognition as well as many of the variables that can affect cognitive functioning. However, most of the research has been directed toward mapping the cognitive system in relation to various structures of the brain. Unfortunately, relatively little research has actually focused on treatments that improve cognition after brain injury.

Another issue in the development of CRT methods is a lack of broad-based theoretical grounding. Although speech/language science and neuropsychology have certainly contributed to the field, many therapists are ignorant of the vast amounts of information that have accumulated in the area of cognitive psychology and the implications for treatment of cognitive dysfunction. This is because there has not been much of an attempt to translate these findings into a form that the average CRT practitioner can use. This may be due to the belief that because most of the findings were obtained with college student populations, the results do not apply to clinically impaired groups. Hertel (1994) provided an especially cogent integration of research dealing with the effects of depression on memory and its implications for CRT. We recommend that others use this as a model for their theoretical extrapolations.

There is also the issue of whom these methods were designed to help. Clearly, a wide variety of clients may benefit from cognitive rehabilitation. The best known targets are those who have suffered closed head injury or penetrating-missile head injury. Indeed, it is fair to say that the field was developed first to help these victims. However, CRT methods are also being used to treat other disorders such as attention-deficit disorder, dementia, and schizophrenia. Potentially, CRT can help elderly clients cope with the cognitive challenges of self-care and self-sufficiency, such as the ability to keep appointments, to recognize others, and to remember others' names. Some methods simplify troublesome cognitive problems that would otherwise induce confusion and anxiety. In some cases, these methods can enable a mildly impaired client to learn an employable skill.

In addition to the rehabilitation of cognitive impairments, CRT methods may be especially useful with learning-disabled students. For example, a brain-injured person may eventually return to school but may have difficulty with certain courses. Students who have long-standing learning disabilities but have never had a brain injury may also benefit from CRT methods. These techniques may also be applicable to those students in early-enrichment environments such as Head Start programs. Clearly the potential is there, but the field is simply too new for the research effort to provide much in the way of guidance for any of these questions. In essence, cognitive rehabilitation is a field of enormous challenge and promise.

PRACTITIONERS OF COGNITIVE REHABILITATION

Because its theoretical roots are interdisciplinary, practitioners of cognitive rehabilitation come from several areas: anthropology, speech/ language pathology, occupational therapy, artificial intelligence, geriatrics, neurology, pharmacology, physiology, psychiatry, experimental psychology, clinical psychology, and social psychology. Although they come from different disciplines, these practitioners have a common goal dictated by a shared understanding of the devastating effects of a neurological insult. Generally accepted procedures for licensing have not been established yet; however, the Society for Cognitive Rehabilitation has created a certification procedure that includes the following criteria for "minimal competency" to provide CRT: (a) at least a master's degree in an allied discipline, (b) either an internship or some other proof of substantial experience in practicing cognitive rehabilitation, and (c) a work sample evaluated by a panel of certified members of the organization.

CONCLUSION

What can CRT currently provide victims of brain injury? Clearly, this population is treated far more successfully than previous generations of clients were (Grafman, 1984). Moreover, it is probably safe to say that CRT methods can arrest cognitive decline and even reverse it. For clients who have experienced a substantial cognitive loss, cognitive rehabilitation can improve the quality of life and reduce the incidence of everyday problems that clients once had to struggle with for the rest of their lives.

CRT is also more widely available than it was in previous years. Until just a few years ago, it was available only in private hospitals and centers for medical research. Additionally, until the past decade, the topic was not addressed in textbooks (Kreutzer & Wehman, 1990) or made the object of professional conferences. In recent years, various hospitals around the country established CRT as part of their treatment offerings. There is now a professional organization, the Society for Cognitive Rehabilitation, that has established certification requirements for CRT professionals.

This text is intended to provide the therapist with basic theoretical background that has been generally lacking in the CRT literature. We have done this by surveying the vast quantities of related literature in cognition and neuroscience and presenting summaries of this literature that the average practitioner can use. Admittedly, in many cases our summaries are speculative. We certainly do not claim to provide the level of detail that is currently available in many of the excellent books that deal with more specific aspects of brain injury rehabilitation. Our attempt to summarize the literature is based on the assumption that the field must have a theoretical grounding and that existing theory is the best place to start. Our hope is that the theoretical discussion we provide will generate many more applied research questions than it answers.

Our primary goal is to provide CRT practitioners with techniques they can actually use with their clients. Unlike most books on CRT, which are basically summaries of published articles, this book applies the research we summarize and provides the therapist with actual therapy strategies along with descriptions of how to apply them. In most cases, these are methods that have worked successfully for us over the years. Wherever possible, we document the efficacy of the technique with published or original research. Our hope is that therapists will use these techniques with their clients and will continue to document their efficacy. We also hope that researchers will use these therapies as a starting point for research and development of better techniques.

Finally, this book assumes that rehabilitation of impaired cognitive skills requires consideration of all the variables that may affect psychological functioning. This approach contrasts with prior approaches, which relied primarily, if not exclusively, on improving cognition through active retraining methods. Thus, although we provide a thorough grounding in the retraining of capacities for attention, perception, comprehension, learning, remembering, communication, problem solving, and creative thinking, we also provide a thorough discussion of other approaches that can be equally effective, such as nutrient and drug treatments, use of external aids, and enhancement of physical and emotional health and social functioning. We believe that the combination of all these approaches can lead to the greatest and most rapid improvement in the client's functioning.

REFERENCES

Barsalou, L.W. (1992). *Cognitive psychology: An overview for cognitive scientists.* Hillsdale, NJ: Lawrence Erlbaum.

Boake, C. (1991). History of cognitive rehabilitation following head injury. In J.S. Kreutzer & P.H. Wehman (Eds.), *Cognitive rehabilitation for persons with traumatic brain injury* (pp. 1–12). Baltimore: Paul H. Brookes.

Bracy, O.L. (1986). Cognitive rehabilitation: A process approach. *Cognitive Rehabilitation, 4,* 10–17.

Butler, R.W., & Namerow, N.S. (1988). Cognitive retraining in brain-injury rehabilitation: A critical review. *Journal of Neurologic Rehabilitation, 2,* 97–101.

Craine, J., & Gudeman, H. (1981). *The rehabilitation of brain function.* Springfield, IL: Charles C Thomas.

Dunnett, S.B., Low, W.C., Iversen, S.D., Stenevi, U., & Bjorklund, A. (1982). Septal transplants to restore maze learning in rats with fornix-limbic lesions. *Brain Research, 251,* 335–348.

Ellis, H.C., & Hunt, R.R. (1993). *Fundamentals of cognitive psychology.* Madison, WI: Brown & Benchmark.

Eysenck, M.W. (1993). *Principles of cognitive psychology.* Hillsdale, NJ: Lawrence Erlbaum.

Gianutsos, R. (1991). Cognitive rehabilitation: A neuropsychological specialty comes of age. *Brain Injury, 5,* 353–368.

Gianutsos, R., & Grynbaum, B.B. (1982). Helping brain-injured people contend with hidden cognitive deficits. *International Rehabilitation Medicine, 5,* 37–40.

Glisky, E.L., & Schacter, D.L. (1989). Models and methods of memory rehabilitation. In F. Boller & J. Grafman (Eds.), *Handbook of neuropsychology.* Amsterdam: Elsevier.

Godfrey, H.P., & Knight, R.G. (1987). Interventions for amnesics: A review. *British Journal of Clinical Psychology, 26,* 83–91.

Gordon, W.A., & Hibbard, M.R. (1991). The theory and practice of cognitive remediation. In J.S. Kreutzer & P.H. Wehman (Eds.), *Cognitive rehabilitation for persons with traumatic brain injury* (pp. 12–22). Baltimore: Paul H. Brookes.

Gouvier, W.D. (1987). Assessment and treatment of cognitive deficits in brain damaged individuals. *Behavior Modification, 11,* 312–328.

Grafman, J. (1984). Memory assessment and remediation in brain-injured patients: From theory to practice. In B.A. Edelstein & E.T. Coutour (Eds.), *Behavioral assessment and rehabilitation of the traumatically brain-damaged* (pp. 102–117). New York: Plenum.

Gross, Y., & Shutz, L.E. (1986). Intervention models in neuropsychology. In B.P. Uzzell & Y. Gross (Eds.), *Clinical neuropsychology of intervention.* Boston: Martinus Nijhoff.

Harrell, M., Parenté, R., Bellingrath, E.G., & Lisicia, K.A. (1992). *Cognitive rehabilitation of memory: A practical guide.* Gaithersburg, MD: Aspen.

Hayden, M.E. (1986). Rehabilitation of cognitive and behavioral dysfunction in head injury. *Advances in Psychosomatic Medicine, 16,* 194–229.

Herrmann, D., & Parenté, R. (1994). The multi-modal approach to cognitive rehabilitation. *NeuroRehabilitation, 4*(3), 133–142.

Hertel, P. (1994). Depressive deficits in memory: Implications for memory improvement following traumatic brain injury. *NeuroRehabilitation, 4*(3), 143–150.

Kolb, B., & Whishaw, I.Q. (1990). *Fundamentals of human neuropsychology.* New York: W.H. Freeman.

Kreutzer, J.S., & Wehman, P.H. (1990). *Community integration following traumatic brain injury.* Baltimore: Paul H. Brookes.

Luria, A.R. (1963). *Restoration of function after brain injury.* New York: Macmillan.

Luria, A.R. (1973). *Higher cortical functions in man.* New York: Basic Books.

Matlin, M.W. (1994). *Cognition.* New York: Harcourt Brace.

McClur, J.T., Browning, R.T., Vantrease, C.M., & Bittle, S.T. (1994). The iconic memory skills of brain injury survivors and non-brain injured controls after visual scanning training. *NeuroRehabilitation, 4*(3), 151–156.

Miller, E. (1980). Psychological intervention in the management and rehabilitation of neuropsychological impairments. *Behavioral Research and Therapy, 18,* 527–535.

Miller, E. (1984). *Recovery and management of neuropsychological impairments.* New York: John Wiley.

Newell, A. (1990). *Unified theories of cognition.* Cambridge, MA: Harvard University Press.

Parenté, R., Anderson-Parenté, J., & Shaw, B. (1989). Retraining the mind's eye. *Journal of Head Trauma Rehabilitation, 4*(2), 53–62.

Parenté, R., & Anderson-Parenté, J. (1991). *Retraining memory: Techniques and applications.* Houston, TX: CSY.

Prigatano, G., & Fordyce, D. (1987). Neuropsychological rehabilitation program: Presbyterian Hospital, Oklahoma City, Oklahoma. In B. Caplan (Ed.), *Rehabilitation psychology desk reference* (pp. 281–298). Gaithersburg, MD: Aspen.

Schacter, D., & Glisky, E. (1986). Memory remediation, restoration, alleviation, and the acquisition of domain specific knowledge. In B. Uzzell & Y. Gross (Eds.), *Clinical neuropsychology of intervention* (pp. 257–282). Boston: Martinus Nijhoff.

Seron, X., & Deloche, G. (Eds.). (1989). *Cognitive approaches in neuropsychological rehabilitation.* Hillsdale, NJ: Lawrence Erlbaum.

Sohlberg, M., & Mateer, C. (1987). Effectiveness of an attention training program. *Journal of Clinical Experimental Neuropsychology, 9,* 117–130.

Sohlberg, M., & Mateer, C. (1989). *Introduction to cognitive rehabilitation.* New York: Guilford.

Wehman, P., Kreutzer, J., Sale, P., West, M., Morton, M., & Diambra, J. (1989). Cognitive impairment and remediation: Implications for employment following traumatic brain injury. *Journal of Head Trauma Rehabilitation, 4,* 66–75.

Wolpe, J. (1973). *The practice of behavior therapy* (2nd ed.). New York: Pergamon.

Wood, R.L., & Fussey, L. (1990). *Cognitive rehabilitation in perspective.* London: Taylor & Francis.

Zimmer, J. (1981). Lesion induced reorganization of central nervous system connections: With note on central nervous system transplants. In M.W. van Hoff & G. Mohn (Eds.), *Functional recovery from brain damage.* Amsterdam: Elsevier.

Chapter 2

A Model for Cognitive Rehabilitation

This chapter introduces a model of cognitive functioning that provides a theoretical backdrop for an eclectic approach to cognitive rehabilitation. It is based on the assumption that cognition and the rehabilitation of cognitive functions can be influenced by many different factors, including the client's physiological state, perceptual skills, emotional status, level of motivation, and social states. These factors affect the client's cognitive functioning as much as does any attempt to teach the client compensatory strategies. Accordingly, cognitive rehabilitation will produce the greatest improvement in a client's cognitive functioning by changing not only the client's thought processes (Ben-Yishay & Diller, 1983; Gianutsos, 1980) but also the client's world. The multimodal model provides a blueprint for a holistic approach to cognitive rehabilitation. It is also grounded in basic and clinical research (Bracy, 1986; Herrmann & Parenté, 1994).

SPECIFIC ASSUMPTIONS OF THE MODEL

The multimodal model assumes that the psychological system is affected by three classes of variables: active, passive, and support. The effectiveness of cognitive processing depends upon the quality of the interaction among them. *Active* variables are cognitive operations that can be learned. *Passive* variables do not involve active mental processing but still exert considerable influence on a person's thinking and memory skill: for example, the client's physical condition and emotional state or use of cognitive-enhancing nutrients and drugs. *Support* variables are variables external to the client that obviate memory and cognitive dysfunction by taking over certain cognitive functions for the client. They include contributions of the client's social network, environmental cues, and prosthetic devices.

Active, passive, and support variables affect the availability of information, the ability to allocate responses, and the client's ability to attend and concentrate effectively (Herrmann & Parenté, 1994). Traditionally, therapists manipulate only the active variables. Our goal in this book is to get the therapist to work with all of the variables because we feel that the passive and

This chapter is adapted from *NeuroRehabilitation,* Vol. 4, No. 3, D. Herrmann and R. Parenté, A Multimodal Approach to Cognitive Rehabilitation, pp. 133–142, © 1994, with permission from Elsevier Science Ireland, Ltd., Bay 15K, Shannon Industrial Estate, Co. Clare, Ireland.

support variables can affect the client's cognition as much as or more than any active mental effort. The variables influencing cognitive functioning are listed in Exhibit 2–1.

ACTIVE VARIABLES

Active variables are cognitive operations that affect the content of the information in the cognitive system; for example, perceptions, thoughts, images, or memories (Grafman, 1989). There are basically two types of active variables:

mental manipulations and applications of mental sets.

Mental manipulations are thought processes that foster encoding of information for transfer to long-term memory, or that cue the retrieval of information. They include operations of paying, shifting, and sustaining attention, as well as strategies such as use of mnemonics and creation of mental images. Mental manipulations are what most therapists think of as cognitive strategies (Ben-Yishay & Diller, 1983; Gianutsos, 1991; Parenté & Anderson-Parenté, 1983, 1991; Parenté & DiCesare, 1991; West, 1985). The ef-

---

Exhibit 2–1 Variables Influencing Cognitive Functioning

Active Variables

- *Mental Manipulations:* cognitive operations that direct attention or foster encoding or cuing of information (e.g., mnemonics, creation of mental imagery)
- *Applications of Mental Sets:* cognitive operations that employ specific concept-learning, problem-solving, decision-making, or reasoning techniques

Passive Variables

Physiological

- *Physical Condition:* acute or chronic illness or disorder, fitness, sensory deficits, pain, daily rhythms of alertness, fitness, exercise, nutrition, sleep, fatigue, relaxation
- *Chemical Intake:* use of common substances such as tobacco, coffee, caffeine, and alcohol; medicines such as antidepressants, antibiotics, antihistamines, and tranquilizers; and illegal substances such as cocaine and marijuana; also passive intake of environmental toxins

Psychological

- *Emotional State:* anxiety about tasks, situations, memory aptitude; annoyance with chronic pain or discomfort, hassles, noise; persistent states of arousal; recent trauma; mood swings, depression; repression; stress
- *Attitudinal State:* extreme religious beliefs; stereotypical beliefs related to age/culture/gender; attitude toward therapy process
- *Motivational State:* distractibility, incentive value of treatment and perceived relevance, goals, pattern of success experiences

Support Variables

- *Prosthetic Devices:* use of tape recorders, calculators, computers, and so forth to compensate for poor memory and thinking skills
- *Physical Environment:* environmental cues, organization of living space or work space
- *Social Environment:* use of collaborative recall with another person, social reminders, social pressure, social feedback and coaching, social tolerance for deficits

fect of mental manipulations varies across individuals with different learning styles. Most people with good memories and thinking skills have well-developed mental manipulation skills. This means that they actively and unconsciously direct attention and manipulate novel information to make it more memorable.

A survey of mental manipulations is presented in Chapters 8 through 18. Teaching mental manipulation skills ensures that the client focuses his or her attention on the organization of the materials or uses specific strategies to process and retain different types of information. The quality of a thought or idea formed by mental manipulation depends on several factors, some of which are under volitional control and others of which operate automatically without awareness (Herrmann & Searleman, 1990). The therapist's goal is to train the client to use different strategies that encode information efficiently and without conscious effort.

Mental sets are strategies for approaching cognitive tasks, such as problem solving, decision making, and concept learning. Mental sets are relatively fixed action patterns that a person applies in a specific situation. For example, we all have certain ways that we perform addition. Most of us start at the top of the column and add downward. However, we still may find specific relationships between numbers that make it easier to add any column and we may opt to simplify the addition process by adding these numbers together first rather than starting at the top. Using mental sets ensures that the client will consider all necessary information before making a crucial decision or when trying to solve an important problem. Mental sets are discussed in Chapters 11 and 14 through 18.

PASSIVE VARIABLES

Whereas active variables directly affect the content of the mental representation, passive variables do not directly affect what is learned or remembered. Instead, they affect a client's disposition, inclination, or readiness to attempt a memory task. They may also make it easier for the client to process information.

Passive variables may be physiological (physical condition, chemical intake) or psychological (attitudes, emotional state, motivational state). Passive variables can change from hour to hour or day to day, and in some cases from minute to minute. But people are usually unaware of these fluctuations and their effects. Clients do not typically monitor passive variables, although many of these can be modified and brought under personal control. Moreover, it is often necessary to modify passive variables before any active manipulations can be successful.

Physiological Variables

Numerous physiological variables affect a person's ability to engage in active processing. For example, physical disease or any other debilitating condition may cause pain, which, in turn, limits cognitive processing. Anemia, brain tumors, dementia, heart failure, low blood pressure, some forms of epilepsy, and syphilis all interfere with the ability to concentrate and perform cognitive functions. Even routine disruptions of health such as the common cold impair cognition.

On a lesser scale are the minor fluctuations in physical well-being and alertness that are determined by exercise, diet, fatigue, restedness, and so forth. Sleep loss generally impairs cognition. The degree of relaxation also can affect cognition. Prolonged strenuous exercise reduces physiological readiness for continued mental activity. A balanced diet with a daily multiple vitamin, a consistent sleep regimen, and a light exercise program can make a dramatic change in a person's cognitive functioning.

In recent years it has been recognized that various chemical substances once seen as beneficial to cognitive processing may actually impair such processing (Squire, 1985). For example, cognition can be impaired by smoking tobacco or by drinking excessive amounts of coffee. Tranquilizers, sedating antidepressants and antibiotics, as well as a variety of illegal drugs, may also lessen memory performance (Herrmann & Palmisano, 1992). Chemical substances can alter a person's neurochemistry; they can also quickly alter physiological readiness for activity. All of these issues are discussed in detail in Chapter 20.

Psychological Variables

Attitudinal, emotional, and motivational states also affect cognitive abilities and the effort that a person puts into cognitive tasks. *Attitudinal state* includes emotional dispositions (positive or negative) toward certain information or people. For example, many clients prefer to work with a therapist of the same or opposite sex. Some prefer to work with therapists who are close to their age. Some have no faith in the therapy process. Often, simply discussing the treatment or the choice of a therapist can greatly enhance the client's progress. Further, it has long been recognized that clients' cognitive performance is affected by their attitude regarding the cognitive tasks they perform (Gruneberg, 1992). A person is likely to perform well when his or her attitude toward a task is positive.

Cognitive performance is also known to be affected by a client's *emotional state*. Generally, high anxiety and depression (Hertel, 1992) interfere with cognitive functioning. Stress, a major factor in mood, has been associated with impaired memory performance in everyday life (Fisher & Reason, 1986). These states can also be modified by discussion and experience. We discuss these issues in Chapter 21.

Motivational states determine the client's tendency to act in specific ways to achieve particular goals. The client's motivation depends on the current incentives. A client's performance will usually improve markedly in situations in which incentives are clear (Herrmann & Parenté, 1994; McEvoy, 1993; Parenté & Anderson-Parenté, 1991). Moreover, if a person can be made to feel in control of his or her goals and rewards, then he or she becomes empowered to acquire the knowledge and methods that will produce better cognitive performance (Parenté & Stapleton, 1993). An incentive-based model of cognitive rehabilitation, along with specific recommendations for creating incentives, is presented in Chapter 23.

SUPPORT VARIABLES

Support variables do not directly affect cognitive functioning. Instead, they are factors in the physical or social environment that obviate or compensate for cognitive deficits, prompt the use of cognitive strategies, or cue memory retrieval. These variables position the person to benefit from the environment, his or her social situation, and various available devices. In essence, the therapist tries to get the world to work for the client rather than against the client.

Prosthetic Devices

Prosthetic devices are electronic and nonelectronic devices that help the client to overcome nagging problems by replacing some damaged aspect of memory or thinking. For example, training the client to use a dictation tape recorder does not improve the client's memory per se, but it does eliminate many of the common problems associated with loss of memory. We provide a detailed description of a variety of prosthetic devices in Chapter 25.

Physical Environment

The physical environment may be manipulated in various ways to foster the encoding of information or to cue information retrieval. For example, the therapist may label drawers in the kitchen, use stacked trays to sort mail, or arrange clothes in the closet for the client. We discuss environmental manipulation in detail at the end of Chapter 14.

Social Environment

The client's social network can also be used prosthetically. For example, arranging for a family member to call the client each day of the week with a reminder of that day's activities can greatly reduce the frustration that most family members feel when the client misses an appointment. Sharing the responsibility among the family members is usually not difficult to arrange.

THE MULTIMODAL MODEL IN PERSPECTIVE

Figure 2–1 presents a summary of the multimodal model described above (Herrmann & Parenté, 1994; Hermann & Searleman, 1992). Active, passive, and support variables together determine what is ultimately perceived, learned, retained, remembered, and reasoned. The bottom arrows in the figure connect the active variables with the sensory, response, and cognitive systems. These lines represent the assumption that active variables operate directly on all three systems. Until recently, manipulations of such variables represented what most therapists would describe as cognitive rehabilitation.

The arrows that connect the passive and support ellipses to the sensory, cognitive, and response systems represent the assumption that passive variables also have effects. These arrows are as thick as the arrows emanating from the active processes because we assume that all these factors can have comparable impact on the person's overall cognitive functioning.

The dark arrows in the center of the figure that connect the sensory system, the cognitive system, and the response system illustrate the flow of information through the system. In general, the model indicates that both active and passive variables operate directly on (a) the sensory input that provides raw information to the cognitive system, (b) the cognitive operations performed on the sensory input, and (c) the ability to express and to communicate what one knows.

We return for the moment to the arrows that connect the active, passive, and support variables to the cognitive system. The large arrows in the upper part of the figure connect the passive variables with the sensory, response, and cognitive systems. The left arrow represents the assumption that passive support variables affect the system's sensitivity or *receptivity* to the sensory input. For example, if a person is ill or depressed,

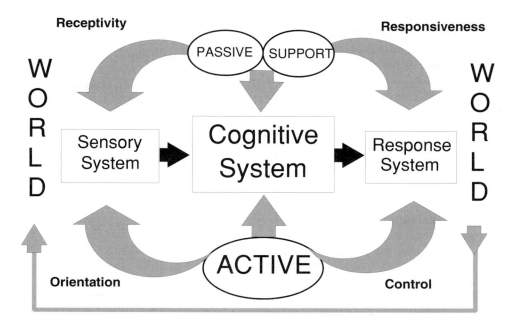

Figure 2–1 A Multimodal Model for Cognitive Rehabilitation

or if his or her hearing or vision is impaired, then he or she may miss pieces of information or fail to perceive some event entirely. The middle arrow shows the influence of passive support variables on the cognitive system and the cognitive operations performed on the input for the sensory store. For example, if the person is depressed or apathetic, then he or she may not process the contents of an important phone call as readily as if he or she were in an alert and attentive and otherwise healthy state. The right arrow represents the assumption that the passive support variables affect a person's *responsiveness* and current ability to express what he or she knows. For example, if the person is taking strong medications, is fatigued, or is emotionally distraught, he or she may not be able to pronounce words easily or clearly.

Returning to the large arrows in the lower part of the figure that connect the active variables with the sensory, response, and cognitive systems, the left arrow shows how manipulations of active variables *orient* a person to perceive something in the environment. For example, visual scanning training may teach the client to orient effectively to certain aspects of his or her environment. Iconic memory training can teach the client how to scan novel information visually to improve reading skills. These techniques are presented in Chapter 8. The middle arrow indicates that manipulations of active variables can alter cognitive processing. For example, training to use any of the rehearsal or memory strategies outlined in Chapters 10, 11, and 12 facilitates active processing. Any of the strategies for solving problems, making decisions, and so forth that we describe in Chapters 14 and 16 alter the client's ability to process facts and other information efficiently. The right arrow represents the assumption that people can control the nature of their responses and choose how to express what they actually know. For example, the ANGER and CALM mnemonics that we present in Chapter 11 are ways for clients to control their agitation and to alter their response in potentially volatile situations.

This is a cybernetic model because it assumes that a person can make a response that changes cues in the environment. The cues, in turn, direct and alter subsequent processing. In essence, the line at the bottom of the figure that runs from the WORLD adjacent to the response system to the WORLD adjacent to the sensory system illustrates the learning component of the model. This means that the person's perceptions and cognitions control the eventual response he or she makes. The response eventually alters the way the person views the world. For example, this loop operates when a person sets an alarm that signals an appointment. The person thereafter learns to use the signaling device for future appointments.

Passive and support variables probably affect memory and thinking via a person's attentional processes (Mullin, Herrmann, & Searleman, 1993). Both modes affect a client's readiness to pay attention or a client's processing capacity at any given moment. The active variables determine the person's ability to allocate attention: that is, the quality of the attention the person gives an object when there are other objects competing for attention.

EMPIRICAL SUPPORT FOR THE MULTIMODAL APPROACH

Three kinds of evidence support the multimodal model: (a) basic research, (b) clinical research, and (c) clinical experience. Each kind of evidence is discussed in detail below.

Basic Research

Numerous mental manipulations enhance learning, remembering, and thinking with head-injured and "normal" populations (Buschke, 1987; Herrmann, Weingartner, Searleman, & McEvoy, 1992; McEvoy, 1993; Parenté & Anderson-Parenté, 1991; Parenté, Anderson-Parenté, & Shaw, 1989; Patten, 1990). Most of these are discussed in Chapters 8 through 18. For example, learning may be enhanced by increasing intervals between successive rehearsals, relating information to a client's personal characteristics or goals, or weaving information to be learned into a story. Similarly, a person may retrieve the name of an acquaintance by simply reciting the letters of the alphabet.

There is also substantial evidence that manipulation of support variables facilitates thinking and memory. Intons-Peterson and Newsome (1992) pointed out that a person may manipulate the physical environment (e.g., position or mark objects, write notes) to enhance acquisition or retrieval or reasoning. Prosthetic devices have long been used to facilitate memory and thought in a variety of settings. *Teaching machines* provide rote learning of basic skills such as typing or academic skills such as reading and math. *Cognitive visual aids* such as signs or cuing cards have long been used to remind a person of danger or of complex actions such as operating a microwave. *Cognitive robots* execute cognitive tasks for a person: for example, they may turn light switches or appliances on or off automatically. *Cognitive prosthetics* provide a device that takes over some memory or cognitive skill. For example, the client may learn to use a tape recorder as a prosthetic memory aid. *Cognitive error correctors* fix mistakes, as in the case of key finders that beep when the client whistles to find misplaced keys. All of these devices illustrate that people can manipulate the physical environment to improve their memory and thinking. This supports the model's assumption of the feedback loop shown in Figure 2–1.

Finally, there is evidence to suggest that manipulations of passive variables, such as training to enhance social functioning or emotional health, can facilitate memory and thinking. For example, Best (1992) reported that people may avoid cognitive failures by interacting with others in ways that affect the rate or substance of conversation, such as using various conversational ploys to buy time for retrieval or to encode information better. In Chapter 12, we present such a method for training clients to form name-face associations: The client is trained to pretend that he or she did not hear the name in order to get the person to repeat it. These social manipulations to improve cognitive performance

also provide evidence for the model's assumption of a feedback loop.

Clinical Research

We know of only one clinical investigation that has examined the effects of a multimodal treatment program. Nevertheless, this investigation, because it was well designed, provides an excellent example of the effectiveness of the multimodal approach, as well as offering some unanticipated benefits. The study addressed the effects of a multimodal program on the memory and cognition of some victims of paint solvent toxicity (Bendiksen & Bendiksen, 1992). Twenty workers from a paint factory in Norway participated in the study. Their performance on 11 tasks from the Rivermead Memory Battery was assessed (Wilson, 1987). Some of these tasks, such as remembering names, belongings, appointments, a story, and the delivery of a message, were targeted for memory training during the rehabilitation program. Other tasks, such as orientation, questioning, and immediate and delayed memory for pictures, faces, routes, and dates, were not targeted for training. Performance of the targeted and nontargeted tasks was assessed at four times. The first assessment, T1, and second assessment, T2, preceded the rehabilitation program. T2 occurred 3 months after T1.

After the second assessment, the rehabilitation program was initiated. The program lasted 9 weeks and consisted of two sessions of 2 hours each per week. Each session was attended by four to seven subjects. One session was devoted to memory training that was appropriate to the targeted tasks. This training involved imparting one or more mental strategies suggested by Herrmann & Searleman (1990). The other session was devoted to psychosocial issues resulting from the memory and cognitive impairments of the subjects. This session involved instruction in coping skills and group discussion of the concerns of the clients about their symptoms. At the end of the 9-week rehabilitation program, a third assessment was taken (at T3).

Memory was assessed one more time, 6 months later (at T4). Relative to the nontargeted tasks, performance on the targeted tasks increased significantly across the study (from T1 to T4). This increase was most pronounced for the story, name, and belonging tasks. The most remarkable aspect of this study was evident when the different kinds of complaints were analyzed across the four assessment times. Complaints about cognitive and emotional functioning decreased significantly after the intervention, and somatic complaints decreased only slightly. In contrast, complaints about social adjustment and economic problems increased after the intervention.

The multimodal approach employed in this investigation resulted in a multimodal outcome. Not only cognitive functioning but also psychosocial functioning was improved. The participants' emotional stability increased because of the socioemotive intervention and because the memory intervention, which demonstrated to the subjects that they could improve their memory functioning, led them to worry less about memory. Increased social and emotional control also prepared subjects to benefit more from the memory training. Because both the memory training and the social/emotional training were effective and resulted in fewer concerns about cognition and emotional issues, subjects were able to allocate more attention to their activities of daily living, directing their worries to relationships with friends and financial matters.

Several investigations have examined the effect of interventions to change a particular class of variables: active, passive, or support. Certain active manipulations have been assessed separately. Cognitive rehabilitation has also been shown to be effectively aided by prosthetic devices (Naugle, Prevy, Naugle, & Delaney, 1988), and the importance of social interactions to rehabilitation has been increasingly recognized (Boake, 1991b). Similarly, each of the passive variables has been separately addressed. For example, the role of pharmacology in cognitive rehabilitation has been assessed (Miller, 1993; Zasler, 1991). A number of studies have examined the importance of rehabilitating a client or

patient emotionally (O'Hara, 1988). Experiments have also shown the value of motivation and incentive in cognitive training (McEvoy, 1993; Parenté & Anderson-Parenté, 1991).

Clinical Experience

Finally, a great deal of support for a multimodal approach exists in the cognitive rehabilitation literature (Bracy, 1986). Recent books on cognitive rehabilitation advance methods tap into different modes of treatment, cognitive and noncognitive (Harrell, Parenté, Bellingrath, & Lisicia, 1992; Kreutzer & Wehman, 1991; McEvoy, 1993; Parenté and Anderson-Parenté, 1991). Our own experience has been that the multimodal approach is useful with a wide variety of clients, including victims of traumatic brain injury, stroke, dementia, chronic alcoholism, and substance abuse. The approach is also useful for caregivers and family members who may be in an especially valuable position to manipulate social and environmental variables. It should be noted that the multimodal approach was previously found useful in psychotherapy (Lazarus, 1989). Because emotional difficulties often accompany neurological impairment and contribute to the level of cognitive impairment, the multimodal approach to cognitive rehabilitation may lessen the negative impact of emotional distress on cognitive functioning.

IMPLICATIONS OF THE MULTIMODAL MODEL

The model presented in Figure 2–1 emphasizes the dynamic and interactive relationship between cognition and physical experience. Cognition is simply part of what we call perception and is embedded between the sensory world and our response to it. The process of cognitive rehabilitation begins by recognizing this embeddedness. This concept has several implications for treatment, diagnosis, and education of professionals in the field.

Treatment

As discussed in Chapter 1, cognitive rehabilitation has focused primarily on active manipulations (Ben-Yishay & Diller, 1983; Boake, 1991a; Gianutsos, 1980). For example, the attention process model (Sohlberg & Mateer, 1989) trains clients to attend selectively, alternate their attention, and sustain attention. Parenté and Anderson-Parenté (1991) described rehearsal procedures to teach clients active control of their rehearsal processes. However, the major implication of the multimodal model is that therapy efforts are best served when the therapist uses a holistic approach. The model presented in Figure 2–1 simply provides a summary of the various areas that compose the whole.

Cognitive rehabilitation researchers and practitioners have recently begun to see the value of holistic approaches to rehabilitation. For example, the *team approach,* in which different clinical specialties such as clinical psychologists, speech therapists, and social workers are represented (Dikengil, Lowry, & Delgado, 1993; Dryovage & Seidman, 1992), emphasizes the contributions of professionals who would work specifically in one or more modalities of the model. The interdisciplinary approach has been found to be very effective, and the multimodal model shows why. The interdisciplinary approach employs two or more modes of treatment and hence is more effective than the early cognitive approach that focused on active variable manipulations alone. This book, by presenting techniques and applications in all of the treatment modes, may augment any professional's knowledge regardless of his or her background or training.

Diagnostic Practices

The model implies that diagnosis should systematically assess not only neurocognitive functioning but also the current status of all other variables that affect cognition and behavior. Currently, there is no standardized assessment method that collects information about the pas-

sive and support variables. An exception to this generalization is the Rivermead Memory Battery, which does provide an assessment of use of external aids in the physical environment (Wilson, 1987). To remedy this situation, we provide a multimodal rating scale in Appendix A. Therapists can use this instrument to guide their treatment according to the multimodal model. This assessment is designed to evaluate the client's use of mental strategies, physical environment, and social environment, as well as the client's physical state, chemical state, attitudinal state, emotional state, and motivational state. Cognitive rehabilitation therapists will want a multimodal performance assessment of the client's active processes. Chapter 7 discusses this issue in detail, and Appendix B is a working example of this type of assessment.

Planning of Cognitive Rehabilitation

Probably the most obvious implication of the model concerns the nature of the treatment plan. We assert that it is no longer sufficient for a treatment plan to focus only on training the client's cognitive processes. The multimodal model points out that rehabilitation yields the quickest and most effective results by optimizing all variables that affect cognitive functioning. The model implies some simple rules of thumb that will be useful to any therapist or family member:

1. If a client's passive variables are not conducive to cognitive functioning, interventions that attempt to improve active processes will have little or no effect. Alternatively, any active intervention will have the greatest effect when the passive variables are brought under control or have been manipulated to work to the client's advantage. This point seems obvious, but in the hectic pace of most rehabilitation services, a client's poor physical condition, mood, attitude, or motivation is often overlooked, ignored, or tolerated rather than directly addressed.

2. In those situations in which a client cannot be helped by training active processes, cognitive performance may still be improved by enhancing passive variables.
3. Working with support variables will probably have the most immediate effect on overall cognitive functions. These interventions may also be the easiest to implement.

Education

To our knowledge, the multimodal model is the first formal model of cognitive rehabilitation. It provides a rationale that therapists can use to explain cognitive rehabilitation to clients, caregivers, new staff, colleagues in related health care professions, and so forth. For example, we have found Figure 2–1 especially helpful when training new staff in cognitive rehabilitation procedures. The figure streamlines the process of explaining cognitive rehabilitation and provides a mnemonic aid to remember the roles of the different modes of treatment in rehabilitation.

CONCLUSION

This chapter has described the multimodal approach to cognitive rehabilitation. The model was evaluated in light of findings from basic research, clinical research, and clinical experience. The basic research findings support the general assumption that cognitive performance can be affected by noncognitive variables. Clinical research findings demonstrate that cognitive impairments can be lessened through interventions that affect one or more noncognitive variables. Clinical experience similarly supports the multimodal approach and indicates that cognitive rehabilitation has the greatest chance for success if treatment manipulates both active and passive variables. Besides accounting for the effects of interventions on particular variables in isolation or in combination, the model also implies a new explanation of the effects of interdisciplinary cognitive rehabilitation, new diagnostic procedures, new and more comprehensive treatment plans, and a rationale for using any or all of these when educating others about cognitive rehabilitation practices.

REFERENCES

Ben-Yishay, U., & Diller, L. (1983). Cognitive deficits. In M. Rosenthal (Ed.), *Rehabilitation of the head injured adult* (pp. 367–378). Philadelphia: F.A. Davis.

Bendiksen, M., & Bendiksen, I.A. (1992). Multidimensional intervention program: Solvent injured population. *Cognitive Rehabilitation, 10*, 20–27.

Best, D. (1992). The role of social interaction in memory improvement. In D. Herrmann, H. Weingartner, A. Searleman, & C. McEvoy (Eds.), *Memory improvement: Implications for memory theory* (pp. 122–149). New York: Springer-Verlag.

Boake, C. (1991a). History of cognitive rehabilitation following head injury. In J.S. Kreutzer & P.H. Wehman (Eds.), *Cognitive rehabilitation for persons with traumatic brain injury* (pp. 1–12). Baltimore: Paul H. Brookes.

Boake, C. (1991b). Social skills training following head injury. In J.S. Kreutzer & P.H. Wehman (Eds.), *Cognitive rehabilitation for persons with traumatic brain injury* (pp. 142–158). Baltimore: Paul H. Brookes.

Bracy, O.L. (1986). Cognitive rehabilitation: A process approach. *Cognitive Rehabilitation, 4*, 10–17.

Buschke, H. (1987). Criteria for the identification of memory deficits: Implications for the design of memory tests. In D.S. Gorfein and R.R. Hoffman (Eds.), *Memory and learning* (pp. 331–344). Hillsdale, NJ: Lawrence Erlbaum.

Dikengil, A., Lowry, M., & Delgado, P. (1993). An interdisciplinary group treatment for the severely brain-injured patient: Participation by four disciplines. *Cognitive Rehabilitation, 11*, 20–22.

Dryovage, J., & Seidman, K. (1992). Interdisciplinary approach to community reintegration. *Cognitive Rehabilitation, 11*, 12–27.

Fisher, S., & Reason, J.T. (Eds.). (1986). *Handbook of life stress, cognition and health.* New York: John Wiley.

Gianutsos, R. (1980, July/August/September). What is cognitive rehabilitation. *Journal of Rehabilitation*, 37–40.

Gianutsos, R. (1991). Cognitive rehabilitation: A neuropsychological specialty comes of age. *Brain Injury, 5*, 353–368.

Grafman, J. (1989). Plans, actions, and mental sets: Managerial knowledge units in the frontal lobes. In E. Perecman (Ed.), *Integrating theory and practice in clinical neuropsychology.* Hillsdale, NJ: Lawrence Erlbaum.

Gruneberg, M.M. (1992). The practical application of memory aids: Knowing how, knowing when, and knowing when not. In M.M. Gruneberg and P. Morris (Eds.), *Aspects of memory* (pp. 168–195). London: Routledge.

Harrell, M., Parenté, R., Bellingrath, E.G., & Lisicia, K.A. (1992). *Cognitive rehabilitation of memory: A practical guide*. Gaithersburg, MD: Aspen.

Herrmann, D., & Palmisano, M. (1992). The facilitation of memory. In M. Gruneberg & P. Morris (Eds.), *Aspects of memory* (2nd ed., pp. 147–167). Chichester, UK: John Wiley.

Herrmann, D., & Parenté, R. (1994). A multimodal model approach to cognitive rehabilitation. *NeuroRehabilitation, 4*(3), 133–142.

Herrmann, D., & Searleman, A. (1990). The new multi-modal approach to memory improvement. In G.H. Bower (Ed.), *Advances in learning and motivation* (pp. 175–205). New York: Academic Press.

Herrmann, D., & Searleman, A. (1992). Memory improvement and memory theory in historical perspective. In D. Herrmann, H. Weingartner, A. Searleman, & C. McEvoy (Eds.), *Memory improvement: Implications for memory theory* (pp. 8–20). New York: Springer-Verlag.

Herrmann, D., Weingartner, H., Searleman, A., & McEvoy, C. (Eds.). (1992). *Memory improvement: Implications for memory theory.* New York: Springer-Verlag.

Hertel, P. (1992). Improving memory and mood through automatic and controlled procedures of mind. In D. Herrmann, H. Weingartner, A. Searleman, & C. McEvoy (Eds.), *Memory improvement: Implications for memory theory* (pp. 43–60). New York: Springer-Verlag.

Intons-Peterson, M.J., & Newsome, G.L. (1992). External memory aids: Effects and effectiveness. In D. Herrmann, H. Weingartner, A. Searleman, & C. McEvoy (Eds.), *Memory improvement: Implications for memory theory* (pp. 101–121). New York: Springer-Verlag.

Kreutzer, J.S., & Wehman, P.H. (1991). *Cognitive rehabilitation for persons with traumatic brain injury.* Baltimore: Paul H. Brookes.

Lazarus, A.A. (1989). *The practice of multi-modal therapy: Systematic, comprehensive, and effective psychotherapy.* Baltimore: Johns Hopkins University Press.

McEvoy, C.L. (1993). Memory improvement in context: Implications for the development of memory improvement theory. In D. Herrmann, H. Weingartner, A.

Searleman, and C. McEvoy (Eds.), *Memory improvement: Implications for memory theory* (pp. 210–230). New York: Springer-Verlag.

Miller, L. (1993). Clinical, neuropsychological, and forensic aspects of chemical and electrical injuries. *Cognitive Rehabilitation, 11*, 6–19.

Mullin, P., Herrmann, D., & Searleman, A. (1993). Forgotten variables in memory research. *Memory, 15*, 43.

Naugle, R., Prevy, M., Naugle, C., & Delaney, R. (1988). The new digital watch as a compensatory device for memory dysfunction. *Cognitive Rehabilitation, 6*, 22–23.

O'Hara, C. (1988). Emotional adjustment following minor head injury. *Cognitive Rehabilitation, 6*, 26–33.

Parenté, R., & Anderson-Parenté, J. (1983). Techniques for improving cognitive rehabilitation: Teaching organizational and encoding skills. *Cognitive Rehabilitation, 4*, 53–65.

Parenté, R., & Anderson-Parenté, J. (1991). *Retraining memory: Techniques and applications.* Houston, TX: CSY.

Parenté, R., Anderson-Parenté, J., & Shaw, B. (1989). Retraining the mind's eye. *Journal of Head Trauma Rehabilitation, 4*, 53–62.

Parenté, R., & DiCesare, A. (1991). Retraining memory: Theory, evaluation, and applications. In J.S. Kreutzer & P.H. Wehman (Eds.), *Cognitive rehabilitation for persons with traumatic brain injury* (pp. 147–162). Baltimore: Paul H. Brookes.

Parenté, R., & Stapleton, M. (1993). An empowerment model of memory training. *Applied Cognitive Psychology, 7*, 34–58.

Patten, B.M. (1990). The history of memory arts. *Neurology, 40*, 346–352.

Sohlberg, M., & Mateer, C. (1989). *Introduction to cognitive rehabilitation.* New York: Guilford.

Squire, L. (1985). *Memory and brain.* New York: Oxford University Press.

West, R. (1985). *Memory fitness over forty.* Gainesville, FL: Triad.

Wilson, B. (1987). *Rehabilitation of memory.* New York: Guilford.

Zasler, N.D. (1991). Pharmacological aspects of cognitive function following traumatic brain injury. In J.S. Kreutzer & P.H. Wehman (Eds.), *Cognitive rehabilitation for persons with traumatic brain injury* (pp. 87–94). Baltimore: Paul H. Brookes.

Chapter 3

The Neuropsychology of Thinking

To provide effective cognitive rehabilitation, the therapist must first understand some cognitive neuropsychology (McCarthy & Warrington, 1990). We therefore begin with a discussion of the physiological circuitry of memory, followed by a discussion of the anatomical areas of the brain that affect behavior and their relationship to learning, memory, and cognition. We discuss Mishkin and Appenzeller's (1987) integrative model of memory and recent research on how memory and habit may be localized in different areas of the brain. The localization of higher cognitive functions such as language, and the causes of memory failure are also addressed. We do not pretend to survey this literature in depth or even completely. However, other authors have done so, and we therefore refer the reader to several excellent published reviews for a comprehensive treatment of specific issues (Kolb & Whishaw, 1990; Squire & Butters, 1984; Wilson, 1987).

THE PHYSIOLOGY OF MEMORY AND COGNITION

Donald Hebb (1949, 1961) was the first to posit the notion of a cell assembly. He theorized that the synapses that connected the cells in the brain eventually became interdependent through learning. The repeated firing of adjacent cells caused a physiological change that the cells all shared. This physiological change produced short-term memory. With repeated sensory stimulation, the entire neural loop would eventually form a *reverberating circuit* that would continue to reverberate even after the stimulation stopped. Eventually, this reverberation would cause the synapses of adjacent cells to grow together and strengthen their connections. The *consolidation* of the cells in this closed circuit—their formation into a working assembly, or cell assembly—was, literally, long-term memory. This notion persists today. For example, the schema theory discussed in Chapter 14 can be viewed as an electronic computer simulation of the Hebbian cell assembly model.

Hebb (1949, 1961) described the process of consolidation as a permanent change in the neural circuit. He assumed that memory consolidation required approximately 15 to 60 minutes to take place. This assumption was based on the fact that head injury usually produces amnesia for events that happened immediately before the injury but leaves intact memories for events that happened over 60 minutes before the injury. Hebb reasoned that the injury would disrupt the consolidation process for memories of events occurring just before the injury and that the disruptions accounted for the amnesia. However, for events occurring over 60 minutes before the injury, the consolidation process for the memory would have already occurred. This assumption is certainly consistent with personal experience. For example, all of us can recall an instance when we could not remember where we put something after being distracted by an important phone call. For Hebb, this would happen because the phone call would disrupt the consolidation process.

Once a memory was consolidated, the neural network could potentially excite others (Herrmann, Ruppin, & Usher, 1993). In a later chapter, we will discuss this mechanism again under the rubric of *spreading activation*. The notion explains many everyday phenomena such as thoughts that come to mind when we are in the middle of a conversation. Some aspect of the conversation stimulates a neural loop that, in turn, spreads the activation to another. This feature, along with almost every other aspect of Hebb's work, has been incorporated into other theories of cognitive functioning. Indeed, some researchers have asserted that Hebb's reverberating circuit theory is a generally accepted fact of memory physiology (Goddard, 1980).

THE LOCUS OF MEMORY

According to Kolb and Whishaw (1990), memory is not located in any one portion of the brain, although certain areas are primarily responsible for processing memories. These authors' review of studies of the persons who had damaged different parts of the brain indicated that memory is usually disrupted, although different types of memory may be affected. No one area of the brain controls the entire process, and it is therefore necessary to discuss the role of several different areas and their control over various aspects of memory consolidation (Dudai, 1989; Squire, 1987; Squire & Butters, 1984). The gross anatomy of these brain structures is presented in Figure 3–1. The areas that control memory are located grossly in the circular region directly beneath the cingulate cortex. These areas include the thalamus, fornix, mammillary bodies, hippocampus, amygdala, basal forebrain, and prefrontal cortex. The limbic system contains all of these structures except the basal forebrain and the prefrontal cortex.

The Temporal Lobes

The temporal lobes of the brain are located near the left and right temples. Milner (1970) showed that damage to the temporal lobes can have devastating effects on memory. He studied patients who had undergone surgical removal of the temporal lobes, specifically the hippocampal region. This type of surgery is often performed to control epileptic seizures. Milner found that the extent of the memory loss was directly related to the amount of the brain that was removed.

Kolb and Whishaw (1990) summarized the work of several authors who had reported similar but more specific findings (Corsi, 1972; Jaccarino-Hiatt, 1978; Petrides, 1985; Petrides & Milner, 1982). For example, removal of the hippocampal region on the right side usually caused impaired visual memory, although these same patients had little problem recalling verbal information. Those patients who had had their left hippocampal area removed had just the reverse problem. That is, they could recall visual images reasonably well but had difficulty remembering verbal information (Corkin, 1965, 1979; Milner, 1965, 1968; Petrides & Milner, 1982; Smith & Milner, 1981). The collective findings suggest that the hippocampus plays a specialized role in memory formation. The left hippocampal region is partially responsible for remembering verbal information, whereas the right hippocampus records visual information.

The amygdala has been shown to be related to long-term memory function (Milner, 1970) and to various emotional and affective aspects of behavior (Pinkus & Tucker, 1974).

Several other areas within the limbic system and frontal brain have also been investigated as possible contributors to memory formation. For example, Assal, Probst, Zander, and Rabinowicz (1976), Rizzo (1955), and Victor, Adams, and Collins (1971) documented the contribution of

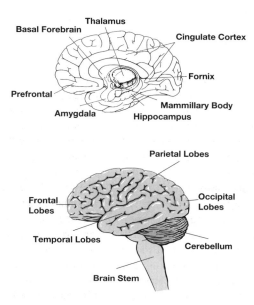

Figure 3–1 Gross Anatomy of the Brain. *Source:* The top portion of this figure is adapted from B. Kolb and I.Q. Whishaw, *Fundamentals of Human Neuropsychology,* 3rd Ed., p. 534, with permission of W.H. Freeman and Co., © 1990.

the mammillary bodies; Lishman (1978), Sprofkin and Sciarra (1952), and Teuber, Milner, and Vaughn (1968) discussed the role of the thalamus; and Mishkin and Appenzeller (1987) demonstrated the role of the basal forebrain.

The Frontal Lobes

Memory deficits often occur after damage to the frontal and prefrontal lobes (Grafman, 1989). This type of injury is common during auto accidents when the person's head hits the steering wheel or the windshield. Prizefighters also experience frontal lobe damage after repeated blows to the head. The memory impairment that typifies frontal lobe damage is not necessarily the same as that which results from damage to other areas of the brain or from removal of areas like the hippocampus. Kolb and Whishaw (1990) also noted that persons with frontal lobe damage have a difficult time with ordering, sequencing, and setting time markers that identify the past versus the present (Petrides, 1985; Prisko, 1963). Also, they may not demonstrate familiar patterns of fatigue as they work. Most of us fa-

tigue when we perform the same task for an extended period of time. The technical name for the fatigue is *proactive inhibition*. However, the average person, when shifted to another unrelated task, will experience *release from proactive inhibition*. This means that the person will be able to perform the new task about as well as he or she could when rested. Persons with frontal lobe injury also experience proactive inhibition, but they experience considerably less release from proactive inhibition. Indeed, there may be no release at all, and their performance may continue to decline. Schacter (1987) noted that the continued decline in performance seems to be unique to the frontal lobe patients. That is, persons with other types of limbic system brain injury do not show the same effect.

The Parietal Lobes

The parietal lobes are the upper sides to the top of the cortex. Damage to the rear parietal areas has been shown to affect memory for where things are located. Warrington and Weiskrantz (1973) showed that damage to the juncture between the parietal and occipital areas also produced short-term memory loss, specifically an inability to recall digit strings presented visually. This same memory failure did not occur when the digits were presented aurally. Damage to the parietal area near its juncture with the temporal lobe had the reverse effect. These patients could recall visually presented digit strings but could not recall the strings when they were presented aurally. These findings suggest that the parietal lobes also play a significant role in forming memories. The left parietal-temporal area partially controls short-term retention of verbal information, and the right parietal-occipital area controls nonverbal information storage.

AN INTEGRATIVE MODEL OF MEMORY CONSOLIDATION

This brief review of the gross anatomy of memory leads to the conclusion that several different portions of the brain, including the hippocampus, mammillary bodies, thalamus, amygdala, basal forebrain, and prefrontal cortex, are responsible for different aspects of memory consolidation. Clearly, head injury can cause a variety of types of amnesia, depending on which area of the brain is damaged. But each of these areas has been investigated in isolation. There have been few attempts to map the relationships among the various mental structures and to determine the contribution of each to the total process that we call memory. We are aware of only one attempt to develop this type of integrative structure-and-function model: that of Mishkin and Appenzeller (1987).

Mishkin and Appenzeller asserted that each area of the brain contributed something unique to the total memory process. Removal of any one area—for example, the hippocampus—could produce serious memory deficits. However, removal of only the hippocampus did not totally obliterate memory. Severe memory loss usually required removal of the hippocampus and the amygdala. Removal of other areas of the brain could also produce amnesia. For example, damage to the diencephalon (the posterior division of the forebrain including the thalamus and hy-

pothalamus), which sometimes results from strokes, head injuries, drug or alcohol abuse, or infections, also produced memory loss. The ability to recognize objects was also affected after damage to those areas of the diencephalon that were connected to both the hippocampus and the amygdala. This type of finding led Mishkin and Appenzeller to conclude that the limbic system and the diencephalon had a common circuitry. Destroying the connection between the two created about as much memory loss as destroying one or the other structure alone. Further, the diencephalon was connected to the basal forebrain and prefrontal cortex. Thus, the entire memory circuit involved the basal forebrain, amygdala, hippocampus, diencephalon, and prefrontal cortex. Each structure played a separate role, but the interaction among the various structures also determined how memories were laid down.

According to Mishkin and Appenzeller's model, information is first processed at a sensory level and then further processed by the amygdala and hippocampus. Some of the information is subsequently processed in the diencephalon, which passes it on to the prefrontal cortex and the basal forebrain. Once processed by these structures, the information eventually returns to the sensory receptors in a feedback loop. This looping process continually updates our memories and alters our perceptions.

The amygdala and the hippocampus have an especially close relationship. Mishkin and Appenzeller found that removal of the hippocampus but not the amygdala from nonhuman primates typically produced specific visual/spatial deficits. They concluded that the function of the amygdala is to correlate different sensory memories. The amygdala also controls the release of opiates that result from emotional states. The opiatelike fibers connect the amygdala to other sensory systems. This network therefore controls the emotional reactions people have in different circumstances.

Mishkin and Appenzeller did not specify the actual mechanism of memory consolidation. They did, however, suggest that it would probably take the form of Hebb's cell assembly. The notion of a reverberating circuit is common to the neural architecture postulated by both models. It is also easy to see how recognition of an experience could simply be the activation of the looping structure described by Mishkin and Appenzeller.

MEMORY VERSUS HABIT

Since the turn of the century, psychologists have discussed learning in terms of a physiological change that results from practice. This discussion has always raised the question of whether two different systems are necessary to explain memory and habit. Some theorists suggested that habit formation occurs more during a training session, whereas memory formation occurs primarily between sessions. None of them, however, felt that habit formation and memory formation could be easily separated or that they were necessarily distinct processes.

Mishkin, Malamut, and Bachevalier (1984) and Mishkin and Petri (1978) were perhaps the first to hypothesize an actual physiological distinction between memory and habit. They argued that habits and memories were stored in different areas of the brain. This explanation, if true, would resolve an issue that has generated enormous controversy among learning psychologists for an entire century. Mishkin and Petri asserted that whereas memory formation requires the contributions of the limbic system, habit formation occurs in the *striatum,* a structure that evolved much earlier. It is a cluster of nuclei located in the forebrain, positioned both to receive information from a variety of different areas of the cortex and to send information to the motor areas. This hypothesis is consistent with the authors' assumption that habits are based on simple connections between the things we perceive and the things we do. Habit formation is not a process that requires high-level thinking. Indeed, it can occur simply by repetition, and the actions can eventually be carried out unconsciously. Psychologists who study animal behavior and habit learning have argued for decades that it is possible to explain most behavior by simply studying habits. But the separate localization of memory in more evolutionarily advanced brain centers is in keeping with the argu-

ments of other psychologists that it is necessary to study higher level cognitions in order to understand complex human behavior fully (Tolman, 1932).

There is considerable evidence for the separation of habit and memory processes. As Mishkin and Appenzeller (1987) pointed out, damage to the striatum in nonhuman primates results in impaired habit learning. These authors also cited research showing that although young and adult monkeys perform at about the same levels on habit-learning tasks, adults do substantially better on memory tests. According to the theory, this is so because the striatum, which mediates habit formation, is fully developed in young as well as adult monkeys, whereas the limbic system, which mediates memory, is fully developed only in adults.

HIGHER COGNITIVE SKILLS

Language

Location of Language in the Brain

A great deal of research and controversy surrounds the localization of language functions. Kolb and Whishaw (1990) provided an elegant summary of the history of this controversy. According to their review, Gall (1880) was the first to hypothesize a relationship between the brain and higher cognitive functions. Dax (1836) first documented several case studies that showed a decrease in language skills after damage to the left hemisphere, and this assertion was reaffirmed by Auburtin (1861). About the same time, Broca (1865) demonstrated most clearly that language skills were localized in the left hemisphere and frontal lobe. These portions of the brain later became known as Broca's area, and it was recognized that damage to this area affected the motor functions of speech production. Wernicke (1875) reported that damage to the temporal-parietal cortex produced language disorders different from those reported by Broca. He reasoned that Broca's area was the locus of language production, whereas his area was the locus of language comprehension.

Although several areas have been implicated as possible loci for language, there is no single area that accounts for this higher cognitive skill. Like memory, some intensive mapping of structures will probably be necessary to account for language. The conventional wisdom is that Broca's and Wernicke's areas are broadly responsible for language production and comprehension. However, other areas also play a role: these include the association cortex in the left hemisphere and the tertiary left temporal cortex. Generally speaking, the left hemisphere is roughly localized for processing syntax, sequence, verbal relationships, rhythm, and grammar.

The contribution of the right hemisphere and the subcortical structures to language is less clear (Kolb & Whishaw, 1990). The left and right hemisphere share processing of physical gestures, voice inflection, word recognition, verbal meaning, concept formation, sequencing, and certain aspects of visual meaning. Although the right hemisphere does not play a role in speech production, it does process certain aspects of language such as auditory information.

Disorders of Language After Head Injury

Persons suffering from head injury manifest a variety of language disorders. *Aphasias* are disorders of language that are apparent in the client's speech; they may include disorders of writing and reading, although these may also be called *agraphia* and *alexia* respectively. *Fluent aphasias* are those that do not involve any severe articulation problems. They are usually associated with damage to Wernicke's area (language comprehension) and generally involve impaired ability to comprehend seen or heard words, to arrange speech sounds mentally to form coherent thoughts, to produce names for objects easily, and to repeat the words of others. *Nonfluent aphasias* are usually associated with damage to Broca's area (language production). Problems include labored speech, articulation disorders, poor repetition, and inability to complete sentences. In general, the person can understand speech but has difficulty speaking coherently (Goodglass & Kaplan, 1983).

Emotional Perception

Several authors have studied the brain's role in processing emotion. Again, these functions are only grossly localized in the right and left hemispheres. The right hemisphere coordinates the perception of others' emotions from their facial expressions and the ability to match emotions to pictures (Dekosky, Heilman, Bowers, & Valenstein, 1980; Kolb & Taylor, 1981). It also controls the ability to judge mood in others and to interpret intonations (Heilman, Scholes, & Watson, 1975; Tompkins & Mateer, 1985). Damage to the left hemisphere results in problems judging propositions and humorous situations (Brownell, Powelson, & Gardner, 1983; Gardner, Ling, Flamm, & Silverman, 1975). In general, although certain areas of the left and right hemispheres control emotional responses, the differences are not as clearly defined as they are for language.

Higher Spatial Skills

Kolb and Whishaw (1990) outlined a model of spatial representation. They postulated that the area to the rear of the parietal cortex is responsible for mentally mapping objects in a spatial coordinate system. However, this area of the brain does not identify or classify the objects. That is the function of the temporal cortex. Each of these areas receives information from the sensory cortex and sends information to other areas of the brain. The frontal cortex functions to direct movement on the basis of past experience. The parietal cortex functions to direct movement within this coordinate system. The hippocampus integrates information from the temporal cortex and from the parietal cortex to associate and remember both location and identity of objects.

Spatial disorders after brain injury are of two varieties. The first involves problems with hand-eye coordination. These disorders probably result from damaged pathways between the sensory cortex and the posterior parietal cortex or from the frontal cortex to the hippocampus. The second variety involves difficulty with orientation in three-dimensional space. These disorders probably result from damage to the pathways between the sensory cortex and the temporal cortex and from the hippocampus to the frontal cortex (Kahn, 1988; Kapur, 1988; Luria, 1963, 1973; Mayes, 1988; Talland, 1968).

THE CAUSES OF MEMORY AND COGNITIVE FAILURE

Wilson (1987) listed a variety of causes of memory and cognitive dysfunction. We begin with a discussion of the factors from her list and proceed through the less frequent causes. However, causes are often multiple. For example, head injuries that result from auto accidents are frequently alcohol related. Many clients will have a history of drug use. The therapist must therefore deal not only with the effects of the injury but also with a substance abuse problem, the effects of withdrawal, and the emotional turmoil that occurs when the client can no longer use the substances for escape and recreation.

Brain Trauma

Traumatic brain injury (TBI) is one of the major causes of memory and cognitive failure. Motor vehicle accidents certainly account for a large portion of the head injuries that therapists encounter. There are, however, many other causes of TBI. Penetrating wounds are common in wartime and in the inner cities. There is usually less overall trauma to the brain from penetrating wounds because there is less impact or global movement of the head (Lishman, 1978). Although it is difficult to predict the overall amount of cognitive disruption after a head injury, the overall severity is roughly indexed by factors such as the extent of the tissue damage, secondary strokes, lack of oxygen to the brain, brain swelling, and cerebrospinal fluid buildup (edema; Miller, 1984). Penetrating wounds can also cause infections, especially if the penetrating object fragments and it is impossible to remove all of the pieces.

Closed head injuries (CHIs) result when there is trauma to the brain but no invasive element

such as a missile wound. For example, in many auto accidents, the person's head hits the steering wheel or the windshield. This can cause not only brain damage at the site of the impact but also equal or more damage to the side opposite (*contrecoup effects;* Bloomquist & Courville, 1947). Closed head injuries also create unpredictable damage to the brain because of the rapid acceleration and rotation of the brain within the skull. This causes a tearing action that damages the tissue and disrupts the vasculature.

It is difficult to predict how much a person will recover after a TBI or CHI. The extent of recovery is grossly related to any of several factors. For example, one good predictor of recovery following head injury is the length of time the person is amnesic (Russell & Nathan, 1946; Russell & Smith, 1961). Brooks (1972, 1974) indicated that this relationship may also vary with the person's age at the time of injury. About 30% to 40% of adults experience permanent memory loss, whereas only about 10% of children do (Klonoff & Paris, 1974; Lidvall, Linderoth, & Norlin, 1974; Russell, 1932; Russell & Smith, 1961). How long the person remains in a coma may also predict recovery as well as the extent of the physical damage to the brain (Evans, 1981; Miller, 1984). In general, older patients with extensive brain damage who demonstrate long-term post-traumatic amnesia are more likely to experience permanent deficits. Chapter 5 presents a complete review of the theories and mechanisms of recovery.

Cerebral-Vascular Accidents

Cerebral-vascular accidents (CVAs) are commonly known as *strokes*. They typically produce memory and cognitive deficits. Strokes can result from a variety of causes, such as blocking of arteries (called *occlusions* or *infarctions*) or breakage of the arteries, which results in hemorrhage. Breakage often results from *aneurysms* (swollen or ballooned areas in the artery that fill with blood), embolisms, or *ischemias* (blood deficiencies in a specific area). These reduce blood supply to various portions of the brain, producing cell death and tissue damage. Blockage of the arteries usually occurs in the posterior areas. The condition commonly produces amnesia and can also restrict the visual fields (Benson, Marsden, & Meadows, 1974; Bouldin, Brian, Pepin, & Barbizet, 1968; Dejong, Itabashi, & Olson, 1969; Victor et al., 1971).

Subarachnoid hemorrhages are caused by rupture of aneurysms that cause blood to flow into the space that surrounds the brain. This type of stroke accounts for about 5% to 10% of CVAs. Aneurysms usually occur where the cerebral arteries merge. If the sac ruptures, the sudden loss of blood causes cell damage in the surrounding area. The breakage can have a variety of symptoms, including memory loss, confusion, impaired speech, and disorientation. How long the disorder persists is related to the extent of the damage and how long the person remains unattended after the stroke, as well as the quality of the care received after the stroke.

Ischemias are due to a temporary constriction of the vasculature, usually in the posterior brain area, that creates a sudden blockage or embolism. They usually produce a global but temporary loss of memory as well as other cognitive deficits (Fisher & Adams, 1958, 1964; Hecaen & Albert, 1978; Patten, 1971; Shuttleworth & Wise, 1973).

Ischemic attacks can have a variety of causes, including severe migraine headaches, concussions, epileptic seizures, and hypoglycemia (Kolb & Whishaw, 1990). These are sometimes called transient ischemic attacks (TIAs) because they do not last long. Nevertheless, there may be a substantial loss of memory, and the attacks may recur (Markowitsch, 1983; Mazzucchi, Moretti, Caffara, & Parma, 1980).

Substance Abuse

Alcohol and drug use often predispose individuals to head injury from accidents. Long-term use of drugs or alcohol, however, can also cause slow but measurable cognitive decline. Long-term alcohol use can lead to a thiamine deficiency that results in memory impairment. This is usually part of a larger complex of symptoms, called Wernicke-Korsakoff syndrome, that includes confusion, disorientation, and uncoordinated movement (Malamud & Skillicorn, 1956). Persons with this disorder typically have problems with short-term memory (Kinsbourne & Wood, 1975). They may also have difficulty recognizing familiar people, places, or things (Butters, 1984, 1979). Tasks that require complex mental switching operations, anticipation, or planning and foresight are also quite difficult (Benton, 1968; Corkin, 1979; Squire, 1982). Korsakoff patients do not, however, show the classic signs of dementia, which include limited intellectual functions and abstract reasoning (Talland, 1965). They frequently undergo a noticeable personality change whereby they become docile and passive (Butters, 1979).

The *Diagnostic and Statistical Manual of Mental Disorders*, fourth edition (*DSM-IV*; American Psychiatric Association, 1994), indexes a variety of substances that may cause memory and cognitive dysfunction during withdrawal, intoxication, or both. For example, marijuana users frequently experience memory failure while they are using the drug, but the effect vanishes after about a month of withdrawal. Heavy caffeine or nicotine use may result in temporary loss of cognitive efficiency during withdrawal.

The *DSM-IV* list also includes alcohol, amphetamines, caffeine, marijuana, cocaine, hallucinogens, inhalants, nicotine, opiates, phencyclidine (PCP), and sedative drugs. Memory and cognitive deficits can result from long-term dependence, abuse, intoxication, or withdrawal. Substance-induced dementia, for example, includes memory impairment, aphasia, limited ability to carry out motor tasks (apraxia), inability to recognize or identify objects by touch (agnosia), and disturbed planning, organization, sequencing, and abstraction.

In our experience, long-term use of specific substances such as inhalants, PCP, alcohol, and amphetamines produces the most damage. Cognitive deficits can also result from exposure to chemicals such as lead or other toxic compounds or from use of certain medications such as Propranolol and Dilantin (Zasler, 1990).

Brain Cancer

Brain tumors will often cause specific cognitive and personality changes. The type of change and its extent depend on the location of the growth (Keschner, Bender, & Strauss, 1938; Selecki, 1964; Williams & Pennybacker, 1954). The problems are exacerbated when the tumors grow to the point at which they substantially increase intercranial pressure (Brain, 1963). Whether the tumor is malignant, whether it metastasizes, and the rate of its growth also have an obvious effect on the change in cognitive status. Several authors have noted that tumors located in the frontal lobes produce dementialike problems, including memory loss and poor insight, planning, and organization (Hecaen & Ajuriaguerra, 1956; Sachs, 1950). Sprofkin and Sciarra (1952) noted that memory loss is most likely when the tumor is located in the brain's third ventricle.

Brain Infections

Viral encephalitis and other types of brain infections can cause severe cognitive defects (Robbins, 1958). For example, the herpes simplex and herpes zoster viruses are known to produce memory loss when the infection occurs in the temporal or frontal lobes (Lishman, 1978). These infections usually do not occur in the diencephalon structures, so the cognitive deficits are more like those of patients who undergo surgery to remove the temporal lobes and less like those of patients with the Wernicke-Korsakoff disorder described earlier. Brain infections can also result from invasive missile wounds, parasites, and ear infections.

Brain Surgery

Surgeries that damage the anterior portion of the hippocampus can produce severe amnesia (Milner, 1966; Penfield & Milner, 1958; Scoville & Milner, 1957). Memory loss does not seem to occur when only the amygdala is removed or damaged. The site of the surgery can have specific effects on memory. For example, removal of the left temporal lobe limits the person's ability to learn and remember verbal information but has relatively little effect on visual information. Just the opposite problem occurs when the right temporal lobe is removed or damaged.

Degenerative Conditions

A variety of degenerative diseases such as Alzheimer's disease, Pick's disease, and Huntington's chorea also produce corresponding memory and cognitive impairment that worsens as the person ages (Wilson, 1987). The behavioral symptoms caused by Alzheimer's disease are similar to those of senility. The disorder occurs in approximately 10% of persons over the age of 65 (Walton, 1971). Memory impairment is usually the first sign, although the condition often progresses to include other symptoms such as disorientation and loss of the ability to abstract and to generalize (Joynt & Shoulson, 1979). Pick's disease begins in the frontal lobes, with resulting change in personality and behavior. As the condition progresses, the symptoms eventually become indistinguishable from those of Alzheimer's patients (Walton, 1971). Both of these conditions can produce rapid deterioration and eventual death within 2 to 5 years after diagnosis. Huntington's chorea is an inherited disease, and the symptoms usually begin after age 40. The most obvious symptoms include poor control of facial muscles, uncontrolled movements, slowness of processing, and memory loss (Albert, Feldman, & Willis, 1974).

Longevity

Most people report that their memory and thinking skills decline with age, and performance on tests of intelligence and reasoning skills typically deteriorates with age. It is possible that the cell assemblies discussed earlier actually change and that the dendrites of the various brain cells establish new connections that interfere with older memories. It is also possible that young children and adults have very different memory systems. Clearly, verbal skills are poorly developed during infancy and early childhood. During these years, it is possible that memory and thinking are mediated by visual/spatial processes.

Most of us have a hard time recalling our infancy, although we have a clearer recollection of childhood and early school years (Campbell & Spear, 1972). Our memories for the early years are usually distorted by selective attention to photographs and the recollections of parents and relatives. Likewise, the elderly often have clear memories of their early life that are impossible to validate.

We probably do not lose stored memories as we get older, but we may lose access to them. For example, we have all had the experience of returning to our hometown and having a flood of memories when we look at the home or neighborhood where we grew up. It is also likely that the priorities of memory and cognitive effort change as we mature. There are a number of explanations for what we observe to be cognitive dysfunction that may not be the result of mental deterioration.

Emotional Status

Our emotional state also determines our ability to think clearly and to remember. Ellis and Hunt (1993) pointed out that particular emotional states are stored along with memories. It may therefore be difficult to recall the information unless the emotional state is reinvoked. The general phenomenon is that people in a sad mood show decreased learning and inability to organize novel information. They have a hard time retrieving the information as well. The problem is certainly consistent with Mishkin and Appenzeller's (1987) view of the function of the amygdala in memory formation. Hertel (1994) provided an excellent summary of the relationship between emotional mood state and cognitive functioning.

Other Causes of Cognitive Dysfunction

Some of the less common causes of cognitive dysfunction include temporal lobe epilepsy, electroconvulsive shock therapy, and commissurotomy (surgical disconnection of the two hemispheres). Epilepsy can destroy cells in the hippocampus. It is commonly a problem that accompanies head injury. Electroconvulsive shock is a procedure that is used for treatment of severe depression. According to Kolb and Whishaw (1990), the effects are similar to those of seizures. The procedure involves applying an electric current to the temporal lobes for about one-half second to create a mild convulsion. Patients receive this treatment several times a week, and the amount of memory loss is related to the frequency of treatment. Memory returns to near-normal levels within a year after the treatments are stopped, but there may be subtle residual memory loss for autobiographical details (Taylor, Tompkins, Demers, & Anderson, 1982).

CONCLUSION

This chapter presented a variety of information concerning the relationship between brain structure, memory, and higher cognitive skills. These relationships have been studied extensively, and certain facts about the structure and function of the brain are well documented. For example, damage to the left temporal region usually results in difficulty remembering verbal information, whereas damage to the right temporal region creates problems recalling visual information. Spatial information is processed in the parietal and occipital regions. The frontal area mediates memory for order, temporal sequence, and priority.

The reverberating circuit proposed by Hebb (1949, 1961) is still generally accepted as the basic physiological mechanism of memory. This model assumes that neurons fire collectively when stimulated and gradually become associated into a circuit that forms the memory. When one neuron is stimulated, its activation spreads throughout the entire circuit, thus reviving the memory.

Although a number of brain structures have been identified that mediate memory and cognition, there are few integrative models that account for the complexity of thought. Mishkin and Appenzeller (1987) proposed a model of memory formation, and Kolb and Whishaw (1990) provided a model of visual-spatial processing. Mishkin and Petri (1978) suggested that habits and memories are stored in different areas of the brain.

Several different factors account for memory and cognitive decline. Among them, closed head injury, stroke, substance abuse, brain cancer, brain surgery, degenerative diseases, and age usually produce the greatest decline. Some of the less common causes include electroconvulsive shock therapy, commissurotomy, and epilepsy.

REFERENCES

Albert, M.S., Feldman, R.G., & Willis, A.L. (1974). The subcortical "dementia" of progressive supranuclear palsy. *Journal of Neurology, Neurosurgery, and Psychiatry, 37*, 121–130.

American Psychiatric Association. (1994). *Diagnostic and statistical manual of mental disorders* (4th ed.). Washington, DC: Author.

Assal, G., Probst, A., Zander, E., & Rabinowicz, T. (1976). Syndrome amnesique per infiltration tumoral. *Archives Suisses de Neurologie et Psychiatrie, 119*, 317–324.

Benson, D.F., Marsden, C.D., & Meadows, J.C. (1974). The amnesic syndrome of posterior cerebral artery occlusion. *Acta Neurologica Scandinavica, 50*, 133–145.

Benton, A.L. (1968). Differential behavioral effects in frontal lobe disease. *Neuropsychologia, 6*, 53–60.

Bloomquist, E.R., & Courville, C.B. (1947). The nature and incidence of traumatic lesions of the brain: A survey of 350 cases with autopsy. *Bulletin of the Los Angeles Neurological Society, 12*, 174–183.

Bouldin, G., Brian, S., Pepin, B., & Barbizet, J. (1968). Syndrome de Korsakoff d'etiologie arteriopathique. *Revue Neurologique, 119*, 341–348.

Brain, W.R. (1963). The neurological complications of neuroplasm. *Lancet, 1*, 179–184.

Brooks, D.N. (1972). Memory and head injury. *Journal of Nervous and Mental Disease, 155*, 350–355.

Brooks, D.N. (1974). Recognition memory and head injury. *Journal of Neurology, Neurosurgery, and Psychiatry, 37*, 794–801.

Brownell, H.H., Powelson, M.J., & Gardner, H. (1983). Surprise but not coherence: Sensitivity to verbal humor in right-hemisphere patients. *Brain and Language, 18*, 20–27.

Butters, N. (1979). Amnesic disorders. In K.M. Heilman & E. Valenstein (Eds.), *Clinical neuropsychology*. New York: Oxford University Press.

Butters, N. (1984). The clinical aspects of memory disorders: Contributions from experimental studies in amnesia. *Journal of Clinical Neuropsychology, 6*, 17–36.

Campbell, B.A., & Spear, N.E. (1972). Ontogeny of memory. *Psychological Review, 79*, 213–236.

Corkin, S. (1965). Tactually-guided maze learning in man: Effects of unilateral cortical excisions, and bilateral hippocampal lesions. *Neuropsychologia, 3*, 339–351.

Corkin, S. (1979). Hidden-figure test performance: Lasting effects of unilateral penetrating head injury and transient effect of bilateral cinglotomy. *Neuropsychologia, 27*, 585–605.

Corsi, P.M. (1972). *Human memory and the medial temporal region of the brain.* Unpublished doctoral dissertation, McGill University, Montreal.

Dejong, R.N., Itabashi, H.H., & Olson, J.R. (1969). Memory loss due to hippocampal lesions: Report of a case. *Archives of Neurology, 20*, 339–348.

Dekosky, S.T., Heilman, K.H., Bowers, D., & Valenstein, E. (1980). Recognition and discrimination of emotional faces and pictures. *Brain and Language, 9*, 206–214.

Dudai, Y. (1989). *The neurobiology of memory: Concepts, findings, trends.* New York: Oxford University Press.

Ellis, H.C., & Hunt, R.R. (1993). *Fundamentals of human memory and cognition.* Dubuque, IA: William C. Brown.

Evans, C.D. (Ed.). (1981). *Rehabilitation after severe head injury.* Edinburgh: Churchill Livingstone.

Fisher, C.M., & Adams, R.D. (1958). Transient global amnesia. *Transactions of the American Neurological Association, 83*, 143.

Fisher, C.M., & Adams, R.D. (1964). Transient global amnesia. *Acta Neurologica Scandinavica, 40*(Suppl. 9), 7–83.

Gardner, H., Ling, H.P., Flamm, L., & Silverman, J. (1975). Comprehension and appreciation of humorous material following brain damage. *Brain, 98*, 399–412.

Goddard, G.V. (1980). Component properties of the memory machine: Hebb revisited. In P.W. Jusczyk & R.M. Klein (Eds.), *The nature of thought: Essays in honor of D.O. Hebb.* Hillsdale, NJ: Lawrence Erlbaum.

Goodglass, H., & Kaplan, E. (1983). *Assessment of aphasia and related disorders.* Philadelphia: Lea & Febiger.

Grafman, J. (1989). Plans, actions, and mental sets: Managerial knowledge units in the frontal lobes. In E. Perecman (Ed.), *Integrating theory and practice in clinical neuropsychology.* (93–138). Hillsdale, NJ: Lawrence Erlbaum.

Hebb, D.O. (1949). *Organization of behavior.* New York: John Wiley.

Hebb, D.O. (1961). Distinctive features of learning in the higher animal. In J.F. Delafresnaye (Ed.), *Brain mechanisms and learning.* London: Blackwell.

Hecaen, H., & Ajuriaguerra, J. (1956). *Troubles mentaux au cours des tumeurs intracraniennes.* Paris: Masson.

Hecaen, H., & Albert, M.L. (1978). *Human neuropsychology.* New York: John Wiley.

Heilman, K., Scholes, M.R., & Watson, R.T. (1975). Auditory affective agnosia. *Journal of Neurology, Neurosurgery, and Psychiatry, 38,* 69–72.

Herrmann, M., Ruppin, E., & Usher, M. (1993). A neural model of the dynamic activation of memory. *Biological Cybernetics, 68,* 455–563.

Hertel, P. (1994). Depressive deficits in memory: Implications for memory improvement following traumatic brain injury. *NeuroRehabilitation, 4*(3), 143–150.

Jaccarino-Hiatt, G. (1978). *Impairment of cognitive organization in patients with temporal-lobe lesions.* Unpublished doctoral dissertation, McGill University, Montreal.

Joynt, R.J., & Shoulson, I. (1979). Dementia. In K.M. Heilman & E. Valenstein (Eds.), *Clinical neuropsychology.* New York: Oxford University Press.

Kahn, A.U. (1988). *Clinical disorders of memory.* New York: Plenum.

Kapur, N. (1988). *Memory disorders in clinical practice.* London: Butterworth.

Keschner, M., Bender, M.B., & Strauss, I. (1938). Mental symptoms associated with brain tumor: A study of 530 verified cases. *Journal of the American Medical Association, 110,* 714–718.

Kinsbourne, M., & Wood, F. (1975). Short-term memory processes and the amnesic syndrome. In M. Kinsbourne and F. Wood (Eds.), *Short-term memory.* New York: Academic Press.

Klonoff, H., & Paris, R. (1974). Immediate, short-term, and residual effects of acute head injuries in children: Neuropsychological and neurological correlates. *Clinical neuropsychology: Current status and applications.* Washington, DC: V.H. Winston.

Kolb, B., & Taylor, L. (1981). Affective behavior in patients with localized cortical excisions: Role of lesion site and side. *Science, 214,* 89–91.

Kolb, B., & Whishaw, I.Q. (1990). *Fundamentals of human neuropsychology.* New York: W.H. Freeman.

Lidvall, H.E., Linderoth, B., & Norlin, B. (1974). Causes of the postconcussional syndrome. *Acta Neurologica Scandinavica, 50*(Suppl. 56).

Lishman, W. (1978). *Organic psychiatry.* Oxford, UK: Blackwell.

Luria, A.R. (1963). *Restoration of function after brain injury.* New York: Macmillan.

Luria, A.R. (1973). *Higher cortical functions in man.* New York: Basic Books.

Malamud, N., & Skillicorn, S.A. (1956). Relationship between the Wernicke and the Korsakoff syndrome. *Archives of Neurology and Psychiatry, 76,* 585–596.

Markowitsch, H.J. (1983). Transient global amnesia. *Neuroscience and Behavioral Review, 7,* 35–43.

Mayes, A.R. (1988). *Human organic memory disorders.* Cambridge, UK: Cambridge University Press.

Mazzucchi, A., Moretti, G., Caffara, P., & Parma, M. (1980). Neuropsychological functions in the follow-up of transient global amnesia. *Brain, 103,* 161–178.

McCarthy, R.A., & Warrington, E.K. (1990). *Cognitive neuropsychology: A clinical introduction.* San Diego: Academic Press.

Miller, E. (1984). *Recovery and management of neuropsychological impairments.* New York: John Wiley.

Milner, B. (1965). Visually guided maze learning in man: Effects of bilateral hippocampal, bilateral frontal, and unilateral cerebral lesions. *Society for Neuroscience Abstracts, 3,* 517.

Milner, B. (1966). Amnesia following operation on the temporal lobes. In C.W.M. Whitty & B. Zangweill (Eds.), *Amnesia.* London: Butterworths.

Milner, B. (1968). Visual recognition and recall after right temporal-lobe excision in man. *Neuropsychologia, 6,* 191–209.

Milner, B. (1970). Memory and the medial temporal regions of the brain. In K.H. Prebram & D.E. Broadbent (Eds.), *Biology of memory.* New York: Academic Press.

Mishkin, M., & Appenzeller, T. (1987). The anatomy of memory. *Scientific American, 256*(6), 80–89.

Mishkin, M., Malamut, B., & Bachevalier, J. (1984). Memories and habits: Two neuronal systems. In G. Lynch, J.L. McGaugh, & N.M. Weinberger (Eds.), *Neurobiology of learning and memory.* New York: Guilford.

Mishkin, M., & Petri, L. (1978). Memories and habits: Some implications for the analysis of learning and retention. In L.R. Squires & N. Butters (Eds.), *Neuropsychology of memory* (pp. 287–296). New York: Guilford.

Patten, B.M. (1971). Transient global amnesia syndrome. *Journal of the American Medical Association, 217,* 690–691.

Penfield, W., & Milner, B. (1958). Memory deficit produced by bilateral lesions in the hippocampal zone. *Archives of Neurology and Psychiatry, 79,* 475–497.

Petrides, M. (1985). Deficits in conditional associative-learning tasks after frontal- and temporal-lobe lesions in man. *Neuropsychologia, 23,* 601–614.

Petrides, M., & Milner, B. (1982). Deficits on subject-ordered tasks after frontal- and temporal-lobe lesions in man. *Neuropsychologia, 20,* 249–262.

Pinkus, J.H., & Tucker, G.J. (1974). *Behavioral neurology.* New York: Oxford University Press.

Prisko, L. (1963). *Short-term memory for focal cerebral damage.* Unpublished doctoral dissertation, McGill University, Montreal.

Rizzo, E.M. (1955). Sulla sindroma de Korsakoff. *Rassegna di Studi Psichiatrici, 44*, 801–816.

Robbins, C.F. (1958). The clinical and laboratory diagnosis of viral infections of the central nervous system. In W.C. Fields & R.J. Blathner (Eds.), *Viral encephalitis.* Springfield, IL: Charles C Thomas.

Russell, W.R. (1932). Cerebral involvement in head injury. *Brain, 55*, 549–603.

Russell, W.R., & Nathan, P.W. (1946). Traumatic amnesia. *Brain, 69*, 280–301.

Russell, W.R., & Smith, A. (1961). Post traumatic amnesia in closed head injuries. *Archives of Neurology, 5*, 4–17.

Sachs, L. (1950). Meningiomas with dementia as the first and presenting feature. *Journal of Mental Science, 96*, 998–1007.

Schacter, D.L. (1987). Memory, amnesia, and frontal lobe dysfunction. *Psychobiology, 15*, 21–36.

Scoville, W.B., & Milner, B. (1957). Loss of recent memory after bilateral hippocampal lesions. *Journal of Neurology, Neurosurgery and Psychiatry, 20*, 11–21.

Selecki, R. (1964). Cerebral midline-tumors involving the corpus callosum among mental hospital patients. *Medical Journal of Australia, 2*, 954–968.

Shuttleworth, E.C., & Wise, G.R. (1973). Transient global amnesia due to arterial embolism. *Archives of Neurology, 29*, 340–342.

Smith, M.L., & Milner, B. (1981). The role of the right hippocampus in the recall of spatial location. *Neuropsychologia, 13*, 51–58.

Sprofkin, B.E., & Sciarra, D. (1952). Korsakoff psychosis associated with cerebral tumors. *Neurology, 2*, 427–434.

Squire, L.R. (1982). Comparisons between forms of amnesia: Some deficits are unique to Korsakoff's syndrome. *Journal of Experimental Psychology: Learning, Memory, and Cognition, 8*, 560–571.

Squire, L.R. (1987). *Memory and brain.* New York: Oxford University Press.

Squire, L.R., & Butters, N. (1984). *The neurospsychology of memory.* New York: Guilford.

Talland, G.A. (1965). *Deranged memory.* New York: Academic Press.

Talland, G.A. (1968). *Disorders of memory.* Harmondsworth, UK: Penguin.

Taylor, J.R., Tompkins, R., Demers, R., & Anderson, D. (1982). Electroconvulsive therapy and memory dysfunction: Is there evidence for prolonged defects? *Biological Psychiatry, 17*, 1169–1193.

Teuber, H.L., Milner, B., & Vaughan, H.G. (1968). Persistent anterograde amnesia after stab wound of the basal brain. *Neuropsychologia, 6*, 267–282.

Tolman, E.C. (1932). *Purposive behavior in animals and men.* New York: Appleton-Century-Crofts.

Tompkins, C.A., & Mateer, C.A. (1985). Right hemisphere appreciation of intonational and linguistic indications of affect. *Brain and Language, 24*, 185–203.

Victor, M., Adams, R.D., & Collins, G.H. (1971). *The Wernicke-Korsakoff syndrome.* Oxford, UK: Blackwell.

Walton, J.N. (1971). *Essentials of neurology.* London: Pitman.

Warrington, E.K., & Weiskrantz, L. (1973). An analysis of short-term and long-term memory defects in man. In J.A. Deutsch (Ed.), *The physiological basis of memory.* New York: Academic Press.

Williams, M., & Pennybacker, J. (1954). Memory disturbances in third ventricle tumors. *Journal of Neurology, Neurosurgery, and Psychiatry, 17*, 173–182.

Wilson, B. (1987). *Rehabilitation of memory.* New York: Guilford.

Zasler, N. (1990, September). *Pharmacologic approaches to cognitive and behavior dysfunction.* Paper presented at the Conference on Cognitive Rehabilitation and Community Integration, Richmond, VA.

Chapter 4

The Dynamics of Attention and Memory

Attention and memory are fundamental cognitive processes, and they are frequently impaired after brain injury. To provide effective rehabilitation for either of these processes, it is first necessary to understand their basic underlying mechanisms. We will therefore present a simplified overview of the various concepts and distinctions of attention and memory before discussing how to retrain these fundamental processes in later chapters.

Attention is a complex mental process. It is *selective,* which means that it is a preferential process that functions to exclude certain aspects of the client's sensory field (Duncan, 1984; Parasuraman & Davies, 1984). It is *modulating* because it involves an allocation of the client's cognitive processes as the situation demands. Attention also has *signaling* and *vigilance* components. This means that attention can alert the person to important aspects of his or her environment and that the person can choose to sustain his or her attention and to control any overload that may occur (Kahneman, 1973; Kahneman & Treisman, 1984).

MODELS OF ATTENTION

Early- Versus Late-Selection Models

An ongoing debate in the early literature on attention was the question of where attention occurs (Ellis & Hunt, 1993). *Early-selection models,* such as the switch and attenuator models discussed below, assumed that selective attention occurs before the information reaches the long-term memory. Information is literally filtered out before it can be processed. *Late-selection models* assumed that all or most of the sensory information registers in the long-term store but that the person simply cannot respond to more than a fraction of it at any one time. Brain injury survivors have problems that are consistent with either of these theories. They frequently seem overwhelmed in situations in which there are several things to process at the same time. However, whether they are screening out most of the information or merely are unable to organize all that they perceive is unclear.

Early-Selection Models

Perhaps the earliest model of attention was Broadbent's (1958) *switch model.* The basic idea was that a person switches attention back and forth between competing sources. Physical aspects of incoming information, such as the volume of a person's voice, control the switching process. The switching occurs rapidly, and we seldom notice the individual focus points. Attention failure results when the switching mechanism breaks down. For example, a person may not be able to stay focused on any individual event or conversation because he or she is constantly switching back and forth between distractions. On the other hand, a person may become fixated because he or she cannot break away from one focus point or another. The implication for cognitive rehabilitation is that remediation must retrain the switching process. For example, training in dichotic listening has been suggested by Craine and Gudeman (1981) as a therapy for attention problems after brain injury. In this task, different messages are played into each ear to retrain the client to switch back and forth between the two.

Triesman (1964) postulated an *attenuation model* of attention. Her basic assumption was that attention is controlled by a filtering mechanism. Both physical and semantic cues control the amount of attention a person gives to any specific event. For example, when one is engaged in a conversation, the volume of the voice of the other person controls attenuation. However, the quality of the message does also. This feature explains a person's uncanny ability to switch attention when he or she detects his or her name in a conversation across the room. Attention is likened to a set of filters that open in relation to the amount of attention the object or event demands. Attention failure may be due to any number of causes: limitations of the size of the filters, inability to open more than one filter, or inability to inhibit the cues that control filtering. It may therefore be necessary to train clients with attention deficits to focus on the dominant filter, eliminate distracting cues, or eliminate internal distractions that arise from thought intrusions.

Late-Selection Models

The fundamental assumption of the late-selection models of attention is that all information registers in long-term memory but that it is difficult to process two different registrations at the same time (Deutsch & Deutsch, 1963; Norman, 1968). The implication is that attention deficit results from an inability to organize a response to seemingly overwhelming information. Accordingly, one can dramatically improve a client's ability to attend by limiting the amount of information that is registered.

Capacity models of attention assume that our ability to attend is related to the process of allocating our mental resources within a limited-capacity system. *Capacity* refers to the amount of the person's consciousness that is taken up with any given task. This theory assumes that attention is the process of allocating, prioritizing, managing, or otherwise organizing a response to incoming information so that various aspects of the task receive appropriate amounts of processing. Attention failure is presumably due to either reduced capacity or limited ability to allocate. Examples of both are quite common after brain injury. For example, clients' digit spans are frequently reduced. Clients also commonly have reduced ability to perform mental control and switching operations. One way to treat these disorders is to develop skills to an automatic level so that they do not take up much capacity. Teaching encoding strategies can also help to compress more information into a form that can be processed by the limited-capacity system.

Selective Attention Models

Duncan (1984) described various types of models of visual attention that differ mainly in terms of the unit of analysis for a person's selective attention. None of these was specifically designed to explain an attention deficit after brain injury, although each makes some interesting theoretical suppositions concerning the nature of attention failure.

Discrimination-based models assume that attention differs in terms of the number of separate discriminations the person can make in a given time frame (Duncan, 1984). For example, an *analyzer theory* assumed that people analyze simple features with specific analyzers. Difficult discriminations involve similar features for which similar analyzers are called into play. Perceptual difficulties arise when similar analyzers conflict with each other. Although there is no strong evidence for this type of theory, it is conceivable that brain-injured persons have difficulty attending because the number and variety of analyzers are restricted or because they are unable to control the various conflicting analyzers present in a particular task.

In *space-based models*, attention is likened to a mental spotlight or a zoom lens (Treisman & Schmidt, 1982) such that information in the focus can be analyzed to the exclusion of everything else. The unit of analysis is therefore the span of the focal area. Accordingly, it is possible that an attention deficit after brain injury is due primarily to a restriction of this mental spotlight. Difficulties arise because the person's restricted range of input creates impoverished selections from the total array of information (Posner, 1980). This theory is consistent with Parenté, Anderson-Parenté, and Shaw's (1989) and McClur, Browning, Vantrease, and Bittle's (1994) iconic memory research. These authors reported restricted iconic memory after traumatic brain injury.

Object-oriented models (Neisser, 1967) are some of the oldest models of attention. The unit of analysis is the number of objects that can occupy the person's perceptual field at any one time. Neisser's model assumes that attention involves a preattentive stage during which the person's focus point is divided into separate areas or separate object groupings. The division is controlled by Gestalt principles such as *proximity, similarity, good continuation,* and *closure,* which occur in parallel. Kahneman and Henik (1977) reported that these groups, once formed, retain their integrity. The second stage involves *focal attention,* which occurs as a serial process across the various object groupings. This means that a person first forms the perceptual groups and then allocates attention to each group in sequence. This model predicts that limited attention may occur because in the first stage the person can no longer form perceptual object groups. In the second stage, the serial search process may be slowed or incomplete or may follow an inefficient path (Kahneman, Triesman, & Gibbs, 1992; Triesman, Kahneman, & Burkell, 1983).

Our discussion of attention theory is admittedly incomplete. Our purpose was to present some of the more well-developed models and to extract any of their implications for brain injury rehabilitation. Regardless of which theory is correct, there is agreement on several points that

may help a therapist understand and treat attentional problems after brain injury. Most theories would agree that attention deficits may be due to a breakdown of basic sensory processes that can often be rectified by simple interventions such as hearing aids or glasses. These theories also point out that there are a variety of forms of attention, such as abilities to allocate mental resources, to avoid distraction, and to switch mentally from task to task. It may therefore be necessary to work with specific aspects in isolation. Attentional problems will usually require restricting the amount of distraction the person encounters. For example, the authors have found that having a client wear earplugs while reading can greatly improve attention. The various theories also point out the value of a hierarchical retraining regimen in which the simpler processes such as orientation and vigilance are retrained first, followed by more complex attentional processes such as selective attention, divided attention, and the allocation of mental effort.

A FUNCTIONAL MODEL OF MEMORY

There are a variety of well-developed models of memory, and excellent summaries of these models are generally available (e.g., Baddeley, 1982; Baddeley & Hitch, 1974; Ellis & Hunt, 1993). Most were never intended for use as models of traumatic brain injury rehabilitation. Parenté and Anderson-Parenté (1991) provided a simplified memory model that could be used to understand memory deficits after brain injury. This model is presented in Figure 4–1.

Figure 4–1 is a diagram of the workings of the multimodal model as it applies to memory. The sensory memory store is thoroughly discussed in Chapter 8. In this chapter, we focus on the working memory. This is a particular portion of the cognitive system that is responsible for processing information so that it can be stored and retrieved easily. Basically, two aspects of the working memory are important to the rehabilitation process. The first involves the person's ability to rehearse information and maintain it in memory for further processing. The second is

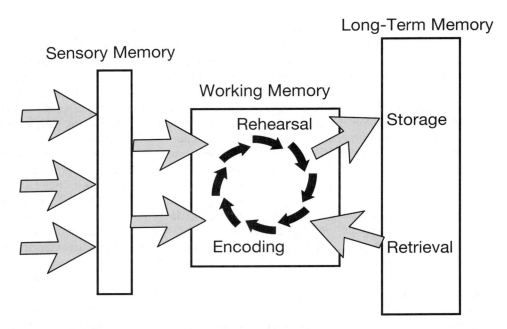

Figure 4–1 Multimodal Model of Memory. *Source:* Adapted from R. Parenté and A. DiCesare, Retraining Memory: Theory, Evaluation, and Applications, in *Cognitive Rehabilitation for Persons with Traumatic Brain Injury: A Functional Approach,* p. 148, J.S. Kreutzer and P.H. Wehman, Eds., © 1991, with permission of Paul H. Brookes Publishing Co.

the ability to transform the information into a form that can be easily stored and retrieved. We will discuss maintenance rehearsal in Chapter 10 and will return again to the topic of rehearsal in Chapter 12.

Once the information has been transformed in the cognitive system's working memory, it is stored in the long-term memory. It is retrieved from long-term memory when the person needs to use it again in some way. After brain injury, there is seldom a problem with storage of information in long-term memory. The usual problems involve (a) inability to generate the appropriate cues that are necessary for retrieval from long-term memory, (b) inability to manipulate information in the working memory, and (c) inability to rehearse effectively.

This model has several implications for brain injury rehabilitation. First, if the sensory system is impaired, then little information will get into the working memory. This is why an entire chapter of this book is devoted to the topic of retraining sensory memory. Second, memory strategy training is only effective if the person is able to rehearse effectively. Without rehearsal, the in-

formation is lost from the working memory, and no strategy will help to store it away in the long-term memory. Finally, it is crucial to focus on the retrieval process during therapy. This involves teaching the client techniques for cuing and also the use of prosthetic devices. This topic is discussed in detail in Chapter 25.

In this chapter, we are primarily concerned with the mechanism that creates mental transformations of information. These mental transformations are called *encodings,* and their purpose is to make storage and retrieval of information quicker and more efficient. The ability to transform information in working memory is central to the process of remembering. Simply rehearsing something over and over again ensures only that we can maintain it in the working memory. The ability to store and to retrieve information from long-term memory depends on our ability to transform it in working memory (Ellis, Parenté, Grah, & Spiering, 1975; Ellis, Parenté, & Walker, 1974). Without encoding, the client is doomed to process most of life's events in a literal form that may be quite difficult to retrieve in its entirety. For example, we can all appreciate the encoding that goes on as we read the pages of this book. We do not remember each word, but rather the gist or meaning of each section. At first reading, the information registers in a literal form. However, with additional reading we combine the meaning with stored experiences, we see meanings that were not initially apparent, and we organize the information into broad themes and subthemes. What we remember are usually the themes. This type of encoding still goes on after brain injury, just at a slower pace. The goal of therapy is therefore to teach the client techniques for speeding up the encoding process. This type of training involves several encoding strategies, the more common of which are discussed below (Ellis, Groggin, & Parenté, 1979).

Image codes are mental pictures that integrate novel information into a visual scene. For example, most of us can conjure up an image of our mother's face or of our favorite movie star. Injury to the right side of the brain may limit the person's ability to use visual imagery. With most clients, however, imagery can be an especially powerful memory aid. For example, we later discuss how clients can use imagery to recall names and faces or to remember what they read in books, magazines, and newspapers.

Verbal labels are symbols, words, or phrases that integrate meaning into a verbal unit. Most verbal labels can take on a variety of different meanings. For example, the letter *A* can suggest the first letter of the alphabet. If printed in scarlet, it can suggest adultery. The word *cat* can suggest a household feline, a lion, a tiger, or an angry woman. Verbal labels are the basis for several different memory strategies, including the word mnemonic (discussed later in this chapter), in which each letter of some word signals recall of some sequence of events. Verbal labels are also especially helpful for encoding unfamiliar visual information. For example, it may be easier to navigate the floor plan of a building if the client is shown that it is shaped according to a familiar letter of the alphabet.

Motor codes are procedures that we learn via some form of motor movement. Often, the only way we can remember them is to perform them. For example, it is difficult for most guitarists to

teach their art without demonstrating chord patterns on a guitar fretboard. Similarly, it is usually necessary for touch typists to demonstrate finger placements on a keyboard to teach their skills. After considerable practice, motor codes may translate into some form of a verbal label. For example, guitar fret patterns become associated with an A minor or an E flat. There is considerable literature that indicates that brain-injured clients can learn motor procedures and perform them quite efficiently. Motor codes are therefore an especially valuable aspect of therapy because, conceivably, most clients can learn and remember motor procedures about as well as anyone else. They may therefore be able to learn employable skills that are combinations of motor codes.

Auditory codes form our memories for what we hear, including conversations, the nonverbal aspects of speech that are carried in voice inflections, music, warning signals, and so forth. Indeed, much of a client's daily experience involves auditory coding of conversation. Listening skills are therefore essential for processing the various aspects of spoken language that convey meaning in conversations, lectures, the media, and so forth. We therefore present a mnemonic that the therapist can use to train clients in effective listening skills.

Distinctions of Memory and Forgetting

There are many types of memory and forgetting, and the therapist will have to understand the difference between the various concepts in order to diagnose correctly and work with a memory impairment. We therefore discuss some of the more common distinctions, along with the implications of each for brain injury rehabilitation.

Recognition Versus Recall

Recall is what most of us think of as memory. Recall is a relatively difficult memory process that requires an active search of memory. In recognition, the information is right before our eyes, and we must either identify it as familiar or unfamiliar or pick out a familiar item from several.

Recognition therefore involves a matching process in which the object in our immediate sensory store is processed directly into the long-term store automatically, essentially bypassing the retrieval process. Brain-injured clients typically do not have as much difficulty with recognition memory as they do with recall. They may therefore have relatively little difficulty in jobs that require inspection of details or recognition of flawed materials or missing features.

Availability Versus Accessibility

This distinction involves the question of whether brain-injured persons lose information from memory or simply lose access to it. The bulk of the evidence seems to favor the latter explanation. For example, when given appropriate cues, brain-injured persons can remember quite well. In general, it is safe to say that they lose the ability to cue themselves spontaneously. The implication for treatment is that the therapist must teach techniques for cuing. These may be internal memory strategies or the use of external prosthetic devices.

Levels of Processing Versus Cognitive Effort

Most would agree that after meeting someone for the first time we have only a shallow understanding of him or her. After years of friendship or acquaintance, we know him or her at a deeper level. According to the levels-of-processing theory, this is because the working memory is constantly processing people, things, and events at different levels. The shallowest level of encoding involves syntactical, acoustical, or concrete features, whereas the deeper levels involve semantic encoding. The deeper the level of processing, the better the recall. Brain injury survivors do not rapidly process information at deep levels.

An alternative to the levels-of-processing theory is the notion of *cognitive effort* (Hasher & Zacks, 1979; Tyler, Hertel, McCallum, & Ellis, 1979). This refers to the amount of the working memory capacity that is taken up with the encoding operation. According to cognitive effort theory, it is not the depth of processing that de-

termines recall but the amount of effortful processing of the information. Although there have been no experimental distinctions between these two concepts with brain injury survivors, it is likely that their memories are also determined by the amount of cognitive effort they invest in the task. It is perhaps safe to say that depth of processing is a manifestation of the amount of cognitive effort afforded the task. The implication for the therapist is that effortful processing will be necessary for a client to recall effectively. The therapist should therefore encourage the client always to actively engage as many senses as possible when trying to learn anything.

Semantic Versus Episodic Memory

Semantic memory is literally a person's mental storehouse of logically related information (Tulving, 1972). For example, we all know that an airplane is a means of transportation, a dog is a canine, and dark clouds suggest a rainstorm. Episodic information is the ability to retain the novel episodes of daily life, such as what clothes we wore yesterday. Episodic memory is the logical precursor of semantic memory because it is likely that we must store several episodes before we can extract meaning or knowledge from them. This distinction is important because brain-injured persons often confuse their memory deficits. For example, they will usually say they have a "short-term memory loss." Actually, their short-term memories are reasonably unaffected by the injury. For example, they can remember most novel information for a few seconds quite well. The real deficit involves episodic memory formation (Kinsbourne & Wood, 1975). The implication is that the therapist will spend the most effort teaching the client strategies for processing novel episodic information.

Anterograde Versus Retrograde Amnesia

Anterograde amnesia is common after a brain injury. Retrograde amnesia is far less common. *Anterograde amnesia* refers to the inability to recall new information. *Retrograde amnesia* is the inability to recall events that happened before the injury. For example, most clients report that they can remember their personal histories well but have difficulty remembering what someone said the day before.

Most clients will demonstrate an episodic memory loss. In some cases, the therapist may be able to build on information and skills the client had before the injury. Because these are spared, the client may be able to return to gainful employment if the task does not involve new learning.

Procedural Versus Declarative Memory

Procedural memories are skills or action patterns the client may learn: for example, typing, operating a machine, or performing any routine or repetitive task. Squire (1982) more formally described procedural knowledge as the ability to "develop in memory a representation based on experience that changes the way an organism responds to the environment without affording access to the specific instances that led to this change" (p. 560). *Declarative memory* refers to the ability to learn things such as words, faces, letters, numbers, and the facts that we deduce from this information.

A fascinating finding is that these two types of memory can exist independently of one another. Brain injury survivors who are taught a skill will often learn the skill but not report any memory of the study sessions (Squire, 1982). The obvious implication is that these clients can learn employable skills but may not remember the training.

Why Brain-Injured Clients Forget

There are several reasons that anyone can forget what he or she experiences. One reason is that memories may decay over time. *Decay theory* is one of the oldest models of memory. Memories are likened to furrows that the rain creates as it runs down the side of a mountain. Forgetting occurs because the furrows are, eventually, effaced by the natural action of wind and sun (Harrell, Parenté, Bellingrath, & Lisicia, 1992). The theory predicts that the best way to remember anything is to renew the memory via rehearsal. The implication of this theory for brain injury rehabilitation is that rehearsal training is

perhaps the most valuable of therapies because rehearsal maintains the memory trace.

Consolidation explanations of forgetting assume that if information is rehearsed, then the brain undergoes structural changes that store the memory permanently. Whereas decay theory assumes that forgetting occurs because of a degrading of the memory trace over time, consolidation theory assumes that memory is a dynamic process that occurs at both a conscious and an unconscious level. Anything that interrupts the consolidation process interferes with the quality of the stored memory. The implication is that clients must ensure that consolidation is not disrupted. The therapist should advise the client that it is important to rehearse information as soon after the original experience as possible to ensure that the consolidation process is completed.

Interference explanations have several variants. All of them assume that forgetting occurs because other information interferes with what we are trying to remember. Proactive interference occurs when our memories are disrupted by a buildup of prior experience over time. We all know that our efficiency lessens after several hours of mental work. For example, waiters and waitresses become progressively less and less able to remember customers' names as the day goes on, due to interference from all of the preceding customers. Retroactive inhibition occurs when we cannot recall something from the past because of something we have just learned. For example, recalling anything from the day before is easier after a good night's sleep than it is after a day of hectic wakefulness. This is because the information from the waking hours retroactively interferes with the information that preceded it. The implication is that memories are strongest when the client rehearses the information and protects the consolidation with a period of relative mental inactivity. For example, making entries into a diary before retiring at night can greatly facilitate memory for the day's activities.

The process of forgetting in clinical populations has also been summarized in the literature on amnesia. Meudell and Mayes (1982) described amnesia as a difficulty in learning new information and recalling old information and poor attention and concentration on an immediate task. In many situations, the client's reasoning and cognitive skills may be intact. Wilson (1987) provided an especially cogent review of this concept.

According to Wilson (1987), one theory of amnesia assumes that brain injury survivors lose the ability to allocate cognitive effort effectively. They may have problems paying attention to incoming information or may be unable to remain attentive for any length of time. Distraction and the inability to screen out irrelevant information may also be an issue. Although the theory seems plausible on the surface, the research evidence is conflicting (Butters & Cermak, 1980; Mayes, Meudell, & Neary, 1978; Meudell & Mayes, 1982; Moscovitch, 1982; Wilson, 1987). Huppert and Piercy (1978) suggested that amnesia is caused by a failure of automatic processing of information. This refers to an inability to process information without effort, almost unconsciously (Hasher & Zacks, 1979). The theory implies that the mechanism for memory may not be damaged as much as the ability to remember without conscious effort.

Wilson (1987) also discussed two types of storage theories. The first assumes that brain injury causes more rapid decay of information. However, there is little experimental evidence for this theory (Brooks & Baddeley, 1976; Huppert & Piercy, 1978). The second type of storage theory assumes that brain injury disrupts the consolidation process. Weiskrantz (1978) pointed out several problems with this theory. For example, amnestics often do well on recognition and cued recall tasks. They can also learn procedures reasonably well. These types of learning could not occur if the consolidation process was disrupted.

Wilson (1987) identified another broad class of explanations for amnesia that implicates the retrieval process. One version assumes that retrieval failure occurs because of interference from extraneous information (Warrington & Weiskrantz, 1970). For example, brain-injured survivors often fail to distinguish familiar from unfamiliar information (Gaffan, 1972). They also have difficulty recognizing how certain information is related to other information (Brooks & Baddeley, 1976). Further, it is difficult for them to distinguish the contexts in which different events occurred (Winocur & Kinsbourne, 1978). These results suggest that information is confused at the time of recall.

CONCLUSION

Despite a great deal of research effort, no clearly plausible theory of amnesia has emerged. There are, however, several findings about memory and memory failure after brain injury that are worth reiterating. The bad news is that brain injury survivors have a difficult time remembering semantically related information or the gist of verbal passages or conversations. They do not store information about the time when an event occurred, incidental facts about the event, or specific details. They do not recognize associations among unstructured pieces of information. They will probably not recall most novel experiences without cuing and will not retain skills without extensive overlearning.

The good news is that amnestics can learn procedures to high levels of proficiency, although they may have no memory for the study sessions (Cohen & Corkin, 1981; Newcomb & Ratcliff, 1979; Starr & Phillips, 1970). They can recall as long as there are appropriate cues provided. They can learn a variety of different verbal and motor skills such as reproduction of line drawings (Williams, 1953), word reproduction (Warrington & Weiskrantz, 1970), response conditioning (Weiskrantz & Warrington, 1979), verbal association (Warrington & Weiskrantz, 1982), and word list recall (Twum, 1994). They also benefit from memory strategy training (Parenté, 1994; Parenté, Twum, & Zoltan, 1994; Twum & Parenté, 1994).

It is our opinion that brain injury limits the person's ability to transform information automatically in the working memory. Before brain injury, memory operations such as attention, rehearsal, organization, and mental transformation of new information occurred at an unconscious level (Huppert & Piercy, 1978). However, a brain injury robs the survivor of his or her ability to execute these mental operations unconsciously.

Consequently, survivors must learn to rehearse, attend, concentrate, and manipulate information consciously in working memory. Eventually, through conscious effort, the processes become unconscious again.

Our research and clinical experience indicates that most survivors have not lost their capacity for memory and thinking. Instead, brain-injured people must make extra efforts to remember while they acquire new compensatory skills. With practice, some of the acquired skills may become automatic, as their native skills were prior to injury.

REFERENCES

Baddeley, A.D. (1982). Implications of neuropsychological evidence for theories of normal memory. *Philosophical Transactions of the Royal Society, 298*, 59–72.

Baddeley, A.D., & Hitch, G.J. (1974). Working memory. In G.A. Bower (Ed.), *The psychology of learning and motivation* (Vol. 8). New York: Academic Press.

Broadbent, D.E. (1958). *Perception and communication.* London: Pergamon.

Brooks, D.N., & Baddeley, A.D. (1976). What can amnestics learn? *Neuropsychologia, 14*, 111–122.

Butters, N., & Cermak, L.S. (1980). *Alcoholic Korsakoff's syndrome.* New York: Academic Press.

Cohen, N.J., & Corkin, S. (1981, October). *The amnestic patient. H.M.: Learning and retention of a cognitive skill.* Paper presented at the meeting for the Society of Neuroscience, Los Angeles.

Craine, J.H., & Gudeman, H.E. (1981). *The rehabilitation of brain function.* Springfield, IL: Charles C Thomas.

Deutsch, J.A., & Deutsch, D. (1963). Attention: Some theoretical considerations. *Psychological Review, 70*, 80–90.

Duncan, J. (1984). Selective attention and the organization of visual information. *Journal of Experimental Psychology: General, 113*, 501–517.

Ellis, H.C., Groggin, J.P., & Parenté, R. (1979). Human memory and learning: The processing of information. In M. Myer (Ed.), *Foundations of contemporary psychology* (pp. 327–358). New York: Oxford University Press.

Ellis, H.C., & Hunt, R.R. (1993). *Fundamentals of human memory and cognition.* Dubuque, IA: William C. Brown.

Ellis, H.C., Parenté, F.J., Grah, C.R., & Spiering, K. (1975). Coding strategies, perceptual grouping, and the "variability effect" in free recall. *Memory and Cognition, 3*, 226–232.

Ellis, H.C., Parenté, F.J., & Walker, C.W. (1974). Coding, varied input versus repetition in human memory. *Journal of Experimental Psychology, 102*, 619–624.

Gaffan, D. (1972). Loss of recognition memory in rats with lesions to the fornix. *Neuropsychologia, 10*, 327–341.

Harrell, M., Parenté, R., Bellingrath, E.G., & Lisicia, K.A. (1992). *Cognitive rehabilitation of memory: A practical guide.* Gaithersburg, MD: Aspen.

Hasher, L., & Zacks, R.T. (1979). Automatic and effortful processes in memory. *Journal of Experimental Psychology, 108*, 356–388.

Huppert, F.A., & Piercy, M. (1978). The role of trace strength in recency and frequency judgements by amnestic and control subjects. *Quarterly Journal of Experimental Psychology, 30*, 346–354.

Kahneman, D. (1973). *Attention and effort.* Englewood Cliffs, NJ: Prentice Hall.

Kahneman, D., & Henik, A. (1977). Effects of visual grouping on immediate recall and selective attention. In S. Dornic (Ed.), *Attention and performance* (Vol. 1, pp. 307–332). Hillsdale, NJ: Lawrence Erlbaum.

Kahneman, D., & Triesman, A. (1984). Changing views of attention and automaticity. In R. Parasuraman & D.A. Davies (Eds.), *Varieties of attention.* New York: Academic Press.

Kahneman, D., Triesman, A., & Gibbs, B. (1992). The reviewing of object files: Object-specific integration of information. *Cognitive Psychology, 24*, 175–219.

Kinsbourne, M., & Wood, F. (1975). Short-term memory and the amnestic syndrome. In D.D. Deutsch & J.A. Deutsch (Eds.), *Short-term memory.* New York: Academic Press.

Mayes, A.R., Meudell, R.R., & Neary, D. (1978). Must amnesia be caused by either encoding or retrieval disorders? In M.M. Grudeberg, P.E. Morris, & R.N. Sykes (Eds.), *Practical aspects of memory.* London: Academic Press.

McClur, J.T., Browning, R.T., Vantrease, C.M., & Bittle, S.T. (1994). The iconic memory skills of brain injury survivors and non-brain injured controls after visual scanning training. *NeuroRehabilitation, 4*(3), 151–156.

Meudell, P.R., & Mayes, A.R. (1982). Normal and abnormal forgetting. In A.W. Ellis (Ed.), *Normality and pathology in cognition functions.* London: Academic Press.

Moscovitch, M. (1982). Multiple dissociation of function in amnesia. In L. Cermak (Ed.), *Human memory and amnesia.* Hillsdale, NJ: Lawrence Erlbaum.

Neisser, U. (1967). *Cognitive psychology.* New York: Appleton-Century-Crofts.

Newcomb, F., & Ratcliff, G. (1979). Long-term consequences of cerebral lesions. In M. Ganannio (Ed.), *Handbook of behavioral neurology* (Vol. 2). New York Plenum.

Norman, D.A. (1968). Toward a theory of memory and attention. *Psychological Review, 75*, 522–536.

Parasuraman, R., & Davies, D.A. (Eds.). (1984). *Varieties of attention.* New York: Academic Press.

Parenté, R. (1994). Effects of monetary incentives on performance after traumatic brain injury. *Neuro-Rehabilitation, 4*(3), 198–203.

Parenté, R., & Anderson-Parenté, J.K. (1991). *Retraining memory: Techniques and applications.* Houston, TX: CSY.

Parenté, R., Anderson-Parenté, J.K., & Shaw, B. (1989). Retraining the mind's eye. *Journal of Head Trauma Rehabilitation, 4,* 53–62.

Parenté, R., Twum, M., & Zoltan, B. (1994). Transfer and generalization of cognitive skill after traumatic brain injury. *NeuroRehabilitation, 4*(1), 25–35.

Posner, M.I. (1980). Orienting of attention: The seventh Sir Frederick Bartlett lecture. *Quarterly Journal of Psychology, 32,* 3–5.

Squire, L.R. (1982). Comparison between forms of amnesia: Some deficits are unique to Korsakoff's syndrome. *Journal of Experimental Psychology: Learning, Memory, and Cognition, 8,* 560–571.

Starr, A., & Phillips, L. (1970). Verbal and motor memory in the amnestic syndrome. *Neuropsychologia, 8,* 75–82.

Triesman, A.M. (1964). Selective attention in man. *British Medical Bulletin, 20,* 12–16.

Triesman, A., Kahneman, D., & Burkell, J. (1983). Perceptual objects and the cost filtering. *Perception and Psychophysics, 33,* 527–532.

Triesman, A., & Schmidt, H. (1982). Illusory conjunctions in the perception of objects. *Cognitive Psychology, 14,* 107–141.

Tulving, E. (1972). Episodic and semantic memory. In N.E. Tulving & W. Donaldson (Eds.), *Organization of memory.* New York: Academic Press.

Twum, M. (1994). Maximizing generalization of cognitions and memories after traumatic brain injury. *NeuroRehabilitation, 4*(3), 157–167.

Twum, M., & Parenté, R. (1994). Role of imagery and verbal labeling in the performance of paired associates tasks by persons with closed head injury. *Journal of Clinical and Experimental Neuropsychology, 16*(4), 630–639.

Tyler, S.W., Hertel, P.T., McCallum, M.C., & Ellis, H.C. (1979). Cognitive effort and memory. *Journal of Experimental Psychology: Human Learning and Memory, 5,* 607–617.

Warrington, E.K., & Weiskrantz, L. (1970). Amnestic syndrome: Consolidation or retrieval. *Nature, 228,* 628–630.

Warrington, E.K., & Weiskrantz, L. (1982). Amnesia: A disconnection syndrome? *Neuropsychologia, 20,* 233–248.

Weiskrantz, L. (1978). A comparison of hippocampal pathology in man and other animals. *Ciba Foundation Symposium, 58.*

Weiskrantz, L., & Warrington, E.K. (1979). Conditioning in amnestic patients. *Neuropsychologia, 17,* 187–194.

Williams, M. (1953). Investigations of amnestic deficits by progressive prompting. *Journal of Neurology, Neurosurgery, and Psychiatry, 16,* 14.

Wilson, B. (1987). *Rehabilitation of memory.* New York: Guilford.

Winocur, G., & Kinsbourne, M. (1978). Contextual cuing as an aid to Korsakoff amnestica. *Neuropsychologia, 16,* 671–682.

Chapter 5

The Process of Recovery

Many different life experiences can produce some form of brain injury that seriously impairs memory and cognition. These experiences include car accidents, degenerative diseases, gunshot wounds, drug overdoses, sports injuries, and toxic chemical exposure. In most cases, it is quite difficult to predict the course of recovery because the traumatic experience differs markedly for each person. In some cases, the problems are mild and the recovery process is quick and complete. More frequently, the recovery process occurs quite rapidly at first, but then the person's cognitive functions level off and eventually stabilize at a level clearly lower than before the injury. Indeed, in many cases the person's cognition never improves to its premorbid level. In most cases, however, rehabilitation can improve the person's cognitive skills to the point at which he or she can function independently around the home or return to some form of self-sustaining employment.

This chapter presents an overview of literature on recovery of cognitive skills after brain

This chapter is adapted from R. Parenté and M. Stapleton, Recovery of Memory After Traumatic Brain Injury, in *Interdisciplinary Handbook of Adult Lifespan Learning,* J. Sinnott, ed., with permission from Greenwood Publishing Group, Inc., Westport, CT.

injury due to trauma, toxins, or disease. This topic is central to the therapy process because most parents and family members will have questions about the client's long-term prognosis. Unfortunately, many therapists are simply unaware of the literature on this topic and are thus unable to give cogent answers. Further, the theories of recovery that do exist are rather poorly developed and vague: Most do not make any clear statements that could be used to direct the course of therapy. Kolb and Whishaw (1990), Miller (1984), and Parenté and Stapleton (1994) have provided the most complete summaries of these theories, and the reader is referred to their reviews for additional information. Miller (1984) was perhaps the first to group these theories into three broad classes: *brain plasticity, functional adaptation,* and *artifact theories.* As he pointed out, these are broad groupings with considerable overlap.

Although the various theories of recovery describe the same process, each is concerned with different aspects. None is generally accepted, nor can any be used to predict an outcome for any individual client. We have interpreted these theories loosely in order to extract any aspects that would dictate an optimal treatment regimen or provide suggestions for treatment that would enhance the recovery process. We do not pretend to explain any of the theories in detail but only provide an overview of the basic concepts. We begin by describing various models and mechanisms of recovery. We end with a developmental model of recovery that summarizes our observations of the return of functioning after brain injury.

THEORIES OF RECOVERY

Brain Plasticity Theory

Anatomical reorganization is the idea that different areas of the brain reorganize as a natural consequence of injury and that the undamaged areas take over the functions of the damaged areas (Devor, 1982; Munk, 1878; Rosner, 1974; Spear, Spear, & Woodruff, 1995). This is, perhaps, the oldest theory of recovery. It assumes that reorganization is hierarchical: that is, the higher cortical areas can take over the functions of the lower, but the process cannot occur in reverse (Taylor, 1931).

Munk (1878) proposed a slightly different notion of brain plasticity. His theory assumed that reorganization would occur only for as long as it was necessary. If one area was damaged and was in a state of recovery, then others would assume its functions until it repaired or recovery plateaued. At that time, the damaged area would resume its previous activity at whatever level was possible. In some cases the recovery would be complete, but in most cases some element of reorganization would remain even after the person's functioning stabilized. Although this aspect of the reorganization model emphasized the importance of training after head injury to facilitate the reorganization process, it did not make any clear suggestions that could be used to direct the treatment.

Functional Adaptation Theory

Alexander Luria (1963) was the first to assert that recovery of cognitive function is largely a process of learning new ways to reach the same goals. He called this process *functional adaptation*. There was no assumption of brain plastic-

ity. Recovery was viewed as a compensatory process whereby one learns new ways of doing what one did before. Although brain plasticity and functional adaptation theories have certain similarities, the latter requires fewer assumptions. For example, there is no need to assume that brain structures reorganize or change their functional status. The only assumption is that humans can learn compensatory behaviors and that brain functions are flexible and can accommodate this type of change. The degree of flexibility along with the extent of the damage largely predicts recovery. Perhaps the major advantage of the functional adaptation model is that it has clear implications for treatment: Treatment should emphasize teaching the person to do what he or she did before.

Artifact Theory

According to Miller (1984), artifact theories assume that damage to the brain produces irreversible effects. Moreover, secondary and temporary disturbances occur in other parts of the brain. Recovery may seem to occur because the disturbances in these secondary areas, such as temporary edema, resolve, thereby producing rapid but incomplete return of function. Nevertheless, the areas of primary loss will never recover completely, so certain functions are permanently impaired.

Von Monakow (1914) discussed one type of transient phenomenon of recovery called *diaschisis*. Although the exact mechanism of diaschisis is unclear, the basic idea is that injury to the brain produces a site of primary damage as well as secondary damage to collateral sites. The secondary damage results in temporary reduction of cognition, and the type of dysfunction may not resemble that which would normally be associated with the primary lesion site. It is as if the primary damage causes a shock wave that traverses the brain and damages the tissue that it passes through (Uzzell, 1986).

As the collateral areas begin to regenerate, the person begins to experience some amount of recovery. But recovery is not assumed to result from regrowth or regeneration of receptors, the regeneration of damaged mechanisms, or the reorganization of brain functions. The various connections between cells that were temporarily disrupted by the shock wave are soon restored, and what appeared to be global dysfunction resolves, leaving the more localized but relatively permanent disorders. Unfortunately, the artifact model can do little to predict the extent of the diaschisis effect, and it provides even less in the way of functional suggestions to expedite recovery.

Miller (1984) provided a lucid summary of artifact, brain plasticity, and functional adaptation theories of recovery. He asserted that there are many similarities between these positions, and that they are best described as interesting notions that are still in the early stages of development. Each explains certain aspects of recovery, but none is obviously superior to the others. Indeed, the major problem is that most lack implications for planning treatment. The various models of recovery simply describe ways therapists can conceptualize cognitive dysfunction.

PHYSIOLOGICAL MECHANISMS OF RECOVERY

Much of what we call recovery may be an artifact of some physiological process that occurs after head injury. However, several well-documented phenomena that occur after tissue damage are known to account for much of what we normally think of as recovery. Most involve changes in the cells or the interrelationship among cells as they regenerate. Although the theoretical mechanisms have been summarized in some detail (Kolb & Whishaw, 1990; Miller, 1984), the underlying psychological processes are neither well researched nor well understood. Consequently, we can only provide the gist of the various concepts and assert that none of the mechanisms discussed here is clearly the most viable description of physiological changes after injury to the brain. It is likely that all of the processes play a role in recovery.

The first two processes involve regeneration of cells or tissues. These include *rerouting* and *sprouting* to re-create an interface among the damaged cells. The last four processes are thought to improve the extent to which the cells can excite one another. These excitatory mechanisms—*vicaration, denervation supersensitivity,* the activation of *silent synapses*, and *disinhibition*—compensate for the lessened area of cortical synapse resulting from brain damage.

Regenerative Mechanisms

Cell regeneration is the process in which brain cells create new connections to an area that was previously damaged. This is a common phenomenon in the peripheral nervous system, and successful regeneration has been demonstrated with amphibians (Sperry, 1965). There have also been attempts to stimulate cell regeneration in brain-damaged adults. For example, Kolb and Whishaw (1990) described a substance called *nerve-growth factor* (NGF) that can be injected into the damaged site to facilitate regeneration. Brain tissue transplants have been used to provide a tissue bridge for the cells to reconnect across a previously damaged area (Kromer, Bjorklund, & Stenevi, 1980). Specifically, transplanting embryonic tissue may have the same effect. These techniques are still in their infancy, although the initial results are promising. This surgical technique is discussed in greater detail later in the chapter.

Sprouting was described by Lynch, Deddwyler, and Cotman (1973), who demonstrated that brain cells will sprout branches that take over the space left vacant by the damaged tissue. The process is quite rapid, usually occurring in 7 to 10 days after the injury. *Rerouting* is the brain's establishment of new connections after cells' normal pathways are disrupted. Although the rerouting and sprouting phenomena provide hope that the brain can regenerate its neural connections, there is little evidence that either process occurs beyond the site of the original insult. Moreover, both types of neural activity are common only in younger, developing organisms. In addition, there is little evidence that rerouting or sprouting can compensate for the degenerative events that typically follow injury to the brain or the onset of a degenerative disease.

Excitatory Mechanisms

Vicaration is a substitution mechanism. Some portion of the brain that was not heavily used before the injury is stimulated into use after the injury because it must now take over the function of a damaged area. For example, the area that is directly adjacent to the damaged area may take over the damaged area's functions. Vicaration cannot be classified strictly as an anatomical reorganization mechanism because the reorganization is not necessarily hierarchical. The takeover of function can occur by any number of different means.

Denervation supersensitivity is a phenomenon of hypersensitivity to neurotransmitters in the brain that is due to an increase in the number of neurotransmitter receptor sites (Ungerstedt, 1971). It is hypothesized that when a brain injury reduces the number of synapses in a given area, receptor sites proliferate and thereby increase neurotransmission in order to compensate. LaVere (1975, 1980) reported that this process is especially noticeable in younger organisms and in cases of brain lesions caused by biochemical toxins.

Silent synapses are hypothetical connections that begin to function only after existing cells are damaged. Brain injury is assumed to activate dormant synapses or to remove inhibition, thereby allowing the previously silent synapses to take over the functions of the damaged cells.

Disinhibition is the removal of the normal inhibitory action on a system that allows the system to function faster or with greater efficiency (Wall & Egger, 1971). For example, the inhibition of acetylcholine production is removed with anticholinesterase drugs such as physostigmine or neostigmine. Geschwind (1974) attributed the recovery of language to disinhibition, arguing that language is learned in both hemispheres and that damage to the dominant hemisphere disinhibits the subordinate hemisphere, thereby leading to the recovery of language.

The variety of physiological mechanisms of compensation for brain injury suggest that the process of recovery cannot be explained by any single physiological mechanism or theory. It is safe to say, however, that for the early stages of recovery, the artifact theory is probably the most accurate account. But in the later stages of recovery, the functional adaptation theory may be most applicable—in which case therapy should emphasize compensatory training. Brain plasticity theory, which is supported by documented phenomena like sprouting, rerouting, and denervation supersensitivity, perhaps best applies to recovery in developing systems, for example, in young children with traumatic brain injury.

A DEVELOPMENTAL MODEL OF RECOVERY

Parenté and Anderson-Parenté (1991) proposed a purely functional model of recovery that was designed to provide suggestions for the course of treatment at each stage. The major purpose of the model is to suggest different types of treatment that are appropriate at various stages of recovery. Consequently, their model is not a formal theory of recovery, although it does generally follow the same stages that were outlined in other treatment models (Ben-Yishay, Piasetsky, & Rattok, 1987; Sohlberg & Mateer, 1987). It is, in essence, a description of successive therapeutic steps, with specific training at each step that will facilitate the next.

Arousal and Orientation

In the earliest stages of recovery, a person may not know his or her name, recognize loved ones, or know the day, month, or year. The first level of recovery concerns regaining these basic faculties. Treatment at this level, typically in the acute care facility, usually begins shortly after the person emerges from a coma. Most of the time, the client is confused, disoriented, combative, and potentially violent. Family members are especially concerned because this is the stage at which the client's behavior is least predictable. It is always disquieting when the client fails to recognize family members and friends who visit or is unable to recall biographical information.

The goal at this stage is to orient the client in time and in place and to person. Most clients gradually relearn names, faces, and once-familiar places and events. The combativeness and verbal abusiveness subside as the client regains a sense of personal identity. The Orientation Remediation Modules may be especially effective at this stage of recovery. Simple paired-associate training with pictures of family and their names can also be effective. Literally, anything that reestablishes the network of personal knowledge is important at this stage. Family members can be especially useful allies because they are usually patient and can provide a wealth of familiar materials, pictures, and personal information (Corregan, Arnett, Houck, & Jackson, 1985).

Attention and Vigilance

After the client regains a sense of personal orientation, he or she will usually begin to show increases in his or her ability to maintain focus and vigilance on a particular task. Attention and vigilance are central to any higher level of cognitive skill (Buchtel, 1987). Attention training is a multifaceted process (see Chapter 9). It assumes that the person is oriented and can maintain attention for some period of time. In the earliest stages, it may not be distinguishable from vigilance, which is simply the ability to maintain focus for increasingly longer periods of time. Attention training does not necessarily require a great deal of mental work. For example, the client may play computer games, and the therapist may record how long he or she can maintain the activity, regardless of the score the person achieves on the game. The first measure is an index of vigilance, and the second is a measure of concentration and performance. The Sohlberg and Mateer (1987) attention process training model may be especially useful during this and the following stage of recovery. Although these activities may require high-level attention and concentration, they usually do not require memory. At this stage, the goal is to get the person to the point at which he or she can maintain focus for some sustained period of time, regardless of whether he or she can remember the activity.

Mental Control

Once the person can maintain vigilance, improvements in concentration or performance become apparent. These improvements are not immediately obvious until the client can maintain focus long enough for the therapist to measure improvements in concentration, active processing, and mental control. We make no clear distinctions among these terms. They all refer to some form of mental activity that results in a measurably correct response. This type of mental activity is essential for the processing of higher level information and for the use of strategies. It is also what most people associate with quickness of thought.

Training at this stage typically involves providing the client with tasks that require active processing but do not necessarily involve rehearsal or memory. For example, the client could practice with tasks that require mental manipulations such as solving anagrams or performing mental math problems. The latter stages of the Sohlberg and Mateer (1987) attention process training program are suitable for use at this stage.

Rehearsal

Many clients report spontaneous recovery of simple strategies such as *repetition*. Indeed, many report that simply going over things again and again is the only method that seems to help them to remember. Usually, they come to this conclusion after having transcended the above stages. Rehearsal is the first stage of recovery of memory skill and must precede higher level memory strategy training. It is the ability to maintain information in memory for some period of time so that the person can then apply various memory strategies that will make the information available and accessible at some point in the future. Memory strategies are usually useless unless the person can first rehearse effectively. Moreover, the client cannot learn to rehearse unless he or she can first attend and concentrate.

Chapters 10 and 11 discuss rehearsal training in detail. Briefly, teaching rehearsal involves training the client first to rehearse at a conscious level. The goal is to get the person eventually to rehearse automatically. The therapist's goal is threefold: to illustrate the importance of rehearsal, to show the client that his or her memory can improve dramatically simply by rehearsing, and to show the client how many rehearsals will be necessary. Rehearsal is perhaps the most important skill at this level of recovery. The extent to which the person can rehearse determines the success or failure of the stages to follow.

Recovery of Episodic Memory

During this stage of recovery, the person regains the ability to remember the novel episodes of life (Johnson & Raye, 1981; Tulving, 1984). It usually requires more than teaching the person to do mental pushups or simply to attend to video games. It requires teaching the person to use memory strategies that he or she has not used before. This level of recovery may take years because the client may have difficulty using the strategies or may not do so spontaneously. Chapter 11 presents a variety of memory strategy training procedures. These are essential for the client to learn because many of the higher level cognitive skills are based on them. However, it is important to emphasize that these strategies are more than just stimulation therapy. They are literally teaching the client a new way of remembering.

Higher Order Cognition

Many clients may never reach this stage of recovery. It involves learning how to reason, solve problems, make decisions, set goals, and prioritize (Sternberg & Smith, 1988). Recovery of these skills obviously depends on a variety of prerequisite skills such as the ability to attend and concentrate, to rehearse, and to remember. Chapters 12 through 15 present specific therapy techniques that may be useful with most clients. As with any of the methods discussed in this text, the therapist must direct the training so that the person sees how each technique is personally relevant. For example, when teaching problem solving, the therapist should focus the technique on the client's personal and current problems. This process is an art and requires a certain amount of creativity on the part of the therapist.

Recovery of Social Competence

The final stage of the recovery process involves regaining the more subtle social skills (Boake, 1991). Retraining these skills may be especially difficult because the client may not have had good social skills to begin with. Nevertheless, this is an especially important area of recovery because it has an impact on every area of the person's social life. In our experience, this stage of recovery is seldom spontaneous or complete. It usually requires a great deal of therapy effort. Unfortunately, there are few discussions of training procedures, and much of what is done may meet with limited success.

For example, the training may involve recognizing subtle social cues such as a person's constantly checking a watch while conversing. The relearning process usually requires active participation such as role playing or modeling, and it may also require new learning of social cues such as body language. For this reason, it is best carried out in a group setting.

Clients do not typically make rapid or consistent progress as they ascend through the various stages. Without any therapy, most clients will reach the middle levels of the recovery process. Some clients may never learn higher cognitive skills, and most severely impaired clients do not attain a high level of social competence. Some may plateau at the first or second stages. It is important to remember that the stages are progressive and that the therapist will not be able to skip any stage. We attribute many failures of treatment to an attempt to ascend the hierarchy of recovery too rapidly.

CONCLUSION

This chapter summarizes several theories and methods of recovery after brain injury. Explanations of recovery after brain injury can be broadly grouped into brain plasticity, functional adaptation, and artifact theories. Brain plasticity models assume that the brain reorganizes itself and that the higher level areas take over the functions of the damaged areas. However, the lower areas cannot assume the functions of the higher ones. The functional adaptation model suggests that the most expedient route to recovery involves teaching the person new ways of doing things that he or she used to do. The artifact model assumes that the damage is permanent and that the recovery that does occur takes place in secondary sites of injury that were only temporarily disabled.

Physiological mechanisms of recovery can be broadly grouped into those that involve the regeneration of connections among neurons and those that involve enhanced excitatory processes among undamaged cells. Regeneration may occur by collateral sprouting, rerouting, or the use of chemicals such as nerve growth factor. Excitatory mechanisms include vicaration, denervation supersensitivity, activation of silent synapses, and disinhibition. Through such mechanisms, portions of the brain that were dormant, inhibited, or little used are stimulated to new or greater activity.

A developmental model of recovery was also presented that emphasizes return of function across a broader time span. Its stages of improvement in orientation, attention, mental control, rehearsal, cognition, and social competence build on each other and must be worked through in order. Different therapy procedures are appropriate at each stage of recovery.

REFERENCES

Ben-Yishay, Y., Piasetsky, E., & Rattok, J. (1987). A systematic method for ameliorating disorders in basic attention. In M. Meier, A. Benton, & L. Diller (Eds.), *Neuropsychological rehabilitation* (pp. 165–181). New York: Guilford.

Boake, C. (1991). Social skills training following head injury. In J.S. Kreutzer & P.H. Wehman (Eds.), *Cognitive rehabilitation for persons with traumatic brain injury* (pp. 142–158). Baltimore: Paul H. Brookes.

Buchtel, J.A. (1987). Attention and vigilance after head trauma. In H.S. Levin, J. Grafman, & H.M. Eisenberg (Eds.), *Neurobehavioral recovery from head injury.* New York: Oxford University Press.

Corregan, J.D., Arnett, J.A., Houck, L., & Jackson, R.D. (1985). Reality orientation for brain-injured patients: Group treatment and monitoring of recovery. *Archives of Physical Medicine and Rehabilitation, 66,* 626–630.

Devor, M. (1982). Plasticity in the adult nervous system. In L.S. Illis, E.M. Sedgwick, & H.J. Glanville (Eds.), *Rehabilitation of the neurological patient.* Oxford: Blackwell.

Geschwind, N. (1974). Late changes in the nervous system. An overview. In D.G. Stein, J.J. Rosen, & N. Butters (Eds.), *Plasticity and recovery of function in the central nervous system.* New York: Academic Press.

Johnson, M.K., & Raye, C.L. (1981). Reality monitoring. *Psychological Review, 88,* 67–85.

Kolb, B., & Whishaw, I.Q. (1990). *Fundamentals of human neuropsychology.* New York: W.H. Freeman.

Kromer, L.F., Bjorklund, A., & Stenevi, U. (1980). Innervation of embryonic hippocampal implants by regenerating axons of cholinergic neurons in the adult rat. *Brain Research, 210,* 153–171.

LaVere, T.E. (1975). Neural stability, sparing and behavioral recovery following brain damage. *Psychological Review, 82,* 344–358.

LaVere, T.E. (1980). Recovery of function after brain damage: A theory of the behavioral deficit. *Psychological Review, 82,* 297–308.

Luria, A.R. (1963). *Restoration of function after brain injury.* New York: Macmillan.

Lynch, G.S., Deddwyler, S., & Cotman, C.W. (1973). Post lesion axonal growth produces permanent functional connections. *Science, 180,* 1364–1366.

Miller, E. (1984). *Recovery and management of neuropsychological impairments.* New York: John Wiley.

Munk, H. (1878). Weitere Mettheilungen zur Physiologie der Grosshirnrinde. *Archives of Anatomy and Physiology, 3,* 581–592.

Parenté, R., & Anderson-Parenté, J.K. (1991). *Retraining memory: Techniques and applications.* Houston, TX: CSY.

Parenté, R., & Stapleton, M. (1994). An empowerment model of memory training. *Applied Cognitive Psychology, 7,* 585–602.

Rosner, B.S. (1974). Recovery of function and localization of function in historical perspective. In D.G. Stein, J.J. Rosen, & N. Butters (Eds.), *Plasticity and recovery of function in the central nervous system.* New York: Academic Press.

Sohlberg, M., & Mateer, C. (1987). Effectiveness of an attention training program. *Journal of Clinical and Experimental Neuropsychology, 9,* 117–130.

Spear, N.E., Spear, L.P., & Woodruff, M.L. (1995). *Neurobehavioral plasticity: Learning, development, and response to brain insults.* Hillsdale, NJ: Lawrence Erlbaum.

Sperry, R.W. (1965). Mechanisms of neural maturation. In S.S. Stevens (Ed.), *Handbook of experimental psychology.* New York: John Wiley.

Sternberg, R.J., & Smith, E.E. (1988). *The psychology of human thought.* Cambridge, UK: Cambridge University Press.

Taylor, J. (1931). *Selected writings of John Hughlings Jackson.* London: Hodder & Stoughton.

Tulving, E. (1984). How many memory systems are there? *American Psychologist, 40,* 385–398.

Ungerstedt, U. (1971). Post synaptic supersensitivity after 6 hydroxy-dopamine induced degeneration of nigrostriatal dopamine system. *Acta Physiologica Scandinavica, 367*(Suppl.), 69–93.

Uzzell, B.P. (1986). Pathophysiology and behavioral recovery. In B.P. Uzzell & Y. Gross (Eds.), *Clinical neuropsychology of intervention* (pp. 3–18). Boston: Martinus Nijhoff.

von Monakow, C. (1914). *Die Lokalisation in Grosshirn und der Function durch Kortikale Herde.* Wiesbaden: J.F. Bergmann.

Wall, P.D., & Egger, M.D. (1971). Formation of new connections in adult rat brains after partial deafferentation. *Nature, 232,* 542–545.

Chapter 6

Transfer and Generalization Learning

Rehabilitation professionals often confuse the terms *generalization* and *transfer*. Learning *transfers* whenever it is applied to another context. In *positive transfer*, what is learned in one context facilitates learning in another context. In *negative transfer,* what is learned in one context impedes learning in another context. Learning *generalizes* when it can be successfully applied to a variety of novel contexts (Parenté, Twum, & Zoltan, 1994). The ultimate goal of any rehabilitation is to teach skills that generalize to novel situations. This type of treatment fosters autonomy and independence (Gifford, Rusch, Martin, & White, 1985; Horner, Sprague, & Wilcox, 1986). For example, occupational therapists may teach clients cooking and other independent living skills that will generalize to any home environment. Speech/language therapists may teach the client how to control the rate and intelligibility of their speech. These therapies are specifically designed to facilitate functioning and communication in a variety of contexts.

Generalization requires the use of memory strategies and thinking skills. Many head injury survivors lose the ability to generalize, but the skills they learn in therapy may still transfer to a similar vocational or independent living context (Cormier & Hagman, 1987; Ellis, 1965). For example, a client may learn mail-sorting skills that are unique to a specific job placement.

Although the terms *generalization* and *transfer* frequently appear in publications about head injury, with the exception of some recent work (Parenté et al., 1994; Woolcock, 1990), remarkably little has appeared concerning transfer theory and its application to rehabilitation. Moreover, with the exception of the excellent work of Singley and Anderson (1987), there has been virtually no discussion of the more recent theories regarding transfer of cognitive skills, nor has there been any experimental validation of transfer theories as they apply to brain injury rehabilitation.

Transfer and generalization theories make specific predictions about how and to what extent skills learned in training programs will carry over to other contexts. This chapter provides the therapist with background information and a theoretical model that allows him or her to develop treatment plans that will carry over into the client's activities of daily living.

This chapter is adapted from *NeuroRehabilitation,* Vol. 4, No. 1, R. Parenté, M. Twum, and B. Zoltan, Transfer and Generalization of Cognitive Skills After Traumatic Brain Injury, pp. 25–35, © 1994, with permission from Elsevier Science Ireland, Ltd., Bay 15K, Shannon Industrial Estate, Co. Clare, Ireland.

A BRIEF HISTORY OF TRANSFER AND GENERALIZATION THEORIES

Ylvisaker (1993) traced the history of concepts of transfer and generalization back to the Greeks. Plato was the first to advocate a model of cognitive training that emphasized teaching abstract skills that would presumably generalize to the real world. The Sophists, however, were quick to point out that only utilitarian, concrete, and specific skills training would transfer. The Platonic model was reborn in the 20th century as a theory of formal discipline. This theory advocated teaching children specific subjects that were assumed to transfer to all other aspects of their academic training. These root disciplines were Latin and mathematics, two topics that were thought to provide generalizable mental skills that not only sharpened the mind but also underlay all other disciplines.

Criticisms of the theory of formal discipline came from psychologists such as Thorndike and Woodworth (1901). These authors advocated an identical elements theory of transfer. Specifically, the theory stated that training in the first of two sequential tasks would carry over to the second, but only to the extent that the two tasks shared identical elements. The more similar the sequential situation's identical elements, the greater the transfer. Indeed, it is unclear whether these authors even believed in the concept of generalization. Like most psychologists of their time, their goal was to describe transfer of learning within the context of a larger theory of learning that explained transfer according to the laws of association between stimuli and responses. Generalization was usually described as the result of "warm-up" or "learning-to-learn" that accrued with repetition.

A similar concept of transfer phenomena was put forth in the Bruce-Wylie laws (Bruce, 1933; Wylie, 1919). These laws stated that the amount of transfer among sequential tasks depended on the number of identical elements that the training and transfer tasks shared. They also stated that the similarity of organization determined whether the transfer was positive or negative. That is, a necessary condition of positive transfer between any training and transfer task was the similarity of organization.

Osgood (1949) summarized much of the existing research and theory as a three-dimensional space that he called the *transfer-surface*. This model of transfer provided a way to predict the amount of transfer that would be likely to occur in similar situations. Osgood's model was firmly rooted in the stimulus-response tradition of mid-20th-century psychology. It therefore defined similarity in terms of the number of identical elements and observable motor responses that the two situations shared. The model did not make any assumptions about how a person might have cognitively organized the tasks. The Osgood transfer surface is still considered an accurate summary of most motor and verbal learning transfer phenomena. It is perhaps less accurate in situations that deal with the transfer of cognitive skills.

Modern theories of transfer emphasize the concept of the problem space (Newell, 1980). Unlike the identical elements theory, which stressed the shared physical characteristics of sequential tasks, the problem space notion focuses on the similarity of cognitive processing demands common to two sequential tasks. Specifically, the theory predicts that positive transfer will occur when a person uses the same knowledge in a similar way in successive tasks (Singley & Anderson, 1987). Common elements do not ensure positive transfer. The number of elements the two tasks share is important; however, the way the person learns to organize the task is a better predictor of how much transfer or generalization will occur.

Problem space models assume that at least two types of old learning can influence new learning. *Declarative learning* is the person's existing storehouse of knowledge and facts. It provides the basis for organizing whatever common elements various tasks have. For example, when learning how to wash clothes, a client may eventually discern that certain types of fabrics require dry cleaning. *Procedural learning* refers to the acquisition of specific skills, such as riding a bicycle or typing. In many cases, procedural skills may apply in only one situation. For example, when preparing a client for a job, the therapist might need to interview the employer to determine exactly how he or she wanted the job performed. The therapist would then teach these specific skills to the client, even though the unique aspects of the job might not apply in any other job the client later acquired.

According to problem space models, declarative knowledge may transfer but will eventually become proceduralized. For example, a head-injured person may learn to perform a skill such as data entry in a training program. When placed in a job, he or she transfers certain aspects of that training, such as knowledge of the generic organization of a keyboard, what a disk drive is, or how to use a printer. However, this declarative knowledge base eventually becomes modified to fit the specific task demands of the new job: use of a specific keyboard with a certain configuration, a Macintosh versus an IBM computer, or a mainframe or local area network. He or she must then learn the intricacies of the different systems.

PREDICTING TRANSFER OUTCOMES

Models for predicting transfer outcomes have been available for years. Although the Bruce-Wylie laws were certainly enlightening and predictive, perhaps the first comprehensive and testable model of transfer was outlined by Osgood (1949). In the head injury literature, Parenté and Anderson-Parenté (1990) and Parenté and DiCesare (1991) modified Ellis's (1965) transfer paradigms and used them to predict the amount of transfer that would be likely to result from various cognitive rehabilitation training procedures. This model was later validated by Twum (1994), whose research is described later in this chapter.

In the cognitive rehabilitation transfer model, training establishes associations between the physical observable aspects of the training task and the unobservable cognitive organizations the client learns while performing the task (Parenté & Anderson-Parenté, 1990; Parenté & DiCesare,

1991). This model differs from Ellis's because it assumes that a cognitive rather than a motoric or observable verbal response is learned. The organization may be a declarative memory trace that can transfer across a variety of different situations. It may also be a procedural characteristic of the task that is specific to a certain situation.

For example, a client may learn different skills through repetition. However, the client may also learn specific job-related mnemonics to ensure that a task is done consistently and accurately. In the former case, the client presumably uses the rehearsal strategy to eventually consolidate some sequence of motor responses that we call a skill. As the reader will see, these cognitions can either facilitate or retard new learning. According to Parenté and Anderson-Parenté (1990), effective cognitive rehabilitation involves teaching clients mental sets and organizations that carry over into their activities of daily living. Moreover, it includes providing clients with practice to use the organizations in a wide variety of real-life situations.

Both the problem space theory and the model proposed by Parenté and Anderson-Parenté assume that positive transfer occurs as long as the same training is used in the same way across a sequence. This same rule has been proposed by Singley and Anderson (1987). All of these theorists agree that therapy facilitates generalization if the therapist can show the client how the organization applies in a variety of different settings. If the client does not see the application, then the generalization is minimal or nonexistent.

Parenté and Anderson-Parenté's transfer conditions are best described by example. The first three are conditions of positive transfer. The physical aspects of the client's therapy are called *task elements* (A). For example, when the client is learning to type, the typewriter, the keyboard, the paper, and so forth compose the task elements of the training context. During therapy, the client also learns to organize specific characteristics of the task. For example, the therapist teaches the client specific ways to position his or her fingers on the keyboard, to adjust the paper, and to format documents such as letters. These are *organizing sets* that the client can use in any new situation that requires the same typing skills. The model assumes that the therapy will transfer as long as the *organizational set* (B) is maintained. If the organization changes, then the client will experience mental confusion. This situation can produce negative transfer.

The A-B:A-B condition produces positive transfer because the conditions of therapy and the real world are literally identical. For example, the client may complete janitorial training and then begin work at the same facility where the training occurred. In this situation, the task elements and organizational sets shared by the training and transfer tasks are identical.

Because there is usually a distinct difference between the training the client receives in therapy and the experience he or she encounters in life, the A-B:A-B paradigm is seldom realistic. This difference can be shown by adding prime symbols (′) to the A and B letters for the real-world condition. Therefore, in the second row of Table 6–1, A′ indicates that the physical elements in the real-world situation differ somewhat from those in the therapy situation. Likewise, B′ indicates that the organization of the task in the real-world situation will differ slightly from what he or she learned in therapy. For example, the client may learn janitorial skills during an on-the-job placement but then begin work in a second placement that is similar, although not identical, to the first. In this situation, the model predicts positive transfer, but less than what occurs in the A-B:A-B paradigm.

The A-B:C-B paradigm describes the conditions of generalization. Here, the training involves task elements (A) that are different from those the client will later encounter (C). However, the task is organized (B) in the same way. This is a necessary condition for generalization. The other necessary condition is that the client must perceive the similarity between the two tasks. For example, the client may learn to sort letters in one placement and then to sort packages in another. The task elements differ (letters versus packages), but the letter sort experience will generalize if the method used to sort both letters and packages is the same and the client is aware of the similarity.

The above examples illustrate a general principle of effective therapy: *In any two sequential tasks, training will promote generalization to the extent that the organizations learned in the first are maintained in the second.* This is basically the same principle originally proposed by Bruce and Wylie. However, we have also found that simply maintaining the organization from one task to another may not produce as much specific transfer as will occur in the A-B:A-B condition, in which both organizational sets and task elements are maintained. The therapist can increase the amount of generalization by varying the physical aspects of the training experience (task

Table 6–1 Transfer Conditions

Therapy		Real World		
Task Elements	Organizational Set	Task Elements	Organizational Set	Amount of Transfer
A	B	A	A	+ + + +
A	B	A′	B′	+ + +
A	B	C	B	+ +
A	B	C	D	+
A	B	A	D	– – –
A	B	A	Br	– – – –

Source: Data from R. Parenté and J.K. Anderson-Parenté, Vocational Memory Training, in *Community Integration Following Traumatic Brain Injury,* p. 158, J.S. Kreutzer and P.H. Wehman, Eds., © 1990, Paul H. Brookes Publishing Co.; and R. Parenté and A. DiCesare, Retraining Memory: Theory, Evaluation, and Applications, in *Cognitive Rehabilitation for Persons with Traumatic Brain Injury: A Functional Approach,* p. 151, J.S. Kreutzer and P.H. Wehman, Eds., © 1991, Paul H. Brookes Publishing Co.

elements) while keeping the organization relatively constant. This aspect of training will illustrate for the client how the same organizational technique can apply in a variety of different situations (Kreutzer & Wehman, 1989).

Many therapists assume that any treatment will benefit the client. There are, however, situations in which the therapy can impede both transfer and generalization. The A-B:A-D and A-B:A-Br conditions describe these situations. In the A-B:A-D condition, the task elements that the client encounters in treatment (A) are similar to those he or she later encounters in the real world. However, the real-world task organization is different (B versus D). For example, an occupational therapist may train the client to recall where various personal belongings are located in his or her room at home. However, unknown to the therapist, a well-meaning family member may decide that the client should move into a new room upon returning home. The client may have a hard time locating different things in his or her new room at home because although the objects in the room and the client's belongings are the same, the organizing context (B versus D) has changed.

The A-B:A-Br condition produces massive negative transfer effects. The little *r* next to the *B* shows that the task elements are reorganized within the same context. For example, after the same therapist trains the client to organize his or her bedroom at home, a well-meaning family member may reorganize the room before the client returns home. The room and the objects within the room are the same, but the client must now reorganize the room mentally. The experience is similar to the one we have all had when we clean and reorganize an office or room and then cannot find anything for several days.

The A-B:C-D condition produces little transfer or generalization because the task elements and the response sets in the two tasks are dissimilar. However, although there are no specific aspects of training that apply to the client's life, there may be general improvements in attention, concentration, vigilance, and immediate memory that do carry over. Stimulation training and most computer-based remediation models conform to this situation. Many clients wonder how computer training with games and other cognitive

rehabilitation computer exercises will help them to regain their faculties. This is a difficult question to answer because there is very little research evidence that documents the efficacy of computer-based or other types of stimulation therapies. The A-B:C-D paradigm also predicts little transfer or generalization because the two situations do not have common elements or organizational sets.

The model of transfer conditions described above has several important advantages. Perhaps the most important of these is that it accounts for both transfer and generalization phenomena. The model predicts that in any sequential situation, transfer of learning occurs when the elements and the organization are similar. Accordingly, the A-B:A-B paradigm predicts maximum positive transfer. It may not, however, produce a skill that will generalize across situations. The A-B:C-B model produces less specific transfer but greater generalization because the client learns a generic organization that applies across situations. Thus, varying the task elements during training while keeping the organization the same produces a more durable organization that increases the potential for generalization.

TRANSFER AND GENERALIZATION OUTCOMES OF CRT METHODS

Parenté and Anderson-Parenté (1990) described how the above model of transfer and generalization can predict the outcome of most cognitive rehabilitation methods. We will reiterate their summary to show how certain cognitive therapies can be modified in accordance with the transfer model to promote either generalization or positive transfer.

Stimulation Therapy

Stimulation therapy is one of the most popular cognitive retraining methods (Schuell, Carroll, & Street, 1950; Gross & Shutz, 1986). Therapists have used a variety of media, although the computer is currently popular. Repetitive mental exercise is a trademark of the stimulation therapy approach. Treatment may involve something as simple as playing video games or as sophisticated as computer software that is matched to the client's pattern of deficits.

Speech/language therapists were the first to use stimulation therapy (Schuell et al., 1950; Taylor, 1950). Indeed, it is still the mainstay of their therapies today. According to the transfer paradigms outlined above, stimulation therapy conforms to the A-B:C-D model because there are no easily identifiable similarities between therapy and the real world. The model therefore predicts that therapy will produce only general transfer. Schacter and Glisky (1986) made a similar assertion about this type of training. In general, there is little evidence for either transferable effects or generalization resulting from most stimulation therapy efforts.

There are, however, some published findings that show how simple modifications to the stimulation therapy procedures can produce marked improvement in functioning. For example, the research outlined in Chapter 11 shows how iconic memory training can improve reading comprehension. Other modifications can also change typical stimulation therapy into a training program designed to produce a transferable effect. For example, many cognitive skills computer packages provide "digit span" training. These programs present number strings that the client then tries to recall. However, rather than training the client to remember random number strings, the goal should be to teach a response set that carries over to a new situation. The therapist should train the client to remember phone numbers by grouping the seven individual digits into a three-digit number followed by two-digit numbers. This process is detailed in Chapter 11. For example, the therapist could read phone numbers to the client as individual digits (e.g., "3, 2, 4, 6, 8, 9, 5"), and the client would learn to organize the digits into three groups and to recall them as "324, 68, 95." This type of training generalizes to any situation in which the client must recall a phone number because the response set allows the client to encode the number string efficiently and to rehearse it rapidly. Therefore, the therapist can recast the same type of digit string training to conform to an A-B:C-B paradigm, which will usually produce dramatic and rapid improvement of memory for phone numbers.

Memory Strategy Training

Chapter 11 describes a variety of mnemonic strategies that the authors have found to be especially effective with head-injured clients. There is also convincing research that demonstrates that mnemonic strategies can improve recall of word lists and text materials (Parenté & Anderson-Parenté, 1990; Wilson, 1987). In general, there is no shortage of evidence that attests to the usefulness of mnemonic strategies. However, clients may not use mnemonics unless these are relevant to some specific aspect of their lives. It is therefore not sufficient simply to show the client how to form mnemonics and then expect that he or she will do so automatically thereafter. It is necessary for the therapist to develop the mnemonic with the client and to demonstrate how it applies to the client's everyday life.

For example, Chapter 11 demonstrates specific types of mnemonics that the client can use to cue recall of important personal information. These can be word mnemonics, rhymes, or mental images. Regardless of the device, the overall strategy conforms to an A-B:C-B paradigm. Once the client learns the mnemonic, the task elements will differ, but the cognitive response will remain the same. For example, if the client learns the rhyme "i before e except after c," he or she can use this rhyme to spell most words that contain ie or ei combinations. In this example, the individual words used in training make up the A portion of the A-B:C-B paradigm, and the rhyme is the organizing rule (B). When the client later encounters a different word, he or she can then apply the same rule to spell it. Therefore, the technique amounts to an A-B:C-B transfer paradigm, which predicts positive transfer.

Academic Remediation

Cognitive rehabilitation sometimes includes teaching functional skills such as reading and basic math. This type of therapy is effective for several reasons. First, most clients see an immediate relevance to relearning these skills. Academic remediation is also effective because it restores declarative memories and procedural skills. The training also conforms to an A-B:C-B condition because the learned techniques apply in a variety of novel situations. For example, teaching the client how to carry digits in column addition is a procedure that the client applies the same way any time he or she adds up a column of numbers. Once the client has learned to organize the task by carrying numbers from one column to the next, the skill will apply to whatever specific numbers he or she may encounter later. In this example, the training problems the therapist provides are the A components of the A-B:C-B condition. The client learns the skill of carrying numbers from column to column, which is the B component of the condition. Thereafter, in any life situation the client may encounter, the digits may differ (C) but the organizing response (B)—that is, the method of column addition—remains the same. This condition, therefore, is designed to produce positive transfer.

Simulation and Domain-Specific Training

Simulated work environments are designed to provide training that shortens the time it takes the client to become job-ready. The simulated work environment trains the client to perform a specific task and continues the training until he or she reaches competitive levels of performance. To the extent that the training matches the actual work environment, the client can begin work with a minimum of adjustment. This type of training is also called *domain specific* (Schacter & Glisky, 1986) because the domain of training closely resembles the real-world domain in which the client will eventually perform the task.

Domain-specific training is effective because it conforms to an A-B:A′-B′ transfer paradigm. However, the training is not without drawbacks. The disadvantage is that the limited therapy focus also limits the range of generalization. The client becomes a robot who is trained to do one

thing. If the task changes, the client will require retraining. This problem undoubtedly underlies what Parenté, Stapleton, and Wheatley (1991) called the *return loop syndrome,* in which clients return for additional rehabilitation once their domain-specific training becomes obsolete or the task demands of the job change in some way.

Evaluation

Two published studies have directly evaluated the transfer conditions described above with head-injured clients. Parenté et al. (1994) described two experiments in which head injury survivors were asked to memorize either a series of number strings or word lists that were presented so that the training/transfer sequence of tasks conformed to one of the transfer conditions. For example, in the A-B:A-B condition, clients first memorized the number string 65-42-71. They then memorized the same number string in the transfer phase. Clients in the A-B:A-C condition first memorized 6-54-271, then learned 65-42-71. In this case, the numbers (A) were the same but the way the numbers were grouped (B) differed. Clients in the A-B:C-B condition first learned 50-69-18 and then learned 65-42-71. In this condition, the elements were different, but the spatial grouping was the same. Clients in the A-B:C-D condition learned strings whose elements and spatial groupings were both different (e.g., 5-06-918 and 65-42-71).

The model predicted that the A-B:A-B clients would learn the second number strings most quickly, followed by the A-B:C-B group and then the A-B:C-D group. The model also predicted that the A-B:A-C clients would actually learn the second number string more slowly than the control group clients. This was precisely the result. Generally, the results indicated that those clients for whom the spatial grouping remained the same from training to the transfer task learned the second number strings most quickly.

Twum (1994) reported a part/whole learning experiment that was designed to test the model discussed above. He had groups of head injury survivors learn two word lists that differed in terms of their individual words and/or their semantic organization. For example, clients in the A-B:A-B condition first learned the following list: "Dog, Cat, Green, Red, North, West." Clients in the A-B:A-C condition first learned "Dog, Green, North, Table, Venus, Man." In the A-B:C-B condition, clients first learned "Lion, Tiger, Blue, Yellow, South, East." In the A-B:C-D condition, clients learned "Pencil, Dime, Ring, Tree, Shoe, Lamp." Each group then learned the longer list, which contained the following words: "Dog, Cat, Green, Red, North, West, Table, Chair, Venus, Mars, Man, Woman."

Clients in the A-B:A-B condition learned the second list most rapidly. Those in the A-B:C-B condition learned the second list almost as rapidly as did the clients in the A-B:A-B group. Those in the control condition (A-B:C-D) actually outperformed those in the A-B:A-C condition. This was surprising because in the A-B:A-C condition, the first list words were actually one-half of the second list. The fact that these clients performed worse than those in the A-B:C-D condition, in which the two lists of words were completely unrelated, indicates that the clients in the A-B:A-C condition were unable to transfer their organization of the first-list words when learning the second list. Performance in this experiment was therefore quite predictable from the transfer model discussed above. A statistical analysis indicated that clients in those conditions in which the semantic organization was maintained from the first to the second list performed the best. Specifically, these were the subjects who were in the A-B:A-B and A-B:C-B conditions. Changing the organization (A-B:A-C condition) actually impeded clients' ability to learn the second list.

CONCLUSION

Although there has been a great deal of transfer research in psychology, there has been relatively little carryover of these research findings into the cognitive rehabilitation literature. This same literature suffers from a general lack of experimental validation of its proposed therapies

and theoretical models of treatment. The author's purpose in this chapter was to trace the history of transfer and generalization theories and to outline a model of these phenomena that would predict the outcome of various rehabilitation methods. The model can also be used to improve the outcome of most cognitive rehabilitation therapies. From it, one can draw the following guidelines that therapists can use to guide their treatment:

1. Teach mental sets that are useful in a variety of different situations. Cognitive rehabilitation strategies will generalize to the real world to the extent that the client learns mental sets that transfer intact. Specifically, therapies that conform to an A-B:C-B model will usually generalize. For example, the problem-solving strategies in Chapter 15, the decision-making strategies in Chapter 16, and the memory strategies in Chapter 11 are all useful in a variety of situations.

2. Teach specific skills that transfer. If the goal is to train specific transferable skills, then the therapy should ideally conform to an A-B:A-B or A-B:A′-B′ training paradigm. This type of training is especially useful when the goal is to expedite return to work. However, the client will learn skills that may not generalize to other situations. For example, the therapist may visit the client's workplace and then create a simulated work environment. This will ensure that the client has the requisite skills to perform the targeted job. However, the same skills may be inadequate or inappropriate for other jobs.

3. Focus on relevant tasks. Therapies are most effective when the client perceives some obvious relevance of the training to his or her activities of daily living. Two types of strategies are relevant. The first is a general rule that the client can use for a lifetime. For example, the "i before e except after c" rhyme is an organizing strategy the client can use forever to recall how to spell most words that contain *ie* or *ei* combinations. The rhyme "righty-tighty, lefty-loosey" can help the client to recall how to tighten and loosen a nut on a bolt. The second type of strategy is one that trains memory for a specific context. For example, teaching the client a specific way of performing a skill on the job may be useful for that job but not for any other. Either type of strategy is useful, and it is easy to show the client how useful it will be.

4. Vary the training examples. Several authors have emphasized the importance of using a variety of training examples when trying to teach clients generalizable strategies (Glick & Holyoak, 1987; Woolcock, 1990). According to the above transfer model, diversifying the training examples will facilitate transfer because a wide variety of task elements become associated with a single organizational response.

5. Provide overlearning and verification. It is not sufficient simply to show the client a strategy and expect that he or she will use it spontaneously. Most clients will need several practice situations with a variety of training examples before they will even remember the skill. The therapist should therefore provide overlearning sessions when teaching a strategy and then test to see if the client has learned the skill by providing new examples.

6. Avoid reorganization. The therapist should avoid training that will eventually force the client to learn new response sets to the same task elements. It is especially important to avoid training in which the same responses are eventually reassociated or mismatched with the same task elements. These situations produce negative transfer, which results in frustration and failure for the client. For example, a therapist trained one client to do data entry by creating a specific template for his keyboard that summarized various function keys. When the client returned to work, he was trained with a different organizing template, so he had to reorganize the keyboard. This created a serious negative transfer problem, and eventually he had to retrain.

In general, the goal of treatment is to promote positive transfer and to reduce negative transfer. However, achieving this goal may be easier said than done. In most cases, however, the therapist will have far greater success if he or she plans treatment by first asking how the therapy will achieve an outcome that carries over into the client's everyday life. If the answer to this question is not forthcoming, the treatment is probably not worth pursuing.

REFERENCES

Bruce, R.W. (1933). Conditions of transfer of training. *Journal of Experimental Psychology, 16*, 343–361.

Cormier, S.M., & Hagman, J.D. (1987). *Transfer of learning: Contemporary research and applications.* Berkeley, CA: Academic Press.

Ellis, H.C. (1965). *The transfer of learning.* New York: Macmillan.

Glick, M.L., & Holyoak, K.J. (1987). The cognitive basis of knowledge transfer. In S.M. Cormier & J.D. Hagman (Eds.), *Transfer of learning: Contemporary research and applications* (pp. 9–42). London: Academic Press.

Gifford, J., Rusch, F., Martin, J., & White, D. (1985). Autonomy and adaptability: A proposed technology for maintaining work behavior. *International Review of Research on Mental Retardation, 12*, 285–314.

Gross, Y., & Shutz, L. (1986). Intervention models in neuropsychology. In B. Uzzell & Y. Gross (Eds.), *Clinical neuropsychology of intervention* (pp. 22–27). Boston: Martinus Nijhoff.

Horner, R.H., Sprague, J., & Wilcox, B. (1986). Intervention models in neuropsychology. In B. Wilcox & G.T. Belamy (Eds.), *Design of high school programs for severely handicapped students* (pp. 179–204). Baltimore: Paul H. Brookes.

Kreutzer, J.S., & Wehman, P.H. (Eds.). (1989). *Community integration following traumatic brain injury.* Baltimore: Paul H. Brookes.

Newell, A. (1980). Reasoning, problem-solving, and decision processes: The problem space as a fundamental category. In R. Nikerson (Ed.), *Attention and performance VIII.* Hillsdale, NJ: Lawrence Erlbaum.

Osgood, C.E. (1949). The similarity paradox in human learning: A resolution. *Psychological Review, 56*, 132–143.

Parenté, R., & Anderson-Parenté, J.K. (1990). Vocational memory training. In J. Kreutzer & P. Wehman (Eds.), *Community integration following traumatic brain injury* (pp. 157–169). Baltimore, MD: Paul H. Brookes.

Parenté, R., & DiCesare, A. (1991). Retraining memory: Theory, evaluation, and applications. In J. Kreutzer & P. Wehman (Eds.), *Cognitive rehabilitation for persons with traumatic brain injury: A functional approach* (pp. 147–162). Baltimore, MD: Paul H. Brookes.

Parenté, R., Twum, M., & Zoltan, B. (1994). Transfer and generalization of cognitive skill after traumatic brain injury. *NeuroRehabilitation, 4*(1), 25–35.

Schacter, D., & Glisky, E. (1986). Memory remediation, restoration, alleviation, and the acquisition of domain specific knowledge. In B. Uzzell & Y. Gross (Eds.), *Clinical neuropsychology of intervention* (pp. 257–282). Boston: Martinus Nijhoff.

Schuell, H.M., Carroll, V., & Street, B.S. (1950). Clinical treatment of aphasia. *Journal of Speech and Hearing Disorders, 20,* 43–53.

Singley, M.K., & Anderson, J.R. (1987). *The transfer of cognitive skills.* Cambridge, MA: Harvard University Press.

Taylor, M.T. (1950). Language therapy. In H.G. Burn (Ed.), *The aphasic adult: Rehabilitation and treatment* (pp. 156–200). Charlottesville, VA: Wayside.

Thorndike, E.L., & Woodworth, R.S. (1901). The influence of improvement in one mental function upon the efficiency of other functions. *Psychological Review, 8,* 247–261.

Twum, M. (1994). Maximizing generalization of cognitions and memories after traumatic brain injury. *NeuroRehabilitation, 4*(3), 157–167.

Wilson, B. (1987). *Rehabilitation of memory.* New York: Guilford.

Woolcock, W. (1990). Generalization strategies. In P. Wehman & J. Kreutzer (Eds.), *Vocational rehabilitation for persons with traumatic brain injury* (pp. 243–263). Gaithersburg, MD: Aspen.

Wylie, H.H. (1919). An experimental study of transfer of response in the white rat. *Behavioral Monographs, 3,* 16.

Ylvisaker, M. (1993, June). *Historical perspectives and general principles.* Paper presented at the conference "Cognitive Rehabilitation: A Practical Approach," Edmonton, Alberta, Canada.

Chapter 7

Assessment

ASSESSMENT APPROACHES

To retrain cognition, it is first necessary to assess which areas of the multimodal system are dysfunctional. Two types of assessment are discussed in this chapter: static and dynamic.

Static assessment methods evaluate the person at a single point in time to determine current level of functioning. Such methods have received the most attention within neuropsychology (see, e.g., Spreen & Strauss, 1991). Because there are so many excellent books on static assessment already available (e.g., Lezak, 1995), we do not go into great detail when describing these techniques.

Traditionally, static assessment has relied upon neuropsychological tests such as the Halstead-Reitan and Luria-Nebraska batteries (Golden, Purisch, & Hammeke, 1985; Goodglass & Kaplan, 1983; Halstead, 1947; Reitan, 1955). Such tests yield raw scores that index the person's ability to do a certain task. This score is compared to scores of a group of "normals" to yield a standard or converted score (e.g., Z score, T score, IQ score). The standard score indicates how well the person performed on the test relative to others who have taken the same test. Typically it is expressed in terms of percentile rank: for example, a client's scoring in the 23rd percentile means that he or she performed better than 23% of the norming group. More recently, static assessment has come to include medical imaging procedures, such as computerized tomography (CT) and magnetic resonance imaging (MRI) to localize brain defects. According to several authors (e.g., Miller, 1984), these technologies may eventually obviate the need for neuropsychological evaluations as we have known them.

Dynamic assessment methods evaluate the person at two or more points in time to determine potential for improvement in functioning. This potential may be learning potential, the ability to improve performance with practice; intervention potential, the ability to benefit from instruction; or transfer potential, the ability to transfer or generalize the newly learned skills. Dynamic assessment, instead of comparing the client's one-shot performance to the normative performance of a large body of people, tracks changes in the client's own performance over time. Thus, standardized tests are not necessary; almost any measure or combination of measures can be used, allowing the therapist far more flexibility in tailoring assessment to the client's particular needs. In dynamic assessment, the significant score is not the standard score, but the *learning score,* literally the difference between performance scores on a test at two different times. For example, on a scale of 1 to 10, a client may score a 5 on the first measurement of performance and a 7 on the second measurement. In this example, the learning score would be 2 (7 – 5). Learning is literally the gain in performance from the first to the second assessment.

STATIC VERSUS DYNAMIC ASSESSMENT

Both static and dynamic assessment methods can provide useful information. For example, static methods can be used to document and to localize a brain injury for legal and medical purposes and to determine which cognitive processes are likely to be impaired as well as the extent of the impairment. Neuropsychological tests in particular provide comprehensive baseline information and can be especially valuable for detecting behavioral and subtle cognitive deficits that are not readily apparent from imaging methods such as MRI and CT.

But neuropsychological testing procedures were originally designed primarily to examine brain-behavior relationships rather than to predict which types of cognitive rehabilitation therapies were likely to be the most successful. This is because the discipline of neuropsychology itself has its roots in diagnosis and has been relatively less concerned with intervention. Consequently, many therapists and family members are left feeling that the test results do not provide the type of information they need to plan a treatment program for the client. They often feel that the test results simply reassert what they already know. The results can indicate what is wrong with the client, but they stop short of making useful recommendations for improvement. Further, it is questionable just how well they predict everyday functioning (Acker, 1986), since the skills demonstrated in the testing situation do not necessarily transfer to real-life contexts. This problem was addressed by Hart and Hayden (1986), who argued that neuropsychological assessment lacks "ecological validity" (see also Wilson, 1987; Wilson, Baddeley, & Cockburn, 1988).

Although it is assumed, in conventional neuropsychological assessment, that one-shot test scores are good predictors of rehabilitation po-

tential, they can in fact be highly misleading. Figure 7–1 illustrates the results of a word-learning task for two clients. The figure shows one client beginning at a considerably higher level of performance than the other. If the evaluator stops testing at this point, results will show only that one client is severely impaired and the other is performing at average levels. A distinctly different pattern, however, emerges with repeated (dynamic) testing (Toglia, 1992, 1994). The client who was initially quite impaired has improved much more rapidly with practice. Because this client's learning curve is steeper, he or she is actually learning faster than the other client. Therefore, we say that he or she has greater learning potential on this task.

In our experience, learning (dynamic) and performance (static) measures can produce quite different conclusions about a client's potential for rehabilitation. This is because rehabilitation is a learning process, and scores on static neuropsychological tests, obtained from a single testing, cannot index learning per se, if *learning* is defined as change in performance with practice (Bower & Hilgard, 1984; Parenté & Anderson-Parenté, 1991). Dynamic assessment, by measuring learning potential, or the ability to change with practice, and intervention potential, or the ability to benefit from instruction, provides far more accurate predictions.

Dynamic assessment also offers guidelines that therapists can use to plan treatment successfully. First, it helps therapists to identify the types of skills the client is capable of learning, and thus the types of skills on which a treatment program can productively focus. As a rule of thumb, skills that improve with practice—and especially skills that improve rapidly with practice—are the best candidates for intervention. Skills on which repeated testing yields no learning effects should not be targeted for interventions, since training will only cause frustration. This rule applies regardless of the initial level of performance. It also applies regardless of whether the client is 6 months or 6 years post injury. Although there has been much controversy over whether therapy should start soon after the injury occurs or be delayed until the deficits stabilize, effective treat-

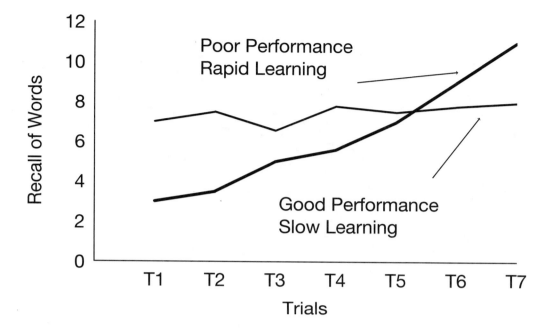

Figure 7–1 Learning Versus Performance Comparison for Two Traumatically Brain-Injured Clients on a 12-Item Word List

ment should be possible whenever the therapist is working with skills that show improvement with practice.

Second, dynamic assessment helps therapists to determine which of several intervention strategies will be most beneficial for a client. Figure 7–2 shows the results of this kind of testing on the effectiveness of three different memory strategies used with the same client. The therapist began with a word mnemonic to help the client learn a word list. Imagery instructions were provided next, followed by a simple repetition of the words. The results indicated that the simple repetition produced the greatest initial gain and the word mnemonic was mildly successful. The imagery instruction seemed to be the worst of the three methods. But when each of the techniques was repeated over several trials, a very different conclusion was reached. With practice, the imagery produced the greatest improvement. The word mnemonic also was helpful and simple repetition was least useful.

Third, dynamic assessment helps therapists to determine what types of training are most likely to transfer or to generalize to the real world.

DYNAMIC ASSESSMENT PROCEDURES

There have been some attempts to develop formal dynamic test procedures (Feuerstein, Klein, & Tannenbaum, 1991), and although these are not yet widely used in clinical practice, they are quite useful for any therapist who is trying to plan a treatment program for a client with traumatic brain injury.

Measuring Learning Potential

Parenté and Anderson-Parenté (1991) outlined a method for evaluating learning potential that can be used with virtually any static test procedure. Their method involves repeated testing until

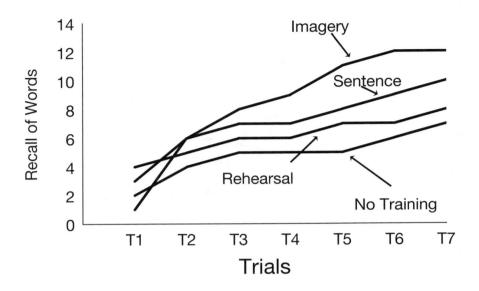

Figure 7–2 Learning Potential Under Four Training Conditions

the client reaches a criterion of average performance. The evaluator begins with any test that has published norms. The norms provide an index of average performance. The client repeats the test until his or her performance reaches average levels. The index of learning potential, then, is the number of repetitions necessary to improve performance to average levels. The therapist need not use standardized tests for this type of assessment. Any measurable behavior can be evaluated to determine if it improves with practice. Moreover, the therapist can create norms from "normal" volunteers at a facility.

For example, a client may require five repetitions on a task before his or her performance reaches a level that would be considered average or above average. With other tasks, performance may reach average levels after one or two repetitions. Learning potential is therefore the number of repetitions necessary to reach the average range. In our experience, tasks that require fewer than five repetitions have clear potential for improvement with treatment. Those requir-

ing more than five repetitions can be treated but will probably respond slowly. Those that require more than 10 repetitions will probably produce frustration.

One advantage of this type of measure is that it is relatively easy to explain the results of the testing to family members. For example, most family members will understand a statement such as "Your son will have to read a magazine article five times before he'll remember it." Another advantage is that the therapist can evaluate almost any ability using this technique. One disadvantage is that the number of trials it takes the person to reach an average level can be misleading because the person may fall in the average range on the first testing but not improve markedly thereafter. Consequently, the technique may create a false impression of the client's learning potential in some situations.

Another measure of learning potential is the slope of the learning curve for any given task. One simple way to determine the task on which the client shows the most learning potential is simply to see which curve has the steepest slant on the graph. This should be apparent after the scores are plotted. A more exact method is to average the client's learning scores (i.e., to average the differences between scores on successive tests). For example, on the scale mentioned earlier (1 to 10), if the client scores a 4 on the first testing, a 6 on the second, and an 8 on the third, the evaluator simply subtracts the first score from the second (difference of 2) and the second from the third (difference of 2), then averages the differences (2 + 2 = 4/2 = 2). On another performance test, the first difference may be 3 and the second 5, yielding an average difference of 4 (3 + 5 = 8/2 = 4). The task that yields an average difference score of 4 shows the steepest learning curve and the greatest potential for new learning.

The advantage of using slope measures is that they need not be compared to an average range. They can therefore be used to assess learning potential with any measure. They also illustrate how much the client is improving with practice. The disadvantage is that they can be labor intensive to compute.

Measuring Intervention Potential

The purpose of testing various interventions is to determine which are most likely to improve the client's thinking and memory. For example, the therapist might train categorization (Parenté & Anderson-Parenté, 1983) and measure performance after each instruction session. The therapist would then compare the client's performance in the second phase with that in the first. If performance improved markedly, then the therapy was effective. If there was no substantial change, then the therapist would try another treatment.

The therapist can use a variety of methods to determine the effectiveness of an intervention. The most common approach is to evaluate the client's performance before and after the intervention to see if there is any improvement. With this approach, the therapist first tests the client without any intervention to evaluate performance when the client is left to his or her own devices.

The client's performance during the intervention stage is then compared with his or her performance during the baseline phase. The difference—termed the *zone of proximal development* by Vygotsky (1978) and the *zone of potential rehabilitation* by Cicerone and Tupper (1986)—measures the client's ability to benefit from the training. The magnitude of the improvement during the intervention phase is an index of the intervention's usefulness. For example, if the client first recalls a paragraph and then is taught to use imagery to learn another, his or her recall of the second paragraph, relative to the first, is an index of the effectiveness of the imagery intervention.

Another approach is to evaluate several potential strategies simultaneously. For example, Appendix B presents a test of preferred organization (see "Multiple Encoding Task"). The task involves presenting a collection of words on a single page and asking the client to study the list and to recall the words in any preferred order. The collection is categorized into semantic groupings. The words can also be grouped by color, by different font styles, and by spatial organization on the page. The client studies the list, then recalls it on a piece of blank paper in any order he or she desires. The study-test procedure continues until a clear organizational preference emerges. Many clients use the semantic organization to recall the words in a list. Others may use the color coding, the font styles, or the spatial groupings. This natural preference clearly indicates the types of strategies the person can recognize and feels comfortable using at a given stage of recovery.

Measuring Transfer Potential

The third aspect of the intervention assessment concerns whether the client is able to carry over his or her strategies to a new situation. Therefore, after training the skill, the next step is to assess whether the training will aid learning and memory in a similar task. For example, after training the client to group number strings, the therapist may have the client call the information operator and require recall of the numbers in grouped fashion. If the treatment does not pro-duce any carryover effects, the therapist should provide further training or abandon it. Clearly, the choice of intervention tasks will be partially dictated by whether there is any obvious trans-ferable quality to the intervention (Twum, 1994).

It is important to distinguish between the trans-fer potential of the strategy and the client's spon-taneous use of the strategy. The strategy may work well for the client, but he or she may not readily implement it. On the other hand, the cli-ent may not find the strategy useful. In the former case, the therapist must realize that training the client to the point at which the strategy is used spontaneously may take quite a long time. *Trans-fer potential* therefore refers to the potential use-fulness of the strategy, not to the client's willing-ness to use it or compliance with the therapist's suggestion to use it.

THE INITIAL ASSESSMENT BATTERY

Despite the problems with conventional static assessment mentioned above, we feel that *both* static and dynamic procedures of evaluation have distinct advantages and should be used when-ever time and resources permit. If a comprehen-sive neuropsychological evaluation is available, the therapist should use it as an estimate of the client's cognitive capacity before beginning treat-ment. However, therapists often do not have ac-cess to neuropsychological test results or cannot get them before they begin treatment. We there-fore provide several tests that any therapist can perform that will also assess a variety of basic cognitive processes (see Exhibit 7–1 and Ap-pendix B for more details on each test and its administration; see also Johnson, 1983). They re-quire no special credentials to obtain or admin-ister, are generally available, and are relatively simple to use and to evaluate. If they reveal any outstanding deficits, however, a complete neuropsychological assessment may be neces-sary. Many other tests will serve the same pur-poses as the ones listed here, and the reader may certainly substitute those that he or she is accus-tomed to using.

Most of the tests in Exhibit 7–1 were chosen because they can be administered repeatedly to evaluate the client's potential for improvement with practice or instruction. This is the dynamic aspect of the assessment battery. But for others, which measure aspects of functioning that are typically viewed as relatively static (e.g., I.Q.), a one-time administration should be sufficient.

We typically administer tasks that involve working/long-term memory first. This is because after the initial learning sessions are finished, a meaningful interpolated task is necessary to keep the client from rehearsing the materials before testing delayed retention. The task should last at least half an hour (preferably 1 hour or more) to be certain that subsequent memory testing is tap-ping long-term retention. In practice, we use the rest of the battery as an interpolated task. How-ever, any interpolated task will work if it keeps the person occupied.

After the interpolated task, the therapist gives three retests for the working/long-term memory tasks that were administered at the beginning. The first is a *free-recall* test. That is, the client recalls all that he or she learned on the memory tasks during the first stage without any prompt-ing. This is a gross index of transfer from short-term to long-term memory. Obviously, if the cli-ent can recall anything after an hour, some information must have been transferred from short-term memory into long-term memory. However, if there is no free recall, this does not mean that no memory transfer occurred.

The client may then be tested for recognition memory of the items. If the client has no free recall but does recognize the items, the therapist should suspect a retrieval problem. This means that the information transferred into long-term memory (LTM) and the client could recognize it but that the information, though available for recall, was not accessible. On the other hand, if the client can neither recall the items freely nor recognize them, the information may not have made it into LTM. The therapist should then sus-pect a storage problem.

Storage and retrieval problems are fundamen-tally different disorders. In our experience, re-trieval problems are more common after head

Exhibit 7–1 Initial Assessment Battery

Cognitive Ability	Test Procedure
Sensory Memory	
Iconic	Brief Duration Flashes
Echoic	Continuous Dialogue Task
Attention/Concentration	Digit Span
	Visual Memory Span
Working/Long-Term Memory	
Rehearsal	Rehearsal Card Games
Verbal Memory	Buschke Selective Reminding
Visual Memory	Rey Figure Recall
	Zoo Picture Task
Memory Strategy	Multiple Encoding Task
Storage/Retrieval	Retesting on any or all of the above tests (1) for free recall, (2) for recognition, and (3) for savings
Thinking Skills	
General Intelligence	Test of Nonverbal Intelligence
	Poison Foods Test
	Kent IQ Test
Reasoning	Tinker Toy Test
Concept Learning	Playing Card Sequence
Cognitive Flexibility	Uses of Objects Test
Expressive Skills	Word Fluency/Figural Fluency
	Draw a Bicycle Test
	Rey Figure Copy
	Writing Sample
	Similar Letter Writing Test

injury. They involve the inability to generate spontaneously the retrieval cues necessary for free recall. Therapy for this type of disorder involves teaching the client retrieval strategies or providing prosthetic devices for cuing (see Chapters 11 and 13). Storage problems are far more difficult to work with and most often resist treatment. It is therefore essential to evaluate storage/retrieval deficits prior to planning interventions.

A final measure of LTM is called *savings*. This measure results from an additional learning trial given after the interpolated task. The logic is simple. After a delay interval, if the client can relearn the original material at a level that exceeds his or her initial learning trial, some amount of transfer must have occurred. The therapist simply readministers the same test once more during the delayed testing, usually after the free-recall and recognition tests. How well the client performs on this task is compared to his or her performance the first time the task was administered (at least half an hour earlier). The difference between the two measures is the index of savings.

We have come to several conclusions using these methods for testing working/long-term memory. Usually, if there is poor recognition, there is poor recall and virtually no savings. However, the therapist may find that the client improves with practice in the training phase (shows learning) but cannot later recognize or recall. Obviously the learning effects mean that some memory transfer has occurred. Such instances do not conform to the neat rules outlined above. However, in most situations, if the client cannot recognize, storage is the problem. If the client can recognize but not recall, retrieval is implicated. Likewise, if there is poor delayed recall but there are savings effects, retrieval is again implicated. Perhaps the most consistent deficit is poor delayed recall with unaffected recognition and clear savings effects.

Our evaluation also involves tests of sensory memory (iconic and echoic; see Chapter 8), attention/concentration, and thinking skills. Thinking skills are divided into several categories. Verbal and nonverbal intelligence can be estimated using the Kent IQ Test and the Test of Nonverbal Intelligence. These provide an index of general knowledge and nonverbal IQ. Clearly, if the therapist has access to other commonly accepted measures of intelligence, these can be substituted. We also provide measures of several specific aspects of thinking skill, including reasoning, cognitive flexibility, and concept learning. Finally, the client's response system is measured with a variety of tests that assess expressive skills.

OBSERVATION

Although the initial assessment battery evaluates a variety of information that may not be available from other sources, it does not look at the client's everyday functioning. Family members and friends, however, do make these types of observations. Thus it may be especially useful to give the questionnaire in Appendix A to both the client and family members. This will typically provide different results. For example, as Anderson-Parenté (1994) discovered, clients can assess the concrete aspects of their behavior quite accurately, but family members are more accurate in assessing the client's ability to deal with abstractions. The combination of the two assessments can provide a useful adjunct to the performance-based testing outlined above.

Observational notes are especially useful during the test phase. For example, the therapist should provide information about the client's optimal style of learning. Does the client learn visual or verbal information more rapidly, and which does he or she retain longer? How many rehearsals are necessary before the client can retain the information? What time of day is the best to work with the client? How long can he or she work before fatiguing? How does the client respond to verbal reinforcement? What is the optimal distribution of practice? Answers to these questions are especially important to other therapists who have to work with the same client later on. Lewkowics and Whitton (1995) presented an excellent survey for this purpose.

CONCLUSION

This chapter presents methods for assessing cognitive functioning and potential for success in therapy. Measures of multimodal performance are presented in Appendix B.

Conventional performance-based assessments and observational measures provide a good starting point for assessing a client. However, other techniques are necessary to evaluate which abilities will respond rapidly to treatment and which will not. Rehabilitation is a learning process. Consequently, it is necessary to measure not only performance at one point in time but also potential for improvement of performance with practice and instruction. The chapter presents dynamic assessment procedures for measuring the client's zone of rehabilitation potential. It discusses several measures of *learning potential*, the client's ability to improve with practice; *intervention potential*, the client's ability to benefit from rehabilitation strategies; and *transfer potential*, the client's ability to apply newly learned skill outside the training environment. All three measures allow the therapist to determine which interventions will have the greatest impact.

REFERENCES

Acker, M. (1986). Relationship between test scores and everyday life functioning. In B. Uzzell & Y. Gross (Eds.), *The clinical neuropsychology of intervention* (pp. 85–118). Boston: Martinus Nijhoff.

Anderson-Parenté, J.K. (1994). A comparison of metacognitive ratings of persons with traumatic brain injury and their family members. *NeuroRehabilitation, 4*(3), 168–173.

Bower, G., & Hilgard, E. (1994). *Theories of learning.* Englewood Cliffs, NJ: Prentice Hall.

Cicerone, K., & Tupper, D.E. (1986). Cognitive assessment in the neuropsychological rehabilitation of head injured adults. In B. Uzzell & Y. Gross (Eds.), *The clinical neuropsychology of intervention* (pp. 59–84). Boston: Martinus Nijhoff.

Feuerstein, R., Klein, P.S., & Tannenbaum, A.J. (Eds.). (1991). *Mediated Learning Experience (MLE): Theoretical, psychosocial and learning implications*. London: Freund.

Golden, G.J., Purisch, A.D., & Hammeke, T.A. (1985). *Luria-Nebraska Neuropsychological Battery: Forms I and II manual*. Los Angeles: Western Psychological Services.

Goodglass, H., & Kaplan, E. (1983). *Assessment of aphasia and related disorders*. Philadelphia: Lea & Febiger.

Halstead, W.C. (1947). *Brain and intelligence*. Chicago: University of Chicago Press.

Hart, T., & Hayden, M. (1986). The ecological validity of neuropsychological assessment and remediation. In B. Uzzell & Y. Gross (Eds.), *The clinical neuropsychology of intervention* (pp. 21–50). Boston: Martinus Nijhoff.

Johnson, M.H. (1983). A multiple-entry, modular memory system. In G.H. Bower (Ed.), *The psychology of learning and motivation*. New York: Academic Press.

Lewkowics, S., & Whitton, J. (1995). A new inventory for exploring neuropsychological change resulting from brain injury. *Cognitive Rehabilitation, 13*, 8–20.

Lezak, M.D. (1995). *Neuropsychological assessment* (3rd ed.). New York: Oxford University Press.

Miller, E. (1984). *Recovery and management of neuropsychological impairments*. New York: John Wiley.

Parenté, F.J., & Anderson-Parenté, J.K. (1983). Techniques for improving cognitive rehabilitation: Teaching organization and encoding skills. *Journal of Cognitive Rehabilitation, 1*(4), 20–23.

Parenté, R., & Anderson-Parenté, J.K. (1991). *Retraining memory: Techniques and applications*. Houston, TX: CSY.

Reitan, R.M. (1955). An investigation of Halstead's measures of biological intelligence. *Archives of Neurology and Psychiatry, 73*, 28–35.

Spreen, O., & Strauss, E. (1991). *A compendium of neuropsychological tests: Administration norms and commentary*. New York: Oxford University Press.

Toglia, J.P. (1992). Generalization of treatment: A multicontext approach to cognitive perceptual impairment in adults with brain injury. *American Journal of Occupational Therapy, 45*, 505–516.

Toglia, J.P. (1994). *Dynamic assessment of categorization: TCA, The Toglia Category Assessment manual*. Pequannock, NJ: Maddak.

Twum, M. (1994). Maximizing generalization of cognitions and memories after traumatic brain injury. *NeuroRehabilitation, 4*(3), 157–167.

Vygotsky, L. (1978). *Mind in society: The development of higher psychological processes*. Cambridge, MA: Harvard University Press.

Wilson, B.A. (1987). *Rehabilitation of memory*. New York: Guilford.

Wilson, B.A., Baddeley, A.D., & Cockburn, J. (1988). Trials, tribulations and triumphs in the development of a test of everyday memory. In M.M. Gruneberg, P.E. Morris, & R.N. Sykes (Eds.), *Practical aspects of memory: Current research and issues*. Chichester, UK: John Wiley.

Chapter 8

Retraining Iconic and Echoic Memory

This chapter focuses on a topic that is usually overlooked in a book on rehabilitation of brain functions. It deals with a brief, fleeting memory system called the sensory register (Ellis & Hunt, 1993; Erdman & Dodge, 1898; Ericksen & Lappin, 1967). This is the first phase of the intake of information. The sensory register holds new information for further processing by the cognitive system. We have devoted an entire chapter to the sensory register for two reasons. First, it is poorly understood, and there is little systematic research concerning deficits after head injury. Second, because the sensory register is the first stage of information processing, if it is impaired after head injury, the remaining information-processing systems will also be impaired. In our opinion, assessment and rehabilitation should always begin with this memory system.

The training procedures discussed later in this chapter are primarily for the visual (*iconic*) sensory register. However, we also discuss the analogous methods for the auditory (*echoic*) register. We provide an in-depth survey of the existing models of iconic memory (IM), summarize results from studies investigating IM deficits and their remediation after brain injury, and provide step-by-step procedures for retraining iconic memory and discuss their transfer to reading and other skills.

ICONIC MEMORY: THE "MIND'S EYE"

Our eyes normally move in brief quick motions called *saccades*. Between the saccades, they focus on the objects that we see. Although our eyes move several times per second, we perceive the world only during the brief fixations (Averbach & Coriell, 1961). In essence, we can think of our visual experience as a rapid sequence of still-life photographs. However, the fixations occur too frequently for us to notice the interval between the snapshots (Haber & Hershenson, 1980).

For decades, psychologists have studied our capacity to scan information during the eyes' fixation periods (Sperling, 1970; Volkmann, 1859). Their research indicates that we continue to see an object for a short time after the physical stimulation ends (Craik, 1973; Haber & Standing, 1969; Sackitt, 1976a). This brief period of visual perception that persists after the object is removed from view is called *iconic memory*. The physical characteristics of IM were originally investigated by Sperling (1960), although the phenomenon was named by Neisser (1967). Iconic memory is more than just an afterimage. A fascinating fact about IM is that it is a fleeting memory that occurs in the brain, not in the eye. This is because the image occurs for a duration that is too brief to permit scanning by moving the eye. Therefore, any attempt to scan the icon must be a totally mental process (Dick, 1974).

On the surface, IM seems simple to define. Physically, it is a brief, photographlike visual representation that is perceptually available for a few hundred milliseconds after the physical stimulus has ended (DiLollo & Dixon, 1988). There are, however, subtly different definitions of IM. According to Chow (1986), IM is (a) a kind of "visible persistence" that allows a person to describe an image (Haber & Nathanson, 1968; Haber & Standing, 1969), (b) the aftereffects that persist when the retina is stimulated (Sakitt, 1975, 1976a, 1976b), and (c) a persistent form of visual information that is precategorical or devoid of meaning or organization (Coltheart, 1980).

It is easy to demonstrate IM. As a simple example, hold your hand directly before your face and shut your eyes. Now blink your eyes once, and immediately keep them shut after a single blink. You will see the image of your hand fade from view in about one third of a second. This is the duration of the icon of your hand. It is literally impossible to maintain the image of your hand in your "mind's eye" for very long. The image will fade too rapidly. There is no way to rehearse or sustain the image in the absence of the actual physical stimulation.

Now pretend you have a different letter drawn on each finger. Without being told which letter to attend to in advance, an average person could report practically any of the letters he or she saw before the hand image faded from memory. But how well could individuals scan the icon of their hand after traumatic brain injury? Could they report the letters on each finger? Would they require another look, perhaps several more, before they could recall the letters?

This example shows that IM stores visual information that is not yet available to any other cognitive system. It also illustrates that our ability to scan an icon determines much of what we eventually perceive of our world. Any event that limits the sensory store—for example, brain damage after head injury—also affects the cognitive system and the response system storage.

Why is it important to study the effect of brain injury on the sensory system? The major reason concerns the paucity of available information about the disrupting effects of trauma on this type of information processing. Although several authors have mentioned IM in their books on rehabilitation of brain functions, we found only three published investigations of IM deficits after head injury (McClur, Browning, Vantrease, & Bittle, 1994, 1995; Parenté & Anderson-Parenté, 1991; Parenté, Anderson-Parenté, & Shaw, 1989). Another reason is that these investigators have found that it is possible to train persons to scan sensory icons and that such training can be an effective therapy after head injury. This is an especially important point in light of Haber's (1983) review of the iconic literature. There has not been much in the way of practical application of the published research findings on iconic or echoic memory. Perhaps the major value of the theoretical literature is that it provides a good understanding of the complexities of the iconic sensory register. Clearly, iconic memory is more than a simple afterimage. Therefore, before we present a procedure for training iconic memory, we will first summarize this literature.

Iconic sensory memory stores a record of the information that is received by receptor cells. Receptor cells on the retina are the specialized sense organs of the eye, and they become activated by physical energy from the environment. The record of this activation is known as the *sensory trace*. Ellis and Hunt (1993) described the sensory register as a holding tank that maintains information until the interpretive processes are activated. In this way, we avoid losing information of the present while we are processing information from the past.

According to Ellis and Hunt (1993), there are three main characteristics of the sensory IM register. First, information is stored in a near-photographic form. Second, the sensory register is a high-capacity storage system. Finally, information remains in the sensory register for only a brief period of time. The information in the IM would be blurred if two scenes were registered in quick succession. For example, one can experience the sensory register by rapidly moving a pencil or a pen back and forth in front of the eye. The image blurs because the icon persists as the pencil changes position.

Sperling (1960, 1963) also made the basic assumption that iconic memory preserves, in raw form, *all* briefly presented information, thereby allowing additional processing. This assumption is consistent with Orenstein and Holding's (1987) report that iconic memory preserves equally both information the person attends to and information he or she does not attend to. This is because it is virtually a photograph of the world at that instant of time, with no priority of processing for any given aspect of the picture.

Measures of Iconic Memory

Several methods have been used to study iconic memory (Eriksen & Lappin, 1967; Loftus & Busey, 1992; Loftus, Duncan, & Gehrig, 1992; Long & O'Saben, 1989; Mewhort, Butler, Feldman-Stewart, & Tramer, 1988). The classic procedure, called *partial report* (Sperling, 1960), was originally used to assess the capacity of IM.

The person initially focused on a cross that indicated the exact spot where a letter matrix would flash on the screen (Exhibit 8–1). The letter matrix was maintained on the screen for approximately 50 milliseconds. Immediately after the letter matrix was removed from view, a high, medium, or low tone sounded that cued the person to report the top, middle, or bottom row of the array. Because the person did not know which portion of the array he or she was to re-

port before the tone sounded, and because the flash was approximately 50 milliseconds, too brief for scanning that would use the slower, mechanical eye-muscle-directed movements, the scanning of the array had to take place in iconic memory.

Using this procedure, most researchers have estimated that humans can perceive 100% of a 9-letter matrix and 75% of a 12-letter matrix. These estimates stem from the fact that the average person can recall any row from a 9-letter matrix using the partial-report procedure. A person can recall only about 3 out of 4 letters in any row from the 12-letter matrix. This same procedure was used by Parenté et al. (1989) and by McClur et al. (1994, 1995) to study the characteristics of iconic memory with traumatically brain-injured clients. Their results indicated that iconic memory was markedly reduced after head injury. Parenté et al. (1989) found that iconic memory improved spontaneously, approaching average levels at 6 months to 1 year post injury. Both studies indicated that training with the partial-report procedure improved the client's performance to the point at which it was comparable to the levels obtained with uninjured participants.

Models of Iconic Memory

There is little consensus about how information is stored in IM. The more recent theoretical descriptions assume a two-stage process. Mewhort et al. (1981) and Orenstein and Hold-

Exhibit 8–1 Classic Partial-Report Procedure

Focus	Display	Cue
	X L D Q	High Tone
+	V N B C	Medium Tone
	P M T Z	Low Tone

Note: The participant first focuses on a cross in the center of a computer screen. An array of consonants is flashed on the screen for about 50 ms. Immediately after the flash, a tone sounds that cues the person to report one of the rows of the array.

ing (1987) outlined a *two-buffer storage system*. In the first buffer, the person processes the basic features of the visual image. In the second buffer, these features are transformed into non-visual characters. Their research indicates that the inability to identify an object results from misperception that occurs in the feature buffer. However, difficulty locating something in space is the result of inability to scan the character buffer effectively. These problems result from incorrect translation of features into characters. If information about the location of an item is not correct, the item's location may be confused with that of a nearby item.

For example, after brain injury, the client may not be able to scan the feature buffer effectively and consequently may misperceive the various features of letters when reading. He or she may therefore misperceive similar letters such as B and D. Ineffective scanning of the character buffer may lead to letter reversals and misperception of words. These problems increase the longer the person has to wait to report from the IM (Mewhort et al., 1988). Therefore, misperception in the iconic store can result from at least two sources and can affect activities of daily living such as reading, driving, or the correct identification of people that one encounters during the day (Coltheart, 1980; Orenstein & Holding, 1987).

Research on Transfer of Iconic Memory Training

One application of IM research involves training head-injured persons to scan visual images without using eye movements. Such training can increase the speed of information processing.

For example, as Posner (1973) pointed out, our past experience with sequences of letters and words eventually allows us to integrate the letters into perceptual units that we perceive as words and phrases. Specific training to perceive words as units without scanning the individual letters via eye movements may therefore improve the head-injured person's ability to identify words rapidly and accurately.

Perhaps the only way to train this skill is to present verbal materials for brief durations. This type of training reduces the tendency to use slower mechanical eye movements to scan the visual array. It may generalize to an activity such as reading because the client learns to process the words as visual units rather than as sequences of individual letters. With extended training, clients may learn to process groups of words as units rather than mechanically parsing series of individual words. The training may therefore improve their ability to identify words, to understand what they read, or to read faster (Schwartz & Reisberg, 1991).

Parenté et al. (1989) were the first to investigate the potential of the partial-report technique as a training process. These authors investigated whether iconic memory could improve with practice and whether the improvement would transfer to another skill such as reading. Their results led to the conclusion that head-injured clients did improve on the IM task. Moreover, various aspects of reading, such as word identification, reading rate, and reading comprehension measures, improved following iconic memory training. In a later study, McClur et al. (1994) compared performances on an iconic training task of two groups of brain-injured participants, one of which had first been trained to scan written materials more rapidly with eye movements and the other of which had not. Their results led to the conclusion that iconic memory was not affected by eye-movement (visual) scanning. They also provided extensive iconic training and training in visual scanning via a computer. These authors (McClur et al., 1995) replicated Parenté et al.'s (1989) finding that iconic training improved performance on a reading comprehension task.

Garner (1994) also investigated the transfer of iconic memory training. His research showed that iconic memory training transferred to the functional task of reading. However, he found that different types of iconic training produced different effects. For example, training with the Sperling matrix enhanced reading rate, but not reading comprehension, on the transfer task. Using meaningful sentences rather than letter arrays during training improved reading comprehension but did not affect reading rate. This result suggests that meaning may be processed in iconic memory, contrary to the previous assumptions that the iconic store is a preverbal stage of memory (DiLollo & Dixon, 1992). It also suggests that this type of iconic training has its effect on the second stage of the various two-stage models discussed above.

McClur et al. (1995) also found that iconic training plus training in visual scanning improved performance on reading comprehension with head-injured patients. The transfer effect therefore seems to hold up in two different populations. Reading speed and comprehension are both related to scanning efficiency, and it is therefore reasonable to assume that if training in iconic scanning is given before training to visually scan, the two procedures will interact to produce an enhanced effect on reading. This is because the client will first learn how to group words efficiently in iconic memory, then learn how to scan the page rapidly with eye movements. Training in visual scanning should therefore be most effective if it is administered after (not before) iconic training and just before a conventional reading task. Its effect should be to amplify the effects described by Garner (1994).

Hamid (1995) replicated Garner's (1994) study using a similar training procedure. Rather than using a simple Sperling letter matrix, she used sentences (e.g., "the tall tree"), nonsense word strings (e.g., "tree tall the"), or random-letter strings (e.g., "hte ltal eret") as training items. These were flashed using a computer program, and afterwards the participants were trained to scan paragraphs of text visually using another computer program. The program presented paragraphs in the form of several short segments of text. The person never saw the entire paragraph, only groups of words that were literally flashed in their appropriate sequential position in the lines of the paragraph. The effect was to force the person both to process the short word segments iconically and to move the eyes in a scanning motion across the screen.

Hamid reasoned that if the client was first trained to process iconically and then taught to scan visually using the computer program, reading comprehension would be improved because the two skills would produce a transferable combination. This was generally the effect. Hamid found that training in iconically processing intact strings of words that formed grammatically correct phrases or sentences followed by training in visual scanning improved reading comprehension on the Nelson Reading Test (Schuell & Schreiner, 1977). Pretraining with the same sentence elements but with the words rearranged to produce nonsense word strings did not produce the same level of comprehension. Training with random-letter strings had little transferable quality.

Implications of Research

The results of Parenté et al. (1989) and McClur et al. (1994, 1995) show that traumatic brain injury can cause serious impairment of iconic memory. The problem is especially apparent during the initial stages of recovery. The deficit is important because IM is the first stage of information processing. If the client is unable to scan information effectively in IM, all of the other systems are adversely affected. Unfortunately, most cognitive rehabilitation requires training hand-eye coordination, memory strategies, or some higher intellectual process. The results presented here suggest that such training memory will have limited effect during early recovery and that early treatment is best focused on more basic sensory and attentional processes.

For some clients, iconic memory can make a full recovery after head injury. The therapist can accelerate recovery with tasks similar to the IM task used in the above-mentioned studies. It is important to emphasize, however, that the specifics of the training task are probably less important than the goal of training. The goal is to train the client to perceive visual sensory information as literal icons. Any task will work if the duration of exposure is short enough to prohibit scanning with eye movements. The studies discussed here demonstrate that training to perceive verbal information presented for brief durations can improve reading skill after traumatic brain injury. Before training, longer words required additional scanning movements. During training, the clients learned to process more information per eye fixation. After training, they were able to process the words as units, in a single glimpse. With extended training, it is conceivable that clients could learn to group clusters of words together into a single unit of meaning.

Sperling (1970) never intended the IM measurement procedures to be used therapeutically. We likewise do not recommend their therapeutic use. The task simply permits convenient measurement of IM. But modifications of the Sperling matrix to feature words and phrases rather than random-letter strings make this procedure a useful tool for training in reading. Indeed, Garner (1994) and Hamid (1995) found that such a modified procedure resulted in better transfer to a reading task than did the Sperling procedure.

One unanswered question concerns whether the effect of this type of training is long-lasting. Does the training simply prime the cognitive system for an immediate but transient effect? Four of the six clients in Parenté et al.'s (1989) experiment were followed to answer this question. None of the reading measures decreased. One person's reading score actually increased. Apparently, the training produced a lasting cognitive skill. In addition, the IM training effects described by Parenté et al. (1989) were not simply due to improved short-term memory or attention/concentration.

This type of training obviously does not work with every client. Those who are disoriented, partially blind, severely depressed, or otherwise uninterested would not benefit. The training requires vigilance, attention, and time. Hundreds of trials may be necessary before significant practical improvement in reading or some other related skill is apparent. The training also requires a computer and the ability to use it. With this theoretical background and practical considerations in mind, we now turn to a discussion of the specifics of iconic memory training.

Retraining Suggestions

What is the most effective way to retrain the mind's eye? We propose the following step-by-step procedure.

1. *Select stimulus materials with practical value*. For example, if the goal is to train reading skill, we suggest using words that are concrete and timely. Use common words or phrases with practical value (Bromberg, Liebb, & Traiger, 1964) such as common warning or hazard signs. Ideally, these materials are selected from the client's everyday environment. For example, we use words the client is likely to encounter during the day, warning signs he or she must process, or symbols that require an immediate response.

2. *Determine target behaviors that are measurable, practical, and convenient*. For example, the therapist could use a commercially available computer program for measuring reading skill. The baseline is necessary for comparing performance after iconic training. Alternatively, the task could involve reading instructions or directions that the client could demonstrate so that the therapist could immediately evaluate whether the client had correctly perceived them.

3. *Train the client to perceive the training materials presented for brief durations*. Computers are ideal for this purpose, and preprogrammed software is available. The program must present the materials for durations short enough to keep the client from using his or her eye muscle movements to scan. The habit of using the eye muscles to scan may be especially difficult to break. It may take hundreds of training trials to produce a lasting effect. We suggest a simpler procedure below that uses a slide projector to achieve the same rapid flash effect.

4. *Reassess improvement of the target behaviors.*

5. *Gradually increase the size or the complexity of the IM display.* For example, use polysyllabic words or two monosyllabic words as training stimuli. Eventually, the client should be able to identify short sentences or phrases.

Perhaps the easiest way to present information for brief durations is to use a standard slide projector. When training reading skill, the therapist begins by typing words and short phrases onto a standard sheet of white paper. It is necessary to leave at least a 2-inch border around each word or phrase. Next, place the paper in a copier and transfer the words onto overhead plastic rather than paper. This involves putting overhead projection plastic (available at any office supply store) into the paper tray rather than copier paper. The therapist should also purchase 35-mm slide binders at a local photographic store. These are generally available and are inexpensive. Using a pair of scissors, the therapist cuts out each of the words or phrases with an approximate 1-inch border, sufficient to fit into the slide binder. The end product is a set of slides that the therapist can use to present words or phrases via the slide projector.

The next step involves putting the slides into the slide tray, leaving empty spaces between successive slides. The tray will therefore have a slide followed by a blank slot, followed by a slide, followed by a blank slot, and so forth. The therapist can then simply hold down the advance button on the projector, which will flash a slide on the screen, then automatically remove it after approximately one-quarter second. Because the next space in the tray is empty, the overall effect is similar to that of a tachistoscope. The therapist then trains the client by flashing all of the words or phrases in the tray and asking the client to repeat them as he or she sees them.

This technique is easy to implement and inexpensive and has the additional advantage that it can be used with groups of clients. In practice, we typically begin with single word flashes, approximately 100. The client next graduates to phrases composed of two words for another 100

flashes. We gradually increase the length of the phrase until the client processes short sentences. The sentences are not random words; rather, each phrase or sentence is a grammatically correct statement. As Garner (1994) and Hamid (1995) found, processing intact statements improved reading comprehension.

We have also used iconic training in other contexts. For example, whenever a client is placed in a potentially hazardous job, the therapist can take slides of common warning signs and hazard symbols and present these for brief durations to ensure the client can recognize them without hesitation. For example, the therapist can use the slide projector technique to present no smoking signs, hazard warning labels, or other common symbols that indicate danger. After the clients see the signs, they should indicate the appropriate response. For example, after seeing a picture of a cigarette surrounded by a red circle with a bar across it, the client should say, "no smoking" or "extinguish all cigarettes." The training forces the client to process the icons or words as units, thereby improving the client's speed of identification and reaction time to potentially dangerous situations.

The training has been especially useful for those who have begun to drive again. With this group, therapy emphasizes rapid processing of common road signs. The client learns to interpret the sign after shorter and shorter durations of exposure. This amounts to taking slides of common road signs in the area where the client will probably drive. These are flashed using the slide projector technique, and the client reports the appropriate action after seeing the sign. The client learns to interpret the sign without having to scan it visually. This training improves his or her reaction time while driving.

ECHOIC MEMORY

Relatively little research attention has been given to echoic memory and its rehabilitation. We have begun to study echoic memory training with a procedure analogous to the one just outlined for iconic memory. The following is a description of this procedure. Our hope is that others will use it with their clients. Our research results are still preliminary, although the general facilitation that occurs in the iconic realm seems also to occur with echoic memory.

The client listens to complex messages via a tape recorder and headphones. The therapist then stops the tape randomly and provides a visual signal to cue the client to recall a specific message on the tape. For example, we commonly use plays in which at least three distinct characters are carrying on a conversation. A different person reads each character's part, and the therapist cues the client at random intervals to recall the last statement made by a specific character. The therapist then continues the tape until the next breakpoint and cues the client to report the last statement made by a different character. This process continues throughout the entire play. The procedure is directly analogous to the partial-report procedure outlined for iconic memory. It is also similar to the procedure outlined by Darwin, Turvey, and Crowder (1972). Any stimulus materials will work, but we recommend using common situations such as plays, conversations, or some other context in which at least three people are carrying on an auditory interaction.

The therapist should use a visual cue to signal which part of the auditory exchange the client should report. For example, we usually use the names of the persons who are in the play, list them on a card, and point to them randomly to indicate which aspect of the conversation the client is to report.

Therapists can use this procedure in a real-world context as well. For example, we worked with one client who was a nurse in an emergency medical center. She was on a team of physicians and nurses who had worked together for several years and who were used to making emergency life-and-death decisions. But after she was assaulted one evening while on her way home from work, she had a difficult time processing information rapidly and dealing with the complexity and emergency of the team's cases. She was simply overwhelmed.

Therapy involved taping several evenings in the emergency room. Because she was familiar with the various nurses and doctors, the task of constructing a chart that the therapist could use

to cue her recall of conversation was quite easy. There were five medical staff in the emergency room, and each person's name was listed on a chart. The therapist played the tape of the emergency room conversation to the client via headphones, and the client was randomly cued to report the last statement by a specific person in the room.

This was a realistic task because the client was forced to attend to auditory information that was similar to what she had to deal with every day on the job. The training had the effect of improving her auditory perception in that context to the point at which she was able to return to work.

CONCLUSION

Iconic and echoic memory occur in the first stage of information processing. They are extremely important processes because if information is distorted at this level, then encoding processes at all the other levels of cognition are affected. This chapter focused primarily on iconic memory because the majority of the available research has investigated this type of sensory register. Several experiments indicated that the iconic memory system is impaired after head injury. However, with time it recovers to near-average levels, and it can also improve with training. Clients can learn to identify word groupings, and this type of training can transfer to a skill such as reading.

The chapter presented a step-by-step procedure for retraining iconic memory and several possible applications of it. We also discussed echoic memory training and presented a method that can be used to retrain this process.

REFERENCES

Averbach, E., & Coriell, A.S.S. (1961). Short-term memory in vision Bet-System. *Technical Journal, 40*, 302–309.

Bromberg, M., Liebb, J., & Traiger, A. (1964). *Absolutely essential words*. New York: Barrons.

Chow, S.L. (1986). Iconic memory, location information, and partial report. *Journal of Experimental Psychology: Human Perception and Performance, 12*, 455–465.

Coltheart, M. (1980). Iconic memory and visible persistence. *Perception and Psychophysics, 27*, 183–288.

Craik, F.L. (1973). A "levels of analysis" view of memory. In P. Pliner, L. Krames, & T. Alloway (Eds.), *Communications and affect: Language and thought*. New York: Academic Press.

Darwin, C.J., Turvey, M.T., & Crowder, R.G. (1972). An auditory analogue of the Sperling partial report procedure: Evidence for one auditory storage. *Cognitive Psychology, 3*, 255–267.

Dick, A.D. (1974). Iconic memory and its relation to perceptual processing and other memory mechanisms. *Perception and Psychophysics, 16*, 575–596.

DiLollo, V., & Dixon, P. (1988). Two forms of persistence in visual information processing. *Journal of Experimental Psychology: Human Perception and Performance, 14*, 671–681.

DiLollo, V., & Dixon, P. (1992). Is the icon's worth apples and oranges? Some fruitful thoughts on Loftus, Duncan, and Gehrig. *Journal of Experimental Psychology: Human Perception and Performance, 18*, 550–555.

Ellis, H.C., & Hunt, R.R. (1993). *Fundamentals of cognitive psychology*. Madison, WI: W.C. Brown and Benchmark.

Erdman, N., & Dodge, R. (1898). *Psychologische unterschungen uber das lessen auf experimenteller grudlage*. Halli: Neimeyer.

Ericksen, C.W., & Lappin, J.S. (1967). Selective memory and very short-term recognition memory for nonsense forms. *Journal of Experimental Psychology, 73*, 358–364.

Garner, R. (1994). *Improving reading skills with iconic memory training*. Unpublished master's thesis, Towson State University, Towson, MD.

Haber, R.N. (1983). The impending demise of the icon: A critique of the concept of iconic storage in visual information processing. *The Behavioral and Brain Sciences, 6*, 1–11.

Haber, R.N., & Hershenson, M. (1980). *The psychology of visual perception*. New York: Holt, Rinehart & Winston.

Haber, R.N., & Nathanson, L.S. (1968). Post-retinal storage? Some further observations on Parkes' camel as seen through the eye of a needle. *Perception and Psychophysics, 3*, 349–355.

Haber, R.N., & Standing, L.G. (1969). Direct measures of short-term visual storage. *Quarterly Journal of Experimental Psychology, 21*, 43–54.

Hamid, M.C. (1995). *Transfer of iconic training in a reading task*. Unpublished master's thesis, Towson State University, Towson, MD.

Loftus, G.R., & Busey, T.A. (1992). Multidimensional models and iconic decay: Reply to DiLollo and Dixon. *Journal of Experimental Psychology: Human Perception and Performance, 18*, 556–561.

Loftus, G.R., Duncan, J., & Gehrig, P. (1992). On the time course of perceptual information that results from a brief visual presentation. *Journal of Experimental Psychology: Human Perception and Performance, 18*, 530–549.

Long, G.M., & O'Saben, C.L. (1989). The changing face of visual persistence. *American Journal of Psychology, 102*, 197–210.

McClur, J.T., Browning, R.T., Vantrease, C.M., & Bittle, S.T. (1994). The iconic memory skills of brain injury survivors and non-brain injury controls after visual scanning training. *NeuroRehabilitation, 4*(3), 151–156.

McClur, J.T., Browning, R.T., Vantrease, C.M., & Bittle, S.T. (1995, October). *Transfer of iconic memory training to reading comprehension with traumatically brain injured patients*. Paper presented at the Medical College of Virginia Cognitive Rehabilitation Conference, Washington, DC.

Mewhort, D.J.K., Butler, B.E., Feldman-Stewart, D., & Tramer, S. (1988). "Iconic memory," location information, and the bar-probe task: A reply to Chow, L. (1986). *Journal of Experimental Psychology: Human Perception and Performance, 14*, 729–737.

Neisser, U. (1967). *Cognitive Psychology*. New York: Appleton.

Orenstein, H.B., & Holding, D.H. (1987). Attentional factors in iconic memory and visible persistence. *Quarterly Journal of Experimental Psychology, 39*, 149–166.

Parenté, R., & Anderson-Parenté, J.A. (1991). *Retraining memory: Techniques and applications*. Houston, TX: CSY.

Parenté, R., Anderson-Parenté, J.A., & Shaw, B. (1989). Retraining the mind's eye. *Journal of Head Trauma Rehabilitation, 4*, 53–62.

Posner, M.I. (1973). *Cognition: An introduction*. Glenview, IL: Scott, Foresman.

Sackitt, B. (1975). Locus of short-term visual storage. *Science, 190*, 1318–1319.

Sackitt, B. (1976a). Iconic memory. *Psychological Review, 83*, 257–276.

Sackitt, B. (1976b). Psychological correlates of photoreceptor activity. *Vision Research, 16*, 129–140.

Schuell, H.G., & Schreiner, R. (1977). *The Nelson Reading Skills Test*. New York: Riverside.

Schwartz, B., & Reisberg, D. (1991). *Learning and memory*. New York: Norton.

Sperling, G. (1960). The information available in brief visual presentations. *Psychological Monographs, 74*, 1–29.

Sperling, G. (1963). A model for visual memory tasks. *Human Factors, 5*, 19–31.

Sperling, G. (1970). Short-term, long-term memory, and scanning in the processing of visual information. In A. Young & D.B. Lindsey (Eds.), *Early experience and visual information processing in perceptual and reading disorders*. Washington, DC: National Academy of Sciences.

Volkmann, A.W. (1859). Das Tachistoscop, in instrument, welches be Understocking des momentanen schens den gerbrauch des electrischen funkens ersetzt. *S.B. Kgls. Sach Ges. Wiss. Lpz.* (Math-Phys.) *11*, 90–98.

Chapter 9

Retraining Attention

Attention has long been considered to be crucial for learning and other cognitive processes (Nissen & Bullemer, 1987). Without the ability to pay attention, people will not register information in memory, solve problems, or respond properly in social situations (Koriat, Ben-Zur, & Sheffer, 1988; Triesman, 1988). Thus, it is not surprising that disorders of attention are some of the most common and pervasive cognitive problems after head injury. Attention deficits may go unnoticed or may be misdiagnosed (Gentilini, Nichelli, & Schoenhuber, 1989). Indeed, many disorders of memory are more appropriately described as disorders of attention (Plude, 1992). Several problems with attention can occur as a result of just a minor head injury. Although the severity of attention deficits usually lessens over time, the problems may persist for years after the injury.

The recent cognitive literature concerning attention reveals that it is a complex phenomenon (Baddeley, 1981; Baddeley & Hitch, 1974; Broadbent, 1958, 1971; Cowan, 1988; Johnson & Wilson, 1980; Posner & Rothbart, 1994; Triesman, 1988). There are several different attentional states and as many ways that attention can be impaired. As a result, the rehabilitation of attention is not a simple matter (Sohlberg & Mateer, 1988).

Whereas in Chapter 4 several general theories of attention were discussed, this chapter discusses specific forms of attention that are often affected by brain injury. These are discussed in some detail because they form the foundation of what most cognitive rehabilitation therapists will have to understand about attention deficits in order to provide effective treatment.

This chapter begins by reviewing the different kinds of attentional phenomena and attentional impairments. We then describe various treatments that can be useful for improving attention deficits after traumatic brain injury. We also recommend that the reader consult Wood (1992) for an especially cogent and recent review of this topic.

TYPES OF ATTENTION

Attention involves a focusing of mental processes on some aspect of the environment or on a concept (Johnson & Dark, 1986). Because attention involves a focusing, there is a limit to the extent to which the person can focus. This limit is called the *span of attention*.

Preattentive Processes

Arousal

Attention is distinguished from *arousal*, which refers to a person's readiness to pay attention

(Posner & Rafal, 1988). Arousal is the ability to remain awake. For example, when people go without sleep, it is more difficult for them to notice a surprising sound. Fatigue and lack of sleep render a person less alert, possibly drowsy, and unresponsive. Low levels of arousal limit a person's attentive powers (Jennings, 1986a, 1986b). However, a person can be sufficiently alert and still fail to pay attention. This is because there are several cognitive responses that are similar to attention and can affect it.

Orientation

Attention can be distinguished from *orientation,* which occurs when someone adjusts some portion of the body in relation to a stimulating source. For example, when we hear sounds, we adjust our heads to perceive them better. Orientation functions to identify those objects, events, or ideas that may deserve attention in the near future. However, a person can be sufficiently oriented and still fail to pay attention.

Attentive Processes

Routine Attention

Simple events of daily life, such as dressing, eating, and performing chores, require a person to focus on what is being done. Routine attention is the ability to perform a task without necessarily exerting a great deal of mental work. Routine attention varies by amount: One can pay little attention or a great deal. It also varies in duration, from momentary to indefinitely long.

Nonroutine Attention

Nonroutine attention involves intense focusing on one or more objects in a simple or complicated fashion. Forms of nonroutine attention are discussed below (see also Sohlberg & Mateer, 1988).

Focused attention involves a rapid increase in focusing, elicited by some unusual event or intentionally directed because an event possesses some importance. For example, men and women often focus attention on an especially nice-looking person of the opposite sex who enters a room in a public place.

Divided attention is a focus on two or more things at once. For example, we all have had the opportunity of trying to write a check or wash the dishes or do some other simple chore while talking on the telephone. Brief pauses in a telephone conversation often indicate that the person is trying to work on the computer simultaneously.

Alternating attention is a shifting of focus back and forth between equally engaging aspects of the environment. Students often try to watch their favorite television program while studying. Another example is that of trying to carry on a conversation on a car phone while driving.

Concentration consists of working with something in one's mind. For example, doing math problems mentally involves a great deal of concentration. Clearly, this activity requires focusing strongly on something, ignoring as much as possible of what is happening nearby, and performing some form of mental work.

Vigilance is the maintenance of focused attention or concentration.

Discrimination involves progressively detecting differences in a perceptual field or in a set of ideas. It is the ability to see differences. For example, most college students are called upon to detect subtle differences among answers on multiple-choice tests. We must discriminate the subtle characteristics of different people to identify someone in a crowd.

IMPAIRMENT OF ATTENTION

After a head injury, a client may experience problems with either routine attention or nonroutine attention. For both kinds of attention, it is important to rule out the possible influence of low arousal or poor orientation before concluding that a client has attentional problems. For example, in Chapter 22 we discuss immediate improvements in attention and concentration that can result from providing monetary incentives to perform. Incentives may thus be one way of ruling out the contribution of low arousal to what seems to be an attention deficit. Often, attention deficits are diagnosed when a client merely has limited sensory functions. Therefore, we recommend that before diagnosing an attention deficit, an eye exam or a hearing evaluation be given to assess the person's ability to orient or to perceive effectively.

A person may be easily distracted even in routine attention tasks. Problems may include difficulty resisting distraction (poor focusing), inability to pay attention to two things at once or in alternation (poor control over shifts of focusing), or difficulty remaining vigilant (fatigue or boredom). Indeed, one or more, or even all, of these attentional disturbances may be evident after a head injury. Perhaps the best way to evaluate the effects of distraction is to have the person perform the task twice, first in a noisy environment and then in a quiet environment, and then to evaluate the extent of the difference in performance.

MODELS OF ATTENTION

We discussed models of attention in detail in Chapter 4. To reiterate briefly, for a long time, attention was thought to involve a single mental switching mechanism. Researchers thought that the attention was a faculty that could be focused, divided, alternated, concentrated, and employed to discriminate, while being kept vigilant or relaxed. In recent years, however, theorists have come to recognize that a person's ability to pay attention is seldom uniform across all of these tasks or across all situations (Eysenck & Keane, 1990). Attentive mechanisms are part of our biological inheritance, but they are affected by experience and current environment. For example, a person may not necessarily pay attention as well at home as he or she can in the clinic, where the environment is contrived to produce optimal attention.

Theoretically, attention processes are governed by preconscious and conscious mechanisms (Logan, 1988; Shiffrin & Schneider, 1977; Spelke, Hirst, & Neisser, 1976). Preconscious mechanisms process perceptions without awareness and can process several things simultaneously. Conscious mechanisms voluntarily execute the attentive processes of focusing, dividing, and concentrating attention and of discrimination. For example, even though we are intensely absorbed in a newspaper or magazine article or television program, we may still be aware that someone else is in the room. Our preconscious processes are making us aware of the presence of another person while our conscious mechanisms are processing the article or program.

RETRAINING ATTENTION AND CONCENTRATION

Because the topic of attention is so complicated, several different models of attention retraining have been developed. Each model has its own emphasis and is best suited to certain kinds of patients with specific disorders. Most models involve a hierarchical approach in which the simple attentional processes are retrained first, followed by the more complex processes.

Orientation-Remediation Module

Ben-Yishay, Piasetsky, and Rattok (1987) developed an Orientation-Remediation Module of attention training (ORM) that has proven effective for rehabilitation of attention deficits after head injury. This is one of the oldest systematic attention training programs (Ben-Yishay et al., 1980). The client proceeds through a series of tasks that are designed to improve attentional processes gradually through the use of a variety of conditioning procedures.

The first goal is to train the client to attend and react to visual signals. The training makes use of a device called an Attention Reaction Conditioner. It trains the client to respond to simple stimulations, measures performance, and provides feedback in a reaction-time task.

The client also learns to shift attention. For example, one technique uses a Zero Accuracy

Conditioner, which trains the client to time his or her responses to a constantly changing stimulus source. The conditioner is a device similar to a clock. The client begins the training by depressing a button that activates a sweep hand. The sweep hand stops when the button is released. Time markings on the clock serve as targets, and the therapist tells the client which time marking to use at random. The client then tries to position the sweep hand as close as possible to the target before stopping it, gradually decreasing errors in placement.

The ORM also includes vigilance and discrimination training with a Visual Discrimination Conditioner. This device consists of a panel with two movable cubes. One cube contains a digital display; the other contains five colored lights. The therapist controls the display of colors, numbers, or color/number combinations. The client's task is to scan the display for predetermined combinations of colors and numbers.

The ORM also focuses on time estimation because it is an integral part of paying attention and remaining vigilant. Time Estimation Training involves learning to perceive the passage of time using a special 10-second stopwatch. The stopwatch can be started and stopped with a special activating lever. The client uses the stopwatch to check his or her estimate of different time intervals.

Another ORM task addresses the client's ability to pay attention to a sequence. This training makes use of the Rhythm Synchrony Conditioner. The client responds to a series of Morse-codelike tones. Eventually he or she learns to anticipate the rhythm and responds in phase, using a telegraph key.

Ben-Yishay et al. (1987) demonstrated that head-injured clients are able to improve their performance on these tasks. Apparently, the training produces a lasting effect because the gains are maintained on 6-month follow-up tests. For example, Ben-Yishay et al. (1980, 1987) demonstrated that performance on the various tasks is significantly correlated with 19 marker variables, including basic psychomotor skills, integrative functions, memory, reasoning, and interpersonal functioning.

Attention Process Training

Sohlberg and Mateer (1986, 1988) developed a systematic method of Attention Process Training (APT). APT retrains focused attention, divided attention, alternating attention, and vigilance. It is designed to increase the client's ability to respond to different kinds of stimulation. This training involves detection and orientation. Clients also learn to activate and inhibit responses selectively and to discriminate among stimuli.

APT is a graded procedure that steps the client through the various levels of training outlined above. Mateer and Sohlberg (1988) demonstrated that the training is effective for improving performance on standardized memory tests and also on informal measures of independent living skills.

The Seven-Level Model of Attention Training

The seven-level model of attention training (SLMAT) was originally proposed by Parenté and Anderson-Parenté (1991). It includes training of (a) basic arousal and orientation, (b) selective attention, (c) divided attention, and (d) complex mental control. The training is hierarchical, and at each level the client receives progressively more difficult information to process. In many ways, the levels are similar to those proposed by Sohlberg and Mateer (1986) and Ben-Yishay et al. (1987). Indeed, the SLMAT was designed to subsume both of these earlier attention training systems. Because it is the most inclusive of all the systems, we detail its levels below and point out the similarities to the ORM and APT systems wherever possible.

SLMAT was not designed with specific exercises. Here we provide training suggestions for each stage and encourage the reader to make up exercises similar to the suggested examples.

Level I: Basic Arousal

This stage of attention training is usually carried out in an acute care facility. It involves training the client to maintain tonic arousal for longer and longer periods of time. For example, the therapist may have the client watch television or interesting videos or listen to the radio. Literally any activity that facilitates arousal can be used. These activities will vary depending on the client's interests (Claridge, 1967). The measure of performance is the length of time the person can maintain the activity.

Level II: Simple Orientation to a Visual-Auditory Stimulus

The general goal is to provide exercises that get the client to adjust his or her body position to perceive a stimulus source correctly. The following are examples of therapy exercises. Therapists are encouraged to develop their own along the same lines.

- Have the client sit blindfolded in a room on a swivel chair. Walk around the room clapping hands. The client swivels in the chair and orients to the clapping sound.
- The therapist can also train orientation with a flashlight in a semidarkened room. The client orients to the flashlight once it is turned on.
- The therapist moves a finger from side to side in front of the client's face. The client follows the finger as it traverses the visual field.
- Using a stereo radio, the therapist plays music and changes the balance control so that the music moves from side to side. The client listens to the music on headphones and points to the ear that is receiving the signal.
- The client orients toward the door in his or her room every time a person passes by.

The measure of performance for all of these exercises is the number of times the client correctly orients. The therapist should not allow the client to go on to Level III until he or she can orient consistently.

Level III: Attention with Discrimination

Discrimination is more difficult than focused attention. To discriminate, the client must not only attend but respond in a way that produces either a correct or incorrect response. The therapist also tries to maintain the same length of time for each therapy session that was achieved for Level III. For example, when the injured person's vigilance improves to half an hour, the therapist should require this same amount of vigilance in Levels III through VII. Here are some therapy suggestions:

- Have the client orient in a dark room to a red light but not to a green one. Alternatively, the client can practice orienting in a lighted room to loud hand claps but not to soft ones.
- Have clients shut their eyes. Then touch their hands with a pencil eraser or point. The therapist may ask, "What do you feel, the point or the head?"
- The client can orient to a male or female person passing by the door, but only to one sex and not the other.
- Present pictures of models cut from department store catalogues, two at a time. Require the client to answer questions such as the following: "Which one has green eyes?" "Which one is taller?" "Which one is blonde?" Have the client pick out pictures of family members from photos that also include strangers.
- Ask the client to sit with eyes closed and identify all the sounds he or she hears in the room, such as the air conditioner, people talking in an adjacent room, and traffic sounds in the street.
- Present different perfumes and ask the client to identify changes in scent.
- Present the same sentence stated in different tones and ask the client to determine the meaning of the sentence from the voice tone.
- Present different soft drinks and have the client discriminate different tastes such as Coke, 7-Up, lemonade, and so forth while blindfolded.

These exercises have the same basic characteristics. None of them requires sustained memory, but all require sustained attention and some degree of discrimination and concentration. Many are similar to those outlined by Sohlberg and Mateer (1988) in the Focused Attention category. Most of them are practical activities that are similar to those the client will encounter in everyday life. The therapist should measure

- vigilance—how long the person can do the tasks
- discrimination accuracy on each task

Level IV: Concentration and Mental Control

These exercises train mental manipulation and cognitive effort. The training materials are always in plain view during the therapy session so that the tasks do not involve a great deal of memory. The following are therapy suggestions:

- Ask the client to solve simple arithmetic problems, such as "2 + 4 − 1." Present the problems on 3-by-5 cards with several alternative answers presented below each problem so that the problem is always in view. This eliminates the need for the client to remember the problem.
- Have the client practice making change mentally, using actual money.
- Have the client solve simple riddles that are presented on cards, such as "What do cats like to chase?"
- Present hypothetical news events, such as "American and Iraqi troops are massing on the border of Kuwait." Then ask the client to choose a likely outcome from alternatives such as (a) "a battle begins" and (b) "the two countries sign a peace treaty."
- Make up simple verbal math problems such as "There are 20 students in a class. Eight are girls. How many are boys?"
- Present scrambled letter strings and have the client unscramble the letters mentally (e.g., TCA = CAT).
- Have the client look at a complex or poorly worded sentence and simplify or clarify it.

The measures of performance are

- whether the client can carry on the activity for longer than half an hour
- the person's ability to respond correctly to the various items
- improvement with practice

The therapist can also manipulate the complexity of the problem (e.g., the number of alternative responses or whether a recall rather than a recognition test is used).

Level V: Distracted Attention

These exercises are similar to those in Sohlberg and Mateer's (1988) Divided Attention category. The reader is urged to use Sohlberg and Mateer's exercises as well as those presented here. The client processes two sources of information but eventually learns to ignore one source while attending to the other. This type of training should directly mimic the real world. The client should learn to attend to various things and screen out distractions such as music or conversations. For example:

- Have the client do arithmetic problems while listening to music on the radio.
- Play simple card games and ask clients to estimate how much time has passed since the game started or since the last query.
- Have the client wear headphones and listen to music while playing video games.
- Dichotic listening procedures are also quite useful for training distracted attention. Ask the client to wear headphones that present different messages to each ear. He or she must repeat the information reaching one ear and ignore the information in the other.

The measures of performance are

- the number of correct responses made to the target task
- the amount of time the person can sustain the dual input task

Level VI: Attention with Immediate Memory

This type of training is designed to improve attention, concentration, and short-term retention. Suggestions for therapy are

- Have the client rock back and forth to the beat of a metronome. Stop the metronome and ask the person to continue rocking to the same beat. Time how long he or she can maintain the rhythm. This exercise is similar to the Rhythm Synchrony Conditioner training of Ben-Yishay et al. (1987), discussed earlier.
- Present familiar sequences (e.g., 2, 4, 6, 8, and so on), then ask the client to continue the sequence (e.g., 10, 12, 14, and so on).
- Ask the client to repeat short sequences of body movements from memory, such as "stand up," "sit down," "turn around," "blink your left eye."
- Claridge (1967) suggested a procedure that requires monitoring sequences of random digits and tapping the top of the table each time a particular sequence occurs. The therapist creates a list of 50 to 100 three-digit numbers and asks the client to tap the table every time he or she hears "123," which is interspaced throughout the digit series. A variation on the theme is to have the client tap his or her finger when odd numbers are presented.
- Have the client trace the correct path in a maze with a finger (rather than a pencil) so that no mark is left on the maze. The therapist measures improvement in speed of performance with practice. The client must remember the maze solution to improve.

Measures of performance for this type of attention training are

- length of time the total session lasts (vigilance)
- number of errors (accuracy)
- how long the person can sustain the activity using his or her recent memory

By this stage, the therapist should have begun to include an additional index of graded-task difficulty. For example, the therapist might begin with simple exercises such as "Continue this sequence after I stop—A, B, C..." or "Stand up, sit down." The next series makes the first task more difficult once the person has reached perfect mastery: for example, "A, D, G..." or "Raise your right hand, raise your left hand, stand up, turn around."

Level VII: Interference Resistance

These exercises train the client to remember something after a second task has interfered with memory for the first. Each involves presenting one cognitive problem, followed by another and then a test on the first followed by a test on the second.

- Ask the injured person to answer simple questions such as "Add 2 + 2 in your head. Now add 4 + 5 in your head. What was the answer to the first problem? What was the answer to the second?" The second activity interferes with the memory for the first, and the client must sustain both answers in memory long enough to answer questions about either. The therapist should gradually increase the number of activities in the sequence to match the client's level of functioning. Again, it is important to bring the person to mastery at any level before making the task more difficult.
- Have the client listen to a simple paragraph. Then read another. Next, ask questions about the first, followed by questions about the second.
- Many of the card games in Chapter 10 (e.g., "Interference Resistance") involve Level VII attention skills.
- Using an extension phone, the therapist can simulate a telephone call to the client. After a brief conversation, the therapist and client carry on a second conversation. The therapist asks the client to recall the contents of the first conversation and then to recall the second.

Measures of performance include

- correct recall of either piece of information
- how long the person can sustain the activity

Additional Training Considerations

Before beginning any of these training exercises, the therapist should collect baseline scores that document the client's initial performance level. It is important to keep a running record of performance relative to the baseline to demonstrate improvement.

We recommend measuring other behaviors after training to determine if there has been any transfer. These should be unobtrusive, such as the length of time spent in conversations with peers or the amount of time the person can play a card game with a friend.

Feedback of results is essential, especially when the task is boring. The activity should be associated with a tangible reward whenever possible, such as money, cigarettes, or time on a favored activity.

Finally, the therapist should adjust the difficulty level of the various activities by extending the duration of the task and/or by increasing task complexity. The client should never end a session making more mistakes than correct responses. This situation can only lead to frustration and despair.

Training attention requires using activities that interest the client, that have obvious transferable quality, and that are relatively simple to implement. Simply exposing the client to the training situation does not ensure participation. Reinforcement and incentives are usually necessary to ensure vigilance and concentration.

Once the client's attention has improved, the therapist should substitute relevant exercises that mimic some real-world activity. For example, after Level III, the client should learn to associate "go" with green and "stop" with red. Better still, the therapist should incorporate these types of exercises directly into the therapy regimen as a concomitant measure of improvement.

During Level V, the client may eventually be able to read while listening to the radio. In Level VII, the client may be able to recall the event of the previous day's therapy after a day of interfering activity. The therapist can also place certain objects such as keys or a wallet or purse in various parts of the room and instruct the client at the beginning of the session to remember where the objects are located. At the end of the session (which becomes an interference activity), the therapist asks the client to find the objects.

Each of these "real-life" activities gives some indication that the therapy is transferring positively to the client's activities of daily living. The reader may wonder, "Why not simply begin treatment with real-world activities?" This point is well taken. If possible, we recommend beginning treatment with real-world activities. However, the contrived exercises mentioned above are usually easier to create and to quantify. Moreover, there may not be any activities of daily living that can be readily adapted for those clients who are in the earliest stages of recovery.

CONCLUSION

This chapter began by providing a brief discussion of impaired attentional processes. Then different models of training attention were examined, including a seven-level model that takes the client through the stages of basic arousal, orientation, attention with discrimination, concentration and mental control, distracted attention, attention with immediate memory, and interference resistance training. The head-injured client must pass through all of these stages before he or she will benefit from other types of memory training, as discussed in later chapters. Attention training is perhaps the most important cognitive retraining the therapist can provide. It has direct transfer to real-life activities. Without attention, higher-level information processing is impossible.

REFERENCES

Baddeley, A.D. (1981). The concept of working memory: A view of its current state and probable future development. *Cognition, 10*, 17–23.

Baddeley, A.D., & Hitch, G.J. (1974). Working memory. In G.A. Bower (Ed.), *The psychology of learning and motivation* (Vol. 8, pp. 47–90). New York: Academic Press.

Ben-Yishay, Y., Piasetsky, L., & Rattok, J. (1987). A systematic method for ameliorating disorders in basic attention. In M. Meier, A. Benton, & L. Diller (Eds.), *Neurological rehabilitation*. New York: Gilford.

Ben-Yishay, Y., Rattock, J., Ross, B., Lakin, P., Cohen, J., & Diller, L. (1980). A remedial module for the systematic amelioration of basic attentional disturbances in head trauma patients. In Y. Ben-Yishay (Ed.), *Working approaches to remediation of cognitive deficits in brain damaged persons*. New York: New York University Medical Center.

Broadbent, D.E. (1958). *Perception and communication*. London: Pergamon.

Broadbent, D.E. (1971). *Decision and stress*. New York: Academic Press.

Claridge, G.S. (1967). *Personality and arousal: A psychological study of psychiatric disorder*. Oxford, UK: Pergamon.

Cowan, N. (1988). Evolving conception of memory storage, selective attention, and their mutual constraints within the human information-processing system. *Psychological Bulletin, 104,* 163–191.

Eysenck, M.W., & Keane, M.T. (1990). *Cognitive psychology: A student's handbook*. Hillsdale, NJ: Lawrence Erlbaum.

Gentilini, M., Nichelli, P., & Schoenhuber, R. (1989). Assessment of attention in mild head injury. In H. Levin, H. Elsenberg, & A. Denton (Eds.), *Mild head injury*. New York: Oxford University Press.

Jennings, J.R. (1986a). Bodily changes during attending. In M.G.H. Coles, E. Donchin, & S.W. Porges (Eds.), *Psychophysiology: Systems, processes, and applications*. New York: Guilford.

Jennings, J.R. (1986b). Memory, thought, and bodily response. In M.G.H. Coles, E. Donchin, & S.W. Porges (Eds.), *Psychophysiology: Systems, processes, and applications*, New York: Guilford.

Johnson, W.A., & Dark, V.J. (1986). Selective attention. *Annual Review of Psychology, 37,* 43–75.

Johnson, W., & Wilson, H. (1980). Perceptual processing of nontargets in an attention task. *Memory and Cognition, 8,* 372–377.

Koriat, A., Ben-Zur, H., & Sheffer, D. (1988). Telling the same story twice: Output monitoring and age. *Journal of Memory and Language, 27,* 23–39.

Logan, C.D. (1988). Toward an instance theory of automatization. *Psychological Review, 95,* 492–527.

Mateer, C., & Sohlberg, M. (1988). A paradigm shift in memory rehabilitation. In H. Whitaker (Ed.), *Neuropsychological studies of non-focal brain injury: Dementia and closed head injury*. New York: Springer-Verlag.

Nissen, M.J., & Bullemer, P. (1987). Attentional requirement of learning: Evidence from performance measures. *Cognitive Psychology, 19,* 1–32.

Parenté, R., & Anderson-Parenté, J.K. (1991). *Retraining memory: Techniques and applications*. Houston, TX: CSY.

Plude, D. (1992). Memory improvement and attention training. In D. Herrmann, H. Weingartner, A. Searleman, & C. McEvoy (Eds.), *Memory improvement: Implications for theory* (pp. 150–168). New York: Springer-Verlag.

Posner, M.I., & Rafal, R. (1988). Cognitive theories of attention and the rehabilitation of attention deficits. In M. Meier, A. Benton, & L. Diller (Eds.), *Neuropsychological rehabilitation*. New York: Guilford.

Posner, M.I., & Rothbart, M.K. (1994). Attentional regulation: From mechanism to culture. In P. Bertelson, P. Eelen, & G. D'Ydewalle (Eds.), *International perspectives on psychological science: Vol. I. Leading themes*. Hillsdale, NJ: Lawrence Erlbaum.

Shiffrin, R.N.J., & Schneider, W. (1977). Controlled and automatic human information processing: II. Perceptual learning, automatic attending, and a general theory. *Psychological Review, 84,* 127–190.

Sohlberg, M.M., & Mateer, C.A. (1986). *Attention process training (APF)*. Puyallup, WA: Association for Neuropsychological Research and Development.

Sohlberg, M.M., & Mateer, C.A. (1988). Effectiveness of an attention training program. *Journal of Clinical and Experimental Neuropsychology, 9,* 117–130.

Spelke, E.S., Hirst, W.C., & Neisser, U. (1976). Skills of divided attention. *Cognition, 4,* 215–230.

Triesman, A.M. (1988). Features and objects: The 14th Bartlett Memorial Lecture. *Quarterly Journal of Experimental Psychology, 40A,* 201–237.

Wood, R. (1992). Disorders of attention: Their effect on behavior, cognition, and rehabilitation. In B. Wilson, & N. Moffat (Eds.), *Clinical management of memory problems* (pp. 216–242). San Diego: Singular.

Chapter 10

Maintenance Rehearsal

Traditionally, *rehearsal* has meant repeating something over and over, and the conventional wisdom is that this process creates vivid and lasting memories. For example, elementary school students are commonly taught that "practice makes perfect." Indeed, most head injury survivors report that their major method for remembering is to simply repeat something over and over until it sticks in memory. There is, however, much more to rehearsal than the simple maintenance of information in memory (Spelke, Hirst, & Neisser, 1976). We have therefore devoted two chapters to this important aspect of treatment. This chapter describes *maintenance rehearsal* and various techniques for training it. Maintenance rehearsal is the simple repetition of information that maintains the information in consciousness. It does not in itself lead to permanent memory storage, but it allows the client to store information temporarily and, if he or she wishes, to transfer it to permanent memory storage through the use of memory strategies and other, more complex rehearsal techniques. Clients must learn maintenance rehearsal and recognize its importance before they can progress to other rehearsal and memory strategies. Chapter 11 deals with the memory strategies and Chapter 12 with the interaction of memory strategies with rehearsal techniques.

WHAT IS REHEARSAL?

The conventional view of rehearsal is that it transfers information from a temporary to a permanent memory state (Atkinson & Shriffrin, 1968). For example, students learn subjects such as history or chemistry by studying their notes over and over. However, rehearsal is not always intended to achieve a permanent memory. Most of us can recall the last time we called directory information and did not have a pencil to write down the phone number. It was probably necessary to say the number over and over subvocally until we dialed it. We therefore remembered the number only temporarily. Indeed, we usually have no need to store in memory many of the events we encounter each day. For example, we seldom memorize the phone number of a dry cleaners, the local dump, or even our favorite pizza delivery shop. If we meet people casually at a party, we often will recall their names during the conversation but not the following day. These examples illustrate common situations in which we rehearse something without intending to learn it. In these situations we are employing maintenance rehearsal (Craik & Watkins, 1973; Rundus, 1977).

There are many situations in which instruction in maintenance rehearsal could help a head-injured person. Recalling a phone number of a business or shop is one example. Remembering instructions long enough to carry out a simple task is another. In each of these situations, the goal is simply to maintain information in memory briefly—just long enough to use it—and then to forget it.

There are several ways to improve maintenance rehearsal (Herrmann, Raybeck, & Gutman, 1993; Payne & Wenger 1992; Pressley & El-Dinary, 1992). For example, a client will maintain information longer if he or she rehearses it with a rhythmic repetition: "Set the table, set the table, set the table, then the napkins, then the napkins." Or *cumulative rehearsal* can be used: "Set the table; set the table, table; set the table, table, table."

In many situations, maintenance is not the ultimate goal. Rather, we seek to store some information in memory permanently. This form of rehearsal is sometimes called *storage rehearsal* because the goal is long-term storage of the information or *elaborative rehearsal* because permanent rehearsal requires one to expand or to embellish the information (Herrmann et al., 1993).

Maintenance rehearsal training is a necessary antecedent for any memory training. Training storage rehearsal requires maintenance rehearsal (Harrell, Parenté, Bellingrath, & Lisicia, 1992; Parenté & Anderson-Parenté, 1991). Without maintenance rehearsal, head-injured clients cannot remember novel experiences for longer than a few seconds. They are therefore doomed to a lifetime of immediate perception. Without storage rehearsal, they cannot store and retrieve information from long-term memory. They are therefore doomed to a lifetime of short-term memory. Consequently, it is essential for head-injured clients to relearn both types of rehearsal.

Most of us employ rehearsal strategies subconsciously and automatically. However, a head-injured person often loses the ability to rehearse automatically (Baddeley, Harris, Sunderland, Watts, & Wilson, 1967). It is therefore necessary to retrain him or her to rehearse consciously and actively at first. With practice, the activity eventually becomes automatic (Harrell et al., 1992).

REHEARSAL PRACTICE

It seems obvious to say that practice in rehearsing is essential for those clients who no longer rehearse automatically or who rehearse ineffectively. Indeed, rehearsal practice has been found to improve memory, often dramatically and substantially (Chase & Ericsson, 1982; Colley & Beech, 1989; Healy & Borne, 1995; Parenté, Twum, & Zoltan, 1994). The ideal exercise for a client to practice is a task he or she will normally have to perform in everyday life. For example, the best practice for learning how to remember someone's name is to experience introductions as often as possible. Unfortunately, life rarely does provide enough introductions for someone to become skilled at learning names. Extra practice is therefore necessary and is usually done in artificial situations.

Training rehearsal, like many other memory processes discussed in this book, is a three-stage activity. First, the therapist must demonstrate that the client's current method of rehearsal is inefficient. Second, the training must be structured so the client is forced to rehearse. Finally, the therapist must demonstrate that the rehearsal process has noticeably improved the client's memory.

Most head-injured clients are impressed by how much rehearsal can improve their ability to learn and remember. When training rehearsal, the therapist should begin by training maintenance rehearsal. Specifically, the therapist must determine the number of rehearsals necessary to bring the client's memory to average levels. For most of us, one or two repetitions are enough. However, head-injured clients typically require many more. Because clients often do not know how many additional rehearsals they need, the therapist must demonstrate that with additional rehearsal, clients' memory can function much better, often at average levels.

Many head-injured clients may be resistant to repeating things several times. There was no need to do so before the injury, and they may not see any reason for doing so now. The different kinds of rehearsal and the training activities proposed in this chapter are therefore designed to force clients to recognize and overcome one of their biggest deficits.

We propose several card games for demonstrating the effects of maintenance rehearsal and for illustrating how many rehearsals will be necessary to improve a person's ability to learn and retain new information. It should be noted that although these games may not have any direct transfer to the person's activities of daily living, the skill they teach does generalize (Deaton, 1991).

The therapist must remember three important points when teaching a transferable memory skill. First, the training must demonstrate how effective and immediately useful the technique can be for the client (Pressley & El-Dinary, 1992). Such a demonstration increases the client's confidence in his or her memory capabilities and the hope that he or she may eventually regain rehearsal skills. Second, acquired memory skills such as rehearsal must be presented in such a way that the client can see their use in certain everyday life activities. Finally, the therapist should demonstrate how maintenance rehearsal applies in a variety of different tasks. The major challenge for the therapist is to get the client to use the rehearsal strategy outside of the therapy context. To further the generalization, the games were developed to mimic several real-life rehearsal situations.

CARD GAMES FOR TRAINING MAINTENANCE REHEARSAL

We suggest several card games to train maintenance rehearsal. Each one demonstrates the immediate improvement that the client will experience with maintenance rehearsal. These games have three purposes. The first is to demonstrate the effectiveness of rehearsal for the client. The second is to demonstrate how much better memory can be if he or she rehearses spontaneously. The third is to determine how many rehearsals are necessary to improve the client's performance to an acceptable level.

The games are easy to learn and require only a deck or two of playing cards. In addition, they improve attention and concentration at least as well as most cognitive rehabilitation computer software. One advantage of these games is that they do not require a computer. Family and friends can play the games with the clients.

The therapist should teach one card game in a therapy session. The client should then play the game between sessions. At the next session, the therapist should determine whether the client demonstrated improvement. Once the client has improved at one game, the therapist should present the client with another game. The therapist should continue the training until the client has learned all the games.

All of these activities have three phases. The *baseline* documents the client's current performance. During the *rehearsal phase,* the therapist forces the client to rehearse consciously; this typically results in immediate and noticeable improvement. Then the therapist asks the client to continue to play the game again and encourages using the newly learned rehearsal strategy. Also, the therapist adjusts the number of rehearsals to the point at which the client no longer makes any mistakes. The goal is to determine how many rehearsals are necessary to improve the client's memory noticeably. Most clients will see that they can improve their memories 100% by simply rehearsing three to five times. Finally, during the *generalization phase,* the therapist shows the client how the technique can be used in the real world by directing the client to perform a variety of practical tasks that employ the technique.

It is vital that the therapist keep accurate records of performance at each phase of training to demonstrate progress. It is also important to assert that what the client has lost is the ability to rehearse *automatically.* That is, it will be necessary to rehearse most things consciously until the process gradually becomes automatic again. It will also be necessary to remind the client that extra rehearsal is not necessary in all situations. It is only necessary in those in which the person must remember something or someone.

Adjusting the number of rehearsals is extremely important. Most of us assume that we need only hear or see things once to remember them. The major purpose of these card game activities is to determine exactly how many times the client will have to hear new information before he or she can retain it effectively. The number of required rehearsals will vary from person to person. However, it is crucial for the therapist to impress on the client that he or she will have to repeat, rehearse, or perhaps rethink new information several times before it will "stick" in memory. Once clients begin rehearsing at this level, their performance on these card games and during the day improves noticeably.

Most of our suggested therapies follow a similar design. First, the client tries a task without instruction. Then the therapist provides instruction and demonstrates improvement. Finally, the person shows spontaneous use of the strategy in a real-world task.

Like any other memory technique, maintenance rehearsal is useful only if clients begin to use it spontaneously in their everyday activities. It is not assumed that the card game activity is therapeutic in and of itself. The basic purpose of the games is to train a strategy that generalizes to the real world. Several games are presented here, and not every head-injured person will play all of them. Perhaps one game will be sufficient to train the strategy with a particular client. Nevertheless, several games are provided because different clients will prefer different games. Thus, it is wise to have a variety from which to choose. The therapist should purchase two inexpensive decks of cards, one with red backs and the other with blue. The decks should be identical in every other way. Each game is discussed below and named according to the type of maintenance rehearsal process it trains. Similar games were discussed by Parenté and Anderson-Parenté (1991).

Interference Resistance

Interference refers to the type of situation in which we experience one event but our memories are interrupted by another that occurs shortly after the first. For example, our activities while cooking dinner are often interrupted by a ringing telephone. We must then resume our cooking where we left it just prior to the interruption. Therefore, this card game trains the client to rehearse in situations in which the second of two

sequential activities interferes with memory for the first (Spelke et al., 1976).

Baseline

The therapist shows the client a card from the deck and asks him or her to say aloud the number/face and suit of the card (e.g., "five of hearts"). The therapist then places this card face down on the table before the client. The client draws a second card, states its number/face and suit (e.g., "jack of diamonds"), and places it face down next to the first.

Now the client must recall the number/face and suit of the first card. If correct, it is placed in the "right" pile (to the client's right). If the client guesses incorrectly, the card is placed in the "wrong" pile (to the left).

The therapist displays a third card, and once again the client says the name and the suit aloud. This card is placed face down next to the second card; then the client says the number and suit of the second card. Thus, after saying the number and suit of one card, the client must recall the number and suit of the card that was seen immediately before. The process continues until the deck is exhausted. The therapist always displays a card and asks the client to say its number and suit. The card is placed face down next to another that the client just previously labeled. The therapist points to the old card and asks the client to identify it. If the card is incorrectly identified, then it is placed in the wrong pile. If it is correctly identified, it goes in the right pile. Another card is displayed, then placed face down, and the client must then identify the old card.

The measure of performance is the number of cards in either the right pile or the wrong pile when the deck is exhausted. This is a measure of how well a client can retain information in the short term. Clients generally miss about every third card. The therapist should either record the number of errors or simply leave the piles on the table to show correct and incorrect responses before beginning the second phase with a new deck. The difference between performance in the rehearsal phase and baseline performance shows that the rehearsal strategy works.

Rehearsal

The therapist should repeat the game, this time forcing the client to rehearse. After the client says the name and suit of the first card, the therapist places it face down (as before). This time, however, the therapist points to it again before showing a second card and asks, "Now, what did you say this first card was?" This modification of the game forces the client to rehearse the face-down card before seeing another. If the client continues to make mistakes, it may be necessary to ask for more than one rehearsal. The goal is to adjust the number of rehearsals until the client does not make any errors.

The game then proceeds as before, with this new rehearsal feature added. That is, before identifying each new card, the therapist forces the client to rehearse the old card that is still face down on the table. Using this forced-rehearsal technique, clients often will not make any mistakes. Most are impressed to see the immediate improvement in their accuracy.

To reiterate, it is critical for the therapist to adjust the number of rehearsals until the client no longer makes errors. The number of rehearsals indicates the number of times the client will have to rehearse most information. This estimate of a client's rehearsals provides a therapist with valuable information concerning the client's recovery. Ideally, the therapist should leave the client with the knowledge that from now on, he or she must rehearse most things at least that many times to remember effectively.

Modification

It is easy to adjust the difficulty level of this game depending on the severity of the head injury. Simply having the person remember the color of the card (red or black) rather than the suit and number makes the game easier. Perhaps the client can recall the number or the suit alone. The therapist can make the task more difficult by having the client use more than two cards. Using three cards is usually quite difficult for most head-injured people. More than three is virtually impossible. Before the therapist makes this game more difficult, however, the client

should demonstrate perfect performance several times with only two cards.

Generalization

Once the client can play the game without substantial errors (typically with fewer than five cards in the wrong pile), the therapist can show how the technique relates to the real world. For example, the therapist can give the client sequential directions and ask for performance of the first after the performance of the second. This activity requires that the client rehearse the first while performing the second. The client can turn on the TV and switch channels. The therapist can then direct the client to switch back to the first channel. This activity requires rehearsing while watching the second channel. The therapist can require that the client perform some activity in the kitchen but not finish it (e.g., boil water for a cup of tea), then do another activity in the living room (e.g., water a plant), and then return to the original activity (continue making tea). The therapist should encourage the client to rehearse each activity as many times as was necessary to eliminate most errors in the card game. These activities are similar to those discussed in Chapter 9 for retraining the later stages in the seven-level model of attention training.

Rehearsing Multiple Sets

This is a form of mental control activity that requires remembering the number of instances that have occurred in various categories. For example, teachers in elementary schools keep mental records of how many times each student has answered questions correctly or has misbehaved. We all mentally track how many times we use certain words in our conversations to avoid overusing them. Salespeople keep mental track of how many of a particular item have sold that day. Each of these activities involves maintaining multiple categories and mentally tallying the number of times each is incremented over time.

Baseline

The therapist shows the client three cards, one at a time, and places each face down after presentation. The client is told to "remember how many there are of each suit." Now the therapist asks the client to say aloud the number of cards he or she recalls from each suit (e.g., "two diamonds and one spade"). The therapist picks up the cards and evaluates if the client's memory was correct. If it was correct, all the cards are placed in the right pile. If it was incorrect, all the cards are placed in the wrong pile.

Rehearsal

The client should initially play the game without forced rehearsals, trying to remember the cards in whatever way he or she can. Now, however, the client learns a rehearsal technique: He or she must keep a running total, out loud, as the therapist presents each card. For example, when displaying the first card, the client might say, "diamond." After the second, the client might say, "one diamond, one spade." After the third, the client might say, "one diamond, two spades." After having seen and rehearsed all the cards, the client repeats how many of each suit there were in the hand. If his or her recall is correct, the cards go in the right pile. If it is wrong, then the cards go in the wrong pile.

Modification

The game can be easily modified to fit the client's abilities. For example, severely impaired persons can count only the number of red and black cards. This makes the game considerably easier. The game is made more difficult by increasing the number of cards from three to five.

Generalization

The therapist can create any real-world task that requires maintaining multiple sets. For example, the client can keep mental track of how many television shows he or she watched between sessions that were of different categories, such as action, sitcom, or talk show. The therapist can have the client browse through a newspaper and keep mental track of the number of articles that deal with sports, politics, or world affairs. The client can keep mental track of how many conversations he or she had with other male versus female clients during the day.

Spatial Rehearsal

Spatial rehearsal deals with memory for people or things in a three-dimensional space. Such memory is commonly used in daily living when we have to recall where something is located or where similar things are found. For example, when we go shopping at a mall, we may not buy a piece of clothing at one store because we recall seeing the same thing on sale in another store. We must therefore recall the store where the matching piece of clothing can be found. Training this skill involves a game that is similar to the popular child's game Memory. This game is also like the television quiz show *Concentration*.

Baseline

The game begins with 16 cards, 4 from each suit (i.e., 4 clubs, 4 spades, 4 diamonds, 4 hearts). Any four cards from each suit will do. The therapist shuffles the cards and arranges them in a 4-by-4 grid. The client turns over any four cards (leaving them in the same position in the grid). If the four cards have the same suit, the therapist puts them in the right pile. If the cards are not all of the same suit, the therapist turns them face down again. The therapist should return incorrect guesses to the same position in the grid. The client must therefore remember the cards' suit and position in the grid.

Next, the client turns over four more cards. Again, the therapist should restate that the goal is to turn over four of the same suit. If they are of the same suit, then all four are placed in the right pile. If not, they are overturned in the same position in the grid. This procedure continues until the entire board is cleared.

Rehearsal

The game begins again, but this time the client rehearses the cards in the face-down set after each attempt. This means that if the client overturns four cards that are not of the same suit, the cards are again immediately turned face down. However, before the client looks at four more cards, the therapist should ask the client to rehearse the position and suit of the four cards that were just overturned. Specifically, the client should point to the four cards that were just seen and identify each card's suit from memory. This procedure usually results in a 100% reduction of the number of guesses necessary to clear the board. If not, the therapist should adjust the number of required rehearsals accordingly.

Modification

The game can be modified by increasing or decreasing the number of cards the client must arrange. The game is made less difficult when the client arranges colors only (e.g., reds on the left and blacks on the right).

Generalization

The therapist may then create a situation using the client's immediate environment. The client can learn a floor plan of the facility and then locate in the floorplan the offices of staff with some shared attribute. For example, the client can try to pick out staff with similar-size offices. He or she can also identify the various therapists of the same sex, with similar hair color, or of approximate age using the floor plan. This can be easily accomplished by using Polaroid photographs of the therapists and placing them on a floor plan of the building in the approximate location of their offices. If the client can ambulate freely, a trip to a mall can be used to identify pairs of stores with similar items.

Rehearsing Changing Sets

We frequently have to identify something as familiar or similar to something we have already seen even though the context is changing. For example, waiters in a restaurant must recall orders from several tables at a time even though the people at the various tables are slowly changing as one or more parties finish and others are seated (Ericsson & Poulson, 1988). Portions of the waiters' spatial memories are constantly changing, whereas other portions are temporarily the same. These tasks require maintaining a set of information in memory, modifying it over time, and maintaining the new set until the next change occurs. The following game comes close to simulating this activity.

Baseline

The client is shown three cards, one at a time, and says them aloud as the therapist places them face down on the table. The therapist shows the client cards from the deck, one at a time, until the client identifies one that is the same face (king, queen, jack, or ace) or number (2 through 10) as one of the three cards that is face down on the table. For example, if one of the face-down cards is a seven and the client sees another seven (any suit), then he or she must identify which of the face-down cards is the match. The therapist checks to see if the cards match and, if so, puts the pair in the right pile. If the pair does not match, it is put in the wrong pile. The therapist shows the client another card from the deck and uses it to replace the one from the set of three face-down cards that was just matched. Therefore, the set of face-down cards will always change as the client recognizes potential matches from the deck.

The therapist continues showing the client cards from the deck, one at a time, until he or she identifies one that matches the face-down set. Those cards that the client feels do not match are discarded. If the client thinks a card matches, its mate is identified in the face-down set. The therapist checks the pair and places the cards in the appropriate (right or wrong) pile. The next card in the deck is used to replace the missing member of the face-down set. This process continues until the deck is exhausted.

Rehearsal

The client continues playing the game but rehearses the current face-down set several times before searching the deck for matches.

Modification

The therapist can make the game more or less difficult by adding or subtracting cards in each suit. Severely impaired people can begin with two cards per suit and gradually increase to four. Less impaired persons can begin with four and increase to five, then six, and so forth.

Generalization

The therapist can create a cooking task in which the client must maintain multiple categories of things that are necessary to cook a particular dish. The client then finds different things from each category. After the client finds the match, the therapist can then add a new category. For example, when baking a cake, the client will need a bowl, spoon, and sugar. The client remembers "bowl," "spoon," and "sugar," then searches the kitchen for any of these materials. When he or she finds any of the items, the therapist can introduce another to the existing set. For example, after the client finds the spoon, the therapist deletes this item and adds flour. The client now rehearses "bowl, sugar, flour," then searches again and retrieves a bowl. The therapist adds butter, and the client rehearses "sugar, butter, flour," and so forth.

Rehearsing Sequence

Throughout the course of a given day, we must all recall order and priority of our actions. Often we try to retrace our steps during the day to determine if or when we did a particular task or chore. When washing the car, we automatically rehearse the sequence of steps that gets the task done quickly and efficiently. When cooking dinner, we arrange the materials and subtasks to create a menu in the shortest amount of time. The following card game trains the client to rehearse this type of sequential activity.

Baseline

The therapist shows the client five cards (one at a time), then places each of the cards face down on the table in a random order. The client must then arrange the cards in order from left to right, lowest to highest. The task requires that the client remember the cards so they can be arranged in the proper order. If the client correctly arranges the card sequence, the therapist places them in the right pile. If all five are not correctly sequenced, all five are placed in the wrong pile. The game continues until the deck is exhausted.

Rehearsal

The client begins the game again, but this time he or she identifies the face-down cards in the various positions before rearranging them from lowest to highest. The goal at this stage is to identify how many rehearsals are necessary to ensure errorless performance. The therapist should encourage at least that many rehearsals from that point on. The client must say the number or face of each of the face-down cards.

Modification

Once again, the game can be made easier or more difficult by using fewer (e.g., two) or more (e.g., five) face-down cards. The game is quite easy if the client arranges only red (first) then black (second) cards in that sequence.

Generalization

The therapist trains the client to rehearse sequences of activities such as those involved in cleaning a house, washing a car, or some other activity of daily living. The therapist can list these on the back of 3-by-5 cards and ask the client to arrange them in the correct order, thus forcing memory for the events in the sequence.

Logical Rehearsal

Many problem-solving tasks require rehearsal of facts that eventually accumulate until the problem can be solved. For example, when the television breaks, we frequently try several possible solutions until one or some combination solves the problem. We must, however, keep a mental accumulation of those things we have tried, such as "It's plugged in—it's turned on—the cable is hooked up," and so forth. Each of these facts eliminates a possible problem until the person eventually identifies the critical one. The following card game can be used to train this type of rehearsal.

Baseline

The therapist gives the client one of the card decks and selects a single card from the other deck. The client asks questions about the card the therapist is holding. The client does not know what the card is, and the goal of the game is to remember the answers the therapist provides. The client must identify the therapist's card correctly and produce it from the other deck. For example, the client might ask, "Is it a red or a black card?" The therapist might say, "red." The client might then say, "Is it a face card or a numbered card?" The therapist might say, "a numbered card." This questioning goes on until the client can produce the correct card.

The critical feature of this game is that the client must remember and use the information the therapist provides to search out the correct card. It may be necessary for the client to sift through the deck after each question until the game procedures become more familiar. The therapist may later require the client to ask all the questions first, before beginning the search. The task thus forces the client to remember the answers to as many as 5 to 10 questions to select the appropriate card.

This game is quite challenging at first, and the therapist will notice that clients repeatedly ask the same questions because they have forgotten the answers. If the client correctly matches the card, the match is placed in the right pile. If the guess was incorrect, the therapist places the card in the wrong pile.

Rehearsal

The therapist should instruct the client to rehearse the answers to the questions and all previous questions before asking another. The game then continues with this forced-rehearsal procedure. The client will be surprised to see a 100% reduction in the number of errors after the therapist adjusts the number of necessary rehearsals.

Modification

The game is made more difficult by requiring the client to identify two cards at a time. The game is simplified by allowing the client to eliminate cards from the deck after each question or perhaps after every other one. For example, the client may say, "Is it a red card?" If the answer is no, he or she eliminates all red cards before asking the next question.

Generalization

The therapist can then ask the client to determine the correct decision to make in a variety of different social situations. For example, the therapist could ask the client which street a friend lives on by asking, "Is it in this neighborhood?" "Is it close to us?" and so forth. The game of charades is similar to this activity.

OTHER EXERCISES TO GENERALIZE REHEARSAL SKILLS

These exercises are certainly not the only ones a therapist could use. They are simply ones that we have used largely because they are convenient and do not require special materials. Regardless of which ones the therapist uses, we recommend choosing exercises that are as closely allied to the real world as possible.

Rehearsing Numbers

Read zip codes, telephone numbers, or social security numbers (Chase & Ericsson, 1982). Ask clients to repeat the numbers over and over. They may be able to recall a zip code without rehearsal. Phone numbers, however, are more difficult to remember and require additional restatement before dialing. The training should acquaint the client with the number of times he or she will have to hear a number to recall it accurately. Usually, this is the same number of rehearsals that were required to play the card games without error.

Name-Face Associations

Name-face association training involves making up flash cards with faces taken from magazines and names randomly assigned from the telephone directory. Pictures are displayed on the front of the cards, and the names are stated by the therapist. The goal is to train clients to rehearse the name several times before going on to the next face. After several cards, they see the same faces again and recall the associated names. The measure of accuracy is simply the number of names the client correctly recalled. The therapist should adjust the number of times the names are rehearsed until the client no longer makes errors and should encourage rehearsing names and faces at least that many times in the future.

Following Instructions

The therapist should provide a series of instructions and ask for restatement before carrying them through: for example, "Write your name, age, social security number, and date of birth." Clients rehearse the command sequence aloud before doing it. The measure of accuracy is simply the number of commands that are correctly carried out. The goal is to determine how many restatements of the instructions are necessary before the client can follow the directions correctly. From that point, the client should rehearse directions at least that many times.

Reading Text

The therapist asks the client to read a passage of text aloud and to repeat the gist of the text from memory. If this is too difficult, the client rereads it one or more times. In addition to demonstrating the effects of rehearsal, this activity teaches a valuable self-monitoring skill: that is, not to read further until the gist of the text can be repeated. This skill is extremely important for those who go on to formal educational training. Most academic topics require sequential reading comprehension as one goes through the text. That is, the client must understand what has been read before going on to something new.

Activity Assignments

We recommend that the therapist, after teaching these games, use other real-life activities as measures of transfer. That is, after each training session, the therapist may choose to assign any common activities to determine if the client uses maintenance rehearsal. As clients learn the strategy of rehearsal while playing the games, they should also notice that this strategy generalizes to these more practical real-life activities such as dialing a phone or taking a message.

DEMONSTRATING IMPROVEMENT

We suggest charting performance on all the tasks as the therapy proceeds. This way, the client can see improvement. Clients should practice each of the games every day. The therapist should not allow a client to transcend one level of difficulty in any game until he or she has demonstrated complete mastery of the previous levels.

The therapist may wonder, "Why use the card games at all?" or "Why not simply begin with the real-life activities?" There are two reasons for beginning with the card games. First, the games are easy to learn, and clients can practice between therapy sessions. All that is needed is a deck of cards. It is more difficult for clients to construct transfer materials such as photographs, digit strings, or text passages. Second, the games are easier to quantify. Photos of different people vary in their ease of learning, and text passages vary in complexity and length, but card games provide a consistent measure that is visible to the client and is easily understood.

REFERENCES

Atkinson, R.C., & Shiffrin, R.M. (1968). Human memory: A proposed system and its control processes. In K.W. Spence & J.T. Spence (Eds.), *The psychology of learning and motivation* (Vol. 2). New York: Academic Press.

Baddeley, A., Harris, J., Sunderland, A., Watts, K.P., & Wilson, B. (1967). Closed head injury and memory. In H.S. Levin, J. Grafman, & H.M. Eisenberg (Eds.), *Neurobehavioral recovery from head injury*. New York: Oxford University Press.

Chase, W.G., & Ericsson, K.A. (1982). Skill and working memory. In G.H. Bower (Ed.), *The psychology of learning and motivation* (Vol. 16, pp.141–189). New York: Academic Press.

Colley, A.M., & Beech, J.R. (1989). *Acquisition and performance of cognitive skills.* New York: John Wiley.

Craik, F.I.M., & Watkins, M.J. (1973). The role of rehearsal in short-term memory. *Journal of Verbal Learning and Verbal Behavior, 12,* 599–607.

Deaton, A.V. (1991). Rehabilitating cognitive impairments through the use of games. In J.S. Kreutzer & P.H. Wehman (Eds.), *Cognitive rehabilitation for persons with traumatic brain injury.* Baltimore: Paul H. Brookes.

Ericsson, K.A., & Poulson, P.G. (1988). An analysis of the mechanisms of a memory skill. *Journal of Experimental Psychology: Learning, Memory, and Cognition, 14,* 305–316.

Harrell, M., Parenté, R., Bellingrath, E.G., & Lisicia, K.A. (1992). *Cognitive rehabilitation of memory: A practical guide.* Gaithersburg, MD: Aspen.

Healy, A.F., & Borne, L.E., Jr. (1995). *Learning and memory of knowledge and skills: Durability and specificity.* Thousand Oaks, CA: Sage.

Herrmann, D., Raybeck, D., & Gutman, D. (1993). *Improving student memory.* Toronto: Hogrefe & Huber.

Parenté, R., & Anderson-Parenté, J.K. (1991). *Retraining memory: Techniques and applications.* Houston, TX: CSY.

Parenté, R., Twum, M., & Zoltan, B. (1994). Transfer and generalization of cognitive skill after traumatic brain injury. *NeuroRehabilitation, 4,* 25–35.

Payne, D., & Wenger, M.J. (1992). Memory improvement and practice. In D. Herrmann, H. Weingartner, A. Searleman, & C. McEvoy (Eds.), *Memory improvement: Implications for memory theory* (pp. 187–209). New York: Springer-Verlag.

Pressley, M., & El-Dinary, P.M. (1992). Memory strategy instruction that promotes good information processing. In D. Herrmann, H. Weingartner, A. Searleman, & C. McEvoy (Eds.), *Memory improvement: Implications for theory.* New York: Springer-Verlag.

Rundus, D. (1977). Maintenance rehearsal and single level processing. *Journal of Verbal Learning and Verbal Behavior, 16,* 665–681.

Spelke, E.S., Hirst, W.C., & Neisser, U. (1976). Skills of divided attention. *Cognition, 4,* 215–230.

Chapter 11

Retraining Memory Strategies

Retraining a client's memory may take months, years, or a lifetime. Much of the therapist's success depends on factors that are difficult to control. Moreover, success in any stage of training cognitive function depends on success at the earlier stages of training. As we pointed out in the previous chapters, rehearsal and attention/concentration are necessary precursors to memory strategy training. If the person cannot attend and concentrate reasonably well, memory strategies are virtually impossible to train (Eysenck, 1982). Likewise, if the person cannot maintain information in memory with rehearsal, then any type of strategy training is impossible (Gianutsos, 1991; Parenté & Anderson-Parenté, 1983; Schacter & Glisky, 1986). We assume, therefore, that the client's attention and sensory memory have already improved, and the client is now ready to relearn the skills of encoding, storage, and retrieval (Duffy, Walker, & Montague, 1972; Goldstein et al., 1988).

In this chapter, we focus on a variety of different memory strategies that the therapist can use to improve the client's ability to process information in working memory. These strategies are specifically designed to help the client store novel information in a form that can be easily retrieved (Atkinson & Wickens, 1971; Baddeley, 1986).

Rehearsal is crucial for encoding because without rehearsal, it would not be possible to maintain the information long enough to encode it. Likewise, encoding operations are crucial for efficient long-term memory functioning because without encoding, it is impossible to transform the information into a form that can be rapidly retrieved. Training to encode is perhaps the most important part of memory therapy (Hannon, de la Cruz-Schnedel, Cano, Moreira, & Nasuta, 1989; Harrell, Parenté, Bellingrath, & Lisicia, 1992; Kertesz, 1979).

Memory strategy training focuses on strategies and skills that transfer to the client's activities of daily living (Bellezza, 1981). Thus, it should be distinguished from other approaches that rely on mental exercise, such as stimulation therapy, which is designed to exercise the mind but not to teach the client strategies or skills. Although stimulation therapy may be useful for improving attention and concentration (Sarno, 1981; Wepman, 1951), it is questionable if it actually improves memory.

Simple mental exercise does not improve memory because no new learning takes place. This is because stimulation therapy approaches do not teach the client ways to process information more efficiently (Crosson & Buenning, 1984; Dansereau, 1985). They provide an environment for the client to practice remembering by using the same inefficient methods. The client can only improve the speed of an inefficient system to a certain level. However, unless he or she learns some new method of processing, the system will never function efficiently (Godfrey & Knight, 1988).

The basic value of stimulation therapy is the practice it affords. It may therefore be best used after the client has learned a number of different memory strategies because it provides an opportunity for practicing them. It can have the effect of priming the person for some type of activity (Payne & Wenger, 1992) or of warming up the memory system (Thune, 1950). However, if stimulation therapy forces the client to practice an already inefficient skill instead of acquiring new compensatory techniques, therapy may accomplish little in the way of improving memory.

Interest and motivation are critical to successful memory retraining. If a head-injured person is not interested in the training, this person will invariably perform at low levels. However, if a task is made interesting, performance will improve dramatically, and the person will attempt to use his or her newly learned skills in novel situations.

We discuss a theory of incentive and its effects on learning and memory after head injury in Chapter 23. Without belaboring these points, it is clear that incentives can be provided in several ways. For example, the therapist can explain the task so that the client understands its relevance. The therapist can provide monetary incentives, making performance potentially lucrative or rewarding. Research with people who have not suffered a head injury has shown that monetary reward improves learning but not remembering. Apparently, a reward disposes people to try harder, but there is less effect on long-term memory (see Chapter 23). However, with head injury survivors, monetary incentives dramatically improve memory and learning in a variety of memory tasks. The improvement from incentives has sometimes been as great as 400% to 600%.

THERAPY EXERCISES

We now present a variety of memory strategies, each suited for recall of certain types of information.

Training Perceptual Grouping of Number Series

We all must remember phone numbers, zip codes, extended zip codes, social security numbers, and other important numbers. Most people, however, recall number strings as sequences of individual digits. The average person can recall approximately 7 digits correctly.

A typical phone number (seven digits) is not difficult to retain because it does not exceed most people's capacity. After head injury, however, the capacity of working memory is substantially reduced (roughly three to four units). Phone numbers, extended zip codes, or social security numbers may, therefore, overwhelm a head-injured person. Because the size of the digit string dramatically affects accuracy of recall, the trick to remembering digit strings is to group the digits into larger numbers. For example, many head-injured clients can recall three multidigit numbers (e.g., "324, 67, 31"), but they cannot recall seven individual digits (e.g., "3, 2, 4, 6, 7, 3, 1"). The therapist should therefore train clients to remember numbers in larger groupings or "chunks." We recommend the following step-by-step process.

Baseline

Present common number strings (e.g., zip codes, phone numbers) and ask the client to recall them. Determine the largest string the client can recall correctly.

Instruction

The first step is to train the client to pronounce groupings of digits as numbers. That is, the therapist should discourage the habit of remembering numbers as series of individual digits. This means that the therapist trains the client to remember two or three digits at a time by presenting them as individual digits but requiring the client to repeat them grouped into larger units. For example, the therapist may say "1, 2" and require the client to repeat the digits as "12." The therapist says "2, 3, 7" and requires the client to say "237." The therapist continues this type of training until the chunking translation is performed consistently and automatically.

Although it is always possible to train clients to use the strategy, it is more difficult to ensure that they learn to use it automatically. It is therefore unreasonable to expect that simply demonstrating the strategy is sufficient to get the client to use it. Most clients will require extensive practice using the strategy. Some clients may learn to do the perceptual grouping operation in 50 trials. Others take hundreds before the technique becomes second nature. The important point is that the client must learn to use the strategy automatically.

The second step is to increase the number of digits and have the client recall multiple higher-order groupings. For example, say "3, 4, 6, 8" and require "34, 68" as a response. The goal at this stage is to get the person to recall numbers the size of a zip code using the grouping strategy. The therapist teaches the client to recall a zip code as a three-digit number and a two-digit number. For example, if the therapist says "2, 6, 8, 5, 4" the client should respond, "268, 54" or "26, 854."

The therapist should assign homework that requires the client to read lists of digit strings and practice the groupings as words. For example, create lists of digit strings such as "3, 4, 5, 6, 3" and have the client practice grouping the various strings (e.g., "345, 63").

Generalization

Once the client groups digits automatically, the therapist can continue training with commonly used numbers such as phone numbers, social security numbers, and extended zip codes. The client should learn to group a phone number as a three-digit number followed by two, two-digit numbers. The client can also learn to re-

member a social security number as a three-digit number followed by three groups of two digits. This same grouping structure works well for extended zip codes. Clients can learn to recall extended phone numbers (with area code) as two three-digit numbers (area code and prefix) followed by two two-digit numbers.

Head-injured persons who internalize this strategy to the point at which they use it automatically do not have any problem remembering numbers. Once again, the difficulty is getting them to use it automatically. To convince them that the strategy is effective, the therapist should test their multidigit, multinumber memory at the beginning of training. She or he can then test it again at the end to demonstrate the improvement when using the strategy.

One test procedure involves finding a phone number in the phone directory and asking the client to call the information operator and get the number for that person. The client then repeats the number to the therapist in grouped form, and the therapist validates it from the directory.

Training Organization

Baseline

Once again, the first step in training any memory skill is to collect baseline data. However, there are so many semantic organizational procedures that it is difficult to specify one as most indicative of the client's skill level. We suggest using a list-learning procedure in which the items can be grouped into several categories (e.g., fruits, vegetables). After reading the list, the client recalls the words and the therapist determines if the words are remembered according to the various groupings. The critical measure here is whether the words are semantically grouped at recall. Usually they are not because the ability to perceive semantic organization is disrupted.

Instruction

The therapist types word lists of various lengths onto 3-by-5 cards and trains the client to sort the cards into the various categorical piles. For example, the client may place all vegetable items in one pile and all dairy products in another.

The first step trains recognition of the hierarchical organization of the list. The client later uses the organizational structure as a retrieval cue. The therapist trains the client to recognize the various categories before attempting to recall the individual elements. The therapist asks the client to recall not the individual items on the list but the structural categories (e.g., vegetables, household materials, meats). This procedure forces recognition of the categories, which will later serve as a cuing aid. The number of categories should never exceed the client's working memory capacity (usually three to five units).

In the second step, the client continues with the sorting and recall procedure but recalls as well the specific words after the category. Once the client has learned the categories, recall of the actual items is relatively easy. Most clients are amazed that after they learn the categories, the words fall into place automatically.

The session should always begin by presenting a body of seemingly disorganized information and having the client try to remember it using whatever strategies he or she may choose. Word lists are easy to construct. Other simple materials such as a random assortment of household or office items also work well. The therapist simply places 10 to 15 items on the table top and asks the client to remember what is there. The person may not be able to recall more than four or five items without the organization strategy, even after repeated study and test. But after training to focus on the organization rather than the elements, it is not difficult for most clients to recall 12 items in five or six study/test sessions, a 100% savings. Showing clients how much they improve their recall with this procedure is the most important portion of the therapy. Once clients see that it works, they are more likely to use it outside of the therapy context.

The therapist should provide the client with at least 50 words and instructions to make up lists of at least 10 words at a time. They can then practice the sequence of steps on their own and demonstrate their skill during later therapy sessions.

When clients are unable to use semantic categories to improve their recall, the therapist should try other organizational categories that are more concrete, such as color categories, acoustic similarities among the words, formal similarity (e.g., coat, boat), or spatial similarity (e.g., in the same room). Ideally, any set of training materials (words, objects, shapes) should have some relevance to the person's daily life, and the training should focus on whatever organizational strategy produces the highest levels of recall.

Generalization

The therapist should continue training with practical activities to determine if the client can generalize the strategy. We recommend the following exercises:

- Family members can provide a simple household task they would like the client to do (e.g., wash the car). The client can then do the task by categorizing the materials needed and the correct sequence of steps to perform the task (e.g., "What is necessary in order to wash the family car? Cleaning materials, washing devices, and so forth"). After the person has recalled the categories, he or she should try to recall the materials individually.

- Alphabetizing names is a simple and useful activity. Ideally, these should be the names of friends or acquaintances so that clients can simultaneously relearn their social environment. Eventually, clients should sort by zip code, north-south east-west portions of their locale, street names, and so forth.

- The family can provide 20 to 30 household items and have the client reorganize them into appropriate categories (e.g., living room, eating utensils, laundry items).

- Have the client read a few paragraphs of text and write an outline from memory. The client should reread the text until he or she can correctly outline the materials.

Training Mediation

Self-Questioning

Mediation strategies involve training clients to establish an association between the new thing they are trying to learn and something familiar. The therapist's goal is to get clients always to ask a certain set of questions about the new thing. These include "What does it look like? What does it sound like? What does it smell like? What does it taste like? What does it mean the same thing as? What groups does it belong to? Who is it commonly associated with?" Such questions simply focus attention on the formal, meaningful, spatial, or other similarity of the to-be-remembered person or event and its association to something the client already knows.

The questions begin with "Who? What? When? Where? How? Why?" Thus, when making a new acquaintance, the client might ask, "Whom does the person look like? What does the person's name sound like? To what nationality does the person seem to belong? What type of perfume or cologne is the person wearing? Where did I meet the person? What were the distinct characteristics of the person's face or body? When (what time) did I meet the person? How did the meeting take place? Why was I introduced?" When the client tries to recall the person later, he or she again tries to answer the same questions. The technique works because it allows the client to establish multiple retrieval routes to the same core memory. When trying to recall the event later, one or more of the retrieval routes is likely to reproduce the memory.

Sentence Mnemonics

Other techniques of mediation, called *mnemonics*, are also quite effective with certain clients. *Sentence mnemonics* are sentences that cue our memories for lists of words or instructions (Bower & Winzenz, 1970; Herrmann, Geissler, & Atkinson, 1973). For example, recalling the words *baby, cow, glass, tree,* and *steel* is considerably easier if a client learns to create a sentence such as "The baby cow eats steel near the glass tree." Clearly, this sentence is bizarre. However, it has the effect of integrating the previously unrelated words into an easily rehearsed unit.

Baseline. Have the client freely recall a list of unrelated words. The initial level of recall is the baseline.

Instruction. First, using a different set of words, teach the client to form a bizarre sentence that relates the words. Record how many trials it takes the client to say the sentence that includes all the words. After the client can say the entire sentence from memory, point out that the sentence also contained the entire list of words. This may be obvious to some clients, but it will not be for most. In any case, the exercise will demonstrate the utility of the technique.

Next, teach the client to use the sentence to recall the words alone—that is, to use the sentence as a mediator. Specifically, the client should speak the sentence subvocally and use the sentence to recall the words.

Last, illustrate improvement of recall using the sentence mnemonic strategy with another set of words. Clients often complain that bizarre sentences are meaningless and irrelevant. Actually, there is no good reason for the sentence to be bizarre. Any sentence will work as long as it integrates the words.

Generalization. After considerable training, clients will begin to produce sentence mnemonics on their own to deal with things they must remember in everyday life. This is the primary goal of the therapy.

Word Mnemonics

Simple words can be especially useful mnemonics. For example, in Chapter 15 we discuss a problem-solving technique that can be summarized by the SOLVE mnemonic: (S)pecify the problem—define it; (O)ptions—what are they? (L)isten to advice from others; (V)ary the solution; (E)valuate the effect of the solution—did it really solve the problem?

Another word mnemonic is designed to help clients control their anger. It includes the two words *anger* and *calm.* The ANGER sequence is as follows: (A)nticipate the signs of anger; (N)ever act in anger; (G)o through the CALM sequence; (E)valuate the situation; (R)eview how you coped. The CALM sequence is as follows: (C)all someone for help; (A)llow yourself to emote; (L)eave the situation; (M)ove about. This is a psychosocial mnemonic that teaches the person to recognize what makes him or her angry as well as the physical signs of anger (e.g., increased body temperature, clenched fist). The client learns never to take any action while angry—that is, before going through the CALM sequence.

The first step in the CALM sequence is to call someone for help and allow the emotion to escape in a sympathetic environment. The client should also make every effort to leave the situation that is causing the anger and to move about in order to dissipate the anger. Once the client has gone through the CALM sequence, then he or she can return to the E portion of the anger mnemonic. At this point, the client is in a better position to evaluate the situation rationally and to determine what it was that caused the anger. Finally, the client learns to review what facilitated coping with the anger and to write it down for later review.

Another word mnemonic, LISTEN, is designed to teach the client effective listening skills: (L)ook at the person who is talking—maintain eye contact; (I)nterest yourself in the topic; (S)peak less than half the time; (T)ry not to interrupt or change the topic; (E)valuate what is said—don't blindly accept it; (N)otice facial expressions and body positions. We have found that rehearsing these points while the client is listening can dramatically improve attention and memory for conversations.

Generalization

Once the client understands the concept of word mnemonics, it is feasible to work with him or her to develop individual mnemonics that may be uniquely helpful. We will typically ask clients to discuss their biggest memory problems to determine if a mnemonic can help. For example, one client was in mechanics training and could not recall all of the things he was supposed to check on a car that came into the shop. He could not use a checklist because it would get greasy and unreadable. We developed the LITE BRACE mnemonic and worked with the client until he had memorized it: (L)ook and listen, (I)gnition, (T)ransmission, (E)xhaust (B)rakes, (R)ear end, (A)ir conditioning, (C)oolant, (E)lectrical. The advantage of this mnemonic for the client was that it solved a major problem. He was therefore quite motivated to learn it and to use it in his training.

Another client sustained a severe right hemisphere injury. Her speech was disinhibited, and there were several complaints that she would go off on tangents and lose the focus of her points in conversation. We therefore developed the BOMS mnemonic for her to remind her of how to explain her points clearly and efficiently: (B)ottom line, (O)mit the details, (M)odulate your voice for emphasis, (S)ummarize your point at the end.

Rhyming Mnemonics

Rhymes are especially effective for training long-term retention of semantic information and procedures. For example, many of us learned the rhyme for remembering the number of days in each month of the year: "Thirty days hath September, April, June, and November. All the rest have 31 except the second month alone, to which we 28 assign, till leap year gives it 29." Rhymes are difficult to create but have lasting effects on memory.

Instruction. First, provide the client with several rhymes that illustrate the concept of rhyming mnemonic. For example, rhymes that most of us learn in grade school, such as "*i* before *e* except after *c*" or "thirty days hath September . . ." are appropriate. These also provide the client with valuable tools to cue specific recall that can be used for a lifetime.

Once the client has mastered these rhymes, original rhymes can be developed. Therapy may never progress beyond the point at which the therapist develops rhymes that the client memorizes. Nevertheless, time spent developing useful rhymes is time well spent. The more the client invests in the process, the more relevance the rhymes will have. Ideally, the client will come to develop personal rhymes with the therapist's assistance at first. For example, one client had difficulty remembering to ask "who, what, when, where, why, and how" in order to organize novel information. He developed, with the therapist, the following rhyme to assist his use of the strategy: "To remember in the here and now, ask who, what, when, where, why, and how. To remember it again, ask who, what, where, how, why, and when."

Last, have the client try related tasks that demonstrate mastery of the rhyme. For example, after memorizing the rhyme "*i* before *e* except after *c* and for sounds like *eigh,* as in *neighbor* or *weigh*," the client should attempt to spell the words (e.g., *conceive* versus *thief*), and after memorizing "thirty days hath September," the client should attempt to tell how many days there are in the various months.

Generalization. Have the family members select everyday behaviors that the client can integrate into a rhyme. For example, lists of things to do before leaving the house are always useful. Rules for operating household appliances have obvious practical value. One client had difficulty remembering to lock her door and turn out lights before going to bed. She lived in the inner city in a neighborhood where there were several break-ins. Her neighbor mentioned that he could see into her apartment window while she was undressing. Her family and she created this rhyme: "Lock the door—turn out the lights. Draw the blinds—block out the sights."

Training Mental Imagery

The visual analogue to the strategies described thus far is mental imagery. Training imagery may not work well with low-functioning clients or those with residual right hemisphere lesions. It does work well with those who have made greater gains in recovery. Training imagery is easiest when the task is to recall concrete items. It does not work well for abstractions. For example, it is easy to remember a visual scene such as a baseball player hitting a home run. How-

ever, it may be impossible to imagine symbolic concepts such as truth, justice, or the American way. Imagery is most effective when the parts of the image actively interact (Higbee, 1988; McDaniel & Pressley, 1987; Richardson, 1992).

Baseline

Collect baseline data on a memory task such as memorizing a word list.

Instruction

First, demonstrate the concept of a mental image. With eyes closed, the client conjures up the image of his or her mother's face. Alternatively, he or she can draw a map of a familiar place. Either of these activities demonstrates the concept of a mental image.

Then demonstrate the power of a mental image. For example, have the client recall a list of 12 words. We typically read the following list and ask the client to recall the words after hearing the list: "Bowl, Passion, Fruit, Judge, Dawn, Bee, Plane, County, Choice, Seed, Wool, and Meal." The therapist reads the list again and the client attempts a second recall. The process continues for several trials. Typically, the client will not recall the words even after several study and test trials.

The therapist then instructs the client to use mental imagery. With eyes closed, the therapist reads another word list and asks the client to form a mental image of the words in his or her mind. For example, we usually use the following list image: "Think of a DOG chasing a CAT up a TREE. Behind the tree is a ROAD. On the road is a CADILLAC. ELVIS is driving the Cadillac. Behind the road is the SKY. In the sky is a full MOON. In front of the moon is a WITCH. The witch is riding a BROOM. Beneath the witch is a STAR. Behind the star is the ENTERPRISE."

After the client hears the image, he or she attempts recall of the word list using the mental image to mediate recall. Most clients can recall the entire word list in two trials, whereas they cannot recall the first word list even after six or more study and test trials. This demonstration illustrates the power of mental imagery.

Generalization

Ask the client to close his or her eyes and imagine a familiar map such as that of the United States. Ask questions such as "What direction would you travel if you went from Chicago to Dallas?" Or ask the client to close his or her eyes, then place a familiar object in the client's hands (e.g., a key). Instruct the client to form a mental image of what it looks like. Then verbally describe it in detail. Repeat this technique with a second and a third object. Eventually give the person an object that is similar or identical to the first. Ask the client to identify it as same or different. If different, ask, "Why is it different?" Begin with five object pairs. For example, use two keys, two coins, pencil and pen, two types of paper clips, and two erasers; then gradually expand the set to 10 items. Show the client pictures of unfamiliar faces and ask for a verbal description or a sketch of each face after removing the picture from view. Have the client, with eyes closed, trace familiar objects with the index finger (e.g., circle, square, triangle). Ask the client to say what the object is. Gradually make the shapes more complex. Give the client verbal directions how to get somewhere, then have the client draw the corresponding map.

Imagery may be quite difficult for most persons with head injury to learn. Nevertheless, it is a powerful memory aid and may be quite useful. In our experience, imagery training is less useful for remembering things like lists but more useful when viewed as part of other, more functional memory tasks such as name-face association or recall of text materials. It is therefore necessary to tell the client that he or she will use imagery in a variety of memory strategies and to point out when it is used. Usually, clients did not knowingly use imagery before their injury. Therefore, they may have no clear idea of what the term *mental image* means. Extensive demonstration of the concept and its power may be necessary before the clients can use the strategy effectively. The therapist should gradually make the images more complex.

Training Associative Memory

Head injury survivors frequently have difficulty forming associations. For example, they may have a hard time recalling names after an initial introduction or learning and associating a phone number with a newly acquired friend. Lack of attention and poor rehearsal are the biggest reasons that they cannot form associations easily. For example, they may avoid eye contact when meeting new people. They seldom realize how many rehearsals are necessary before the information will stick in memory. As with the other memory tasks, retraining associative learning is a sequential process.

It is usually best to start with relatively simple associations and gradually progress to the more difficult ones. Again, we recommend constructing training materials that are similar to those the client will encounter in everyday life.

Baseline

Present the client with word-picture associations to learn. For example, the therapist could make photographs of everyone the client sees in the rehabilitation center or outpatient clinic and write these names on the back of each picture. The therapist would then present these pictures one at a time and ask the client to recall the names. The therapist should then record the number of study and test trials necessary to associate the names correctly.

Instruction

Initiate the training by providing the client with the letter mnemonic NAME: (N)otice the person—maintain eye contact; (A)sk the person to spell and pronounce his or her name; (M)ention the name in conversation; (E)xaggerate some facial feature.

Rehearsal of the names and faces is a psychosocial skill that trains the client to do whatever is necessary to elicit enough rehearsal of the name. For example, pretending that he or she did not hear the name or asking the person to spell it are useful for getting the person to say the name again. The client must hear the name several times in order to ensure adequate rehearsal.

Provide feedback about the number of rehearsal trials necessary before the client can learn the name-face association. From that point on, require that many rehearsals before attempting recall.

If snapshots are not available, construct flash cards with pictures selected from magazines. Each card should display a person's face with no name. Initially, ask the client to make up names that would fit the faces. This forces attention to facial features that will cue the name.

Next, show pictures of faces and ask the client to sketch cartoons of the faces exaggerating some facial feature. This activity promotes effective scanning and attention to salient facial cues. The technique is similar to that used by political cartoonists who exaggerate one facial feature (e.g., Richard Nixon's nose, Jimmy Carter's teeth). The cartoon creates an unforgettable image of the person in the public eye. Likewise, drawing a cartoon image of a new acquaintance on the back of a business card or next to his or her phone number in an address book can aid recall of the person later on.

Now have the client practice the introduction and rehearsal process with another person and videotape the encounter. Afterward, play the tape and ask which aspects of the NAME process the client did well and which ones need work.

The client should go through the sequence of steps whenever he or she is introduced to someone. Eventually, the sequence becomes second nature, and the client's memory for names and faces improves noticeably.

Generalization

The best evidence that clients have learned to associate names and faces is to observe whether they use the strategies just outlined spontaneously when they are introduced to new people. The therapy should continue until clients implement the techniques without prompting.

CONCLUSION

This chapter provides step-by-step instructions for training various memory encoding strategies.

It emphasizes only strategies that are simple and have proven effective. Perceptual grouping of number strings into chunks typically facilitates rehearsal and memory of number strings. Training rhymes can improve memory for specific sets of activities. Training mental organization will improve the client's ability to formulate retrieval cues (Ellis & Hunt, 1993).

For all of these strategies, training involves collecting baseline data, providing instruction, determining if instruction improves retention, and, if so, continuing training. It is also necessary to determine if the training generalizes to real-world activities.

The eventual goal of therapy is to train the client to use the strategies spontaneously. Long-term episodic retention involves continued training with the encoding skills outlined above. The client will probably always demonstrate some impairment of long-term retention for episodic information. However, the mnemonic strategies, along with the prosthetic aids outlined later in this book, are excellent compensatory strategies.

Initially, the client may feel that mnemonics are too difficult to use or they require too much cognitive effort. Eventually, however, the person will realize that it is easier to remember and use the devices than it is not to use them. But this type of training requires patience, long-term persistence, and application in a real-world context. Generalization of the strategies may not occur for several months, perhaps a year or more. It is, therefore, never sufficient simply to demonstrate the procedures and assume that the client will spontaneously apply them from that point on.

Training memory is an art. It requires patience and time. Many of the strategies outlined above may not work with a particular client. Therefore, one of the therapist's functions is to assess the various strategies until one or more can be isolated that are uniquely suited to a particular client. If the client learns even one strategy and utilizes it spontaneously, the time taken to learn it was well spent.

REFERENCES

Atkinson, R.C., & Wickens, T.D. (1971). Human memory and the concept of reinforcement. In R. Glaser

(Ed.), *The nature of reinforcement*. London: Academic Press.

Baddeley, A.D. (1986). *Working memory*. New York: Basic Books.

Bellezza, F.S. (1981). Mnemonic devices: Classification, characteristics, and criteria. *Review of Education Research, 51*, 247–275.

Bower, G.H., & Winzenz, D. (1970). Comparison of associative learning strategies. *Psychonomic Science, 20*, 119–120.

Crosson, B., & Buenning, W. (1984). An individualized memory retraining program after closed-head injury: A single-case study. *Journal of Clinical Neuropsychology, 6*, 287–301.

Dansereau, D.F. (1985). Learning strategy research. In J.W. Segal, S.F. Chipman, & R. Glasser (Eds.), *Thinking and learning skills* (Vol. 1). Hillsdale, NJ: Lawrence Erlbaum.

Duffy, T.M., Walker, C., & Montague, W.E. (1972). Sentence mnemonics and the role of verb-class in paired-associate learning. *Psychological Reports, 31*, 583–589.

Ellis, H.C., & Hunt, R.R. (1993). *Fundamentals of cognitive psychology*. Madison, WI: W.C. Brown and Benchmark.

Eysenck, M.W. (1982). *Attention and arousal: Cognition and performance*. Berlin: Academic Press.

Gianutsos, R. (1991). Cognitive rehabilitation: A neuropsychological specialty comes of age. *Brain Injury, 5*, 353–368.

Godfrey, H., & Knight, R. (1988). Memory training and behavioral rehabilitation of a severely head-injured adult. *Archives of Physical Medicine Rehabilitation, 69*, 458–460.

Goldstein, G., McCue, M., Turner, S., Spanier, E., Malec, E., & Shelly, C. (1988). An efficacy study of memory training for patients with closed-head injury. *Clinical Neuropsychologist, 2*, 252–259.

Hannon, R., de la Cruz-Schnedel, D., Cano, T., Moreira, K., & Nasuta, R. (1989). Memory retraining with adult male alcoholics. *Archives of Clinical Neuropsychology, 4*, 227–232.

Harrell, M., Parenté, R., Bellingrath, E.G., & Lisicia, K.A. (1992). *Cognitive rehabilitation of memory: A practical guide*. Gaithersburg, MD: Aspen.

Herrmann, D.J., Geissler, F.V., & Atkinson, R.C. (1973). The serial position function for lists learned by a narrative-story mnemonic. *Bulletin of the Psychonomic Society, 2*, 377–378.

Higbee, K.L. (1988). *Your memory* (2nd ed.). Englewood Cliffs, NJ: Prentice Hall.

Kertesz, A. (1979). *Aphasia and associated disorders: Taxonomy, localization, and recovery*. New York: Grune & Stratton.

McDaniel, M.A., & Pressley, M. (1987). *Imagery and related mnemonic processes: Theories, individual differences and applications*. New York: Springer-Verlag.

Parenté, F.J., & Anderson-Parenté, J.K. (1983). Techniques for improving cognitive rehabilitation: Teaching organization and encoding skills. *Journal of Cognitive Rehabilitation, 1*(4), 20–23.

Payne, D., & Wenger, M.J. (1992). Memory improvement and practice. In D. Herrmann, H. Weingartner, A. Searleman, & C. McEvoy (Eds.), *Memory improvement: Implications for memory theory* (pp. 187–209). New York: Springer-Verlag.

Richardson, J.T.E. (1992). Imagery mnemonics and memory remediation. *Neurology, 42*, 283–286.

Sarno, M.T. (1981). Recovery and rehabilitation in aphasia. In M.T. Sarno (Ed.), *Acquired aphasia*. New York: Academic Press.

Schacter, D.L., & Glisky, E.L. (1986). Memory remediation: Restoration, alleviation, and the acquisition of domain-specific knowledge. In B. Uzzell & Y. Gross (Eds.), *Clinical neuropsychology of intervention* (pp. 257–282). New York: Martinus Nijhoff.

Thune, L.E. (1950). The effect of different types of preliminary activities on subsequent learning of paired-associate material. *Journal of Experimental Psychology, 40*, 423–438.

Wepman, J.M. (1951). *Recovery from aphasia*. New York: Ronald.

Chapter 12

Rehearsal Revisited

Although we have all heard the saying "practice makes perfect," actually, the only function of repetition is to keep new information in memory long enough to develop strategies such as those outlined in Chapter 11. Whether these strategies generalize to other situations depends largely on the client's ability to rehearse their use. Therefore, rehearsal skill is not just for maintaining information in memory but also for rehearsing the *organization* of novel information (Anderson, 1981; Ericsson, 1985). This latter type of rehearsal allows us to encode information so that we can retrieve it later.

Our purpose in this chapter is to develop the concept of rehearsal of organization and specifically to show how this rehearsal skill interacts with the memory strategies discussed in Chapter 11. Those exercises taught the client to recognize the organization that binds together the seemingly unrelated elements of his or her experience. In our experience, the concept of rehearsing organization is especially difficult for most head-injured clients to grasp. Most will spend hours repeating separate pieces of their daily activities without any thought to rehearsing the organizing structure that binds the pieces into a coherent episodic memory. The therapist should therefore teach the client that recognizing and rehearsing organization is of primary importance. If he or she can recall the organiza-

tion, the individual elements will usually fall into place. In Chapter 11, we discussed some techniques for illustrating the concept of rehearsing organization. One involved dumping a variety of objects on a table and asking the client to rehearse the types of objects he or she saw rather than the individual objects per se. We recommend that the reader review these techniques before proceeding.

TYPES OF REHEARSAL

There are four basic kinds of rehearsal (Herrmann, Ruppin, & Usher, 1993). The simplest kind is *maintenance rehearsal,* which was discussed at length in Chapter 10. This type of rehearsal strengthens a memory record via simple repetition (Rundus, 1977). For example, rehearsing a phone number by repeating it out loud will, as described earlier, maintain information in the client's consciousness. It will not, however, lead to a permanent memory unless the repetition helps the client to transform the number in some way and unless the mental transformation makes it especially memorable.

The second kind of mental rehearsal fosters the *encoding of attributes* of the information—attributes that otherwise would not be included in the memory trace (Underwood, 1969;

Wickens, 1970). For example, pointing out some unique quality of a person's face may help the person to recognize the person later and to recall his or her name. Businesses capitalize on encoding of attributes. For example, some businesses may choose a phone number whose sequence is easy to remember, such as 666-7777 or 123-1234. Such numbers are easy to rehearse because the sequence creates an obvious organizational rule for memory. The person does not rehearse the number because, by remembering the rule, he or she can generate the string.

The third kind of mental rehearsal fosters association *of novel information with more familiar information* already in memory (Tulving & Madigan, 1970). For example, noticing that Mr. Girard has an especially long neck may allow the client to associate him with a giraffe. The client then rehearses the image of a giraffe with Girard, a strategy that facilitates later recall of his name. Instead of repeating the name Girard over and over again, the person focuses rehearsal on the relationship between the name and the familiar association.

A fourth type of rehearsal is a *physical reminder* (Chase & Ericsson, 1982; Herrmann et al., 1993). Physical rehearsals create a mental duplicate or a cue that ensures that the client can rehearse the information when the need arises. For example, a client may use a tape recorder to make a physical backup of an important phone conversation. The client can then rehearse the entire conversation whenever necessary. Diaries allow us to rehearse the events of our lives. Physical reminders also involve other people whose task is to remind us of some event. For example, bill collectors seldom let you forget when a debt comes due. These systems force rehearsal of some event or activity that requires attention. Each of the rehearsal techniques discussed below is based on one or more of these types of rehearsal.

REHEARSAL TECHNIQUES

Much of what we call memory involves forming vivid first impressions. However, the strength or permanence of this first impression depends upon the extent to which the person actively rehearses it after the actual event has passed (Baddeley, 1995). There are several ways of ensuring that the rehearsal process provides adequate strength (Bellezza, 1981; Higbee, 1988). The therapist should train the client to use each of the methods discussed below whenever there is a need to store information mentally.

In *scene rehearsal,* the client, when attempting to remember a scene, scans it systematically, then closes his or her eyes and asks questions about the scene (Biederman, Mezzanotte, & Rabinowitz, 1982). This is a form of physical rehearsal that creates an eidetic or photographic copy of the scenario. For example, when trying to remember a meeting, the client should close his or her eyes and rehearse the scene by conjuring up pictorial answers to questions such as "Who was there?" "What were the people wearing?" and "Where were they sitting?" The zoo picture task discussed in Appendix B is a good example of this type of rehearsal skill (Biederman et al., 1982).

Spaced rehearsal ensures that the person continues to rehearse the new information over time (Landauer & Bjork, 1978). The therapist encourages the client to attempt to remember the event at intervals that increase in length. Each interval is twice as long as the preceding one. The client may therefore try to remember the gist of a conversation 1 day later, then 3 days later, then 6 days later, and so forth.

Fact rehearsal is a method of focusing attention on specific aspects of the information that the client needs to encode. Several techniques can be used to facilitate fact rehearsals. For example, questioning is a technique in which the client asks specific questions about the information, such as "Who? What? Where? When? Whose? Why? Under what conditions? How? How much? How many? How often? For how long?" Questioning directs the client's attention to the critical aspects of the event (Loisette, 1886). If the client cannot answer the question, he or she must rehearse the event once again. For example, when reading, the client should stop after each paragraph and try to answer as many of the above questions about the paragraph as possible, then reread the paragraph until the answers come to mind. In some situations, a fact rehearsal is similar to a scenario rehearsal. The two are literally identical when the person is rehearsing a visual scene. However, when reading books, the client may simply try to rehearse critical verbal facts.

Self-referencing is a method of relating the new to the old. The goal is to hook novel experiences into the client's existing associative network via rehearsal. In so doing, the client can access the novel information by thinking of things that are related to it. One or more of these associations will eventually lead to recall of the novel event. Self-referencing usually involves paying attention to the ways the information could be personally categorized (Greenwald & Banaji, 1989). For example, when meeting someone new, the client may ask, "How is this person like someone I already know?"

In *semantic rehearsal*, the therapist teaches the client to organize items into groupings and to rehearse their similar meaning (Tulving, 1983). For example, when learning a new word, the client learns synonyms for the word that define its meaning. The words do not actually have to be synonymous with the original: they might be opposites, sound the same, or belong to the same category. For example, when teaching vocabulary, the therapist can teach the client to rehearse the word along with its synonym and its homonym. Each of these techniques essentially puts information in different places in a client's memory. Having the memory record in two different places makes it much less likely that the client will forget what has been learned.

Loci rehearsal is similar in some ways to scenario rehearsal. Loci rehearsal differs from scenario rehearsal because the latter is designed to improve memory of novel events and places, whereas the former uses a familiar place to organize a person's possessions (DiBeni & Cornoldi 1985). For example, the therapist may teach the client to organize items or events into spatial areas and then to rehearse the spatial organization. He or she may later recall where something is located in a house by retrieving the context and mentally searching this space to recall a specific item contained within it. We all use loci rehearsal to some extent when someone

asks us where something is located in the house. Most people mentally search some area of the house that they are reasonably certain contains the desired object.

One consequence of the rehearsal techniques described above is that the client tends to remember more attributes of the event than he or she would otherwise. This is because as the client repeats the information over and over, his or her mental energy directs attention to the subtle attributes of the memory record that would otherwise go unnoticed. We have all noticed these phenomena when we go to the same movie twice and see things that we missed the first time. The client may also draw new conclusions, suppositions, and inferences about the event that were not apparent initially.

Acrostic rehearsal techniques were discussed in Chapter 11, so we will only briefly discuss them here. Acrostic rehearsal is especially useful for improving rote recall of some information. The client forms a sentence, poem, or series of words that reminds him or her of whatever he or she wants to recall later (Loisette, 1886). The goal is to recall the acrostic, which, in turn, cues recall of the desired information. For example, the client could rehearse "My Dear Aunt Sally." The first letter of each word cues recall of the order of operations in arithmetic: that is, Multiplication, Division, Addition, Subtraction.

Use of the *first-letter mnemonic* involves arranging the first letter of each to-be-recalled item to form a word (Morris & Cook, 1978). For example, the NAME mnemonic cues recall of the steps needed to remember names and faces: (N)otice the person, (A)sk the person to repeat his or her name, (M)ention the name in conversation, and (E)xaggerate some special feature.

Use of the *near-word abbreviation* involves forming a smaller nonsense word by using the first letters of several words the client wants to remember. This technique is similar to the first-letter mnemonic, but it uses a "near-word" that can be rehearsed but would not be found in the dictionary. The BOMS mnemonic in Chapter 11 is an example of a near-word. BOMS is not a word, but the letters cued the client to respond appropriately when answering questions:

(B)ottom line the answer, (O)mit the details, (M)aintain eye contact, (S)ummarize your point.

In *sentence generation,* the client learns to generate a sentence that contains the items that need to be recalled (Duffy, Walker, & Montague, 1972). For example, when learning a list of things to do before leaving home the client might rehearse "Lights the door, iron the stove." This sentence cues the person to turn off the lights, lock the door, check that the iron is unplugged, and turn off the stove.

SUGGESTIONS TO THE THERAPIST

The therapist can maximize the benefit of rehearsal training by employing the following guidelines.

1. *Customize the training.* Mnemonic strategy training may be too abstract or may require attentional demands that are beyond the client's ability. Nevertheless, clients who cannot generate their own mnemonics may be able to use some mnemonics if these are personally relevant. In general, it makes no sense to teach rehearsal as an abstract process because the client will not typically use it spontaneously. However, with guidance, the client and therapist can generate specific acrostics that are especially useful to the client. Once the client sees the usefulness of the mnemonic, he or she is likely to buy into the general process.
2. *Vary the context.* Many clients learn a mental strategy but do not use it because they fail to recognize that the strategy would be useful in a particular situation. It is therefore necessary to rehearse not only the strategy but also its use in a wide variety of situations (Davies & Thomson, 1988). This ensures that the client will see how the strategy applies.
3. *Review periodically.* The strength of any memory, skill, or strategy is increased markedly by scheduling times when important information is reviewed. For example, if the client needs to recall the staff names and faces in the facility, he or she can re-

view these names with pictures of the staff each day. It is seldom sufficient simply to teach the client a strategy and then to assume that he or she will remember to use the strategy without extensive review.

4. *Rehearse real-life scenarios.* The client should rehearse imagined situations in which he or she might be called on to remember certain information and to imagine further using the information in that context (Hardy & Ringland, 1984). For example, the therapist might direct the client to imagine recalling his or her social security number when filling out various job applications.

SUGGESTIONS FOR THE CLIENT

Clearly, effective rehearsal training is more than just teaching the client to rehearse. Whether the client tries to form a vivid first impression of a novel event or tries to scan an existing body of information in memory, the therapist must teach the client to manage his or her efforts in accordance with the demands of the situation (Schoenfeld, 1985). Managerial strategies will help the client to choose which types of rehearsals will make the information most memorable. These are presented below:

1. *First scan, then select, then rehearse.* Rehearsal is most effective if the client has already selected the most important aspects of the display. When presented with a complex array of information or situations, the client should (a) scan the entire array, (b) select the most important aspects of the information, and (c) rehearse only the important information.
2. *Use a whole/part scanning strategy.* Learning is most efficient when the big picture or global organization is rehearsed rather than the individual parts.
3. *Vary the rehearsal strategy.* The client should use more than one kind of manipulation when possible to encode the same material. Most experts believe that the use of different techniques leads to a more du-

rable and accessible memory trace. For example, at a party, the client could first rehearse attributes of various guests, such as their hair or eye color. Next, the client could rehearse social groupings of the guests.

4. *Distribute rehearsal sessions.* Ideally, the client will learn to rehearse consistently over several sessions. Trying to learn everything at once usually leads to much less learning than distributing the learning over different occasions.

5. *Put in the time.* The therapist should impress on the client that whatever method he or she uses, the amount learned is directly related to the amount of time spent practicing.

6. *Self-test.* The therapist should train the client to self-test repeatedly during learning. The goal is to overlearn the material if it is especially important or detailed. That is, after learning 100% of the new material, the client should study the material and self-test further. The major value of self-testing is that it acquaints the client with the aspects of the information that he or she does not know well. It therefore focuses rehearsal on those aspects that require the most review. For example, when reading a text, the client should recall the gist of each paragraph and then spend the most time reviewing the paragraphs that were most difficult to recall.

7. *Rehearse when rested.* Rehearsal is functionally useless if the client is not attending to the information. It is therefore important to ensure that the client is rehearsing when he or she can attend and concentrate adequately.

CONCLUSION

This chapter presented various techniques for integrating rehearsal skill with various techniques of memory strategy training (Harrell, Parenté, Bellingrath, & Lisicia, 1992; Parenté & Anderson-Parenté, 1991). Rehearsal is the mechanism that allows us all to keep informa-

tion in the cognitive system. Without rehearsal, we would forget most things we heard or saw in a matter of minutes (Higbee, 1988). After traumatic brain injury, clients lose the ability to rehearse automatically. The goal of treatment is to train the client to rehearse, at first consciously and later automatically. However, the rehearsal process is most effective if the client rehearses the strategy or organizational structure of the information rather than the component parts.

In Chapter 10, we discussed several card games designed to illustrate the value of maintenance rehearsal. The techniques outlined in this chapter are designed to integrate the basic maintenance rehearsal skills with memory strategies that are discussed in Chapter 11. Together, these two techniques interact to create vivid and lasting memories. These strategies increase strength of a memory by increasing the number of attributes of information being learned, by increasing the number of connections between the information being learned and other information already in memory, and by developing other backup records of the information being learned.

REFERENCES

Anderson, J.R. (1981). *Cognitive skills and their acquisition.* Hillsdale, NJ: Lawrence Erlbaum.

Baddeley, A.D. (1995). Applying psychology of memory to clinical problems. In D. Herrmann, C. McEvoy, C. Hertzog, P. Hertel, & M. Johnson (Eds.), *Basic and applied memory: Theory and context.* Hillsdale, NJ: Lawrence Erlbaum.

Bellezza, F.S. (1981). Mnemonic devices: Classification, characteristics, and criteria. *Review of Educational Research, 51,* 247–275.

Biederman, I., Mezzanotte, R.J., & Rabinowitz, J. (1982). Scene perception: Detecting and judging objects undergoing relational violations. *Cognitive Psychology, 14,* 143–177.

Chase, W.G., & Ericsson, K.A. (1982). Skill and working memory. In G.H. Bower (Ed.), *The psychology of learning and motivation* (Vol. 16, pp. 141–189). New York: Academic Press.

Davies, G., & Thomson, D.M. (1988). *Memory in context: Context in memory.* Chichester, UK: John Wiley.

DiBeni, R., & Cornoldi, C. (1985). Effects of the mnemonotechnique of loci in memorization of concrete words. *Acta Psychologica, 60,* 11–24.

Duffy, T.M., Walker, C., & Montague, W.E. (1972). Sentence mnemonics and the role of verb-class in paired-associate learning. *Psychological Reports, 31*, 583–589.

Ericsson, K.A. (1985). Memory skill. *Canadian Journal of Psychology, 39*, 188–231.

Greenwald, A.G., & Banaji, M.R. (1989). The self as a memory system: Powerful but ordinary. *Journal of Personality and Social Psychology, 57*, 41–54.

Hardy, L., & Ringland, A. (1984). Mental training and the inner game. *Human Learning, 3*, 143–226.

Harrell, M., Parenté, F., Bellingrath, E.G., & Lisicia, K.A. (1992). *Cognitive rehabilitation of memory: A practical guide*. Gaithersburg, MD: Aspen.

Herrmann, M., Ruppin, E., & Usher, M. (1993). A neural model of the dynamic activation of memory. *Biological Cybernetics, 68*, 455–463.

Higbee, K.L. (1988). *Your memory* (2nd ed.). Englewood Cliffs, NJ: Prentice Hall.

Landauer, T.K., & Bjork, R.A. (1978). Optimum rehearsal patterns and name learning. In M.M. Gruenberg, P.E. Morris, & R.N. Sykes (Eds.), *Practical aspects of memory* (pp. 625–632). London: Academic Press.

Loisette, A. (1886). *Assimilative memory: Or how to attend and never forget*. New York: Funk & Wagnall.

Morris, P.E., & Cook, N. (1978). When do first letter mnemonics aid recall? *British Journal of Educational Psychology, 48*, 22–28.

Parenté, R., & Anderson-Parenté, J. (1991). *Retraining memory: Techniques and applications*. Houston, TX: CSY.

Rundus, D. (1977). Maintenance rehearsal and single level processing. *Journal of Verbal Learning and Verbal Behavior, 16*, 665–681.

Schoenfeld, A.H. (1985). *Mathematical problem solving*. Orlando, FL: Academic Press.

Tulving, E. (1983). *Elements of episodic memory*. Oxford, UK: Oxford University Press.

Tulving, E., & Madigan, S.A. (1970). Memory and verbal learning. *Annual Review of Psychology, 20*.

Underwood, B.J. (1969). Attributes of memory. *Psychological Review, 76*, 559–573.

Wickens, D.D. (1970). Encoding categories of words: An empirical approach to meaning. *Psychological Review, 77*, 1–15.

Chapter 13

Retrieval from Long-Term Memory

In Chapter 11, we discussed encoding strategies that can be used to improve the client's ability to recall everyday information such as phone numbers, name-face associations, and seemingly unrelated events. These techniques are designed to improve the person's ability to store information in long-term memory in a way that ensures rapid and efficient retrieval later on. In this chapter, we focus on the retrieval aspects of the working memory store (Baddeley, 1986). Specifically, we discuss techniques for training the client to extract stored information from the long-term store (Humphreys, Bain, & Pike, 1989).

RETRIEVAL OF EPISODIC MEMORIES

Factors That Inhibit Retrieval

Poor Acquisition

What seems like forgetting is sometimes not a true memory problem at all. For example, clients may appear to have forgotten something because they never learned the information in the first place or because they do not understand what they are supposed to remember. For example, many clients will say they understand instructions or remember directions after hearing them once. However, they did not adequately process the information, and their incomplete memory is due more to poor storage or encoding than to a retrieval failure. The therapist can ensure adequate storage by asking clients to repeat information in their own words and insisting on additional rehearsals when necessary.

Poor Perception

Clients may forget something because poor eyesight or hearing prevented them from noticing relevant cues (Cutler & Grams, 1988). Often a new set of glasses or a hearing aid can have a remarkable effect on memory. Old age can change clients' priorities for what is important to remember. Medications, depression, or life changes such as menopause can create temporary changes in memory efficiency. It is therefore necessary to postpone a diagnosis of amnesia until other factors such as hearing or vision limitations are ruled out. It is worthwhile investigating these issues because often a simple physical intervention can save the therapist hours of needless and unproductive memory therapy effort.

Inability To Generate Cues

The importance of cuing cannot be overemphasized (Tulving, 1983). Often, head injury survivors forget, not because the information did not get into long-term memory, but because they are no longer able to generate the cues that are necessary to retrieve the information from the long-term store. Consequently, the treatments presented here are designed to facilitate the cuing process. The therapist should therefore advise the client that he or she will, at first, have to make a conscious effort to generate memory cues. After a long period of conscious effort, the cuing process will eventually happen relatively effortlessly.

Strategies That Do Not Work

There are several reasons why strategy training may not produce immediate improvement. Clients may continue using a strategy that doesn't work and may resist trying others the therapist may suggest. Certain strategies may work in one situation but not in any others. Using strategies may seem to require more mental effort than the client is willing to invest. It is usually necessary to try several strategies over an extended period of time to find those that work for the client. Despite these frustrations, the therapist should emphasize to the client that using strategies will, more often than not, improve recall.

Factors That Improve Retrieval

Generally, the accessibility of information in memory depends on how it was initially stored. Storage determines four characteristics that affect the ability to retrieve the information (Herrmann, 1990): the *strength* of the memory, its characteristic *attributes,* its *associations* with other memories, and the client's *reconstructions* from other memories. The art of training retrieval involves getting the client to attend to these four attributes when creating memory cues.

Strength

All of us have hunches, best guesses, and feelings about certain events that we cannot recall. These are usually based on a subjective feeling of memory strength. For example, sometimes

we are not able to recognize a particular person, place, or thing immediately, but we can make a choice based on a subjective feeling of familiarity that results from the strength of the memory trace. Head injury survivors can use such subjective feelings of memory strength to make guesses about a vague memory. For example, when they are trying to remember a person's name, the name that seems the most familiar is likely to be the correct name or at least similar to the correct name. The therapist should therefore advise clients to attend to their subjective feelings of familiarity as a way of initiating the retrieval process. Even though the initial recall may not be correct, it may spur an association that in turn triggers correct recall.

Attributes

Clients can also jog their memory by partial recall of some component of the larger memory. For example, when trying to cue recall of a person, they might try to conjure up a mental image of the person or to use some physical characteristic to cue recall. Sometimes a person can remember one or a few attributes of an event, place, or person but still cannot retrieve the entire memory. These partial cues eventually produce a correct recall. For example, we have all had the experience of trying to find a particular text passage in a book. We cannot recall the content of the passage, but we can remember that it was located on the top of the page about halfway through the book. These attributes then direct and limit our search for the passage. The therapist should therefore encourage the client to use these attributes to cue recall of the complete picture. In many cases, recalling only the single aspect will lead to the larger item.

Associations

Clients can also cue recall by focusing on those things that are associated with the information in question. For example, recalling attributes according to the time when something happened, who was present during an introduction, where the event occurred, and so forth can provide a useful triggering association. The "who, what, when, where, how, and why" method discussed in Chapter 11 is a useful technique for encoding and storing information in an organized format. However, the client can also use the same words to trigger recall later. For example, when trying to recall a name, the client can ask, "Who is the person associated with? What conditions led to our introduction? When were we introduced? When did I see the person last? Where did I last see the person? How did we encounter each other?" These questions force the client to produce one or more associations that lead to recall of the event or person.

Reconstructions

Memory reconstructions are based on all of the above attributes of retrieval. Reconstructions lead the client to conclusions based on a rehearsal of a previous sequence of events (Barclay, 1986). For example, if the client is trying to find his wallet, he might sit down and mentally rehearse the course of yesterday's activities. What clothes was he wearing? Where was he going that day? Where did he last see his wallet? In which pocket of a jacket did he place the wallet? These questions often lead to a new conclusion that directs the client to locating the object. He may conclude that he last saw his wallet 2 days ago on the table. He does not recall picking it up and putting it in his jacket. It may therefore still be on the table from 2 days ago.

Specific Retrieval Therapies

Several additional strategies presented below may help a client to retrieve information from memory (Adams, 1985). Most are based on one or more of the principles outlined above. All of them may help a client, and we advise therapists to try them all to determine if any are useful with a particular client.

Alphabet Search

The therapist trains the client to search memory using the letters of the alphabet as a cue. For example, the client may say, "I think her name began with an A? a B? a C?" and so

on through Z. This technique can often cue recall of the correct name.

Free Generation of Attributes

The client free-associates and recalls anything that may be associated with the information in question. Some aspect of the free-generation process may cue recall of the target memory. For example, clients may think of women's names at random, places they have been recently, or people who come to mind freely. Any of these freely generated memories can trigger recall of the target.

Reinstating Mood

Powerful moods and emotional states can often cue recall (Blaney, 1986). The client therefore tries to recall any mood or dominant emotions that were associated with the memory. For example, we can all recall incidents in which a person or group of people became emotional and cried or laughed heartily. Storing the mood by actively paying attention to the emotional state of the person or to oneself at the time of the incident certainly helps recall later because the mood becomes associated with the scenario at the time of storage.

Tip-of-the-Tongue Method

When a memory is on the tip of the tongue, usually the first letter comes to mind before the actual memory. Therefore, the therapist should advise the client to use the alphabet method to cue recall of the first letter, which is usually enough to cue recall of the larger memory (Burke, MacKay, Worthley, & Wade, 1991). This technique will be especially effective in situations in which the memory has almost surfaced or the client feels that it is on the tip of the tongue. For example, when trying to recall a person's name, the client may use the alphabet cuing method to bring to mind the first letter of the person's name. Once the name is on the tip of the tongue, the client can guess names that begin with that letter until the correct name comes to mind.

Other attributes may also trigger a memory. These may include the length of a word, unusual letter combinations, or homophone qualities of the word. The basic strategy is to encourage the client to generate cues rather than to struggle searching for the actual memory.

Retracing

This technique involves reconstructing chronologically the events that preceded or followed the one the client would like to remember. Usually, the client tries to recall the circumstances that produced the event or situation. For example, some clients may go into a room and immediately forget what they entered the room to retrieve. Simply retracing the sequence of events that led up to entering the room can cue recall of why he or she is there. For example, the client may be wrapping a package and need a pair of scissors. The client may forget that he or she went into the kitchen to get some scissors to complete the task. Recalling the previous activity will therefore cue recall of the reason for going into the kitchen.

Return to the Scene

Recreating the original surroundings where the event occurred can cue recall. For example, simply walking into a room, a store, or a neighborhood can cue recall of important information such as the location of an object, a friend's house, or an office. For example, the therapist should advise clients who return to school to study for a test in the same room where they will eventually take the test. The room will then serve as a cue for recall of the information at the time of the test.

Suggestions to Clients

Effective remembering requires more than simply learning a variety of retrieval strategies. A client must also be able to manage these strategies according to the demands of different situations (Herrmann, Raybeck, & Gutman, 1993). The therapist should therefore train the client to adopt different behaviors and attitudes that may

facilitate recall. The following are suggestions that therapists should make to their clients.

Relax

Tension seldom improves recall (Yesavage, Rose, & Spiegel, 1982). In most situations, adopting an attitude of relaxation will facilitate recall. Even when the information comes to mind, hurrying can lead the client to miss recalling important details. The therapist should therefore train the client to use simple relaxation methods such as stretching, short meditations, and head/neck rotations to produce a relaxed state of mind. Trying to recall in the period just before falling asleep can also improve retrieval.

Vary the Method

If one of the above methods does not work, then another might. The client should always make a systematic attempt to try any and all of the above techniques before giving up on the retrieval process. With practice, the client will find that certain techniques work well for certain types of retrieval and others work well in different situations. Often, simple persistence in trying different methods will eventually lead to recall (Morris, 1984).

Use Primacy and Recency

The primacy-and-recency effect is a well-documented memory phenomenon that occurs when we try to recall sequences of information. There is a tendency to remember what happened last and first in a sequence best. The center portion of the sequence will not be as memorable. Consequently, the therapist should advise the client that in situations in which the information is serial or sequential, he or she is most likely to recall what happened last, followed by what happened first, followed by what happened in the middle. Recalling the first and last sections can cue recall of the middle.

Any new learning situation is a time-ordered sequence. Clients can therefore structure this sequence to capitalize on the primacy-and-recency effect to improve retrieval. When learning anything new, clients should try to rehearse and summarize the information at the end of the session. This will ensure that the summary occurs during a section of the sequence that is remembered best. Clients should also distribute their practice over several short sessions rather than massing all the learning in one marathon session. Distributed practice produces better retrieval because frequent practice sessions provide more first and last segments of learning sessions, thereby offering more opportunity to capitalize on the primacy-and-recency effect.

Give It a Rest

If clients feel that their memories are blocked, the best strategy is to take a break. It may therefore be best to use the above techniques just before falling asleep at night. Often the person will awaken during the night with recall of the information. Sometimes it will come to mind the following morning.

Monitor Accuracy

The therapist should monitor the client's correctness and provide an assessment of any systematic distortions or embellishments that occur consistently. The therapist should also train the client to take these distortions into account when evaluating recall. For example, if the therapist notices that the client usually overestimates characteristics such as beauty, weight, or speed, then the client can use this information to correct his or her recollections in the future.

RETRAINING RETRIEVAL OF PERSONAL INFORMATION AND SKILLS

The above techniques are designed to train clients to retrieve episodic information. However, retrieval from long-term memory involves other types of information as well. For example, head-injured persons' personal histories are usually intact even though there are sometimes "islands of memory" and some personal facts are inaccessible. In the earliest stages of recovery, how-

ever, the client may be disoriented and unable to recall personal information. This is an especially frustrating state, and the therapist may have to spend considerable time reinstating these memories before working with episodic retrieval strategies. These techniques are described as *retraining* methods because they are designed to recreate an existing long-term memory. They are specifically useful for retrograde amnesias, whereas the training methods outlined earlier for retrieval of episodic information are better suited for anterograde amnesias. These methods may also be especially useful with elderly clients who suffer from dementia or for clients with progressively degenerative conditions. With such clients, the correct recall of personal information may be all that can be accomplished.

Personal Information

Retrieval of personal history is best retrained by getting a number of personal facts from the family members and recording them on tape. Useful facts are birth date, children's names, phone numbers, street addresses, names of high schools or colleges attended, and so forth. The therapist should then require the client to listen to the tape over and over each day, using headphones to ensure adequate attention. Having the client repeat the information out loud as he or she hears it can also help to re-establish the memories. We frequently purchase a Walkman-type tape player and give it to the client for this purpose. The therapist should make up a list of the facts and test recall of each one on the tape until the client demonstrates perfect mastery of his or her personal information. The therapist can then collect another set of facts from the family and repeat the process as many times as necessary.

The same result can be accomplished with a family photo album. The therapist can use the photos as flash cards, showing them to the client one at a time and asking for recall of the event, person's name, year, city, and so forth. This technique also works well in conjunction with the tape recorder training method.

Academic Skills

Academic remediation of previously learned skills is usually a rote process. It is valuable to assess clients' reading, math, and spelling skills and then to provide commercially available academic remediation materials. The difficulty level of the materials should be about one-half year below the client's assessed grade level. Computers are especially good for this type of training. Most software stores have shelves of excellent academic remediation software and games for all grade levels. Math training should emphasize rote learning of functional skills such as multiplication, division, and eventually fractions and percents. Previously learned skills such as typing are also retrained this way.

Reading should stress comprehension, finding the main idea, and extrapolation beyond the concrete facts. Spelling and vocabulary should retrain understanding of current word meanings. Books such as *Absolutely Essential Words* (Bromberg, Liebb, & Traiger, 1984) are useful for establishing a vocabulary of current words. The therapist can use a thesaurus to memorize opposites, synonyms, and homonyms to increase the number of alternative retrieval routes to the desired words. This type of memorization usually decreases the incidence of word-finding and word substitution problems after head injury. It is also useful to train clients to recognize Greek and Latin roots so that they can figure out the meaning of novel words from the roots.

Other techniques for retraining reading skill may also prove to be effective. For example, clients may benefit from reading text materials into a tape recorder, then replaying the tape while rereading the text. This technique produces both visual and auditory rehearsals. We recommend that clients who return to school learn to dictate notes from text into a tape recorder rather than writing them down. This process is much quicker, and it forces clients to restate or translate the information while they read it.

Once again, translation of written text and other materials into one's own words produces an encoding that is especially easy to retrieve later on. We recommend using the "who, what, when, where, how, and why" method for training reading translations. This training involves teaching the client to translate text materials by answering the above questions after each paragraph. If the client cannot answer the questions, then it will be necessary to reread the paragraph. Under no circumstances should the person go on to the next paragraph until he or she is able to answer the questions about the current paragraph. This procedure provides a self-monitoring system for reading comprehension. It also ensures that the client can use the words as retrieval cues later on.

CONCLUSION

This chapter presents techniques for training retrieval and self-cuing skills. We began with a discussion of the retrieval of episodic information. Factors that inhibit retrieval include the inability to generate cues and strategies that do not work, as well as conditions that cloud the diagnosis of a true memory impairment—for example, poor acquisition or a sight or hearing deficit. Factors that improve retrieval include the client's attention to four attributes of memories: their strength, characteristic attributes, associations with other information, and surrounding context. Specific techniques for cuing recall include the alphabet method, free generation, reinstating the mood, tip-of-the-tongue guesses, retracing, and returning to the scene of the memory. Additional factors that facilitate retrieval include the ability to relax, to use primacy and recency to the client's best advantage, to give the process a rest when retrieval becomes too difficult, and to monitor accuracy for any systematic distortions at the time of recall.

This chapter also discusses methods for recreating memories of personal history or previously acquired skills. Recall of personal information can be conveniently accomplished by having the client listen to a tape recording of personal facts followed by regular quizzing of those facts. Photo albums also provide convenient sources for flash cards that the therapist can use in the same manner as the tape. The therapist can use the large body of available computer software to retrain academic or job-related skills that the client may need to return to work.

REFERENCES

Adams, L.T. (1985). Improving memory: Can retrieval strategies help? *Human Learning, 4*, 281–297.

Baddeley, A.D. (1986). *Working memory*. New York: Basic Books.

Barclay, C. (1986). Schematization of autobiographical memory. In D.C. Rubin (Ed.), *Autobiographical memory*. Cambridge, MA: Cambridge University Press.

Blaney, P.H. (1986). Affect and memory: A review. *Psychological Bulletin, 99*, 229–246.

Bromberg, M., Liebb, J., & Traiger, A. (1984). *Absolutely essential words*. New York: Barrons.

Burke, D., MacKay, D.G., Worthley, J.S., & Wade, E. (1991). On the tip of the tongue: What causes word finding failures in young and older adults. *Journal of Memory and Language, 30*, 237–246.

Cutler, S.J., & Grams, A.E. (1988). Correlates of self-reported everyday memory problems. *Journal of Gerontology, 43*, 582–590.

Herrmann, D.J. (1990). *SuperMemory*. Emmaus, PA: Rodale.

Herrmann, D.J., Raybeck, D., & Gutman, D. (1993). *Improving student memory*. Toronto: Hogrefe & Huber.

Humphreys, M.S., Bain, J.D., & Pike, R. (1989). Different ways to cue a coherent memory system: A theory of episodic and procedural tasks. *Psychological Review, 96*, 208–233.

Morris, P.E. (1984). The cognitive psychology of self-reports. In J. Harris & P. Morris (Eds.), *Everyday memory, actions, and absentmindedness*. London: Academic Press.

Tulving, E. (1983). *Elements of episodic memory*. Oxford, UK: Oxford University Press.

Yesavage, J.A., Rose, T.L., & Spiegel, D. (1982). Relaxation training and memory improvement in elderly normals: Correlations of anxiety ratings and recall improvement. *Experimental Aging Research, 4*, 123–137.

Chapter 14

Retraining Organizational Skill

Head injury survivors may often seem disorganized, may have difficulty keeping track of things, or may seem unable to do things systematically or in a timely fashion. The purpose of this chapter is to suggest ways for head-injured persons to improve their organizational skills. The chapter begins with an overview and summary of the various theories of mental organization. Although these theories were never intended to explain deficits of organization that occur after head injury, we feel that they all have implications for head injury rehabilitation. We discuss schema theory in detail because it appears to be the most likely candidate for a comprehensive theory of organizational deficits after head injury. We also present some original research that tests the basic assumptions of the various organizational models. The chapter ends with a discussion of rehabilitation techniques that follow from these theories, along with a description of principles of environmental organization.

MENTAL ORGANIZATION

Theories of Mental Organization

Before we can retrain mental organization, it is necessary to understand how mental representations of the world are created. Although there is considerable literature that describes the process of mental organization with college students, there is comparatively little that describes how information becomes disorganized after head injury. We therefore briefly describe various theories of mental organization and extract from them any implications for head injury rehabilitation.

Propositional Theory

Kintch and van Dijk (1978) proposed a classic and widely accepted theory of mental organization. This theory is similar to another proposed by Anderson and Bower (1973). The general idea is that comprehension is the process of forming *propositions,* or relationships that integrate an existing body of information. For example, Figure 14–1 illustrates a hypothetical propositional network that relates the elements of the statement "Alice sells fresh bagels to Tony, who owns a restaurant." The network on the left illustrates an intact propositional structure. The various lines indicate relationships that bind together the subject, object, and recipient portions of the network in some way. For example, the line between *fresh* and *object* indicates that the object *bagels* is related to *fresh.* Likewise, *sells* is related to the subject *Alice.* The elements are grouped in this way into the larger cluster depicted in the figure. The theory assumes that information is stored in memory according to propositional

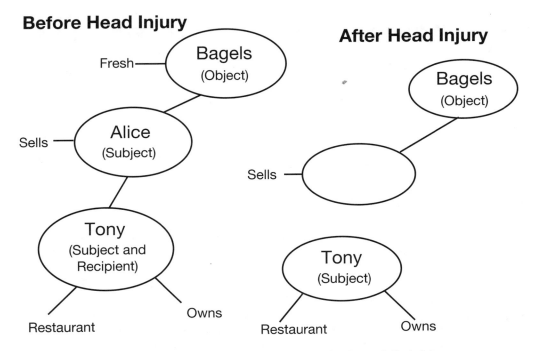

Figure 14–1 Hypothetical Propositional Network Model Before and After Traumatic Brain Injury

structures. The structures are modified and developed by the person's past experience, goals, and values. Larger groups of propositions eventually become organized around central themes.

Head injury could have any of several effects on the network. By breaking connections among the subnetworks, it could eliminate an entire subnetwork from the larger structure. For example, it could disconnect "Tony, who owns a restaurant" from "Alice sells fresh bagels" simply by eliminating the relationship between "Alice" and "Tony," as depicted in the right-hand portion of Figure 14–1. It might also change the relationship markings in the network. Regardless of the combination of effects, the result is an altered cognitive state with unpredictable consequences.

The implication of the propositional network model is that the therapist must focus on reconstructing the propositional structure of the network. The primary goal of therapy is therefore to teach the client to relate pieces of novel information to a meaningful structure. When confronted with a novel situation, the client generally asks, "How are these things related to one another?" This question forces the client to focus on the propositions that relate episodic information in memory. We describe a method of questioning later in the chapter that can be used for this purpose.

Associative Network Theory

This type of theory assumes that knowledge is stored in a hierarchy. The first such theory (Quillian, 1968, 1969) was actually a computer program called the Teachable Language Comprehender (TLC). Quillian devised a method for storing information in a computer such that the program could answer questions in a flexible fashion, much as humans do. An example of his method is presented in the left-hand portion of Figure 14–2.

Quillian's model has *superordinate categories* with attributes attached to them. These are depicted from top down as the dots or nodes of the hierarchy. Beneath each of these are *subordinate categories* with attached attributes. Individual instances are stored at the bottom of the hierarchy with their associated attributes.

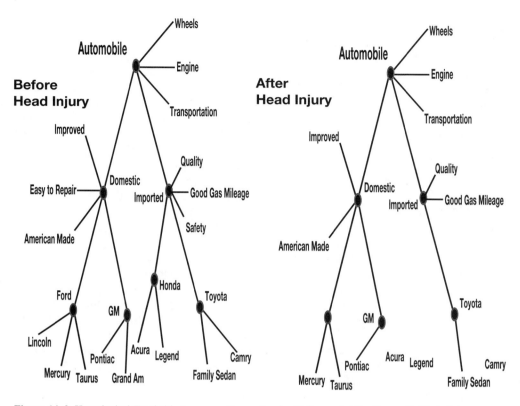

Figure 14–2 Hypothetical Teachable Language Comprehender Before and After Traumatic Brain Injury

The program answers questions simply by tracing the query through the hierarchy. For example, when asked, "Is a Ford an automobile?" the program traces the word *Ford* to the superordinate category and locates the word *automobile,* thereby producing a yes response. Although the process is relatively simple, the program can account for a variety of human performances.

Quillian's model assumes that efficiency of thinking is partially related to the ability to organize information into superordinate categories. Without the structure, retrieval from memory is clearly limited to the capacity of the working memory (about four to five units of information after brain injury). However, when the information is organized into a superordinate and subordinate structure, then speed and accuracy of processing can be greatly improved.

Head injury could disrupt the structure by erasing one or more of the connections between nodes and from a node to an adjective that describes it. These possibilities are presented in the right-hand portion of Figure 14–2. Note that *easy to repair* and *safety* have been omitted from the head-injured person's organization. The implication is that the therapist should teach organization via superordinate, subordinate, and examples. That is, the therapist should teach the client to organize information so that there is a clear hierarchical structure that allows the client to build or to re-establish his or her functional networks.

Feature Set Theory

Originally proposed by Smith, Shoben, and Rips (1974), feature set theory emphasizes the importance, for memory retrieval, of the attribute features of information rather than the hierarchical structure, as in associative network theory.

According to Smith et al.'s theory, knowledge is the sum of the features that describe a particular concept. In essence, there is no need for superordinate nodes in feature set theory because the attributes alone are sufficient to define the concepts. This aspect of feature set theory explains why we can seldom describe some concepts even though we can give many concrete examples of them. For example, the word *beautiful* conjures up any number of examples of things we believe are beautiful, but no single definition of *beauty*.

Smith et al. (1974) distinguished between what he called defining features and characteristic features. *Defining features* are central to the meaning of a concept. What Quillian (1968, 1969) called superordinate categories, then, are simply collections of objects that are considered members of the same class because they have similar defining features. *Characteristic features* are features that may be associated with an object but are not necessary to define it. For example, a defining feature of a Ford is that it is American made. A wheel is a characteristic feature of the superordinate category of *simple tool*.

The implications of this theory for head injury rehabilitation are that the client's concept of an event will depend on his or her ability to extract the defining and characteristic features of the event. For example, teaching the client to make a mental listing of the physical features of a person to whom he or she is introduced should help to make that person more memorable. The NAME mnemonic discussed in Chapter 11 helps the client to extract features when forming name-face associations.

Spreading Activation Theory

The spreading activation theory is a hybrid of the associative network and feature set theories (Collins & Loftus, 1975). It is also a precursor to the modern schema theories that are discussed in detail below. It is similar to associative network theory in that it includes nodes that represent superordinate concepts. However, it differs in that each instance within a superordinate category is connected with other instances and with other superordinates as well (Klix, 1986).

Several assumptions of this theory are unique. First, it is assumed that when a person perceives anything, the effect of the perception spreads through the entire mental network. In Figure 14–3, the length of the line that connects the various elements is the probability that one instance or superordinate will activate another. For example, activating the subordinate category *Ford* is more likely to activate the memory of *Taurus* than the memory of the superordinate category *Domestic*.

The term *spreading activation* refers to the assumption that any instance, subordinate, or superordinate that is stimulated is assumed to spread some amount of activation to another portion of the network. The strength of the activation will then trigger other portions of the network to fire, and these, in turn, will stimulate others. For example, saying *Toyota* will probably trigger *Imported* and may also trigger *Camry*. Whether these are triggered depends on the strength of the original stimulus and the associations that have developed over the years. *Imported* and *Camry* will also activate other portions of the net that may evoke other associations, depending on their strength. The spreading activation notion is an important part of the schema theory discussed in detail below.

According to this theory, cognitive dysfunction would be due to network damage in the form of weakening of activation among certain elements, with widespread ramifications for activation among the rest. The goal of rehabilitation would therefore be to repair the network through exercises that teach organization of semantic information. Further, because memory and thinking depend on establishing functional connections among instances and categories, the training would need to include association of these characteristics. The theory also explains many of the seemingly tangential thinking processes that occur after head injury. This could happen when the connections between the instances and ordinates are broken or altered.

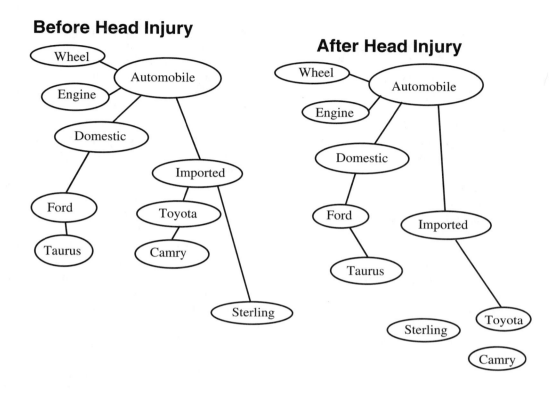

Figure 14–3 Diagram of Cognitive Structures According to Spreading Activation Theory

Research on Organizational Theory

The common assumption of the four theories just discussed is that humans naturally organize information and that the way they organize determines the efficiency and accuracy of their thinking as well as the ability to retrieve information from memory (Herrmann & Chaffin, 1986). It is therefore reasonable to assume that a head-injured person's ability to recall semantic information depends on his or her ability to organize the information initially. Twum and Parenté (1994) tested this hypothesis as part of a larger experiment.

Persons with head injury received lists of words that were organized semantically. The lists, such as *red, green, Mars, Venus, table, chair, hand, foot, north, west, dog, cat,* implicitly contained several semantic categories (colors, plan-

ets, furniture, body parts, directions, and animals). The words were mixed up so that the semantic organization was not apparent. The authors hypothesized that persons who perceived the organization would recall more of the words. In essence, retrieval of the words for each of these head-injured persons depended on his or her ability to perceive the organization of the list. This was precisely the result. Those who recalled the words in an organized fashion usually remembered the entire list of 12 words. Those who did not perceive the organization seldom recalled more than half the list, even with repeated study and test.

After half an hour, the clients were asked to recall as many of the words as they could remember. When they could no longer recall any more of the words, the authors prompted them by providing the category of those words that they had not recalled. This cuing procedure generally resulted in recall of all the words. However, giving only one of the categories usually led to recall of words from other categories as well. This result suggested a spreading activation component to the client's recall.

Elliot and Parenté (1995) followed up on this experiment to determine how to train clients to enhance their recall of the word lists. Several conditions of pretraining were evaluated. In one condition, head-injured and learning-disabled clients were asked to memorize a list of words that was semantically arranged in a way that primed the person to discover the organization of the larger list that he or she would memorize next. For example, clients would first learn the list *yellow, blue, sun, moon, south, east.* They would then learn the list *dog, cat, table, chair, red, green, Mars, Venus, north, west.* Each of these lists was presented in a random order. The first contained several of the categories that were also part of the second but none of the same words. Another group learned the category labels but not any of the words from the second list. For example, these clients learned the words *animals, furniture, colors, planets, directions* before learning the larger 10-word list. In both conditions, the clients learned the second list much more quickly than did a group of clients who had first learned a list of words that was totally unrelated to the second list.

Both of these experiments illustrate the importance of organization for improving thinking and memory with head-injured clients. Teaching clients to organize information initially not only allows them to learn it more quickly but also improves their ability to remember it over the long term.

Schema Theory

Schema theory is one of the oldest and also one of the most controversial concepts of how humans form mental representations of the world. We describe this theory in greater detail than the rest because we feel that of all the theories of organization, it has the greatest potential for explaining memory and cognitive dysfunc-

tion after head injury. Indeed, the theory has already been used to explain the mechanism that underlies amnesia (McClelland & Rummelhart, 1987). Schema theory has also undergone a great deal of development in recent years (Bransford & Johnson, 1972; Neisser, 1976). We begin with a brief discussion of early work in this area and then describe the more recent developments along with some initial tests of the schema theory with head-injured clients.

Schema theory is both old and new. It dates back to the time of Kant (1787/1987) and has been discussed most recently by McClelland and Rummelhart (1987). Basically, a schema is a body of organized information that summarizes our experience and attitudes about any aspect of life. For example, the theory assumes that we have schemata for dinner, vacations, work, and so forth. Schemata differ from person to person, as evidenced by statements we have all heard, such as "That's not my idea of a good time," "He's a good speaker," or "She's beautiful." Each of these statements implies some inner representation that the person can use to make judgments about the world.

Schemata do not necessarily imply propositions, hierarchical structure, or categorization. Some schemata are organizations of time, space, or sequence (Mandler, 1984; Rabinowitz & Mandler, 1983). For example, most people can conjure up a mental representation of the last 10 minutes, their backyard, or the series of events they go through when starting a car. Some schemata are *scripts* that describe sequences of events that we expect to occur in certain situations (Schank & Abelson, 1977). For example, there is a certain script sequence we expect a waiter or waitress to follow when we go out to a restaurant for dinner. *Scene* schemata (Mandler, 1984) represent the spatial representations of things in a common or familiar space. For example, we all have a scene schema for the furniture in our living room.

Early work on the schema concept did not describe it concretely and had little practical value. Kant (1987), for example, discussed the concept of a schema in philosophical terms. Bartlett (1932) described schemata in relation to the recall of text materials. Piaget (1952) also used the term *schema* to explain the development of human cognition. Because of the vagueness of the term, the idea of a mental schema was generally considered philosophical and too diffuse to be of any practical value. More recent discussions, however (Bobrow & Norman, 1975; Minsky, 1975; Rummelhart, 1975; Schank & Ableson, 1977), use the term to describe data structures for storing information in memory. These are likened to three-dimensional pictures of the outside world that describe situations, events, actions, and sequences.

Bartlett (1932) concluded that humans generally form a schema of everything they read and try to integrate new information into their existing store of experience. This is why the same event can have such different meanings to different people. Since the time of Bartlett, several basic processes of schema formation have been identified (Alba & Hasher, 1983; Eckhardt, 1990). These are especially relevant for therapists because they have direct application to head-injured persons.

The first process is *selection*. Whether people will relate something new with things they already know depends on whether they allow the information to come in contact with the schema. For example, a person may not allow anyone's medical advice to alter his or her opinion unless that person is a physician. However, once the person selects certain information for processing, the selected information is then *abstracted*. This means that irrelevant details are ignored and/or dropped before the core features are incorporated into the schema. The abstracted information is then *interpreted*. This means that the person forms inferences (additional facts that could be true) and presuppositions (additional facts that must be true) from the new information and that these also become part of the larger schema. This is the process of *integration*.

New information may be integrated in one of three ways. It may be (a) readily assimilated into the schema, (b) tagged as similar but a little different, or (c) mentally labeled as an acceptable variation to the general rule. Schema formation

is also an actively changing process that is unique to the cultural experience of the individual.

The basic implication from this overview of schema theory is that persons with head injury must learn to focus on the thematic content and try to affix novel experiences to an existing schema. Clearly, however, there are several subprocesses, and the therapist must first identify which process is deficient. For example, the client may have difficulty selecting information at input or integrating the information once it gets into memory. Unfortunately, there has been little research in the head injury field that describes these processes or what therapies are appropriate for their retraining.

McClelland and Rummelhart (1987) have proposed a parallel distributed processing (PDP) model of schema formation that is actually a connectionist computer program that can be used to simulate human cognition as well as cognitive dysfunction. The underlying logic of their model departs from those described above because it assumes that the brain does not store physical representations of the world per se. Rather, it creates them. The PDP model assumes that schema formation is a constructive process that occurs when something in the world stimulates or activates some portion of the schema, in turn spreading the activation to the rest of the schema. The resulting schema may vary markedly depending on the extent of the original stimulation. These processes are thought to be unconscious and to depend on the person's prior learning and values and the amount of information available. In essence, schemata are the mental representations that result when a person tries to interpret his or her environment.

More specifically, the PDP concept is that the mind is composed of receptors that are sensitive to simple features. Combinations of the features create higher level organizations such as words or shapes. At this level, schema theory is similar to the feature set theory mentioned earlier. Both assume that features are interconnected and that environmental stimuli can activate any part of this connected network. The activation then spreads through this mental landscape, either activating other portions or inhibiting them. The pattern of activation and inhibition develops via experience. However, the schema formed will differ depending on which aspects of the array are stimulated or inhibited. For example, when we see a person from afar, his or her gross features may activate the schema for a certain friend or relative. However, this same person's features may remind us of someone else as he or she gets closer.

Schema theory assumes that what is stored in memory is a set of connections that are probabilities. These connections vary from person to person and from moment to moment. After a head injury, they can be altered or destroyed or the process of forming them can be changed. It therefore stands to reason that persons with head injury will perceive the world differently because the schema formation process has been altered in some way.

McClelland and Rummelhart's (1987) PDP model is especially useful because it is designed as a computer program that can be used to model the neural functioning of the brain. It is unique because it assumes that humans do not form hardwired schemes to represent the novel experiences of life. Their assumption is that all information is represented in a probabilistic manner by a series of mental associations. Activation of an associative network spreads and can potentially trigger a variety of other schemata. Throughout life, all of us have repeated experiences, and these increase the probability of conjuring up certain schemata in memory. Therefore, a certain schema is likely to arise for a given person when he or she is confronted with a certain set of events. For another person, a different schema is likely to arise from exactly the same set of events. For example, a young child in a store may see a young women who is standing in line as *mother,* whereas a senior citizen standing in the same line may see the same woman as *young lady.* The cashier may see the young woman as *customer.* Each of these schemata may dictate different behavioral actions.

There have been many different uses of the PDP model for simulating human thinking and memory. One concrete example involves the program's ability to perceive common words the same way humans do. Consider the following explanation of word identification using the PDP (Figure 14–4).

When reading the word *cow* or *sky,* the program perceives several different characteristics of the word at the same time. At a feature level (the bottom line in Figure 14–4), the program analyzes separately the angles, lines, and halflines of the various letters. These features and their combinations determine possible letters (middle line). At the same time, the letters determine a set of possible words in memory (top line). The computer program then constructs a list of possible words that the feature and word analysis generates.

The model is called a PDP model because it assumes that processing occurs with all information simultaneously. For example, when we perceive the word *cat,* we process each letter at the same time. The model also assumes that we process the part and the whole simultaneously. We see each letter and the entire word in parallel—that is, at the same time. Therefore, the feedback from the word can influence our perception of any particular letter.

In Figure 14–4, all the features are interconnected, as are the letters, as are the words. When any feature, letter, or word is activated (thick arrows), the activation travels throughout the entire model. All letters and words are activated, although differentially depending on their preset strengths. There are also inhibitions (thin arrows) at each level that limit the next excitement of a letter or a word. The words also feed back to the letters, which also exert control on the net impact. At the feature level, the slanted line in the middle bottom will activate the letter W because this letter contains a slanted line. It will also inhibit the letter C because this letter does not contain a slanted line. At a letter level, the letter W will activate the word *cow,* but it will inhibit the word *sky.* At the word level, *sky* will activate the letter Y, but it will inhibit the letter C.

In the PDP model, knowledge is the connection among the units, not the units themselves. This is a big departure from the earlier theories that we discussed. The assumption is also consistent with the widely held view that the brain

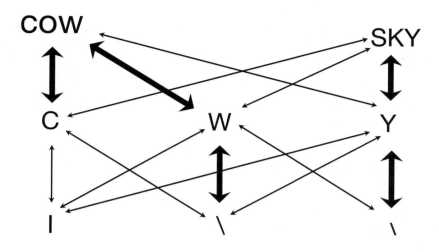

Figure 14–4 Hypothetical PDP Model of Word Storage, Activation, and Inhibition in Memory

functions by *mass action*. Action is not localized to one exclusive structure such as a single neuron or a specific site.

Research on Schema Theory As Applied to Head Injury

Hart and Parenté (1995) explored the PDP model's application to head injury by comparing the ability of persons with and without head injury to process ambiguous words. The study involved three groups: a group of 17 persons with mild head injury, a group of 17 persons with severe head injury, and a control group of 17 college students with no head injury. Each group saw the same words, and each word was obscured with blotches over one of the letters. The words were flashed for one-tenth of a second, and the participants were asked to write down what word they thought they had seen.

Control subjects were able to identify 100% of the words correctly. The mildly impaired subjects identified 71%, and the severely impaired subjects recognized 66% correctly. Each group generated a variety of responses to the words, and the pattern of responses differed from group to group. Given the differences in the groups'

responses, Hart and Parenté examined how the PDP model could explain the differences: What modifications to the PDP computer program would be necessary to get the model to simulate the pattern of correct and incorrect guesses that were obtained from each group? Because persons with traumatic brain injury are known to have difficulty inhibiting responses, changing the inhibition levels in the PDP program might allow the program to simulate the pattern of responses that were obtained with the head-injured groups. Head-injured persons also complain of slower processing. Hart and Parenté therefore predicted that the program would process at different rates depending on which group of subjects it was called upon to simulate.

Hart and Parenté (1995) analyzed the same words with the McClelland and Rummelhart (1987) PDP computer model. The program allows the user to modify several different processing characteristics. Among them are activation levels for the feature-to-letter portion of the analysis and for the letter-to-word analysis. Activation is the extent to which the feature, the letter, or the word stimulates a response and spreads to some other portion of the associative network. Inhibition levels are also reported for these two types of analysis. Inhibition is the degree to which the features, letters, or words suppress a response throughout the net. McClelland and Rummelhart's interpretation of activation and inhibition is that the former is analogous to the person's ability to construct choices, whereas the latter represents the ability to inhibit the possibilities. A measure of cycling was also manipulated. This is the number of times the program analyzes and reanalyzes the word before converging on a specific word. Cycling is analogous to the speed of processing prior to forming an impression.

Once again, Hart and Parenté (1995) reasoned that the inhibition and cycling parameters of the computer program would be the most likely candidates to modify because problems with inhibition and speed of processing are reported after head injury. They manipulated all components of the PDP model to determine if it could reproduce the pattern of word selections that resulted from each of the head-injured participant groups. For example, for the word *work,* these groups may have generated alternatives such as *word* or *worn* consistently. The program was then modified until it produced an identical distribution of correct and incorrect alternatives. This procedure was carried out with all three groups. Again, the goal was to determine how the program's thinking process had to be altered to simulate the performance of the different levels of head injury.

The results indicated that the most accurate simulation occurred by manipulating the inhibition and cycling parameters. Manipulating the activation parameter had relatively little effect. The program provided a nearly perfect reproduction of college student performance. Lowering the inhibition and cycling parameters produced almost perfect reproductions of mild and severe head injury group performances.

This finding has several implications for head injury rehabilitation. First, head injury seems to affect the person's ability to inhibit. This is certainly consistent with literature that states that head-injured persons are impulsive. It also explains the difficulty head-injured persons have with concentration and attention. This may result from the inability to inhibit the flood of ideas and information that comes to mind. They also

do not cycle as quickly or as much before settling on a schema that leads to a response. The results imply that therapists should teach clients to inhibit responding and to process more before settling on a response. For example, we teach clients to rehearse their statements mentally before saying them. Many of the processes discussed in the chapters on decision making are designed to force the client to process the situation thoroughly before making a decision or acting.

From Theory to Practice

The various organizational theories suggest several techniques that will help clients with head injury to organize more effectively (Mayer, 1983). Common to most of the theories is the notion that mental efficiency is the result of organization. Therefore, the basic goal of therapy is to train the client to extract the structure of whatever he or she experiences. A simple method for introducing this process is to force the client to recall organization rather than individual elements. This type of exercise demonstrates clearly how much faster and more accurate thinking and memory can be when the information is organized. It also illustrates the basic premise of the schema and TLC theories that elements automatically attach themselves to the organization.

We use a simple procedure for training perception of organization. In one variant of the exercise, clients see a page that contains 12 words: *red, dog, table, north, hand, Mars, Venus, foot, west, chair, cat, green.* The words are grouped semantically, by color of type, by size, by font style, and by position on the page. Thus, the client may organize the words in a variety of ways.

The client studies the page for a minute. Then the therapist asks him or her to recall the categories, not the words. The client may recall semantic categories: "Some were animals, some were body parts, some were planets," and so forth. Or he or she may recall categories of position on the page, color, size, or font style. The study-test procedure continues until the client settles on a specific organization. Afterwards, the therapist asks for recall of the individual words. The client then can use the organization to recall the individual elements. Usually, he or she is amazed to see that the words come to mind once the organization is stored.

A similar exercise serves the same purpose. The therapist dumps a number of unrelated household materials on the table. Scissors, tape, a knife, a fork, a rubber band, a paper clip, a toothbrush, and a comb could be used. The therapist lets the client study these materials, then removes them from view. The client must then describe the types of materials that are there rather than the individual items: for example, metal items or things found in an office. Once the client can recall the types of materials, the therapist should ask for recall of the individual items.

Both of these exercises not only show the client the value of organizing to improve recall but also allow the therapist to see the types of dimensions the client naturally uses to organize. It is important not to force the client to use an organization method that he or she does not feel comfortable using. The therapist should encourage the client to use any of the dimensions as long as it works. In our experience, organization by concrete features such as color or size is usually used in the early stages of recovery, whereas semantic organization is preferred by higher functioning clients.

The organizational theories also dictate that efficient processing is directly related to how well novel information is integrated into memory. Questions that force the client to discover the similarity of new and old information are helpful because they force the process of integrating the new information into the existing mental network. Therefore, as we discussed earlier in Chapter 11, we train clients to ask and answer "who, what, when, where, how, and why" questions when confronted with a novel situation: What is this the same as? What category does this belong to? What does this sound like? Look like? Smell like? Taste like? When did this occur? What social group does this person belong to? A similar procedure works when training reading comprehension. The therapist trains the client to extract the gist of the information by stopping after each paragraph and asking questions such as "Who is discussed? What is the paragraph about? When did the event take place? Where did it occur? Why did it happen? How did it occur?" This process is especially effective if the person summarizes the information into a tape recorder and can rehearse the summaries later.

According to schema theory, therapists should train the client to inhibit any response without first adequately processing the situation. This can be accomplished by training the client to spend more time thinking about a situation before making a decision. For example, we frequently teach clients to count to three mentally and to say a sentence in their mind before speaking. Adequate processing may also result from untimed test situations, forced rehearsal techniques, rereading of text passages, and self-paced instructional materials that promote errorless discrimination. For example, when clients receive instructions, they should repeat them to keep them from rapidly converging on an incorrect understanding of the instructions. When reading, they should reread several times to ensure that they do not immediately settle on a surface-level comprehension of the material. All of these techniques teach the client to inhibit responding until the situation has been fully processed.

ORGANIZATION OF THE EXTERNAL ENVIRONMENT

So far, we have discussed methods for organizing the client's mental knowledge base. These methods are certainly useful with most clients. But methods for organizing the client's external world are also quite helpful and relatively easy and expedient.

Attitude Adjustment

The therapist should begin by discussing several misconceptions about organization the client may have (Winston, 1989). One misconception is that being organized means being neat. Another is that neatness is a moral issue, so that not being neat means the client is a bad person. Organization means only that the client's system is functional. Regardless of how neat the person is, the real issue is whether he or she can find something when it is needed.

Unfortunately, most people are not taught how to organize when they are children. Many people grow up with poor organizational skills that they must unlearn and replace with more efficient organizational habits. The therapist will therefore have to teach many clients new skills, and the process may take quite a while. Clients may have problems with authority stemming from their relationship with their parents and teachers. They may see organization as something imposed on them by an outside authority. They may unconsciously resist authority even though they are now the authority figure. Some clients may rebel against organization because they do not want to be controlled by some external structure. Likewise, many clients are not punctual because they do not want to be controlled by time. These issues may surface during the course of treatment, and it is usually best to deal with them up front.

Teaching the client a part/whole strategy will greatly facilitate his or her ability to organize space and time effectively (Chaffin, Herrmann, & Winston, 1988). A part/whole strategy involves approaching every task as a large collection of smaller tasks. The client's first response to any task is to break it down into manageable subtasks. For example, if the client has to clean the car, the first step is to arrange the materials, such as soap, water bucket, window cleaner, and cloths, that are needed to perform the task. The second step is to move the car to a spot where the materials can be used conveniently—for example, next to a water spigot. Only when all the pieces are in position can the whole task be completed.

In many cases, completing the whole task is impossible within a limited time frame. The goal is then to complete some portion of the task and keep a record of what remains. It is important for the person to write down or record on a tape recorder what portion of the task he or she has completed. This is especially important for a client who has memory problems because writing down which subtasks were completed keeps the client from repeating them as well as reminding him or her of the whole task.

With these things in mind, we now suggest some specific strategies for training clients to organize their living and work spaces.

Organizing the Environment

Organizing the client's living and work spaces involves five basic principles. These are *consistency, accessibility, separation, grouping,* and *proximity.* The best way to teach these principles is immediately to apply each of them to the client's personal space. The goal is to make the environment work for the client rather than against him or her (Evans, 1980). To accomplish this goal, the therapist must first evaluate the client's living and/or work environment and work with the client, his or her family, employers, and so forth to arrange the space according to the above principles.

Consistency is literally the old adage *a place for everything and everything in its place.* For example, we typically recommend that a client or his or her family place a bowl on a pedestal table next to the front door. The client learns always to place important things like keys and wallet in the bowl immediately on entering the house. The rule of thumb is that a minute spent putting these things in the bowl is usually worth an hour spent looking for them later on. This same principle can be applied to other parts of the house. The goal is to get the client always to put things back in the same place. This principle capitalizes on the loci memory technique discussed in Chapter 11. The client begins using the mental image of the house as a memory aid.

Accessibility means that those things the client uses most often are physically closest and those that are less frequently used are placed furthest away. For example, the client may use the same plates and cups daily and may use others only occasionally or on special occasions. The dinnerware that are used most often are arranged in a cabinet that is closest to the daily activities of the kitchen. The other dinnerware or appliances are placed on shelves that are further away. The client's desk space is arranged so that the materials such as pens and paper are closest, whereas special books or other materials that are infrequently used are on shelves further away. The rule of thumb for accessibility is that the client should be able to stand in any room and physically reach out and almost touch those things he or she uses most often.

Grouping means physically aggregating those things that are commonly used with one another. For example, cups and plates are stored in the same cabinet. Coffee and the coffee pot are stored in the same place. Raincoats and umbrellas are stored in the same portion of the closet. This principle helps the client to remember where various things are located because they are physically related to those things with which they are used. Again, these techniques works quite well because the scene schema the client forms of the living or work space serves as a memory aid.

Separation means keeping things in logically distinct locations, categories, or time frames. For example, organizing clothes in a closet can be performed in several ways depending on the needs of the client. It may be necessary to organize the clothes by season of the year: that is, putting all the winter clothes on one side of the closet and all the summer clothes on the other side. Other clients may prefer organizing by type of clothing—for example, putting all the coats on one rack, the pants on another, and the shirts on a third. It is often a good idea to put mail into two piles based on the time frame for acting on a given letter, so that letters that require an immediate response go in one pile, whereas those that are interesting but do not require immediate action go into another. The best type of separation for any client will become clear only after a great deal of discussion and considerable trial and error.

Proximity means that items that are used with one another are at the same point of use. For example, cooking utensils should be hung as close as possible to the stove. We frequently suggest installing carousel racks above a client's island stove. Pots, pans, and utensils can be hung there

to ensure proximity to the cooking area. Computer supplies should be stored near the computer in an office context, and materials for the copier such as paper or toner should be kept next to the copier. This principle eliminates a great deal of wasted motion and searching for things.

Although these five principles of organization may seem simple, they usually require quite a bit of time to implement. We have found that organizing the entire house or workplace this way may take several days or weeks. The process should be done with the client so that he or she can learn the schema as it is being developed. It is also important to encourage the client always to return things to their proper place. In addition, once the schema is formed, the therapist can reinforce the image by asking the client to shut his or her eyes and then mentally walk through the house and describe where certain things are located. Once the client becomes accustomed to the schema, it is especially important to avoid reorganizing it. According to the principles of transfer outlined in Chapter 6, this would create an A-B-A-Br paradigm that would be extremely confusing, difficult to unlearn, and potentially dangerous.

CONCLUSION

This chapter described how humans organize their experiences and how head injury may limit a person's ability to organize effectively. We began with a discussion of several theories of organization and the implications of these theories for rehabilitation after head injury. The gist of this discussion was that we all organize new experiences unconsciously. After head injury, this automatic process may be destroyed. The therapist must therefore retrain the client to seek out the structure in new situations consciously. The schema theory of mental organization was discussed in particular detail because we feel that this is probably the best working model of organization. An experimental test that confirmed its usefulness as a model of cognitive dysfunction after head injury also suggested that clients may lose the ability to inhibit responding after head injury. They may therefore perform most tasks without adequate processing, which leads to an incorrect response. Several suggestions for treatment were discussed that were based on the implications of these theories.

REFERENCES

Alba, J.W., & Hasher, L. (1983). Is memory schematic? *Psychological Bulletin, 93*, 203–231.

Anderson, J., & Bower, G. (1973). *Human associative memory*. Washington, DC: Winston.

Bartlett, F.C. (1932). *Remembering: An experimental and social study*. Cambridge, UK: Cambridge University Press.

Bobrow, D.G., & Norman, D.A. (1975). Some principles of memory schemata. In D.G. Bobrow & A. Collins (Eds.), *Representation and understanding: Studies in cognitive science* (pp. 131–149). New York: Academic Press.

Bransford, J.D., & Johnson, M.K. (1972). Contextual prerequisites for understanding: Some investigations of comprehension and recall. *Journal of Verbal Learning and Verbal Behavior, 11*, 717–726.

Chaffin, R., Herrmann, D.J., & Winston, M. (1988). A taxonomy of part-whole relations: Effects of part-whole relation type on relations naming and relation identification. *Cognition and Language, 3*, 1–32.

Collins, A.M., & Loftus, E.F. (1975). A spreading activation theory of semantic processing. *Psychological Review, 82*, 407–428.

Eckhardt, B.B. (1990). *Elements of schema theory*. Unpublished paper, University of New Mexico, Albuquerque.

Elliot, A., & Parenté, F.J. (1995). *Conditions of positive transfer in part/whole learning*. Unpublished master's thesis, Towson State University, Towson, Maryland.

Evans, G.W. (1980). Environmental cognition. *Psychological Bulletin, 88*, 259–287.

Hart, P., & Parenté, R. (1995). First tests of a parallel distributed processing model of word perception after traumatic brain injury. *Monographs of the Human Learning, Cognition, and Information Processing Laboratories, 1*, 1–10. Towson, MD: Towson State University.

Herrmann, D.J., & Chaffin, R. (1986). Comprehension of semantic relations as a function of definitions of relations. In F. Klix (Ed.), *In memoriam Herrmann Ebbinghaus: The proceedings of the Ebbinghaus Centennial Conference*. Amsterdam: North Holland.

Kant, E. (1987). *Critique of pure reason* (2nd ed., N. Kemp Smith, Trans.). London: Macmillan. (Original work published 1787)

Kintch, W., & van Dijk, T.A. (1978). Toward a model of text comprehension and production. *Psychological Review, 85*, 363–394.

Klix, F. (1986). Recognition processes in human memory. In F. Klix (Ed.), *In memoriam Herrmann Ebbinghaus: The proceedings of the Ebbinghaus Centennial Conference*. Amsterdam: North Holland.

Mandler, J.M. (1984). *Stories, scripts, and scenes: Aspects of schema theory*. Hillsdale, NJ: Lawrence Erlbaum.

Mayer, R.E. (1983). *Thinking, problem solving, cognition*. New York: W.H. Freeman.

McClelland, J.L., & Rummelhart, D.E. (1987). *Parallel distributed processing: Explorations in the microstructure of cognition: Vol. 2. Psychological and biological models*. Cambridge, MA: MIT Press.

Minsky, M. (1975). A framework for representing knowledge. In P.H. Winston (Ed.), *The phychology of computer vision* (pp. 211–277). New York: McGraw-Hill.

Neisser, U. (1976). *Cognition and reality*. San Francisco: W.H. Freeman.

Piaget, J. (1952). *The origins of intelligence in children*. New York: International University Press.

Quillian, M.R. (1968). Semantic memory. In M. Minsky (Ed.), *Semantic information processing*. Cambridge, MA: MIT Press.

Quillian, M.R. (1969). The Teachable Language Comprehender: A simulation program and theory of language. *Communications of the Association for Computing Machinery, 12*, 459–476.

Rabinowitz, J.C., & Mandler, J.M. (1983). Organization and information retrieval. *Journal of Experimental Psychology: Learning, Memory, and Cognition, 9*, 430–439.

Rummelhart, D.E. (1975). Notes on a schema for stories. In D.G. Bobrow & A. Collins (Eds.), *Representation and understanding* (pp. 211–236). New York: Academic Press.

Schank, R., & Abelson, R. (1977). *Scripts, plans, goals, and understanding*. Hillsdale, NJ: Lawrence Erlbaum.

Smith, E.E., Shoben, E.J., & Rips, L.J. (1974). Structure and process in semantic memory: A featural model of semantic decision. *Psychological Review, 81*, 214–241.

Twum, M., & Parenté, R. (1994). Maximizing generalization of cognitions and memories after traumatic brain injury. *NeuroRehabilitation, 4*(3), 157–167.

Winston, S. (1989). *Getting organized*. New York: Simon & Schuster.

Chapter 15

Retraining Problem-Solving Skill

The task of solving problems after a head injury is usually difficult and frustrating. Nevertheless, certain techniques may be helpful to persons with head injury or to anyone who wants to apply a systematic and efficient method to solving daily problems (Bransford & Stein, 1984). The purpose of this chapter is to summarize much of the literature on problem solving and to make it useful for those individuals who may have cognitive limitations due to head injury.

We begin by reviewing some of the classic theories of problem solving and taking from them, wherever possible, the more practical aspects that have implications for work with traumatically brain-injured clients. We then describe the characteristics of good problem solvers along with some common problem-solving styles. We describe in detail the stages of problem solving, review several methods for generating solutions to problems, and discuss personal barriers to problem solving. Finally, we discuss a mnemonic that we use to teach problem-solving skills to head-injured clients.

THEORIES OF PROBLEM SOLVING

A problem arises whenever a person is unable to think of a means to achieve a certain goal.

Therefore, problem-solving skill is the ability to discover the means that will achieve some desirable result. There are several theories of human problem solving. Our brief review focuses on three well-documented theories that have specific implications for teaching this type of skill to head-injured persons. Other authors, such as Ellis and Hunt (1993) and Wickelgren (1974), provide a more comprehensive presentation of these and other theories of solving problems.

Stimulus-Response Theory

Perhaps the earliest theory of problem solving came from the stimulus-response theory of animal learning. This explanation assumed that as we develop, we learn a number of problem-solving habits through the process of stimulus-response conditioning. These are used to solve any new problem. We remember those that are successful and tend to use them again; however, we may use some more frequently than others (Hull, 1930). Techniques are organized hierarchically (in a *habit hierarchy*) according to how frequently we use them. When one does not work, we try the next. Those that consistently solve the problem are the ones we are most likely to try first in any new problem-solving situation.

Stimulus-response theory predicts that head-injured clients begin their therapy with a set of prelearned problem-solving strategies that may no longer be organized in a hierarchy. Some clients may have more intact or more efficiently organized problem-solving habit hierarchies. Some may have a greater number of habits at their disposal. The theory suggests that the goal of therapy is both to organize the hierarchy and to provide the person with new strategies that will be useful in a variety of different situations. It is also necessary to practice problem-solving strategies so that they eventually become habitual.

Gestalt Theory

The gestalt theory of problem solving is not as well defined as the stimulus-response theory. The basic idea is that problem-solving skill depends on the person's ability to visualize the problem context (Kohler, 1947; Wertheimer, 1945). Good problem-solving skill is literally the ability to reorganize or negotiate either the context or the goal to achieve a solution. The gestalt school emphasizes the mental processes of insight and creativity, which are crucial for effective problem solving. It also underscores the need for periods of long pondering before the person will achieve the insight that produces the solution. Unlike the stimulus-response theory, which describes the gradual development and organization of a problem-solving strategy, the gestalt approach describes an all-or-nothing process of insight.

The problem-solving process, according to gestalt theory, involves four distinct stages. In the first stage, the person *identifies* the problem. This may require a great deal of thought and analysis. In the second stage, the problem and its possible solutions incubate. The person literally tries not to think about the problem. In the third, the person experiences a period of *illumination* whereby the solution suddenly comes to mind. In the fourth stage, the person *applies the solution* and evaluates whether it produces the desired result.

The methods of problem solving discussed below draw heavily on the gestalt problem-

solving approach. The therapist first trains the client to visualize the problem context and to spend a great deal of time thinking about it and pondering the possible solutions. The client eventually learns that problem solutions seldom occur slowly over time but more often all at once, usually when he or she least expects them to occur. In addition, it is necessary to train the client to use creative problem-solving strategies that produce solutions that are novel or unique to the specific situation. This will keep the client from using only one method that may or may not be useful in all situations.

Information-Processing Theory

The information-processing approach suggests that humans create mental recipes that will produce a solution to a problem. The recipes also dictate action in situations in which a failure to solve the problem is experienced. Newell and Simon (1972) specified three necessary characteristics of information-processing models of problem solving (Simon, 1987). The first involves the *data* that must be fed into the human computer. These include things like historical facts about the problem, assumptions, constraints of the situation, and other specific facts the person should consider. The second involves the *problem space,* which includes the person's global assessment of the problem or hunches about the solution. The third characteristic is the existence of an *operation,* or a specific course of action that the person can use to carry out the solution.

This theory implies that problem-solving skills break down after a head injury for many different reasons (Hallux, 1990). The person may not be able to collect the necessary data. The client's set of potential solutions may also be limited or too highly structured. This is quite common after damage to the frontal lobes, which limits cognitive flexibility. It may also be difficult for the person to analyze the available facts in a way that leads to an appropriate course of action. Many of the techniques and strategies mentioned below involve building skills that would improve each of these areas of human information processing.

As the reader will see, each of these theories has influenced the development of the methods described below. Although our proposed therapy approach borrows heavily from the gestalt approach, we suggest that each theory has merit. Perhaps the major value of any of these theories is that it forces us to think about the possible ways for people to solve problems and the various things that we must do to teach this skill effectively. Along these lines, it is also helpful to describe the characteristics of people who are good problem solvers. In this way, we can illustrate ways clients can change their thinking and their behavior to facilitate problem solving.

CHARACTERISTICS OF GOOD PROBLEM SOLVERS

Ellis and Hunt (1993) identified several personality characteristics of good problem solvers. Good problem solvers are typically *preoccupied with the problem*. They devote a great deal of mental effort to the solution and do not simply put it aside or procrastinate taking action until the situation becomes critical at some later date (Reisbeck, 1987). Good problem solvers are seemingly challenged by the problem and feel a sense of urgency about solving it. Consequently, the solution becomes a priority for them.

Good problem solvers *frequently dream solutions*. They often think about the problem just before they go to sleep at night and will sometimes awaken to a solution or experience the solution upon waking. The solution will frequently come to mind when they least expect it. The fact that the solutions come to mind unexpectedly suggests an insightful process.

Good problem solvers are *set breakers*. This means that they frequently shift from one solution to another until one is found that solves the problem. It is therefore important to teach head-injured clients that there is no single correct solution in most situations. There are usually two or more solutions that solve any problem; 10 different people may produce 10 different solutions. It is also important to teach the client to use favored methods but to discard solutions that do not produce a result and then to try another.

Clients should always consider the broadest possible range of solutions. No solution should be immediately rejected because it is too unconventional. None should be excluded from consideration. The therapist should therefore teach the client to consider as many solutions as possible, to evaluate each one, and to add others to the list as they occur.

Good problem solvers *do a dry run of solutions* before committing to any one. This allows them to experience unexpected problems before they actually waste considerable time, money, or effort on an unsuccessful attempt to solve the problem. Much of the therapist's time will be spent creating mental simulations of problem solutions and training clients to ask the question "What would happen if I were to implement this solution?"

Good problem solvers *break the problem down into pieces*. If the problem is large, good problem solvers will reduce it to a series of smaller problems and then attack these one at a time. The therapy process involves taking a client's personal problems, breaking them down into manageable pieces, and then solving the pieces to illustrate the gradual solution of the whole.

Good problem solvers *clarify problems and solutions* by explaining them to others. Explaining the problem to someone forces the client to organize the problem, to summarize it, and to eliminate parts of it that are vague or misunderstood. Discussing potential solutions with others clarifies the client's assessment of these solutions and allows others to give feedback and to suggest alternative solutions.

Good problem solvers *listen to others' proposed solutions*. Therapists should therefore encourage clients not only to explain the problem to others but to solicit advice from others before committing to a possible solution. It is also important for the client to determine consensus opinion about which solutions are most likely to work. In many cases, simply doing what most people suggest will produce the fastest solution.

Good problem solvers purposely *create incubation time*. The therapist should therefore remind clients that when the solution evades them, they should put it aside and expect that at some future time, usually when they least expect it, the solution will come to mind.

To summarize, the characteristics of good problem solvers suggest an insightful process whereby the person carefully considers a variety of solutions, does a dry run of potential solutions, discusses the various solutions with others, and then makes a decision (Bedard & Chi, 1992; Chi, Glaser, & Farr, 1988; Ericsson & Smith, 1991; Schoenfeld, 1985). These characteristics are consistent with gestalt theory, and it is difficult to see how the other theories would explain all of them. Regardless of which theory is correct, the major issue for the therapist who works with head-injured clients is that clients must learn and adopt these behaviors as part of their overall approach to problem solving. We therefore typically discuss these behaviors in detail with our clients and encourage clients to adopt them in response to any novel problem-solving situation.

STAGES OF PROBLEM SOLVING

Ellis and Hunt (1993) outline several stages of problem solving. These stages were also discussed by Polya (1957), who documented the process in students who solved math problems (see also Schoenfeld, 1985). We elaborate on these stages later, but for now we simply describe the various steps.

Understanding the problem is perhaps the most important step because without a clear representation of the problem, it is difficult to obtain a clear and accurate solution. The person will have to understand not only the problem but also the costs and benefits that are associated with each potential solution. This is especially difficult in situations in which the problem may be emotionally based or difficult to represent or frame.

The next step, *generating possible solutions,* is similar to Polya's (1957) concept of devising a plan. It implies that we develop not only one plan of action but others as well and select the one that is the most likely to succeed. One problem that head-injured persons share is their fixation on a single solution or option to the exclusion of others. It is therefore necessary to teach the cli-

ent to generate as many possible options as possible before committing to any one (Runco, 1990). It is also helpful to acquaint the client with the types of solutions he or she may generate.

It is worthwhile elaborating the generation stage of problem solving because it is so crucial to forming a solution. Ellis and Hunt (1993) pointed out that most problems can be broken down into one of three types: those that require the person to see some unifying relationship that summarizes the problem, those that require a conversion solution, and those that involve rearrangement. The first type of problem is commonly observed on analogy tests in which the person discovers the relationship between four words. For example, the analogy "Color is to painter as car is to mechanic" requires an abstraction that relates the words in a meaningful and predictable way. Abstracting these types of unifying relationships is often difficult for a head-injured person.

Conversion solutions require changing something into something else. A common example involves converting a word problem into a mathematical formula to solve it. Conversion solutions are difficult for many head-injured clients. For example, clients who have difficulty with their marriages after a head injury have a hard time converting this rather complex situation into observations that link facts with social consequences—for example, "I am no longer working, so our lifestyle has deteriorated because our income has been reduced by two-thirds."

Most people extract these observations from experience (Lave, 1988). Head-injured clients, however, may need a great deal of coaching and help from family members before these conversion rules will become apparent in real-life situations. It may take months before a person may see or accept these rules. Psychosocial group training is an effective way to help the person see how his or her behavior can have consequences and the general rules that predict a social outcome. This usually involves asking the person what social problems he or she has and then trying to break each problem down into a conversion rule. For example, one client could not understand why others did not talk to her. After one group session, the other clients pointed out that she constantly interrupted and dominated the conversation. The group then converted the client's problem into a solution rule: "Speak less than half the time."

Rearrangement solutions involve taking existing elements and putting them in a different order or sequence to effect a solution. These solutions are relevant when the person has everything necessary to solve the problem but needs to organize the solution. For example, a head-injured client may have difficulty finding things in the home. The problem may be solved by simply organizing the home and training the client to maintain the organization. This same procedure is also necessary when training time management. Head-injured clients often have a difficult time arranging their days so that they can avoid wasted effort and time. To-do lists and appointment calendars can be quite effective as a solution to this type of problem.

Evaluation, the next stage of problem solving, occurs after the client has generated a possible solution. In this stage, the person tries to determine whether the solution is likely to succeed. He or she then makes a mental ranking of the options that are possible and thereby limits the set to those he or she will try.

The last stage, *following through,* involves not only trying one of the solutions but also evaluating, after the fact, whether it solved the problem. All too frequently, we assume that simply doing anything will solve the problem, only to find that what we did had little or no effect at all. It is therefore important to teach head-injured clients that they need to ascertain whether the solution produced the desired result. If it did not, the person must go through the same stages again until he or she finds an acceptable solution.

In our experience, training problem solving with head-injured clients is a difficult but rewarding process. Much of what the therapist does with the client involves training the person to step back and visualize a larger picture. For example, the relationship may simply involve teaching the person to recognize that certain behavior patterns result in social rejection, certain physiological signs indicate anger, or frequent symptoms represent a certain medical condition. The training will usually require drill and practice and is best

performed with individual problems that are unique to the client (Mayer, 1987). The overall process works best when the therapist trains the client to devote about 60% of his or her time to representing or understanding the problem. This is especially important in situations in which the problem is emotionally based. The other factors require about 40% of the solution effort. These factors include things like defining options, criteria for evaluating whether a solution had the desired effect, and limitations to the possible solution options. These aspects of the total problem-solving process are certainly important; however, nothing can replace a correct problem representation.

FORMULAS AND STRATEGIES FOR PROBLEM SOLVING

Clients may use a formula or a strategy method of problem solving. According to Cohen (1971), *formulas* are set procedures that will always work, but not necessarily efficiently. *Strategies* are rules that may produce a quicker solution but may not always solve the problem. There are advantages and disadvantages to each method. Formulas are best used when the problem has potentially few solutions. For example, if the client knows to call one of three numbers in case of an emergency, he or she can try all of them in sequence until one solves the problem. This method will always work, assuming the person has the time to call all three numbers. The strategy method is to call the number that is most likely to solve the emergency the fastest. This may result in a quicker solution, although if the other person does not answer, the client may still have to call each number to get help.

Teaching strategies is often difficult but may be the only way a client will ever be able to solve problems. This is because many problems are too complex for formula solutions to solve efficiently. Consequently, we discuss strategy solutions in detail and point out their applications in a variety of different contexts. The therapist should understand that all clients will have some strategies for solving problems. Their strategies are usually inefficient, however, and the goal for the therapist will be to acquaint the client with more efficient action plans and to illustrate how each works in the real world.

The Trial-and-Error Strategy

This strategy involves thinking of a possible solution and then trying it out until the person determines whether the problem was solved. There may be a large number of possibilities, and to try them all would take a long time. The number of possible solutions is a rough index of the person's representation of the problem. It is also an index of what Newell and Simon (1972) have labeled the problem space. In situations in which there are many possible solutions—that is, the problem space is quite large—the trial-and-error strategy can be quite cumbersome and inefficient.

The trial-and-error method may also be inefficient in situations in which the person has never encountered the problem in the past. In these novel contexts, the problem space and the range of possible solutions restrict the client's ability to generate solutions. Unfortunately, many clients attempt trial-and-error solutions even when they are obviously ineffective or when there are numerous possible solutions. The therapist must then redirect the client's strategy.

The Action-Goal Strategy

This is a strategy that requires breaking a complex problem up into its simplest parts or subgoals. The client first specifies the overall goal, then defines what is necessary to reach that goal in forward sequence. The action-goal strategy is appropriate when the problem-solving situation involves goal setting and the attainment of subgoals along the way.

The action-goal strategy is also appropriate for solving more common problems. For example, when the television does not turn on, the client may learn to break the problem up into simpler subgoals. The question "Is the television getting electricity?" is a first step. This subgoal may lead the person to check to see if the television will function with other wall outlets, to check the plug, or to see if there is a blown fuse. Assuming that the television is getting electricity, will it work on any channel? With or without the cable hookup? Answers to these questions narrow the range of possible solutions to the problem by proceeding in a forward direction from simplest to more complex solutions. As the client answers questions at each stage, the possible cause of the problem and the range of solutions narrow until the most appropriate response emerges.

The Backwards Strategy

This strategy is roughly the reverse of the action-goal strategy (Bransford & Stein, 1984). The person first defines the solution or goal, then asks what would have been necessary to achieve it in backwards sequence. For example, if the client's goal is to increase the number of friends and acquaintances, then the appropriate question is "How does a person who has many friends behave?" This form of thinking requires the person first to assume that the goal has been achieved and then to ask what would have been necessary to achieve it. For example, many people find it easier to solve mazes by starting at the finish and backtracking steps to the start box. Criminal investigators are forced into backward problem solving by virtue of their job. They must always ask what must have happened for the criminal to have been able to commit the crime.

Training the person with head injury to use the backwards strategy requires that the person first define the goal or the problem clearly. Only then can he or she determine what behaviors or conditions could have precipitated such an event. For example, we recall one distraught client whose girlfriend had recently broken off their relationship. This was a big problem because he had become quite depressed and isolated. The therapist first asked the client to define the problem and any acceptable solutions. After several redefinitions of the problem, the client finally realized that his girlfriend wanted to be married and to have a family. He recognized that this was literally impossible because he would be unable to support a family for many years to come. Once he accepted the loss of his girlfriend, he was able to form a new goal, which was to have friends and to meet other women. He observed that others who had reached this goal were cheerful and pleasant most of the time. They placed themselves in situations where they could meet people their own age. Using the backwards strategy, he and the therapist were able to work out a clear strategy that would help him to eventually move beyond the loss of his girlfriend.

The outcome of this story is rather interesting. Although the client wanted to form new friendships, he was reluctant to meet people in face-to-face social situations. He therefore began using his personal computer and communicating with others on local bulletin board systems via electronic mail and conferencing systems. He was able to establish several regular "cyberfriends" this way and eventually started meeting them in person. He now regularly communicates with many friends internationally on the Internet.

The Contradiction Strategy

As the name implies, the contradiction strategy implies that to solve a problem, the person does just the opposite of what would be necessary to solve a problem: He or she asks, "What would I have to do to keep from solving this problem or ever achieving my goal?" The value of this question is that the person often realizes that his or her behavior is actually causing the problem.

For example, one of our clients was becoming increasingly reclusive and depressed and potentially suicidal. When the therapist said to her, "Let's assume that you wanted to be very depressed and reclusive. What would you have to do to get to that point?" she answered, "Stay indoors all day, watch soap operas, get high, and eat." Others in her group began to point out that these were precisely the behaviors she exhibited. The fact that she had generated the response was the first step toward realizing that her behavior was completely contradictory to her goal. The solution to her problem was to behave in exactly the opposite manner.

This strategy is best exercised in a group context. As Parenté and Stapleton (1993) pointed out, "Clients listen to clients." That is, a client is more likely to listen to and remember a point that a certain behavior is maladaptive when it comes from the group than when it comes from a therapist.

The Explanation and Consensus Strategy

This strategy is crucial during the later stages of the problem solution. Once the solutions have been identified, it is necessary to evaluate which ones are the most likely candidates for success before the person wastes time on the unlikely candidates. Explaining the problem to others is perhaps the best way to ensure that the person will organize the problem mentally. This is because the person must organize the problem and the possible solutions to explain them so that another will understand them. We commonly insist that the client explain each potential solution without using common filler phrases such as "you know" or vague assertions such as "I just think or feel that way!" This method ensures that the person will not retreat into vague explanations.

We also insist that the client explain the problem to at least three different people who listen and offer an opinion concerning the feasibility of his or her solutions. The usefulness of this technique will usually depend on the time frame for the solution. At a minimum, however, explaining the problem to even one person will help the client clarify and organize the problem space and also make it easier to evaluate the possible solutions.

Obtaining a *consensus* involves mentally averaging the opinions of all the persons to whom the client has explained the problem. The value of consensus-based solutions has been known for decades (Parenté & Anderson-Parenté, 1989). Generally, the consensus solution of a group is more accurate than the solution that any individual in the group would have reached.

The Giving-the-Problem-a-Rest Strategy

This strategy may actually result in a quicker solution in the long term. Most of us have had the experience in which the solution to a nagging problem simply popped into our minds when we were in the shower, brushing our teeth, or asleep. Often, the fatigue associated with a problem prohibits the solution. Taking a break reduces the fatigue and allows the solution to surface. One additional trick is to think about the problem just before going to sleep. This method will sometimes facilitate dreaming the solution.

PERSONAL BARRIERS TO PROBLEM SOLVING

Therapists will usually have to retrain problem solving by overcoming bad habits that the client has used over the years. There are at least three bad habits. The first involves a client's tendency to solve each new problem using the same strategy. This is called a *set fixation*. The second concerns a client's failure to perceive that different elements of a problem may have different roles when they occur in another problem. This is called an *element fixation*. The third is the client's inability to generate novel solutions, which is a major problem that often predates the head injury. This is called *rigid creativity*.

Set fixations occur when a person tries a certain rule or strategy and initially experiences some success with it (Mayer, 1983). According to the stimulus-response theorists, the set is rewarded and becomes the dominant way of solving the problem. The client may therefore continue to apply the rule or strategy despite the possibility that some other strategy may lead to a faster solution. Only with lack of reward or punishment will the dysfunctional set be eventually replaced in the hierarchy. Until it is, the old problem-solving strategy may keep the client from solving a problem because he or she does not perceive that the situation has changed. For example, one client who had sustained a frontal lobe injury had been an athlete before his injury. He had always solved his physical problems by exercising. After his injury, he persisted in physical exercise as a means of solving what was now a different kind of problem. Only after years of unemployment, social isolation, and limited cognitive gains was he convinced to try another

problem-solving solution. Unfortunately, the only way to deal with set fixations is to let the person continue to use the dysfunctional set until it fails.

Element fixation is the tendency to see the elements of a problem in only one way. We fail to realize that the same element can function in a variety of ways depending on the problem. The person fails to see the solution to the problem because he or she does not see the changed role of some part of it. For example, a client who was getting a divorce tended to blame his wife for every negative aspect of his life since his head injury. Because she had rejected him, he could only see her as an enemy. He could not accept that she cared for him and wanted to create a supportive friendship despite their divorce. Because of his tendency to see this element of his life myopically, he resisted any effort of help if she were involved. For a time he ended up homeless because he refused to accept a living arrangement she had negotiated. He quit a job that she had helped to find. He could not solve his major problems in life because of his fixation with his wife as an enemy and his inability to accept that she could play a positive role in his rehabilitation even though they were no longer married.

Rigid creativity is more than just set and element fixation. It is the inability to expand the problem space, to develop novel solutions, or to take risks. It often is the result of personality variables that were in effect long before the person's head injury. Creative persons tend to be individualistic, intuitive, self-accepting, introverted, and independent. With respect to problem solving, they are interested not only in generating a solution but in coming up with novel and unique solutions. They purposely try to redefine the problem so that it can be solved in a novel manner. Training the production of original ideas can improve this type of problem-solving process.

THE SOLVE MNEMONIC

We created the SOLVE mnemonic to help persons with head injury remember the problem-solving procedures outlined above. These steps have been conveniently summarized by the word SOLVE, which is used to provide the client with a step-by-step process that he or she can invoke in any novel problem-solving situation.

The first step in using the SOLVE mnemonic is to have the client memorize it to the point at which he or she can repeat the steps dictated by each letter. The therapist should give the mnemonic to the client and quiz his or her recall of the information during each session. Once the client learns the mnemonic, the next step is to provide practice using it in real life. We usually ask the client to provide an actual problem, which the client and therapist then analyze using the mnemonic. This works well in a group situation, in which each client can participate in the problem-solving process.

1. *(S)pecify the problem.* To specify means both to define and to analyze the problem. We recommend that clients spend at least 60% of the problem solution time specifying the problem parameters. This entails several tasks.

The first involves identifying the data that define the parameters of the problem. Along these lines, the client must determine the magnitude of the problem, its urgency, and its possible ramifications. For example, a client who is faced with an impending divorce must ask if he or she will be able to function without the support of a spouse. What will happen to the family finances? What effect will a separation have on the children?

A second aspect is the necessity of defining the problem in concrete terms. This is usually difficult to do when the problem is emotionally rooted. It is, however, imperative that the client specify the problem in concrete language to make the solution tangible. This aspect of the specification process may take quite a while. Often a client will specify a problem in vague terms— for example, "I'm not happy!" It may therefore take a great deal of discussion before the person can respecify the problem as "I am not happy with the social isolation I am experiencing since my head injury."

The third stage involves getting the client to ask questions such as: Is this a problem that demands a solution right now? Is this really my problem, or does it belong to someone else? What

would happen if I were to do nothing? Such questions may lead the client to realize that he or she may not be responsible for the problem or its solution. This type of realization can often provide relief from endless hours of mental preoccupation and perseveration. This is because clients often obsess about a problem only to conclude, at some point, that there is nothing that they can do to solve the problem anyway. If possible, the client should come to this realization sooner rather than later.

For example, one client reported that his major problem was that he could no longer do anything or go anywhere with his daughter. He felt that he was now an embarrassment and a burden to her and that she did not want to be seen with him in public. His daughter had recently begun college in a different state and was no longer living at home. His problem was therefore less relevant than he had imagined because it was physically impossible for him to interact with her as he once did.

2. *(O)ptions.* What are the possible actions or solutions to the problem? This step requires writing out on paper any option that is even remotely feasible. These should be specified in concrete terms and the list should be inclusive. We usually write out a list of possible options underneath a definition of the problem, preferably on the same page. This sheet is then given to the client as a summary of the session and as an example of how the client should approach the process in the future.

3. *(L)isten to others' advice.* Once the problem has been defined and the potential solutions delineated, the next step is to discuss these issues with others. This process has two purposes. First, it gets the client to output the problem, and the process of discussing the problem helps the client to organize it and to form a clear mental representation. Second, others will provide feedback about the client's clarity of explanation, ask questions that point out specific areas of vagueness, and provide insights the client may never have considered. They will also suggest options that may have previously gone unnoticed.

As mentioned earlier, one of the main reasons for listening to others' advice is that the group consensus opinion will usually be superior to any other solution the client may have devised. This is simply to say that if the client decides to do what the majority suggests, that solution will usually be correct. At a minimum, the client can rest assured that this simple formula will be sufficient to solve more problems. Additionally, a client may often be more receptive to the suggestions made by a group than to those of the therapist simply because the members of the group have experienced head injuries, whereas the therapist usually has not. This is consistent with a well-established principle of social psychology that people tend to trust others who are most like them.

4. *(V)ary the solution.* The therapist will have to walk the client through all of the different strategies mentioned above. The goal is to look at the problem from as many perspectives as possible. The therapist should go through all of the possible strategies, from the action-goal strategy through the contradiction strategy, before making any firm decisions concerning a course of action. It is also important to use the opportunity to point out any clear examples of set or element rigidity. As with the other steps, the therapist should write out the results of the session so the client can review the materials.

5. *(E)valuate if the solution actually solved the problem.* Once the client has decided upon a solution, it is necessary to determine if the solution actually solved the problem. Often, clients will fall into the trap of thinking that any solution they decide to implement has solved the problem. They never go back and see if the solution actually hit the mark. They may then believe the problem has been solved, only to realize too late that it has not. The evaluation process depends on a clear specification of the problem in the first place. Evaluation usually implies measures of one form or another that are used to identify changes in the problem space. The client must then monitor the measures to determine if the solution has had a desired effect.

As an example of the SOLVE mnemonic, consider the client who is faced with an impending divorce.

1. *Specify the problem.* The client's initial representation of the problem is "My wife doesn't want me around anymore!" The therapist works with the client to respecify this problem by accurately specifying the problem space. Questions such as "How does your wife see you as a different person now?" and "How has your role in the family changed?" clarify the global complaint. After much discussion, the client realizes that the real issue is that his wife is now forced into a provider role, and there has been a role reversal.

The next stage involves specifying the problem space in concrete terms. The therapist and client agree that the real issue is that the client's wife is no longer a housewife and that she can no longer be as attentive as she once was. She is also faced with work-related stresses that she has never dealt with before. The client also acknowledges that he now spends the majority of his time at home and virtually none of his waking hours at work. His wife now expects that he will take on some of the duties that she used to perform around the home because he is there most of the day.

The focus of conversation turns to the client's willingness to do anything about the role reversal problem. He decides that he is willing to redefine the problem and that the first step is to ask his wife whether she still wants to continue their marriage and to ask her to clarify her perceptions of their marital difficulties. He concludes that an attempt on his part to change roles may save the marriage.

The client and therapist discuss the urgency of the problem. They both agree that if something is not done soon, the marriage will end in divorce. Therefore, doing nothing could have disastrous results. The client agrees that he and his wife share responsibility for the problem and for the effectiveness of the proposed solution. They both reaffirm their commitment to saving their marriage through mutual change. The wife reaffirms her respect for her husband but qualifies the feeling by saying that her respect is partially dependent upon her perception of his willingness to change and to work within his limitations.

2. *Options.* The client lists a variety of options that vary from doing nothing and letting the marriage deteriorate to making changes that he and his wife mutually agree upon. He considers separating and living alone, going back to

work in his former job, getting a new job, or starting a home-based business. The therapist and client discuss the feasibility of each of these options and conclude that trying to change the marriage roles is the easiest to implement and that he should try this first before making any other drastic lifestyle changes.

3. *Listen to others' advice.* The client has several family members that he trusts, and he agrees to discuss the various options with each of them prior to making a final decision. One suggests formal marriage counseling. Another suggests that the client use his free time to go back to school and retool for a different profession. Most agree that attempting a mutually agreed-upon role reversal would be the best first step. They also agree that marriage counseling would be helpful to facilitate the role reversal process as it progresses. There is no clear agreement about long-term vocational goals, only that the deteriorating marriage is the most important problem and needs an immediate solution. The client then agrees to accept the consensus opinion of his family members, to begin taking on household duties, and to seek out marriage counseling.

4. *Vary the solution.* The client and therapist discuss several different ways of looking at the problem. The action-goal method suggests that they define a series of subgoals and work toward each in sequence. Several of these have already been established and accomplished. For example, the first step is to commit to solving the marital problem. The next step is to define possible alternative employment goals for the client. A third step is to attempt one or more of those employment goals. In this way, the client and therapist develop a road map that clearly specifies the long-term goal and the subgoals necessary to reach it.

With the backwards approach, the client first defines his long-term goal. This is quite difficult to do in a concrete manner. It is hard for the client to know what type of training or job options he would like to pursue. There are simply too many possibilities, and many of his options depend on the extent of his recovery. His only conclusion is that he wants to contribute to the family income and that he would like to work from home. He concludes that he therefore has

to get additional computer training and establish a home-based computer system to accomplish this goal.

With the contradiction strategy, it is easier for the client to visualize an outcome. He concludes that if he wished to thwart his efforts he would procrastinate any positive effort simply by doing more of what he is currently doing, which is nothing. This brings him to the conclusion that his current behavior is actually counter to all of his stated goals.

5. *Evaluate.* Six months later, the client and therapist go through the SOLVE mnemonic again, redefine the problem, and develop a new solution. Briefly, the client begins a home-based business doing bulk mailings. The client and his wife agree to begin going to church activities. The client agrees to return to therapy every 6 months to go through the SOLVE mnemonic.

CONCLUSION

This chapter evaluated three theories of problem solving: stimulus response, gestalt, and information processing. None of these theories has been specifically applied to head injury rehabilitation. Several personality characteristics of good problem solvers were discussed. Generally, good problem solvers are preoccupied with the problem and devote a great deal of mental effort to the solution. They are seemingly challenged by the problem and feel a sense of urgency about solving it. Consequently, the solution becomes a priority for them.

Good problem solvers frequently dream solutions. They are set breakers and frequently shift from one solution to another until one is found that solves the problem. They always consider the broadest possible range of solutions. They attempt to do a dry run of solutions before they commit to any one solution. They break down the problem into pieces and clarify solutions with explanation. They listen to others' proposed solutions and will typically implement the consensus opinion. When no solution comes to mind immediately, they deliberately create incubation time.

The chapter also examined the general stages of problem solving that most cognitive psychologists have investigated. These include generating possible solutions, evaluating the feasibility of each option, and following through with the most likely candidate. The methods most people use to come up with a solution are either formulas or strategies. Formulas are set procedures that will always lead to a solution but may be time consuming and cumbersome to implement. Strategies are shortcut methods that will probably produce a solution in most cases. These include the trial-and-error strategy, the action-goal strategy, the backwards strategy, and the contradiction strategy.

Explanation and consensus opinion are crucial to the problem-solving procedure. Requiring clients to explain their thinking verbally at each stage forces them to clarify their representation of the problem. Listening to other representations and implementing what the majority feel is the best solution will usually produce a correct solution.

There are several personality barriers to effective problem solving that therapists should discuss with clients. These include set fixation, element fixation, and rigid creativity. Set fixation is the tendency to use the same method of problem solving in all situations. Element fixation is the tendency to see elements that are common to different problems in exactly the same way in every problem. Rigid creativity is the tendency to restrict the output of potential options.

The chapter ended with a discussion and example of the SOLVE mnemonic. The letters of this mnemonic provide a framework that can be used by head-injured clients in a variety of different problem-solving contexts. The S reminds the client to *specify* and define the problem. The O is a reminder to generate possible solution *options* and to evaluate the feasibility of each. The L is a reminder to discuss the various options with others and to *listen* to their advice. The V reminds the client to *vary* the solution. Finally, the E is a reminder to *evaluate* any solution option the client decides to implement.

Teaching problem-solving skills is an art. It usually is most effective with higher functioning clients, and it is always most successful when the therapist applies the principles outlined above to the client's unique problems. It is easy to train in a group situation because clients typically enjoy applying the process to other people's problems as well as their own. It is important for the therapist to encourage clients to discuss their problems during the session so that they can serve as real-life examples of the process.

REFERENCES

Bedard, J., & Chi, M. (1992). Expertise. *Current Directions in Psychological Science, 1*, 135–139.

Bransford, J.D., & Stein, B.S. (1984). *The ideal problem solver.* New York: W.H. Freeman.

Chi, M.T.H., Glaser, R., & Farr, M.J. (Eds.). (1988). *The nature of expertise.* Hillsdale, NJ: Lawrence Erlbaum.

Cohen, J. (1971). *Thinking.* Chicago: Rand McNally.

Ellis, H.C., & Hunt, R.R. (1993). *Fundamentals of cognitive psychology.* Madison, WI: W.C. Brown & Benchmark.

Ericsson, K.A., & Smith, J. (Eds.). (1991). *Toward a general theory of expertise.* Cambridge, UK: Cambridge University Press.

Hallux, K.J. (1990). Problem solving. In D.N. Osherson & E.E. Smith (Eds.), *Thinking.* Cambridge, MA: MIT Press.

Hull, C.L. (1930). Knowledge and purpose as habit mechanisms. *Psychological Review, 57*, 511–525.

Kohler, W. (1947). *Gestalt psychology: An introduction to the new concepts on modern psychology.* New York: Liveright.

Lave, J. (1988). *Cognition in practice.* Cambridge, UK: Cambridge University Press.

Mayer, R.E. (1983). *Thinking, problem solving, cognition.* New York: W.H. Freeman.

Mayer, R.E. (1987). Teachable aspects of problem solving. In D. Berger, K. Pezdek, & W. Banks (Eds.), *Applications of cognitive psychology.* Hillsdale, NJ: Lawrence Erlbaum.

Newell, A., & Simon, H. (1972). *Human problem-solving.* Englewood Cliffs, NJ: Prentice Hall.

Parenté, R., & Anderson-Parenté, J.K. (1989). *Delphi inquiry systems.* In G. Wright & P. Ayton (Eds.), *Judgemental forecasting* (pp. 129–156). New York: John Wiley.

Parenté, R., & Stapleton, M. (1993). An empowerment model of memory training. *Applied Cognitive Psychology, 1*, 585–602.

Polya, G. (1957). *How to solve it.* Garden City, NY: Doubleday.

Reisbeck, C.K. (1987). Realistic problem solving. In P.E. Morris (Ed.), *Modeling cognition.* Chichester, UK: John Wiley.

Runco, M.A. (1990). *Divergent thinking.* Norwood, NJ: Ablex.

Schoenfeld, A.H. (1985). *Mathematical problem solving.* Orlando, FL: Academic Press.

Simon, H.A. (1987). Information-processing theory of human problem solving. In A.M. Aitkenhead & J.M. Slack (Eds.), *Issues in cognitive modeling.* Hillsdale, NJ: Lawrence Erlbaum.

Wertheimer, M. (1945). *Productive thinking.* New York: Harper & Row.

Wickelgren, W.A. (1974). *How to solve problems.* San Francisco: W.H. Freeman.

Chapter 16

Training Conceptual Skills

Conceptual skills are the most fundamental aspects of thinking (Whorf, 1956). They are the skills that allow us to understand our surroundings and to make sense of the events that occur there. Conceptual thinking occurs whenever something becomes clear to us. For example, conversations frequently include statements such as "Do you see what I mean?" or "Now I get the point." Our language is replete with phrases that imply getting the big picture and images of mental light bulbs that suddenly turn on at the moment of comprehension. Conceptual skill is a centerpiece of the cognitive system. Indeed, much of what we call cognition is the process of understanding concepts, learning rules, and testing hypotheses (Bourne, 1966; Mayer, 1983).

Concepts, rules, and hypotheses are slightly different from each other. A *concept* is a special combination of ideas that has a particular meaning. For example, most people can picture a police officer, but this mental image may differ from our concept of a detective or private investigator. *Rules* are concepts that direct behavior by attaching consequences to the behavior. For example, the rules of our legal system specify that homicide will be punished by imprisonment or possibly death. A *hypothesis* is a prediction that certain concepts are related in a specific way. For example, a detective may hypothesize, on the basis of the available evidence, that a certain person committed a homicide. The cognitive skills of forming concepts, rules, or hypotheses may be impaired after a traumatic brain injury.

Our goal in this chapter is to explain how concept learning occurs and to identify things that affect the process. We therefore begin by defining concept learning along with other related ideas such as rule learning and hypothesis testing. We will then present a method for explaining new concepts to head-injured persons. The same method can be used by head-injured persons to express themselves clearly.

THE CONCEPT OF A CONCEPT

Concepts are called by various names, including *abstractions, schemas, ideas, structures, and understandings* (Hampton, 1981). We form concepts almost every day, typically when someone is explaining something to us that we do not understand or with which we have no familiarity or previous experience. People with head injury have a difficult time forming concepts. They may also have a difficult time explaining their ideas to others. The challenge, when teaching concept learning to head-injured persons, is to develop a method of making concepts clear to clients and helping clients make themselves clear to others. This technique usually involves teaching other skills, such as categorization and hypothesis testing.

Categories are groupings that are defined by their attributes or the rules that either distinguish them or connect them in some way (McCloskey & Glucksberg, 1978; Mervis & Rosch, 1981; Smith & Medin, 1981). Categorization is the process of seeing these groupings among our experiences. This is, perhaps, the basis of concept and rule acquisition. For example, the fact that a square and a triangle have straight lines is a concept. This concept becomes a rule when we misidentify a circle or square on a geometry test and suffer some consequence as a result of the misidentification.

Concepts and categories are not necessarily the same thing. Concepts are usually thought of as more complex categories. For example, a concept can be an idea such as the theory of relativity, which contains several categories of thought such as mathematics and physics. However, in some situations, concepts and categories are the same.

Categories/concepts can be verbal and semantic, visual and perceptual, fuzzy, or basic. *Verbal/semantic* categories refer to the types of abstractions we form when using language. For example, whenever we see similarities between two authors' writing styles, we form a verbal category. *Visual/perceptual categories* are those that involve physical traits that are seen or felt. For example, we frequently learn "the feel" of driving different types of cars. We can learn the categories of modern versus classical art from exhibits in a museum.

Zadah, Fu, Tanaka, and Shimura (1975) discussed the notion of *fuzzy concepts,* which are ideas with uncertain boundaries. For example, a person's concept of art is obviously fuzzy because of the broadness of the field. Barsalou and Medin (1986) described fuzzy concepts as having "graded structure" in the sense that examples can vary in their ability to define the category. For example, the word *computer* typically conjures up the idea of a desktop model seen in most offices. However, the fuzzy boundaries of the concept include a variety of different types of computers including laptops, notebooks, sub-notebooks, palmtops, and personal data assistants.

Rosch, Mervis, Gray, Johnson, and Boyers-Bream (1976) described *basic-level concepts* that are tangible, concrete, and easy to learn. Basic-level concepts define a category's distinctive features but are also rooted in common experience. They are usually defined by words that are common in the language of the speaker. They are easy to understand and particularly useful because other people are readily familiar with the terms. For example, *dog* and *cat* are easier to understand than *canine* and *feline* or the names of particular breeds such as *boxer* or *Siamese*. Basic-level concepts are easy for most people to visualize. For example, many people have a difficult time imagining a four-wheel drive vehicle. It is easier to think of a "jeep." This is because although we have some idea of the attributes that define a four-wheel drive vehicle, we are more familiar with the concept of the jeep. Similarly, although we all have a fuzzy image of a copier, we often visualize a Xerox machine.

The above discussion leads to several practical conclusions that are useful when working with head-injured clients. First, it is instructive to explain to the client that the idea of a concept is not easily defined. This is because there are many types of concepts and it may be difficult to define their graded or fuzzy boundaries precisely (McCloskey & Glucksberg, 1978). Second, training concept learning involves teaching the client to focus on commonalities of their experience that define a concept. Third, explaining concept learning is most effective when the process is personally relevant to the client. Fourth, concepts are best presented at a basic level (Mervis & Rosch, 1981), in simple, common terms, using examples that are readily available in the culture. To clarify these points, it is first necessary to survey briefly the available literature on concept learning and to abstract from it what is relevant to the retraining process.

THEORIES OF CONCEPT LEARNING

At least three theories of concept acquisition have been described. Medin (1989) described the *attribute theory,* which assumes that humans define concepts and categories by creating mental lists of features (Bourne, 1966). For example, to learn a concept such as *Roman,* the person creates a list of mental attributes such as *legion, Rome, Ben-Hur,* and so forth. Each of these examples and features is equally descriptive of the concept because they all share the element *Roman* (Smith & Medin, 1981).

The implication for training concept learning is that the therapist must teach the client to recognize and list mentally attributes that define the concept in order to make it clear and precise. Indeed, the longer the mental list of attributes, the clearer the concept.

Prototype explanations of concept learning assert that we learn and remember the gist or core features of a concept. The common features that we extract from different examples define the prototype. The prototype is stored, and thereafter, the person uses it to identify new examples. For example, we all have a prototype of a U.S. president, a superhero, and a college professor. Prototypes vary from person to person and may or may not be accurate. They change with experience and age. Prototypes are similar to basic-level concepts except that prototypes can apply to technical concepts that are too esoteric to be considered basic level. For example, most physicists have a prototypical concept of a nuclear reaction. The average person may have heard this phrase but cannot visualize the concept.

More recent explanations of prototype learning involve the notion of the *schema,* discussed earlier in Chapter 14. McClelland and Rummelhart (1986) defined a schema as a network of cells in the brain that lies dormant until it is somehow activated by various stimulus features such as visual or auditory sensations. The more features that are present, the greater the chance that a particular schema will be activated. For example, when someone calls on the telephone and we do not know who the person is, we can frequently activate his or her schema by certain characteristics of the voice.

The implication of prototype and schema theories for head injury rehabilitation is that the number of relevant features determines the ease with which the concept can be learned. Moreover, both theories assert that learning both features and prototypes is important for concept learning.

Accordingly, the best way to teach the concept of a four-wheel drive vehicle to a head-injured person would be to show a Jeep, a Hummel, a Land Rover, a Bronco, and so forth and then to point out the common features.

Exemplar theory is actually the reverse of the prototype theory. According to exemplar theory, examples of concepts are stored in memory and continuously updated with new instances. This theory predicts that our ability to categorize new instances of the concept is based on the similarity of the new instances to the existing set of examples. For example, although the Hummel is probably the best example of a prototypical four-wheel drive vehicle, until recently it was used only by the military. Most civilians would not have recognized it or categorized it as a four-wheel drive vehicle because it was not a member of the existing set of examples. Now that it is available for civilian use, it is mentally integrated into the set of four-wheel drive vehicles that many of us would recognize.

The implication of exemplar theory for head injury rehabilitation is that a client's understanding of a concept depends on the therapist's ability to generate real-life examples that define it. Because the theory assumes that the client does not store prototypes, the more examples the therapist uses, the clearer the concept will be.

RULE LEARNING

As we mentioned earlier, rule learning is similar to concept learning but involves not only understanding a system but also associating some consequence with it. Rule learning refers to the person's sense of a system, order, or structure. It also refers to the ability to respond appropriately within this structure (Wason, 1960). For example, most people know how to behave in restaurants because they have been socialized to behave appropriately in this type of situation. They know the rules, so to speak. However, in some social situations, they may not know the rules—for example, rules for laying out a formal dinnerware place setting. This may require training to ensure that they do not do something inappropriate.

Persons with head injury may have difficulty learning rules and understanding social concepts. This is because they may be unable to foresee consequences and have a very difficult time testing hypotheses. The therapist may therefore have to teach them systematic methods for behaving in various social situations. This type of training may be quite difficult to implement. Many rules cannot be taught by experience because of the danger involved when an inappropriate behavior is punished. For example, we cannot teach head-injured persons that they are hypersensitive to drugs and alcohol by letting them try these substances. This practice may result in injury or arrest. Therefore, most rule learning involves paired-associate training with descriptions of situations and behaviors that the therapist labels as appropriate or inappropriate. The process may be quite tedious because clients may not remember the rules. One way to enhance the learning is to provide simulations and role playing to ensure that clients form a mental image of the situations that define the rules.

CONCEPTUAL STRATEGIES

Hypothesis testing, rule learning, concept learning, and problem solving are all interrelated skills (Bourne, 1966; Bruner, Goodnow, & Austin, 1956; Mayer, 1983). It is therefore difficult to discuss them separately. However, one difference is that hypothesis testing is an activity that typically precedes the formation of a rule or concept or the solution to a problem. Hypothesis testing is the process of trying out several different possible concepts, solutions, or rules in some systematic way and determining which is the most useful.

There are several methods of testing hypotheses and forming concepts and rules, some of which are more effective with head injury survivors than others. The therapist will probably find that many clients have never heard of these techniques, although some may use them unwittingly. Many clients will default to the trial-and-error method. Wherever possible, we suggest that the therapist direct the client's conceptual strategies to the conservative focusing and focus gambling approaches.

We have found that the *conservative focusing* method leads to the most rapid concept acquisition with traumatically brain-injured clients. It involves gradual manipulation of one aspect of a complex situation at a time until the correct concept is formed. It also involves mentally ranking the various attributes of the situation and manipulating first those that are most likely to produce some result. For example, if the toaster in the kitchen will not work, we must first determine why it is broken before we can fix it. We may conclude that the socket may be defective. We then decide to plug it into another socket. If it still does not work, we have eliminated the socket as a potential explanation of "brokenness." We may next suspect a blown fuse, so we replace it. However, if we were to replace the fuse and then try a different wall outlet, we would be manipulating two possible explanations at the same time. We would then never know which one was the correct concept.

The major implication for training after head injury is that the person should learn to manipulate only one aspect of the situation at a time. Although this process may seem tedious, it typically leads to the most rapid concept learning and problem solutions. It is especially important when the concept involves some form of problem solving. Unfortunately, many persons with head injury may not have the frustration tolerance to withstand the process. They may therefore resort to a *focus gambling* strategy.

Focus gambling differs from the conservative focus technique in that several possible hypotheses may be tested simultaneously (Bruner et al., 1956). Many head-injured clients test hypotheses this way, and they often achieve some degree of success. Indeed, the method does produce more rapid concept acquisition and rule learning than a trial-and-error process. The obvious problem, however, is that the person may not ever identify the core concept. He or she may think that the concept or rule is clear, only to find later on that some other aspect or relevant feature was the true concept.

For example, one client told us that his wife complained that their marriage was deteriorating. She told him that "she did not know him any longer, and they were becoming strangers."

He decided to do something about the problem and began to buy her gifts, spend more time at home, do more housework, and try to behave in a manner reminiscent of his premorbid personality. This tactic manipulated several aspects of the concept simultaneously in an attempt to focus on the problem and to eliminate it, thereby saving the marriage. The client was gambling on the hunch that one or more of these changes would regain his wife's affections. The situation did improve, although his wife eventually told him that his being around more often and sending her gifts had little to do with her affections for him. His personality change was the major problem for her, and she appreciated most his efforts to regain his previous personality.

Perhaps the most efficient method of focus gambling uses a *split-half* strategy. The person first identifies the possible set of things that make up the concept and then splits the set in half and manipulates one half at a time. In our example above, the client's optimal method would have involved abandoning half of the set of behaviors he changed when it did not change his wife's attitude. He would then work on the remaining set of behaviors and change these until he finally hit upon a set that made an obvious improvement in her response to him. He could eventually split this set in half, repeatedly, until he finally limited the set to the behaviors that were crucial.

Clearly, it would have been easier simply to ask his wife about her dissatisfactions and adjust his behavior accordingly. However, there are many concept-learning situations in which this will not work. If the person uses a focus gambling strategy, the split-half method will probably be the best approach. But it is difficult and often tedious, and it typically requires a great deal of initial coaching and guidance from the therapist.

Scanning involves forming global hypotheses about a concept and modifying them in accordance with rewards and punishments. For example, we may all drive slightly over the speed limit until we are stopped by a police officer and ticketed. At that point, the concept of speeding may change along with our behavior so that we no longer exceed the speed limit on that particu-

lar stretch of highway. We may, however, still speed on other highways. We learn that speeding is permitted, but only on certain roads, whereas other areas have more strictly enforced limits. This type of hypothesis testing usually goes on until an intricate, although often incorrect, rule structure is acquired.

Scanning does not usually produce rapid concept learning because it assumes a relatively passive method of testing hypotheses. The person continues doing something until he or she is punished. The individual may then modify the concept slightly until he or she is forced to modify it again. Scanning also requires a good memory because the person must recall what rules were tested in the past and what outcomes resulted. This is one reason why a scanning strategy does not work well for head-injured clients.

Trial and error is one of the more common hypothesis-testing procedures. Many head-injured clients will say that they "just keep going until something works." This method, however, produces the least rapid concept learning and least efficient means of testing hypotheses or learning rules. We usually alert the client to the fact that it is easy to fall into using the trial-and-error method but that in the long run it will not work nearly as well as the other methods outlined above.

Which of these methods works the best will depend upon the client's level of functioning. In our experience, persons with mild head injury can master the conservative focusing strategy. However, moderately to severely impaired clients do not possess the frustration tolerance that this strategy requires. The focus gambling strategy is one that many clients prefer and use spontaneously. They are usually unaware of the split-half method but can learn to use it. The scanning strategy is one that we never endorse or train. This is because it usually yields slow solutions and requires a good memory for complex rule structures. Unfortunately, this method is one that many clients adopt. Therefore, our goal is to acquaint the client with the pitfalls of the scanning and trial-and-error strategies and to try to dissuade their use. We then try to teach or to substitute the conservative focusing or focus gambling strategies.

TRAINING CONCEPTUAL SKILLS

In our experience, persons with head injury form concepts, learn rules, and test hypotheses in much the same fashion as those who have not had a head injury. They simply do so more slowly and are usually less able to articulate the process. We therefore define the process for them and break it down into several distinct stages. These include (a) identifying attributes; (b) manipulating the concept, rule, or hypothesis; and (c) eliminating inappropriate responses. With respect to social rule learning, suppose the client is trying to understand the rules associated with an appropriate social greeting. It is first necessary to identify the elements of social greeting, such as handshakes, salutations, and eye contact. The client must then manipulate these and gain experience with how each affects the other person's behavior. The client may then focus on those aspects that have the greatest discernible effect on the social exchange.

These three steps can also improve social problem solving. For example, suppose the client does not comprehend why no one understands his or her speech. The first step is to identify all the things that could affect speech reception, such as the rate, quality of pronunciation, clarity of word usage, and so forth. The next step is to manipulate each of these, one at a time, and notice the effect on others' comprehension. Finally, the person must focus on those that seem to improve the intelligibility of his or her speech.

Ellis and Hunt (1993) provided several specific suggestions for training concept acquisition. These include (a) generating new examples of the concept, (b) considering both positive and negative examples, (c) thinking of a variety of different examples, and (d) focusing on the relevant features of the concept. We agree with this listing, although we suggest that therapists teach clients to do them in a specific sequence. Our system is explained below.

Like the Ellis and Hunt (1993) method, this procedure involves teaching concepts by example. The method is used with clients as well as with those therapists who work with the clients. The goal is to get all who are involved in the therapy process to participate in a common concept communication process.

The first step involves teaching the client to identify the concept. This happens most rapidly by using examples that illustrate what the concept is. These are called *positive examples*. For example, if we wished to explain the concept of "'90s fashions for women," clearly the best way to get our concept across would be to use photographs from present-day women's magazines. After seeing several of these, most people would have some idea of how we conceptualized 90s fashions for women. We would use this as a means of establishing the prototype or the schema. However, the prototype would still have fuzzy boundaries because there would be so many variations in makeup, hairstyle, dress, height, weight, and so forth. We could never know if our concept was anything more than a fuzzy prototype. Nevertheless, this is the best way to establish the initial core concept.

At this point, it is necessary to have the client form hypotheses about the underlying concept. For example, we would ask the client to state verbally what he or she thinks defines the therapist's concept of '90s fashions for women.

The next step is to use *negative examples*. These provide the client with information that eliminates some of the irrelevant details and focuses the client's attention on those aspects that are central to the concept. For example, we could go to women's magazines from different decades and select pictures that did not conform to our concept of '90s fashions for women. These could include pictures from the '60s, '70s, and '80s. Over the years, we have found that it is crucial to follow positive examples with negative examples but that the reverse order does not work. That is, traumatically brain-injured clients seem to learn the concepts more rapidly when the positive examples are presented first, presumably because they form the prototype and subsequently refine it. Once again, the therapist asks the client to verbalize any hypotheses that may come to mind during this stage.

The third stage involves *sharpening* the concept by pointing out irrelevant features. For example, hair color or height may be an irrelevant aspect of our concept. This may not be apparent when the client sees the pictures, and he or she may require our pointing out the irrelevancy. This tends to make the features more distinctive. Enhancing the distinctiveness can be accomplished by having the person verbalize the concept in his or her own words. Another technique is to present the positive and negative examples simultaneously and point out the irrelevant features. This technique relieves the burden on the person's memory, whereas the first technique encourages active processing of the examples.

The final stage of concept acquisition involves *verification*. This simply means that the therapist must now ask the client to identify new instances of the concept. In our example, we show clients new pictures and require identification of those that express our concept of '90s fashions for women. This is the final test to see that the concept has been acquired and is usable. If the client can do this, we are satisfied that he or she has acquired the concept to the point at which it is functional.

Two additional procedures enhance the training of conceptual skills and rule learning. The first is verbal explanation. We typically ask clients to explain something to the rest of the group and videotape the explanation. Ideally, the topic will be something that the rest of the group members know nothing about. We have accumulated many of these tapes and use them to illustrate the concept of a clear presentation. After reviewing several of the tapes, we first show those that are especially good examples of clear explanations. We ask the clients to form hypotheses about why these presentations were so easy to understand. We next show tapes in which the presentations are especially unclear and follow these with questioning to facilitate hypothesis formation. Finally, we ask the clients to isolate those aspects of talks that determine their clarity. Verification occurs when the clients again try to explain something to the group.

The same procedure can be used to train the concept of clear writing. We have collected many short writing samples from clients on a variety of topics ranging from "my biggest problems in life" to "what I'm interested in doing vocation-

ally." We present the clearest of these samples first to illustrate the concept of clear written expression. After reading about 10 of these examples, we ask the client to form hypotheses about what makes the paragraphs easy to understand. We then show the client negative examples—those that are illegible, tangential, extremely brief, or otherwise poorly written. This is followed by further discussion of hypotheses about why they are poorly written. The next step is to focus on those aspects of the paragraphs that are central to the concept of clear writing. Finally, we verify that the person understands the concept by having each person write another paragraph and share it with the group.

This concept- and rule-learning method also applies when teaching social skills. This usually involves modeling procedures and videotaping. For example, the therapist shows the client tapes of someone asking out a potential date. The client first sees tapes that illustrate obvious successes. He or she generates hypotheses about why the approach was successful and what things will affect whether the person accepts the invitation. For example, how well do the two people know one another? How nicely is the asking party dressed?

The person next sees tapes that illustrate refusals and generates hypotheses about what went wrong. For example, one tape shows a person approaching a total stranger on the street. Another illustrates a person asking for a date in the negative—for example, "You wouldn't want to go out with me, would you?" Another shows an unshaven and unbathed man approaching and getting refused because of his appearance. Clients generate hypotheses about why these attempts failed. Finally, the client verbalizes what aspects of the social approach determined whether the person succeeded.

Ellis and Hunt (1993) also outline other crucial features that affect concept acquisition and rule learning. The following are aspects of their discussion that are relevant to head injury rehabilitation:

1. *Orderly arrangement.* Head-injured persons will often require a great deal of struc-

ture and perceptual clarity. It is therefore necessary to define the concept or rule as concretely as possible and to arrange the concept demonstration in a logical sequence. For example, when explaining the concept, it is first necessary to explain it in words and then go through the step-by-step sequence outlined above (use of positive examples, use of negative examples, sharpening the concept, and verification) to limit the amount of information presented at one time.

2. *Compactness of the display.* Concepts are often difficult to understand because they are too broad or expansive. It is therefore necessary to break the concept down into smaller pieces or to limit discussion of the concept to easily processed examples. For example, the wife of our client above would be well advised to stay away from explanations such as "You're just not the same" because these present a picture that is too vague and difficult to understand. A more concrete and specific statement of the problem, such as "You leave all the decisions to me now," is much clearer.

3. *Consistency of concept in sequential problems.* If the purpose is to teach a general rule or strategy, then it is necessary to display the rule or concept as clearly as possible in each example. For example, if the goal is to show how to ask a person out for a date, the elements of a successful attempt must be apparent in each example. If the goal is to illustrate how to write a clear paragraph, examples of clarity must be presented until the person forms the core concept.

4. *Saliency of the examples.* The ability to understand the concept will depend on the saliency of the examples the person uses to explain it. The more abstract concepts (Hampton, 1981) are obviously more difficult to explain because it is hard to find concrete examples. The goal is to choose examples that make the concept clear. The general rule of thumb is that the more salient the examples, the more quickly the client will understand the concept. It is also best to begin with a very salient example and gradually to introduce more abstract ones.

5. *Use of color for highlighting.* Color helps establish a vivid first impression. It also adds interest value to the process. For example, the concept of '90s fashions for women is best explained using color photos. In the writing example, sections of the article that best illustrate clarity or expression can be highlighted in red.

6. *Complexity and the number of relevant dimensions.* The number of relevant dimensions also determines the person's ability to understand concepts. The implication is that for the client to learn a new concept, he or she must first identify its relevant dimensions. It is therefore necessary to have the client define these dimensions up front. This may lead to the conclusion that the concept is too difficult or fuzzy to describe.

7. *Concept novelty.* This aspect determines the person's ability to find relevant examples. The therapist should impress upon the client that if there are no examples of this concept, then it may be impossible to explain.

8. *The importance of feedback.* This is, perhaps, the most important aspect of teaching conceptual skills. It is essential for the therapist to impress upon the client that feedback is a two-way street. To understand a novel concept, the client must get the other party to provide examples in the manner outlined above. At a minimum, he or she should always ask, "Can you give me an example of what you mean?" This question will force the person who is explaining the concept to provide the positive examples that are so crucial for the person's understanding. We typically train our clients to say one of three things: (a) "Can you give me an example of what you mean?"; (b) "Here is an example of what I mean. Tell me if it's clear"; or (c) "Let me see if I can think of an example of what you're telling me. Please tell me if I get it." These questions elicit verification of a client's understanding.

CONCLUSION

We have shown the similarities between concept learning, rule learning, and hypothesis testing. All of these higher cognitive skills involve learning by example. It does little good to explain concepts or rules to clients in the abstract. The person must see examples and test hypotheses with real-world information. The optimal order of examples will proceed from positive to negative. This sequence will help to establish the prototype and facilitate the gradual elimination of the irrelevancies. Once the concept or rule has been established, the therapist should focus on the critical features that define it. Finally, the therapist should verify that the client understands the concept or rule by giving concrete examples that require using the rule to generate an appropriate response.

REFERENCES

Barsalou, L.W., & Medin, D.L. (1986). Concepts: Static definitions or context-dependent representations? *Cahiers de Psychologie Cognitive, 6*, 187–202.

Bourne, L.E. (1966). *Human conceptual behavior.* Boston: Allyn & Bacon.

Bruner, J.S., Goodnow, J., & Austin, G.A. (1956). *A study of thinking.* New York: John Wiley.

Ellis, H.C., & Hunt, R.R. (1993). *Fundamentals of cognitive psychology.* Madison, WI: W.C. Brown & Benchmark.

Hampton, J.A. (1981). An investigation of the nature of abstract concepts. *Memory and Cognition, 9*, 149–156.

Mayer, R.E. (1983). *Thinking, problem solving, and cognition.* New York: W.H. Freeman.

McClelland, J., & Rummelhart, N. (1986). *Parallel distributed processing: Explorations in the microstructure of cognition.* Cambridge, MA: Bradford.

McCloskey, M.E., & Glucksberg, S. (1978). Natural categories: Well defined or fuzzy sets? *Memory and Cognition, 6*, 462–472.

Medin, D.L. (1989). Concepts and conceptual structure. *American Psychologist, 44*, 1469–1481.

Mervis, C.B., & Rosch, E. (1981). Categorization of natural objects. *Annual Review of Psychology, 32*, 89–115.

Rosch, E.H., Mervis, C.B., Gray, W.D., Johnson, D.M., & Boyers-Bream, P. (1976). Basic objects in natural categories. *Cognitive Psychology, 8*, 382–439.

Smith, E.E., & Medin, D.L. (1981). *Categories and concepts.* Cambridge, MA: Harvard University Press.

Wason, P.C. (1960). On the failure to eliminate hypotheses in a conceptual task. *Quarterly Journal of Experimental Psychology, 12*, 129–140.

Whorf, B.L. (1956). *Language, thought, and reality.* Cambridge, MA: MIT Press.

Zadah, L.A., Fu, K.S., Tanaka, K., & Shimura, M. (1975). *Fuzzy sets and their application to cognitive and decision processes.* New York: Academic Press.

Chapter 17

Retraining Decision Making

This chapter presents strategies for retraining decision-making skills. It begins with a discussion of decision making and the various skills that allow a client to frame a decision, to define it, and to come to the best possible decision, given the available input. The techniques described below are similar to the method of cost-benefit analysis that is commonly used for making business-related decisions (Larrick, Morgan, & Nisbett, 1990; Wheelwright & Makridakis, 1980). We then present a simple method that therapists can use to teach clients a procedure that will apply in most decision-making situations. The chapter ends with a discussion of examples of how the decision-making training procedure would apply with specific clients.

WHAT IS A DECISION?

The word *decision* implies that there is a set of possible actions and that the person must decide among two or more options. Most decisions can be framed in one of three ways. The person can either make a definite response or not make it. The person can either react in some way or not react. Finally, the person can decide among a variety of different actions. This latter position implies that there are several options and that the person has identified them beforehand.

Perhaps the most difficult part of making a decision is to determine exactly what the person must decide (Doerner, 1987). This is also the most important part of the decision-making process because the set of possible decisions may not include the correct one unless all possibilities are carefully considered in advance. The process therefore entails spending considerable time identifying options (Janis & Mann, 1977; Kahneman, Slovic, & Tversky, 1982; Reason, 1990).

One problem with teaching decision making is that most head-injured persons will require a rather simple method that they can retain and implement on demand and with a certain amount of flexibility. Conventional methods of cost-benefit analysis may be too complex for most head-injured persons to appreciate or to see how it will be useful in their everyday lives. However, the same principles can be reworded in ways that are easy for most clients to understand and use.

TECHNIQUES OF DECISION MAKING

The Analytic Method

One method of decision making involves answering eight questions about the decision before taking any action (Dawson, 1993). This method can be useful to head-injured clients because it helps them to comprehend the complexities of the decision. We recommend beginning the decision-making process by having the person consider the decision according to the following eight frames of reference.

1. *What are the boundaries or limits of the decision?* What options fall within those limits? Whatever options satisfy the limits are the ones that deserve consideration. For example, the client may have to decide whether to go to one of several movies. Each of the movies may be equally attractive. Let us assume that one limit the client must consider is what time he or she will return home after the movie. If only one of the movies ends by that time, then the decision is made for the client because only the one movie satisfies the constraint.

2. *Does the decision involve a problem or an opportunity?* Often what seems to be a problem can result in substantial gain if the person views the situation as a potential opportunity. For example, many head-injured clients believe they are faced with only two options: returning to work or accepting Social Security disability payments. This seems like a problem until the client discovers that both are possible on a trial basis. The problem then becomes an opportunity because a third option is to receive SSDI payments and work, perhaps part time, at the same time.

3. *Is there an existing policy that dictates the decision or will otherwise override any decision the person may make?* If there is, the client must investigate existing policy and make a decision that accords with that policy. For example, many clients want to drive again after their injury. However, the decision to drive is often aborted by state laws that first require medical examination, retaking the written driving examination, and medical clearance.

4. *Can the decision be classified?* One common type is the *go/no-go decision,* which requires deciding to do something or not to do it. Usually the person has only one option and must decide whether to exercise it—for example, whether to go to the movies. *Right/wrong decisions* involve determining the correctness of a decision. That is, several potential solutions are available or

apparent, and the client must discover which one of them is correct. For example, solving a math problem will usually require making a right/wrong decision. The *evaluation decision* assumes that several potential solutions are known and the person must evaluate which is the best. For example, the client may have to decide which of several movies he or she should attend. *Discovery decisions* involve identifying potential options in situations in which none are known. It is therefore necessary for the therapist to acquaint the client with the various types of decisions and to discuss how they apply in everyday life. For example, one client's water heater broke for the first time since he had moved into his house. The therapist and client used these techniques to decide which of several water heaters would replace the original.

5. *Is the problem real or imagined?* Decisions or opportunities can be unnecessary or unrealistic. To answer this question, the client must determine the tangible characteristics of the decision and decide if the problem actually affects him or her and therefore requires a decision. For example, one client obsessed over the unnecessary decision of whether to file suit because his neighbor's dog frequently soiled his lawn. Another client anguished over an unrealistic decision to apply to NASA to become an astronaut for future Mars exploration.

6. *Does the decision involve money or people or a combination of both?* Money decisions usually involve training the client to choose the solution that yields the best financial outcome. With people decisions, we teach clients to choose a solution that creates a "win-win" situation—that is, one in which everyone involved either benefits from the decision or, at a minimum, does not lose as a result of the decision.

7. *What would happen if the person decided to do nothing?* Many decisions are unnecessary because the need to make the decision would dissipate spontaneously if nothing were done. For example, one client's marriage was in a state of rapid decay. He decided that if he did nothing to rectify the situation, his wife would leave him. He also admitted that his marriage had been deteriorating before his injury and that his wife had decided to leave him then. He therefore con-

cluded that his wife would leave him anyway, even if he did nothing to save their marriage.

8. *Is the problem unique?* When it is especially difficult to frame the decision, it is usually because the person has not encountered it before. The solution is to consult someone who has made a similar decision in the past. The second possibility is that no one has ever made a similar decision. This requires a unique solution, which is usually a combination of decisions that may have worked in other similar situations and that may also work with the situation the client faces.

We have found that these eight questions are easy for most head-injured clients to understand and are useful in practically any decision-making situation. We therefore train clients to begin thinking about the decision by asking and answering each of the eight questions. We also suggest that the client consider the decision using the *hat method* outlined below. The primary goal is to ensure that the client considers the decision thoroughly before committing to any course of action (Fox, 1987). The value of both methods is that they force the client through a structured process that keeps him or her from making an ill-considered response.

The Hat Method

The hat method has been tested with several clients over the years and has proven to be an exceptionally easy-to-use and potent decision-making tool. It is a modification of a technique suggested by Bono (1990), who developed it as an offshoot of his "lateral thinking" method. This method was originally designed to harness the various aspects of personality that may improve the group decision-making processes in the business world. Business executives have different styles of thinking. For example, one business person, the *information collector*, will collect all available information about a decision before making it. The value of this approach is that it forces the group to collect all necessary information before making a final decision. However, the person may also tend to overcollect information, often to the point at which the decision is

never made because too much time is spent collecting information. Another person, the *option generator*, may spend most of his or her time defining options but never making a decision. This approach may be especially important because often, in our haste to make the decision, we neglect to define all the options. However, the person will also often overdefine the decision. Another personality is the *born skeptic*. Given any option, this person will tell you everything that is wrong with it. Unfortunately, the person seldom sees what is right with it. The opposite of the born skeptic is the *eternal optimist*. This person sees every option as a wonderful possibility. He or she seldom, however, sees the flaws with the various options. The *gut-level thinker* relies on intuition to make decisions. Such individuals seldom use the word *think* to describe their decision-making process but will usually rely on feelings and emotion. Often, these people have a good decision-making track record, although there is no easy way to define their thinking process. Clearly, each of these approaches has its value. The best decisions would therefore arise from harnessing the best parts of each personality into a combined decision-making process.

Bono (1990) reasoned that all of these personalities could provide valuable input into the decision-making process as long as no one personality was allowed to dominate. He therefore decided to allow each personality to make his or her unique contribution for the group's consideration. Because most people will postpone making decisions until the last minute and then make a gut-level response, the approach Bono developed facilitated consideration of all aspects of the information before the decision was made.

The same method may be used by an individual. The technique requires training the head-injured person to consider all aspects of the decision according to the personality styles outlined above. To create a clear picture at each stage, the therapist asks the client to imagine wearing various colored hats that bring to mind the different personality components of the decision-making process.

We recommend that the therapist purchase a number of hats of different colors. Inexpensive hats work well. There must be, however, at least a white hat, a red hat, a green hat, a blue hat, and a yellow hat. If the therapist works with groups of clients, it will be necessary to have several hats of each color, depending upon the size of the group.

The hats are used to depict different aspects of the decision-making process. Each client wears the hats to remind him or her of what type of thinking is necessary at each stage. The thinking process therefore proceeds sequentially, with the hat colors dictating which type of thinking is necessary at each stage. We now describe the thinking that each hat depicts.

White Hat: This hat represents the process of *generating information necessary to make the decision.* That is, while the client is wearing the white hat, he or she can only generate information necessary to make an informed decision. Any other discussion of the pros or cons of various options is not allowed.

During the white hat session, the therapist should write down the information that the client generates on paper so that it is readily visible. This provides the client with a tangible record of the decision-making process and also a record of all the information and procedures that underlie the decision.

At the end of the session, the client and therapist should have a listing of all relevant information. If the client is unclear about certain information, then any further action should be postponed until the necessary information is complete.

Yellow Hat: This hat signals the client to *generate options.* Generating options can only occur once all of the information relevant to the decision has been collected. The therapist should write down the options for the client and should discuss each option, regardless of whether it is feasible. At the end of the session, the client should have a listing of options that are potential candidates for further consideration.

Red Hat: This hat reminds the client to think only of the *negatives* associated with each option. The questions are "What could go wrong?" "Why is this a bad idea?" "How can this option create more problems than it solves?" and so forth. Only negative thinking is allowed. The therapist should write down the negatives next

to each of the options. The session continues until the negatives are exhausted.

Green Hat: This hat reminds the client to think *positively.* It is exactly the reverse of the red hat thinking process. The client and therapist think of only the positives associated with each possible option: for example, "What can I gain from this option?" "How am I better off by doing this?" and so forth. Again, the therapist writes down the positive opinions next to the appropriate options. At the end of the session, the decision begins to take shape in the form of a structured cost-benefit analysis of each option. Alongside the various options are the associated thoughts about costs (red hat) and benefits (green hat).

Blue Hat: The client is no longer allowed to think, only to *feel.* He or she puts aside all logical thought and asks the question "What is my gut-level feeling about this option?"—in essence, "How do I feel about it emotionally?" This hat allows for the affective side of personality to influence the decision-making process but not to dominate it. The hat method assumes that emotion and intuition do play a role in decision making and should provide input into the final product. However, the contribution of emotion is given equal weight with all of the other hats. The therapist writes down the gut-level opinion of the client next to the various options, alongside the logical positives and negatives outlined above.

Once the entire decision has been framed in the above manner, the therapist and the client can make the final decision. This usually comes about after perusal of the fact sheet that was developed during the session. The final decision is usually obvious but not necessarily desirable. This is, indeed, the purpose of the process. The technique shows the client that the best decisions are not always the easiest, most lucrative, or least time consuming. Clients also see that decisions are more than just a gut-level response to a last-minute emotional need to do something, regardless of how uninformed or ill considered. When the process is structured in this manner, the client comes to realize that decisions require careful analysis and consideration. The purpose of the hat method is to provide the client with a simple technique that can be used to structure practically any decision.

During the course of the decision-making process, clients will often come to the conclusion that the decision needs reframing. That is, the way the original decision was framed no longer makes sense, and the process must begin anew to restructure the decision in a manner that accords with the new line of thought. The process therefore forces the client to assess whether the decision is actually correct. For example, one client wanted to decide what type of new car to purchase. After going through the hat method, he came to the conclusion that all of his choices were too expensive. It was therefore necessary to reframe the decision to ask whether he should purchase a new car or a used one.

After the decision is made, the therapist sends the client off to implement the final product. The client then returns and reports on the success or failure of the decision. If it does not work out, the therapist and client go through the same process again.

APPLICATION OF METHODS

Each of the above methods of decision making, Dawson's eight questions and the hat method, is applied, by way of example, to a client's decision of whether to begin a training program or get a job or simply to apply for Social Security disability insurance. This is a decision that many clients face. We use it as an example because the methods have been especially effective for making this type of decision. We begin by using the analytic method to frame the decision, then shift to the hat method to refine it further and to establish an action plan. In general, we recommend this as a two-stage process in which the client structures the decision by answering the eight questions first, then goes through the hat method before making a final decision.

The Analytic Method

1. *What were the boundaries of the decision?* The client qualified for SSDI benefits and would probably get them if he applied. The client would probably be able to live on the benefits alone,

although the quality of life would be less than what he currently enjoyed. The client would be bored after a time not working and would probably lose a great deal of self-respect. There were at least three options: to work, to collect benefit payments and not work, or to do both and gradually phase out one or the other source of income.

2. *Did the decision present a problem or an opportunity?* The client concluded that the decision created an opportunity because there was the opportunity to work and to receive benefits at the same time. He also saw that the system was quite flexible and that it created more options than it closed off.

3. *Was there an existing policy that determined the decision?* After talking to a social security counselor, the client learned that there were guidelines that determined the decision to grant benefits. These would affect his decision to apply for benefits. He qualified, however, so the decision to apply was strictly personal.

4. *Could the decision be categorized?* Yes, it could. It was not a simple go/no-go decision. It was best categorized as an evaluation. As such, it required assessing several different options. The best course of action was to call Social Security to get any additional information about different programs that were available and to determine which were the most attractive options.

5. *Was the decision real or imagined?* The answer to this question was quite clear. The problem was real because it involved the client's long-term source of support.

6. *If you did nothing, would the situation go away?* Again, the answer was quite clear. The financial situation would obviously worsen and become critical if the client did nothing.

7. *Did the decision involve money or people or both?* The decision involved both because it affected the client's livelihood and the respect of his family.

8. *Was the problem unique?* No, it was not unique. It was a rather common problem that most people with serious disabilities would eventually face. It would be useful, however, for the client to determine what most other people had decided to do in this situation and to determine what factors dictated their individual decisions.

As a result of this process, the therapist summarized the decision with the client. There were at least three options: (a) collecting benefit payments but not working, (b) working but not collecting benefit payments, and (c) doing both, with the gradual phasing out of one income source or the other. The client concluded that this was actually an opportunity rather than a problem because he had the option of receiving both types of income. Because he qualified for benefits, there was no existing policy that governed his choice of any option, although there were policies that limited his options once a choice was made. The decision conformed to an evaluation because it involved choosing among several available options whose costs and benefits were known. This type of decision therefore boiled down to an analysis of several factors and a judgment about which one was best for the client, based on the analysis. The problem was quite real. The person was currently disabled and unemployed. For this client, the decision involved both money and people because the client's self-respect and the family's perceptions were equally weighted. The client believed that if he did nothing, the situation would worsen and eventually become critical. The problem was not unique, and it would be useful to talk to others who had made similar decisions in order to evaluate their reasoning and whether they felt they had made the right decision.

The Hat Method

This technique can be used in lieu of the analytic method or along with it. We teach both methods and encourage our clients to use the hat method after answering the eight decision-making questions of the analytic method. In some cases, the decision will be obvious after using either method alone. Moreover, using both methods will obviously not work in situations in which a decision is required immediately or on the spur of the moment. However, when there is time to process the decision, both methods can work together to produce the most appropriate decision plan. As a general rule, the more time the client

processes the decision, the better the eventual decision will be.

White Hat: After considerable research, the client determined that he would make about the same amount of money working as he would if he were receiving SSDI payments. He also determined that there were programs available that allowed him to work at a job for a period of time and still receive a portion of his SSDI benefits. Only after working for a year or more successfully would he lose his benefit payments entirely. He could receive SSDI payments while he was in a formal training program. SSDI would also pay for course work at community colleges and four-year institutions.

The client was generally unaware of these various options and had thought that there were only two options: to go on SSDI or to work and not to receive it.

Yellow Hat: The client and his therapist listed the various options:

1. Receive SSDI benefit payments and not work. Reassess the situation later on.
2. Work and live off a paycheck without SSDI.
3. Apply for and receive SSDI; go to school and have SSDI pay for courses.
4. Work and receive a paycheck and have SSDI benefits gradually reduced over a year interval and eventually phased out.

Red Hat: The client and therapist discussed and wrote down all of the drawbacks that were involved with each option. With respect to the first, the major drawback was that the client would eventually become bored sitting around the house all day. He also enjoyed work for its mental and social stimulation value. He was afraid that the longer he remained unemployed, the less motivated he would be to return to work ever. He was also afraid that his family would no longer respect him if he did not change.

Option 2 was also fraught with potential difficulties. The client had few salable skills and might not make as much money working as he would collecting SSDI. He would require some amount of training before he would be able to work, a period of time when he would be unemployed with no income at all. He was not certain that he could hold down a full-time job. He wondered what advantage there would be to not taking some amount of money from SSDI as a backup position. The therapists reminded him that this was the Red Hat thinking stage and the last statement was not allowed because it did not deal strictly with the negative aspects of each decision.

The third option was difficult because the client had not been to school in many years. He was therefore uncertain if he would be able to compete in a formal classroom training environment. He did not have a high school diploma, and although he could take community college courses, he would eventually have to get a GED certificate to graduate from a community college. He was uncertain how long SSDI would fund his course work, especially if he was unsuccessful for the first few semesters. He was basically afraid to go to school because he had not done well in high school and had never developed the requisite skills to succeed. He felt embarrassed about taking remedial, noncredit courses because he was afraid that his wife and child would think he was not intelligent.

Option 4 had the same problems mentioned earlier. There were several difficult questions. How much money could he make? How long could he sustain the job? What if he worked for a year and eventually lost his benefits because of his successful employment but then got fired or laid off?

Green Hat: The therapist reminded the client that he was allowed only to list the positive aspects of each decision. The first option was certainly the easiest. He would simply collect a check each month, approximately half the amount of his former paycheck. He could pay the rent on his apartment and most of the bills. His wife's paycheck could be used for any other family needs. The couple did not need day care because he could watch their child during the day. He felt that he had paid into the system and deserved the money now that he needed it.

The second option was attractive because he had always worked hard and enjoyed work. He wanted his child to grow up with a father who worked and supported his family. He wanted the respect of his wife and wanted her to perceive that he was trying to make something of his life despite his injury. One of his therapists warned him that many marriages break up after one person suffers a head injury, and he felt that his might also if his wife felt he was no longer making an effort.

Option 3 was attractive because he had always wanted to go to school and to learn a technical skill such as electronics. He felt that this would be an opportunity to finish his education and get some advanced training. He wanted his child to view him as an educated person and not to make the same mistakes educationally that he had made. His wife had an A.A. degree, and he had always felt inferior to her because of the difference in their educational level. He wanted to show himself that he could still think. He could devote all of his time to studying because he had SSDI income. SSDI would also pay for the courses.

The fourth option made sense because, as he put it, "Work is what I know." He felt confident that he could do his old job or something similar to it even though the doctors had warned him that it would not be feasible for him to return to work doing what he did before. If he were fired, he would still retain his benefit payments. He would be around people and have the social stimulation he enjoyed in the past. His wife and child would respect him because he was working again.

Blue Hat: The therapists reminded the client that it was time to feel. He should put aside all thoughts of logic and simply ask himself how he felt about each of the options and which one he felt most comfortable with. The client, after much silence, decided that he felt the best about the first option. It made him feel secure to know that some money was coming in. He also felt that he could make logical decisions better after a longer period of recovery. He wanted more time to think about the situation.

Decision: The client decided to receive the SSDI benefit checks and not to work right away. He would live off the checks until he tired of the free time or became bored. At that time he would make the decision either to work or to go to school.

CONCLUSION

Decision making is one of the core elements of cognition. It is similar in many ways to problem solving because decisions are often due to problems or our attempts to solve them. It differs from problem solving because the options are often known and the client's task is to simply discover them and to decide among them. This chapter outlines two techniques for teaching head-injured clients to make correct decisions. The first is an analytic approach that involves answering eight questions: (a) What are the boundaries of the decision? (b) Is the client dealing with a problem or an opportunity? (c) Is the decision covered by some existing policy? (d) Is the decision a go/no-go choice, an identification of the correct solution, a discovery of unknown options, or an evaluation of existing options? (e) Is the problem and the need for a decision real or imagined? (f) Does the decision involve money, people, or both? (g) If the person decides not to decide, will the situation rectify itself? and (h) Is the decision unique? Answering each of the questions allows the client to frame the decision effectively and usually leads to a correct decision.

We also discussed another method of decision making that was originally proposed by Bono (1990). This involves training the client to imagine wearing various colored hats. Each color suggests a step in the decision-making process that precedes the final decision. The white hat process involves collecting all relevant information that is necessary to make the decision. The yellow hat involves identifying options among which the client will eventually decide. Once the options are identified, the red hat requires listing all of the things that could go wrong with

each of the options. The green hat requires listing the benefits of each option. The blue hat requires the client to identify his or her emotional feeling about each option.

Both methods of decision making have been useful with our clients. Generally, the first is more complex and may be best used with higher functioning clients, whereas the hat method will work with most clients and is especially useful with lower functioning ones. Whenever possible, we suggest that the therapist use both methods and encourage clients to answer the eight questions first before beginning the hat method. This is especially valuable when the client has to make difficult or very important decisions. The major value of each method is that it forces the client to go through a structured thinking process before making a decision.

REFERENCES

Bono, E. (1990). *The machine of mind.* New York: Penguin.

Dawson, R. (1993). *The confident decision maker.* New York: Simon & Schuster.

Doerner, D. (1987). On the difficulties that people have in dealing with complexity. In J. Rasmussen, K. Duncan, & J. Leplat (Eds.), *New technology and human errors.* London: John Wiley.

Fox, J. (1987). Making decisions under the influence of knowledge. In P.E. Morris (Ed.), *Modeling cognition.* Chichester, UK: John Wiley.

Janis, I.L., & Mann, L. (1977). *Decision making: A psychological analysis of conflict, choice, and commitment.* New York: Free Press.

Kahneman, D., Slovic, P., & Tversky, A. (Eds.). (1982). *Judgements under uncertainty: Heuristics and biases.* New York: Cambridge University Press.

Larrick, R.P., Morgan, J.N., & Nisbett, R.E. (1990). Teaching the use of cost-benefit reasoning in everyday life. *Psychological Science, 1,* 362–370.

Reason, J.T. (1990). *Human error.* Cambridge, UK: Cambridge University Press.

Wheelwright, S., & Makridakis, S. (1980). *Forecasting methods of management.* New York: John Wiley.

Chapter 18

Retraining Reasoning and Comprehension

Reasoning and comprehension are central to the process of cognition (Rips, 1990; Sternberg & Smith, 1988). Indeed, they are core processes in the center portion of the model of rehabilitation that we explained in Chapter 2. Like all concepts, however, they mean different things to different people. It is therefore important to define the concepts of reasoning and comprehension before we explain how to retrain them.

We define *reasoning* as the process of comparing, making deductions, and forming if-then relationships in order to understand something. Reasoning involves connecting and organizing information so that we can make inferences and generate hypotheses. It is therefore the process that defines our comprehension of the world. All of us reason, some more quickly than others. The basic process can be impaired after a head injury and usually is. However, some individuals are better at reasoning than others because they understand basic flaws in the reasoning process and do not fall prey to them. Our goal in this chapter is to acquaint the reader with these logical flaws and to demonstrate how a head-injured person can use this knowledge to reason more effectively.

Comprehension is the state of our understanding at any given point in time. It is our grasp of the gist or essential meaning of something that we have experienced. For example, when we try to "get the point" of a movie, a book, or a conversation, we are seeking comprehension of it. Comprehension is thus the result of the reasoning process.

Often, when something is difficult to understand, we comprehend it in stages, first at a surface level, then more deeply as we continue to study the situation. Our comprehension becomes more complete as we continue to reason with the facts. With continued exposure, our comprehension of the situation becomes relatively settled. For example, we all are called upon to reason in order to learn a skill such as division or multiplication. Eventually, however, we come to comprehend these concepts and can use them rather mechanically (Smith & Medin, 1981). Detectives and police investigators continue to reason with the available facts until, at some point, they form a clear comprehension of the situation that must have occurred at the crime scene. At this point, the reasoning process slows and the comprehension becomes fixed.

Many head-injured persons comprehend their injury in stages. They may have no knowledge concerning the specifics of their injury and may simply wake up in a hospital with no comprehension or memory of the accident. However, a relative may tell them that the accident occurred on a specific road that was icy and that the front of the car was demolished. Given this core knowledge, they use the reasoning process to elaborate and expand their comprehension of what must have happened. For example, when told the facts, they may infer that they must have been driving home from work. If the road was icy, then they quite possibly skidded on some ice. Because the front of the car was demolished, the collision must have been head on.

These examples illustrate the difference between reasoning and comprehension. Comprehension is an understanding of certain events or relations that a person extracts from facts. Reasoning, however, is the mental work that creates this understanding. Reasoning and comprehension also involve *integration,* or the combination of relevant details into a common theme. The way the facts are integrated can either enhance or distort the person's comprehension of the material. For example, we have all played a party game in which one person whispers a story to another, who in turn whispers it to another, and so on until the last person relates the story to the group. The distortion of the general theme is dramatic and usually produces a humorous version of the original. Each person in the group may integrate the facts differently until the final version is distorted beyond recognition. Any one person's comprehension of the story may be quite different from that of the next person in the sequence or the person from whom he or she heard the story. This is why gossip can distort the truth and keep us from making accurate judgments. On the other hand, we have all known someone who seems to "get to the bottom" of an issue rapidly—someone whose capacity for quick and accurate abstraction of a basic underlying theme or idea is impressive. Clearly, there can be no substitute for this valuable skill.

Head injury affects the reasoning process in several ways. The reasoning process is typically slowed after a head injury, so the resulting comprehensions may be ill considered or incomplete. The person may lose the ability to abstract the essence or main idea quickly and efficiently, to generate facts through "if-then" reasoning, or to eliminate information that does not make sense in some way.

This chapter focuses on retraining head-injured clients to understand novel situations, to

get the point, and to reason quickly and efficiently. We begin with a discussion of themes and go on to discuss the reasoning processes of presupposition, inference, and deduction.

THEMES

Themes are the dominant ideas that underlie most written materials and life experiences. Themes also form the basis of what we remember from any episode of life. Head-injured persons are notoriously concrete. They often seem unable to abstract the gist of movies, books, or social encounters. Head injury survivors who return to school have special difficulty writing papers in which the theme or structure is clear. Therefore, much of what the therapist does will revolve around teaching clients skills for extracting the theme from what they read or hear or expressing the gist of their ideas.

This is an important aspect of therapy because the theme is the most likely piece of information to be remembered (Bransford & Johnson, 1973; Sulin & Dooling, 1974). The client's ability to recall any event will depend upon his or her ability to abstract a theme. The details of any of life's episodes will come to mind only after the person recalls the theme of the event. Themes are therefore central to comprehension. Their purpose is to initiate and to organize our recall.

PRESUPPOSITION AND INFERENCES

Reasoning involves a variety of processes, among them the process of *presupposition.* Much of what we see or hear can be understood only if we presume beforehand, or "presuppose" something to be true. This type of reasoning is often distorted or impaired after a head injury. The client may therefore understand new situations only at a surface level because of an inability to generate accurate presuppositions about the event. This inability frequently distorts clients' recollections or their understanding of certain events. For example, one African American client reported that his instructor in a mechanics training program was trying to keep him from graduating and presupposed that this was occurring because the instructor was racially biased. The situation created a great deal of tension, and the topic became a focus of therapy.

The therapist listed several facts from the client's description of the interactions between him and the instructor during training. These were listed on a piece of paper so that the client could review them again between sessions: (a) the instructor had given the client high marks on his early performance evaluations, (b) approximately equal numbers of African American and Caucasian students had failed their examination, and (c) several students had received unsatisfactory ratings at this point in their training.

From these facts, the therapist and client developed a list of presuppositions: (a) the instructor wanted the client to succeed, as evidenced by the high marks on the early performance evaluations; (b) because most of his peers were also having difficulty in this portion of the training, it was likely that this was simply a difficult point in the course; and (c) because equal numbers of African Americans and Caucasians had failed the examination, it was unlikely that the client's failure was racially motivated. These and other presuppositions were sufficient to change the client's attitude about the instructor and the training.

Using presuppositions as a therapy tool is therefore a two-step process. The therapist begins by listing a variety of possible facts about the phenomenon. The therapist and client then begin to generate lists of presuppositions that must have been true for the facts to be true. For example, in the situation described above, the therapist and client listed several facts and discussed presuppositions for each in relation to the instructor's behavior. The critical thing to remember when creating presuppositions with the client is that they are statements about what is likely to have preceded a certain event that has already occurred. The presupposition therefore partially explains the event. If the presupposition does not accord with the situation, then either the client's perception of the situation is inaccurate or the presupposition is wrong. The therapy proceeds until the facts of the situation and the presuppositions correlate.

The words *presuppositions* and *inferences* are difficult for most clients to understand. In speaking with clients, we therefore call presuppositions *ideas about possible causes* and inferences *ideas about likely results*.

INFERENCE

Reasoning also involves forming *inferences*. Once an event has occurred, it usually has certain results or implications. Inferences differ from presuppositions in that they are logical extensions of a current situation (Mayer, 1983; Nisbett, 1993). Presuppositions are logical precursors to the same situation (Johnson-Laird, 1983). Thus one presupposes by determining what is likely to have preceded a certain situation, and one infers by extrapolating the logical consequences of an event.

Forming inferences is also an "if-then" process. With the client discussed above, the therapist began forming inferences by listing the likely implications of the situation as the client now perceived it. For example, given that most of the client's peers had difficulty with this section of the training, it was likely that they all had to meet some stringent standard before going on to the next level of training. This inference also made sense given that the client was in a self-paced training program and that many of the students had failed their competency test several times but still remained in training. The therapist then inferred that failure at this stage was a natural and common occurrence that was necessary to ensure a standard of knowledge required for mastery of the new material in the next stage.

Presuppositions and inferences are especially important aspects of thinking skills training because they structure our comprehension of any situation. Moreover, clients with head injury, especially those with frontal lobe injury, often get fixed in one mode of thinking and fail to break that set. It is therefore important to teach them a method of thinking that ensures that their conclusions are feasible or accurate. Teaching clients to list presuppositions and inferences also keeps them from fixing on a conclusion too soon. Another reason for teaching this type of reasoning is that much of what we call communication involves forming inferences or presuppositions. Without these skills, the client is doomed to form comprehensions based on surface facts.

The ability to integrate information also depends on our ability to generate inferences and presuppositions rapidly. Perhaps the biggest value of this type of training is that it forces clients to develop a picture of their world that is based on a coherent and interrelated body of evidence that makes sense. Clients therefore learn to check their comprehension of a life situation by determining if it makes sense relative to the inferences about what is likely to result from the situation and the presuppositions about what is likely to have preceded it (Halpern, 1995). The process also forces clients to think about and plan for the future on the basis of the inferences.

THERAPY TECHNIQUES

Training reasoning involves teaching a broad range of skills and vocabulary (Nisbett, Fong, Lehman, & Cheng, 1987; Sternberg, 1987). First, the person must understand the importance of *facts* and *evidence*. Correct reasoning can occur only when there has been a complete and accurate listing of the facts. This reasoning process is beset by several common errors of reasoning that the client must learn to avoid (Kahneman, Slovic, & Tversky, 1982). Misconceptions may arise from being locked into one way of seeing a situation (*fixated mind-set*), jumping to conclusions based on incomplete evidence, mistaking evidence for proof, initially misperceiving something, screening out unwanted information, focusing on negative self-assessments and fears, and succumbing to circular reasoning. Each of these reasoning errors is discussed in detail below.

Identifying Facts and Evidence

The first step toward training reasoning is to show the client how to list facts and to evaluate evidence. Facts are the basis of reality. Like them or not, we must use them to construct a clear

picture of the world before drawing any conclusions about it. The ability to generalize is based on the ability to cluster facts that lead to the same conclusion. Facts are not necessarily evidence, though clients often take them to be evidence for a particular conclusion. For example, one client observed his wife eating lunch with her boss at work and took this fact as evidence that she was having an affair with him. The critical point in this stage of the therapy is to teach the client always to make a clear listing of the facts surrounding any situation. The client should not draw any conclusions until the listing is complete and only after considerable time has been spent drawing presuppositions and inferences from the facts.

Inductive and Deductive Reasoning

Once the facts have been identified, it is possible to train the client to work with them. The client can either deduce or induce new information from the facts. *Deductive reasoning* involves forming a conclusion about particulars from general premises. *Inductive reasoning* involves forming a generalized conclusion from particular instances. For example, one client after asking several of his peers how long they had resided at the rehabilitation facility, induced from their responses that the average stay was 6 months. Then, from this generalized conclusion, he deduced that he was likely to reside there for about that long.

Common Errors in Reasoning

The following logical flaws of reasoning are presented as a checklist for therapists to give to clients to check their reasoning in any given situation. These reasoning errors are presented as statements about one's reasoning process, and examples are provided for each. The therapist should go over each reasoning error and try to generate examples from the client's personal life.

Our discussion of these reasoning errors is based on unpublished research with 20 head injury survivors. The group was given a listing of the italicized statements presented below. These described common reasoning errors, and each was explained in detail. The clients then rated each in terms of how often they committed the error. The errors were then listed in rank order, from the most to least frequently reported.

The list of reasoning errors originally came from Ruchlis (1990) in his book *Clear Thinking*. These errors are often described as common media distortions. However, the therapist did not present them as distortions of truth that clients would, for example, encounter while watching television, but rather in a personal framework, as forms of illogical thinking in which clients themselves might engage.

The research was designed to determine which reasoning errors clients would be most likely to commit. Below, we discuss the most frequently cited problems along with therapy techniques that have proven to be effective treatments with a majority of clients. Therapy is a two-step process. The first step is to acquaint the client with all the different forms of distorted thinking. The second is to determine which reasoning errors are most problematic for an individual client and to use these as a focus of treatment.

1. Fixated mind-set: "I tend to see things in only one way." The most commonly cited problem was cognitive rigidity (Mayer, 1983). Most clients reported that they became locked into one mode of thinking and that it was virtually impossible for them to see a situation from any other perspective. The therapy for this problem that has worked best over the years is to play devil's advocate. The therapist presents social problems that are currently popular in the media, and the client must take several positions on each issue and justify his or her position from a variety of perspectives. For example, the client may try to justify either side of the assault weapon ban or the abortion issue. Once the therapist has played this game with several social issues, the client tries the same game with some personal issue. For example, one client complained that his wife no longer seemed to be attracted to him. He was asked to pretend that he was his wife and to describe her affections for him. He was then asked to play the role of a strange woman and to describe her perceptions of him and what she found attractive about him. This latter stage of the game

can lead to a great deal of tension for the client because it deals with emotionally charged personal issues. The therapist should therefore begin the game with common social issues that are not so personal and only begin the second stage when the client seems strong enough emotionally to handle it.

2. Jumping to conclusions: "I form impressions of people or things without first considering all the available information." This was also cited as a major problem after head injury. It overlaps with the first error just discussed above because the person creates an intransigent mindset quickly and then generates conclusions from an incorrect comprehension of the situation.

An effective therapy for this type of thought disorder is to have the client list all the facts about a certain situation on a piece of paper and keep listing until all the facts of the situation are known. This will force the client to postpone forming any conclusions until all the relevant information is available. Again, it is best to begin with impersonal social issues and gradually work into more personal problems. The therapist should list the facts on paper and encourage the client to do so as he or she learns to apply the technique.

3. Mistaking evidence for proof: "I immediately interpret ambiguous situations as proof of one position or another." For example, one client saw his instructor having lunch with another client in the rehabilitation center. He felt that this was proof that the instructor favored this client over any other.

The technique of *scenario interpretation* has proven effective for working with this disorder. This involves presenting several scenarios and asking the client to interpret them in as many different ways as possible. For example, the therapist might ask the client to interpret the following scenario: "A woman wearing a tight, short skirt is standing on a street corner late at night." The client might say, "She's a prostitute," "She's an undercover policewoman," or "She's a cocktail waitress waiting for a cab to take her home to her husband and five children." These types of short scenarios are easy to create and usually lead to a variety of interpretations. The goal is to get the client to increase cognitive flexibility by providing ambiguous evidence and showing how it can be interpreted in a variety of ways. The game teaches the client that even the most concrete evidence is rarely proof of any specific position.

4. Initial misperception: "I seldom have a clear idea of what people tell me." Most clients reported that they simply did not understand many communications and often left a situation with a totally incorrect comprehension. Frequently the client would do something wrong and would have to spend hours fixing the problem simply because he or she did not understand what to do to begin with.

The therapy for most misperceptions is to get the client in the habit of repeating what others say in his or her own words. Each time someone speaks to the client, he or she should say, "Let me see if I can say this in my own words." The client should then do so and ask the person to verify if the concept has been correctly communicated. This simple procedure helps clarify the extent and the types of misperceptions the client is most prone to form. It also provides the client with additional rehearsal, restatement, and practice in expression, all of which are essential elements of good memory (see Chapter 11).

5. Selective attention: "I often see and hear only the things I want to." Many clients reported that they would selectively screen out information or criticism that was painful or difficult to understand or that did not accord with their personal values. For example, one client stated that he ignored people who noticed that he had a problem pronouncing words, walking, or using his left arm. He would tell them not to help him because he did not have any problems in those areas. He would, however, listen to those who noticed improvement in his cognitive and physical state. Both groups of people noticed a problem, but the client attended only to those who noticed improvement.

Therapy techniques for this type of problem are best carried out in a group. The therapist asks the client to list his or her major problems. The therapist goes around the room and asks each client in the group to say whether the targeted client's self-perceptions are accurate. The targeted client must then restate these criticisms in his or her own words. For example, Client A stated that her major problem was that she was shy and could not establish the type of friendships she desired. Client B reassessed her condition by saying that her shyness seemed to be primarily the result of low self-esteem. Client C agreed with the second assessment and added that Client A was also quite fearful of evaluation. This interaction caused Client A to reassess her problems and eventually to change her behavior.

As Parenté and Stapleton (1993) pointed out, this type of treatment works well because clients listen to other clients and are far more likely to accept their criticisms and perceptions than those of the therapist. The therapist plays a crucial role in this situation because he or she must determine if the client is ready to hear the other clients' assessments. Moreover, many clients may phrase their assessments in an unacceptable fashion, and the therapist may need to abort an offensive statement or reinterpret it in a way the client will accept. Often, the exercises must wait until the target client trusts the others in the group to the point at which their input will be valued rather than immediately denied and rejected.

6. Personal mudslinging: "I focus on the negative about myself and pay little attention to my good qualities and achievements." Clients typically say that they are preoccupied with negative thought patterns. They focus on their failures and do not recognize improvement over time. In addition, they are sensitive to criticism. Part of the problem stems from low self-esteem, which may have been a premorbid personality problem. It is also true that head-injured persons have experienced a great deal of personal rejection over the years and have come to expect that this is the way others will automatically relate to them in the future. Some become fixated on their deficits; others deny them. Most gradually become accustomed to their growing social isolation. A few make an effort to focus on improvement and to adopt an optimistic attitude.

Therapy for such negative self-evaluation involves any number of interventions. Perhaps one of the easiest interventions is having the person come to a support group or a psychosocial training group. The group can make the topic of personal mudslinging a focus of their discussion and come up with common strategies. Frequently cited strategies include (a) making a list of the person's strengths and posting them on the wall, (b) making a list of positive things that happened each day, (c) posting a chart of performance on therapy tasks or in school so the client can see improvements, (d) posting goals and checking them off as the client achieves them, and (e) soliciting assessment of the client's progress from infrequently seen family and friends. These people are most likely to see change in the client's functional status.

The technique of *personal success review* may also help to reduce the effects of mudslinging. This method was originally developed for helping salespeople to develop a positive attitude before attempting a sale (Bernstein, 1994). The same technique works well with head-injured clients. The therapist asks the client to think of several success experiences he or she has had over the years. For example, many clients recall standing on the stage wearing a cap and gown at their high school graduation. Some report a specific triumph during an athletic event. Others report getting a highly desirable job or a letter of acceptance to a university or college. Most clients can, with the help of the therapist, conjure up between 5 and 10 personal success experiences. The therapist then writes clients' description of each of these on 3 × 5 cards and instructs the clients to review each card whenever they begin to become preoccupied with negative feelings about themselves. Clients must close their eyes, imagine the various success experiences, and try to rekindle the feeling of success that went along with it. We have found that the negative feelings and depression will often dissipate after clients review all of the cards.

7. Self-scaring: "I can't get these fears out of my mind." Self-scaring is similar to the personal mudslinging problems discussed above. The client usually begins by focusing on his or her deficit areas, then begins to infer all of the problems that could result from it: for example, "What will I do when my parents die and I'm left all alone?" "I'll never be able to have children; no one would want me now, and I couldn't take care of them anyway"; "If an emergency situation arose, I would not be able to help myself." Clients often become preoccupied with these types of thoughts to the point at which they dominate their thinking. In many cases, such thoughts are reasonable given the severity of their disorders. However, perseveration on these problems is always maladaptive and unproductive.

Therapy involves first asking the client to state his or her biggest fears. Facing the fears is always difficult and will often evoke an emotional response. The next step is to list them and to discuss strategies for dealing with them. For example, in one case, the therapist dealt with the personal emergency fear by getting the person a medical warning monitor. The client simply pressed the device to signal an emergency.

The remaining reasoning flaws were less frequently rated by clients as problems. Nevertheless, we do recommend discussing each of them with clients. We often watch television commercials with the clients as a means of identifying the reasoning flaws. Reading newspapers can also serve the same purpose. The goal is to acquaint clients with problems in reasoning that they will see every day. Because clients in our survey did not rate these highly, we discuss them only briefly below.

8. Statements taken out of context: "What people say and do is all that matters. I don't care what caused them to say or do it." This is the problem of not considering a statement or an action in light of the situation that either precipitated it or surrounded it. For example, clients occasionally report irritation when they hear family and friends discussing them because they are not aware of the context that led to the discussion. One therapy that helps to overcome this problem is to train the client always to ask others to explain the context that precipitated an action or statement.

9. Circular reasoning: "I firmly believe certain things, and no one can tell me they are wrong." Many clients become overly religious after their injuries as a way of finding some meaningful explanation for the drastic changes in their lives. Because all religions are based in faith, it is impossible to prove or to disprove their validity. Other clients develop deeply rooted beliefs that are also based in faith. These convictions are not necessarily wrong, nor are they necessarily maladaptive or unproductive. Often, they are the only thing that is helping the person to adjust. Occasionally, however, clients are attracted to convictions and attitudes that create problems for the therapist. For example, some clients become overzealous religious fanatics and try to convert others to their beliefs. Others become devoted to the therapist and believe that anything he or she tells them is true. The therapy for this type of problem amounts to teaching the client to verify independently the conviction or the person. For example, in what tangible way is the client's life better since adopting the faith?

10. Externalization and scapegoating: "When things go wrong, it is usually someone else's fault." This attitude allows clients to deny their deficits or to assume that others, not themselves, are having difficulty adjusting to their disability. It often is manifested in frequent excuses, inability to accept responsibility, and interpretations of events that shift responsibility for failure onto someone or something else. For example, one client recently dropped a valuable piece of china and justified the situation by claiming that her sister did not dry it well. Another explained that his therapies were progressing so slowly because all of his therapists were incompetent. We deal with this problem by training the client to explain an event in the first person—for example, "I dropped the china"—before offering any additional explanation.

11. Slippery numbers: "Test scores and numbers usually tell the story." This attitude reflects a belief in the ultimate truth of data and numerical analysis. Clients seldom understand that for every statistic, there is usually another that can be used to "prove" just the opposite point. It is important to acquaint the client with the fact that test scores do change and that the various statistics they learn are based on studies of groups of individuals. The individual client's recovery often differs markedly from the statistical projections. In addition, the statistical estimates never factor the motivation of the client into the equation.

12. Identification: "If I really respect people, I will usually see things their way." Clients will occasionally model after therapists, friends, relatives, or others who accept them and spend time with them. They occasionally begin to adopt similar attitudes, behaviors, or opinions. This modeling can have positive effects if the person is a positive role model. However, some clients may model after media stars, groups of unsavory friends, or others whose opinions and attitudes are maladaptive or dangerous. For example, one client began modeling after "gangsta rappers" and started talking about shooting police officers. Perhaps the only way to deal with this problem when it occurs is to discuss issues such as who is the real source of the opinion, whether the client understands the opinion, and whether the client is willing to accept responsibility for any action the opinions lead to.

13. Sweet deal: "I am often convinced to buy things because they seem like such a good deal." Many clients are easily persuaded by media campaigns that describe deals of a lifetime. They will occasionally fall prey to this type of advertisement, act impulsively, and experience financial difficulty. For example, one client wanted to buy a computer because he felt that playing computer games would improve his memory. He went to a computer store and was persuaded by a salesman to take out a store charge card to purchase a $7,000 system. He was persuaded by the argument that if he used the charge card, he would not have to make any payments or pay any interest for 6 months. He did not realize that because he was living on public assistance, he would not be able to pay for the computer for 6 years. After the client had gone through the long, embarrassing process of returning the computer, the therapist asked the client to memorize the old adage "If something sounds too good to be true, it usually is."

14. Vague emotion: "I feel that the only things in life worth going after are fulfillment, happiness, love, and truth." Clients and their families often fall prey to this reasoning flaw. In many cases they do so because they do not know what to expect from the recovery process. The emotional abstractions are often easy to accept but difficult to achieve. For example, many clients will describe their major goal in life as "being happy again." Although this is certainly a laudable goal, it is difficult to validate. The therapist should ask the client to state his or her goals in concrete terms. The client should try to explain his or her emotions specifically and should use concrete, rather than abstract, words whenever possible.

15. Thought diversion: "If someone else does something, why can't I?" Some clients will complain that they should be allowed to do something because someone else does it. They should not be sanctioned for having done something because someone else did it and was not sanctioned. For example, one client was admonished by his mother for leaving a candle burning in his room. He replied, "You leave candles burning at the dinner table all the time." The client shifted attention away from his action by pointing out another observation that somehow justified it. The therapist pointed out that this observation was indeed correct. Candles should never be left unattended. However, the instance that the client observed did not justify his own action.

16. People like me: "You can usually believe people who are just like you." Clients occasionally place their beliefs in groups or individuals who behave as they do, are from similar backgrounds, or have had similar life experiences. This is different from identification, in which the person adopts the opinions of someone else out of respect. Occasionally, the opinion or attitude can be useful. For example, one client who had been a member of a motorcycle gang began to identify with the lifestyle of friends from his old neighborhood who attended a local church. Problems may arise when clients adopt the lifestyle of those whom they have outgrown. For example, one client began to identify with those high school friends who were part of a drug culture. Usually, clients will identify with those individuals who accept them. If they perceive that those individuals are culturally similar to them, a stronger or more rapid identification process may ensue. The therapist can use the identification to the client's advantage if the attitudes produce an improvement in the client's functioning.

17. Everyone's doing it: "If everyone is doing something, it must be all right." We all fall prey to fads, and persons with head injury are no exception. Occasionally, however, the client's desire to be accepted leads to behavior, dress, or mannerisms that create more problems than they solve. For example, one client refused to wear shoes other than high-top tennis shoes even though his leg braces were not compatible with the shoes. The leg braces caused the shoes to wear on his ankles, and this in turn caused an infection. Another client began drinking on weekends because all his friends did. Clients have a difficult time explaining to those who accept them as friends why they choose not to adopt similar behaviors, dress, or attitudes. We spend considerable time with each client discussing why his or her behaviors may be inappropriate or potentially dangerous. The client eventually learns to ask the basic question "Is it right for me?"

18. Great person: "If a famous person says something, I will usually believe it." The media commonly display overweight ex-football players advertising a certain brand of beer, hardware, or automobiles. Characterizations of Albert Einstein are sometimes associated with "the smart choice." We will occasionally watch TV commercials with our clients to illustrate the "great person fallacy." The client comes to ask the question "Does this person have any expertise in relation to this product or service?"

19. Science has shown: "Scientific discoveries are always true. If a scientist says something, I will usually believe it." Many clients tend to equate science with truth. They seldom ask whether the scientific discovery has been replicated, whether it is generally accepted, or what are the limits of the discovery. This has been especially apparent in discussions of nutrients and drugs that might improve memory or thinking. Most clients will listen to the available research and immediately conclude that a particular compound will improve their functioning. The best therapy is to tell the clients that a single experiment does not prove or disprove anything. Scientists investigate and replicate findings until there is a consensus that evolves from the bulk of the research. A scientific discovery is never fact until the scientific community agrees that it is.

CONCLUSION

This chapter describes the basic components of rational thought. Persons with head injury, like most of us, are prone to irrational thinking. Many have not been taught how to reason logically. It is therefore necessary to begin by distinguishing the types of reasoning and how they can be used to shape our comprehension of the world. We discussed the deductive, or general-to-specific, process and its opposite, the inductive, or specific-to-general, process. We also described presuppositional and inferential reasoning and several therapy techniques for training reasoning and comprehension. Other techniques for training reasoning include teaching the client to distinguish facts from evidence and to identify a variety of common logical errors. Common reasoning errors, ranked by 20 head-injured clients in terms of how often they found them to be problems in their own lives, were discussed in detail, along with therapy techniques for working with the most commonly reported problems.

REFERENCES

Bernstein, M. (1994). *The Masters 100.* Baltimore: Human Equations Corporation.

Bransford, J.D., & Johnson, M.K. (1973). Consideration of some problems of comprehension. In W.G. Chase (Ed.), *Visual information processing.* New York: American Press.

Halpern, D.F. (1995). *Thought and knowledge* (3rd ed.). Hillsdale, NJ: Lawrence Erlbaum.

Johnson-Laird, P.N. (1983). *Mental models.* New York: Cambridge University Press.

Kahneman, D., Slovic, P., & Tversky, A. (Eds.). (1982). *Judgements under uncertainty: Heuristics and biases.* New York: Cambridge University Press.

Mayer, R.E. (1983). *Rules and reasoning.* Hillsdale, NJ: Lawrence Erlbaum.

Nisbett, R.E. (1993). *Rules for reasoning.* Hillsdale, NJ: Lawrence Erlbaum.

Nisbett, R.E., Fong, G.T., Lehman, D.R., & Cheng, P.W. (1987). Teaching reasoning. *Science, 238,* 625–631.

Parenté, R., & Stapleton, M. (1993). An empowerment model of memory training. *Applied Cognitive Psychology, 7,* 595–602.

Rips, L.J. (1990). Reasoning. *Annual Review of Psychology, 41,* 321–353.

Ruchlis, H. (1990). *Clear thinking.* New York: Prometheus.

Smith, E.E., & Medin, D.L. (1981). *Categories and concepts.* Cambridge, MA: Harvard University Press.

Sternberg, R.J. (1987). *Intelligence applied: Understanding and increasing your intellectual skills.* San Diego: Harcourt Brace Jovanovich.

Sternberg, R.J., & Smith, E.E. (1988). *The psychology of human thought.* Harvard, MA: Cambridge University Press.

Sulin, R.A., & Dooling, D.J. (1974). Intrusions of a thematic idea in retention of prose. *Journal of Experimental Psychology, 103,* 255–262.

Chapter 19

Executive Skills Training

This chapter deals with retraining the client's ability to self-regulate, control, and organize behavior (Brown, 1978; Miller, Galanter, & Pribram, 1960). These aspects of behavior are usually impaired after head injury, especially if there is damage to the frontal lobes. Friends, family, and the therapist will often notice that the client has difficulty setting goals, prioritizing, and executing plans (Case, 1992; Duncan, 1986; Lezak, 1993; Pollens, McBratnie, & Burton, 1988). In addition, the client may not be aware of how he or she presents to others and may have a hard time initiating behavior or inhibiting it, thinking strategically and sequentially, and evaluating progress toward goals. Good executive skills also determine the client's ability to solve problems, to act in a mature and nonegocentric fashion, and to transfer newly learned skills to novel situations. These skills define the person's social competence and are therefore especially important for getting along in the world of work (Ylvisaker, 1995).

The chapter begins with a definition of executive functioning and discussion of its importance in social and work situations. We next discuss how to evaluate self-awareness and executive functions informally after head injury. We then turn to specific intervention strategies that have proven effective over the years.

Several authors (Baddeley, 1986, 1990; Janowski, Shimamura, Kritchevsky, & Squire, 1989; McCarthy & Warrington, 1990; Ylvisaker, 1995) coined the term *metacognitive functions,* which are thinking skills that are closely related to executive functions. Metacognition has both a static and dynamic component. The static component is the person's awareness of his or her cognitive processes and the appropriate procedures for improving performance. The dynamic component is the person's ability to exercise control of his or her cognitions and to initiate appropriate action (Sternberg, 1985). These two components can vary independently of one another. For example, the client may be aware of what he or she wants for dinner but not be able to plan dinner or prepare it. This reflects intact static metacognitive ability but relatively poor dynamic skill. Retraining executive skills is therefore not only a matter of making clients aware of their deficits but even more a matter of teaching clients how to control their thoughts and actions.

Much of our executive skill develops during infancy and childhood (Welsh & Pennington, 1988). This is evident in the preschool and elementary school years, when parents and teachers will often see improvement of the ability to solve problems, control attention, and regulate conversation. Executive skills continue to deelop throughout adolescence and into adulthood. Retraining executive skills may be quite difficult because the person may have been intellectually limited or learning disabled before the injury, so that the head injury exacerbates a preexisting developmental disorder.

INFORMAL ASSESSMENT OF EXECUTIVE FUNCTIONING

Perhaps the best way to determine if the client's executive skills were limited before the injury is to interview the client's family, friends, or coworkers concerning behavioral changes before and after injury. Anderson-Parenté (1994) indicated that clients and family members can estimate different aspects of the client's level of functioning. Clients can evaluate accurately the more concrete aspects of their behavior, such as their motor functioning, but family members can more accurately estimate the more abstract aspects of clients' behavior, such as social skills or abstract reasoning capacity. Anderson-Parenté suggested assessing the client's executive skills by asking family members to answer questions such as the following: Can the client set goals and follow through with attaining them? Can the client plan and prioritize? Can he or she organize a task, living space, and time? How well does the client self-initiate, self-inhibit, self-monitor, and self-evaluate? Can the client solve problems, make decisions, and anticipate the consequences of his or her behavior? How does the client's current level of functioning in each of these areas compare with that of his or her premorbid state? Has there been any noticeable improvement with therapy?

Simply asking the family to reflect on the client's ability to do these types of things before and after the injury can be of enormous benefit when assessing executive functioning and potential for improvement. In many cases, self-report and family observation may be the only ways to estimate the more abstract qualities of the client's behavior. They may also be the only ways to assess the person's premorbid executive capacity (Diller & Ben-Yishay, 1987).

We have already discussed organizational, problem-solving, and decision-making skills in previous chapters. We now turn to a discussion of retraining self-monitoring, goal setting, and social competence.

SELF-MONITORING

Self-monitoring is the ability to evaluate and regulate the quality or quantity of our behavior. This skill can be and often is diminished after a traumatic brain injury (McGlynn & Schacter, 1989). The problem is exacerbated by the fact that skills of self-monitoring are seldom taught early in life, so that the therapist may have to teach the skills without any prior learning to build on. We therefore describe several techniques for training the client to regulate his or her performance on the basis of previous behavior. This list of techniques is not exhaustive. We selected the techniques for discussion because they are methods that have worked in the past.

Behavioral Charting

Behavioral charting is a technique that forces the client to see the changes in his or her behavior over time and to notice the relationships among various behaviors. The therapist and client begin by listing several behaviors the client wants to change. These can be specific and measurable things, such as weight or amount of time spent with the family that day, or vague qualities, such as perceived happiness. Ideally, the client lists the behaviors on a 10-point scale. The therapist must therefore assist the client with developing the list and with scaling the behaviors such that each can be easily rated every day. For example, one client was interested in the behaviors mentioned above as well as severity of daily headaches and number of cups of coffee he drank each day. Weight was measured on a 10-point scale that surrounded his current weight (160–170 lb.). Because the client seldom weighed less than 160 or more than 170, the scale ranged from 161 lb. (1) through 170 lb. (10).

Coffee consumption was rated from a single cup per day (1) to 10 cups per day (10). Severity of daily headaches was scaled from *very low* (1) through *severe* (10).

Each client will choose different variables because the desired changes differ from person to person. We have found that putting everything on the familiar scale of 1 to 10 is easiest for most clients to understand and work with. For intangible variables such as depression, however, anchoring with verbal labels at the beginning, middle, and end of the scale may be necessary. Depression, for example, can be scaled from 1 (*not depressed at all*) through 5 (*unhappy and tired*) through 10 (*cries and is miserable every day*).

The selection of behaviors and the definitions of the scales may therefore take several sessions to complete. An example of the rating form is presented in Exhibit 19–1.

Once the client and therapist identify the behaviors of interest and make up the rating scale, the client rates each variable on a scale of 1 to 10 every day or at some other mutually agreed-upon interval. The client can enter these behaviors on the chart or rate the behaviors on a separate rating form and give it to the therapist, who charts it. Either way, the result is a picture of the client's behavior across several different dimensions. The chart also provides a picture of how the different behaviors interact with one another.

The therapist and client discuss the chart as it develops. A sample set of ratings and their corresponding chart are presented in Figure 19–1. Interpreting the chart is a matter of asking several questions. The first question is whether the various behaviors are at acceptable levels or if it is necessary to increase or decrease them. For example, does the client continue to rate depression with scores of 8 and 9, which indicate a serious problem? Which scores are increasing or decreasing most rapidly? Which scores does the client want to decrease or increase, and are these behaviors going in the right direction?

It is also important to look at the relationship between the behaviors. Those that follow the same trend are usually directly related to one another, whereas those that follow an opposite trend are typically inversely related. For example, the client in Figure 19–1 found that his headaches were directly related to the amount of coffee he was consuming each day. This is because the rated severity of headaches followed the same upward trend on the chart as did the number of cups of coffee he drank each day.

This simple technique shows clients that everything they do can affect everything else. Clients learn which aspects of their behavior are related by inspecting the chart and looking for consistent trends among the ratings. They are often surprised to see that specific behaviors they thought were related to one another are not. Other relationships that they never suspected emerge clearly on the chart. These relationships become the focus of therapy discussions.

Clients eventually learn to predict any future behavior by making mental note of behaviors that turn out to be related to it. For example, the client in this example learned that he would usually get a headache when he drank more than three cups of coffee a day. He learned to limit his intake of coffee in order to decrease the severity of his headaches.

Exhibit 19–1 Sample Behavioral Rating Form

```
_____ Coffee (cups per day)
_____ Anxiety (1 = low to 10 = high)
_____ Depression (1 = low to 10 = high)
_____ Headaches (0 = none to 10 = severe)
_____ Memory (1 = poor to 10 = excellent)
_____ Thinking (1 = poor to 10 = excellent)
_____ Energy (1 = low to 10 = high)
_____ Attention (1 = low to 10 = high)
```

Predicting Behavior and Its Consequences

The therapist should also train the client to predict his or her performance in most tasks and then to evaluate the accuracy of the predictions. To get an idea of how well the client predicts,

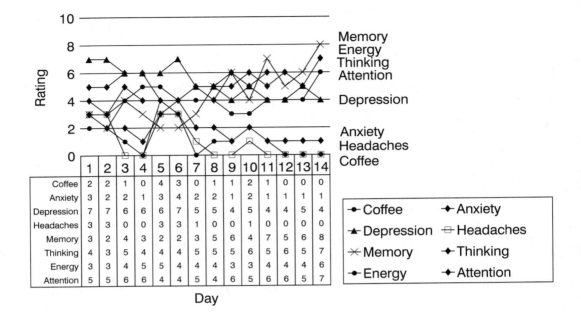

	1	2	3	4	5	6	7	8	9	10	11	12	13	14
Coffee	2	2	1	0	4	3	0	1	1	2	1	0	0	0
Anxiety	3	2	2	1	3	4	2	2	1	2	1	1	1	1
Depression	7	7	6	6	6	7	5	5	4	5	4	4	5	4
Headaches	3	3	0	0	3	3	1	0	0	1	0	0	0	0
Memory	3	2	4	3	2	2	3	5	6	4	7	5	6	8
Thinking	4	3	5	4	4	4	5	5	5	6	5	6	5	7
Energy	3	3	4	5	5	4	4	4	3	3	4	4	4	6
Attention	5	5	6	6	4	4	5	4	6	5	6	6	5	7

Day

Figure 19–1 Sample Behavioral Chart

the therapist can begin by asking the client to estimate his or her performance on various tasks during the initial evaluation. For example, we usually ask clients to predict their performance on the various subtests of a neuropsychological evaluation.

We usually find that clients cannot evaluate accurately due to a tendency either to overpredict or to underpredict their performance. During therapy sessions, we frequently ask clients to predict how they will perform on the various tasks. Family members can also ask the client to predict performance, feelings, physical states, and so forth and then later validate the predictions. The general goal is to get the client in the habit of predicting and evaluating as a matter of daily routine. Clients may have difficulty accepting this type of feedback. They may become frustrated and occasionally irritated when their predictions are inaccurate. The therapist and family members should tell clients that this is a necessary aspect of therapy and that their predictions will gradually improve.

Videotaping

Videotaping may also be an effective vehicle for training self-monitoring. This involves taping the client during a session and then reviewing the tape later to show the client how he or she performed. We describe this procedure for training name-face association in Chapter 11. However, the therapist can use this same procedure to facilitate self-monitoring of virtually any skill. We find that it is most useful for training more complex or abstract social skills, such as communication or social interaction.

Verification

We have also discussed the value of verification of behavior in various sections of this book. This means that the therapist trains the client to ask others to verify whether he or she received a certain communication correctly. The client learns to follow each interchange with a statement such as "Let me repeat what you just said" or "Let me see if I have this correct." This type of statement usually forces the other person to repeat the statement, which ensures adequate rehearsal for the client. It also gives the client the opportunity to put the information in his or her own words and to have the other person verify that the concept was correctly understood. The general rule of thumb is that 1 minute spent doing this is worth 1 hour spent later trying to fix the problems that arise from a miscommunication. The procedure gradually shows the client how to monitor verbal exchanges, and it gives the family a convenient way of monitoring improvement in the client's comprehensions.

SETTING GOALS

When asked to define their goals, clients often say something like "I live my life day by day." This type of response reflects an inability to anticipate and plan for the future (Cicerone & Wood, 1987). The therapist's goal is therefore to define for the client a clear vision of the future and an action plan that the client can use to achieve it. This is the process of teaching goal setting and prioritizing.

The first step toward defining goals is to ask the client certain questions that force him or her to think about the future and to define priorities. For example, we usually ask such questions as "What do you want to have accomplished in 5 years?" This forces the client to define a long-term goal. We spent several sessions discussing priorities and manageable subgoals. We then list the final product for the client and use the list as a focus of discussion. The outcome of these sessions is to define a set of tangible long-term goals for the client, along with a set of short-term goals that he or she can pursue en route to achieving the long-term goals. This becomes an action plan and the focus of the client's therapy.

It is important for the goals to be *tangible, concrete,* and *measurable.* Many clients will begin by defining vague goals, such as "I want to be happy and fulfilled." These are certainly laudable goals, but they are difficult to evaluate in

terms of final achievement. Goals such as "I want to be self-supporting and live in my own home" are far more useful. Some criteria for creating tangible goals include whether (a) the goal can be stated in concrete terms, (b) the client can set a date for when the goal will be accomplished, (c) it is possible to create an action plan that will attain the goal, and (d) the client can record progress toward the goal.

Subgoals are aspects of a long-term goal that are feasible to achieve in 1 year and are necessary precursors to attaining the long-term goal. These are listed on paper and should be posted in the home so that the client can see them each day. We typically make the goals into a poster so that the client can tape it to the door or to a wall where it will be in plain view.

The next step is to have the client memorize the GOAL mnemonic, which details the procedure for creating goals and then acting on them. The mnemonic works well with the behavioral charting technique mentioned above.

> (*G*)*o over your goals every day.* This reminds the client to spend some small amount of time rehearsing his or her goals every day. This increases the client's awareness.
>
> (*O*)*rder your goals*—short and long term. The therapist will usually do this with the client initially, breaking the overall goals into 5-year and 1-year categories.
>
> (*A*)*sk yourself two questions each day:* "What did I do today to achieve my goals?" and "What could I have done differently to achieve my goals?"
>
> (*L*)*ook at your goals each day.* It is useful to post the client's goals next to his or her behavioral chart to show how the behaviors are related to the goals.

As an example of goal setting, consider the client mentioned earlier in this chapter. His initial goals were "to be happy and to have a fulfilling life." The therapist redefined these goals into short- and long-term components by first asking what the client would find fulfilling and what would make him happy. The client concluded that being happy and feeling fulfilled were highly related. Both involved working at a stable job, having friends, and being independent. His long-term goals were therefore to get a job and to get his own place to live. His short-term goals included getting the training necessary for the job and completing the training in 1 year.

The client entered a program in janitorial/custodial training that he could complete in 1 year. He and the therapist developed a self-monitoring sheet that included his weekly performance evaluations from his training plus his daily self-ratings of how he did that day. The chart also included self-ratings of headache severity, attention to detail, and other qualities that he felt were necessary for success in the program. He posted these charts on a wall in his room in the rehabilitation center and reviewed them every day in accordance with the GOAL mnemonic outlined above.

SOCIAL COMPETENCE

This aspect of the client's behavior is, perhaps, the most important of any that we will discuss. It is the ability to behave in a manner that others find socially acceptable. It is the best predictor of whether the person will be able to maintain employment, have friendships, and feel socially accepted. It is also the most difficult of skills to train, probably because it involves a vast array of interrelated behaviors.

Over the years, we have identified several characteristics of socially competent individuals. We review these here because they clarify our view of the type of person we are trying to create with the therapies described below. Socially competent individuals project a unique image. This is not a flashy image or one that is designed to draw attention. It is uncommon, competent, attractive, and memorable. These individuals display a sense of social control and resist social pressure. They listen well and communicate clearly with others. They respond to social feedback and change even though they may not like what others tell them. They consider the history of a social situation before taking a stand or responding. They understand the importance of timing of responses in social encounters. They do not force themselves on others socially but rather initiate friendships and relationships subtly. They praise their friends' appearance and accomplishments. They do not make the same mistakes twice.

Forward Thinking

Most of these personality characteristics require an abstract ability we call *forward thinking,* which is the skill of thinking in advance. This is an abstract skill that includes planning, prioritizing, and anticipating the consequences of behavior and then selecting behaviors in accordance with the predicted consequences. We retrain forward thinking with two games. Each of these games can be carried out in a group or with individuals. Both involve the ability to think ahead and to consider current behavior as a precursor to something that may occur in the future.

One game is called "What Would Happen If?" The therapist begins this game by asking the client to define a major problem. For example, the client might say, "I hate living at home with my family." The therapist then asks what the client wants to do about the problem. The client might respond, "I want to move out on my own!" The therapist then asks, "What would happen if you did that?" The client must then respond with possible problems that might arise if he or she moved out. For example, the client would then have to find a place to live, pay rent, function independently, and so forth. As the client generates each of these consequences, the therapist asks the same question, for example: "What would happen if you had to pay rent?" The client then generates possible consequences, such as "I'd have to get a job." The therapist responds with "What would happen if you had to get a job?" and so on. The goal of the session is to get the client always to ask the question "What would happen if . . . ?" before taking any action. The exercise demonstrates quite clearly that all behaviors have consequences and that even the simplest action can create a variety of consequences that the client must consider before acting impulsively.

Another game is called "Scenario Generation." This game begins with the therapist's asking client to describe an ideal world or life situation. The exercise is easiest to implement after the client has gone through the goal-setting session outlined above because the ideal world usually accords with the client's long-term goals. After the client has described his or her ideal world, the therapist asks the client to define those behaviors he or she feels will create that situation most rapidly and completely. Again, these are usually variations on the short-term goals outlined in the above goal-setting exercises.

The therapist next asks the client to take the opposite or reverse-logic position. Specifically, the client lists those behaviors that would ensure that he or she would never reach the ideal world. Another way of asking this question is to list behaviors that will ensure a "worst nightmare" scenario. The value of this exercise is that many clients, when asked to play the reverse-logic component of the game, realize that their current behaviors are more likely to lead to their worst nightmare than to result in an ideal scenario.

Self-Expression

Another aspect of social competence involves expressing oneself in a manner that is efficient and easy to understand. In the chapter on retraining concept learning, we mentioned that clear expression involves training the client to explain by example, using positive examples first and negative examples second and then focusing in on the relevant aspects of the concept. In addition to this procedure, we recommend another exercise that involves training the client to express a thought with progressively fewer and fewer words. We begin by asking the client to state his or her biggest problem. The next step is to have the client restate the problem in fewer words and to continue this process until the problem is stated as clearly and with as few words as possible. This exercise works well in a group setting, with each person being asked to redefine the problem in his or her own words but by using fewer words than the person before.

This process will often result in a redefinition and clarification of the person's biggest problems. For example, one client stated that her biggest problem was that she "couldn't go to the mall without spending all of her money on clothes or movies or jewelry." The next person in the group redefined the problem as "She can't control her spending." The third person restated

the problem as "poor impulse control." The client listened and agreed with each of these redefinitions. She also came to the conclusion that the gist of the problem was not that she could not resist buying clothes. It was that she could not control her impulses and that spending was simply the most obvious example of poor impulse control. The value of this exercise is that clients learn to focus on the core elements of their problems. They are also more likely to accept the analysis because it comes from other clients rather than from the therapist. In addition, they learn how to express their ideas in a focused manner.

Care of Appearance

Social competence also encompasses behaviors of caring for one's appearance, such as dress and grooming. We encourage clients to dress neatly and in attire that is just slightly better than the situation calls for. We have found that dressing in this manner will usually improve the client's mood. The more important consequence is that others relate to the client differently than they would if the client were not so nicely dressed. This becomes apparent when the client goes out into the everyday world. Store owners, police, and passersby on the street treat the person with greater respect and take the person more seriously.

Listening Skills

Listening skills are a critical component of the person's social competence. We use the LISTEN mnemonic to help the client remember these skills:

> *(L)ook at the person to whom you are speaking.* This will usually require some training to get the client to maintain eye contact. The goal is to teach the client to focus on the nonverbal aspects of communication that are carried in facial expressions.
> *(I)nterest yourself in the conversation.* Ask questions about the statement the other person is making. Comment occasionally on the conversation. Use social fillers such as "Uh huh," "I see!" or "Tell me more about that."

(S)peak less than half the time. This is especially important for clients with head injury because some aspect of the conversation may trigger another schematic thought that leads to a tangential discussion.

(T)ry not to interrupt or change the topic. The problem arises when, some portion of the conversation triggers a memory. The therapist therefore must train the client to ask questions only about the topic at hand or to relate additional ideas about that topic.

(E)valuate what is said. Question the content. Do not blindly accept it.

(N)otice body language and facial expression. We typically use pictures of individuals in different body-expressive states and train the clients to recognize these when shown the pictures. Pease (1981) is a good source for these pictures.

After the client learns the mnemonic, the next step is to create a conversation and to videotape the exchange. After about 5 minutes of conversation, the therapist stops the tape and replays it for the client. The purpose of this exercise is to have the client identify which aspects of the LISTEN mnemonic were adhered to or violated during the conversation.

PERSONAL TIME MANAGEMENT

Organization of time involves teaching the client to plan, to set priorities, and to use external aids as a day planner and to-do lists. It also requires that the client begin to change attitudes about time and social behavior. One begins by discussing with the client some common misconceptions about time. Topics include procrastination, completion anxiety, and various common principles of time management. Much of this information may be new to the client and somewhat difficult to understand.

Procrastination and *completion anxiety* are very different problems, and many clients suffer from both. Procrastination is the problem of delaying initiation of a project. Completion anxiety is the problem of finishing 95% of the task but never completing the last 5%. The root cause of procrastination is usually a fear of commitment to a task that seems overwhelming. The underlying cause of completion anxiety is fear

of evaluation: that is, the fear that others will not approve of the final product. It is important for the therapist to discuss these problems with the client and to point out these problems as they arise.

Managing time effectively also involves changing the way we do things during the day. One important change is first to identify peak performance times and to protect them from interruption as much as possible. For example, many clients will be fresh during the morning hours but tire at the end of the day. Others will be more efficient at the end of the day or during the evening. The therapist teaches clients to organize their day so that their important tasks are done during their peak hours. This time needs to be protected; that is, clients must alter their behavior so that they are not interrupted during the peak times. Many clients will have to resist the temptation of talking to friends, sitting in public areas, or making themselves available for conversation during peak time. However, most clients will be amazed how many things can be accomplished if there is a clear agenda that they try to accomplish during peak time.

Another behavioral change involves teaching the client to use bits of time. Many clients sit idly during the day for periods that range from minutes to hours. These are times when the client can perform some form of productive activity. To use this time effectively, the therapist trains the client to bring different projects or portions of projects with them so that smaller tasks can be performed during those smaller time intervals that would normally be spent doing nothing. It is first necessary, however, to teach the client the concept of breaking down larger projects into smaller ones. Usually, only the smaller ones can be completed during these smaller time intervals.

Teaching time management skills is much easier if the therapist first gives the client an appointment calendar that is also a day planner. We recommend a particular planner, made by E-Z Record Company (see Chapter 25). This has several unique features that make it ideal for work with head-injured clients. First, each day is marked off in half-hour increments, and the time is listed in the margin of the page for that day.

The client can then circle the time of the appointment and write a reminder next to the time.

The calendar also has blank lined paper next to each day so that the client can make notes about directions or instructions for that day. The goal is to get the client to list all appointments for the following day on the night before. The therapist also teaches the client to mark the time in the DayTimer and to write any directions or special instructions next to the appointment.

It is important for the client to organize his or her appointments so that there is as little duplication of effort as possible. This particular calendar also comes with insert pages for to-do lists. These may be useful for some clients, although they are seldom necessary because the client can also create to-do lists on the lined paper. Regardless of how the client does this, it is important that he or she write a list of tasks to be completed that day and divide them into two groups. The first group includes two or three tasks that must be done that day. The second group includes tasks that would be nice to complete but are not crucial to complete that day. It is important for the client to check off these tasks after completing them.

One advantage of writing out to-do lists is that it forces the client to structure the day. In addition, writing out the to-do list the night before forces the client to anticipate all the things he or she will need to prepare in advance in order to complete the tasks the following day. Therefore, the training involves not only writing out the to-do list but also listing the things the client will need to do first, to find, to collect, and to have ready for the next day's activities.

Time marking involves several procedures. One is the use of a beeping watch to provide the client with an hourly time sense. Simply wearing the watch and hearing it beep at regular intervals will gradually give the client a clear concept of an hour. Asking the client to estimate time since the last time it was mentioned is another simple procedure that forces the client to keep mental track of how much time has passed. Asking the client to estimate how long it will take to finish a task is also effective for instilling a sense of future time.

CONCLUSION

This chapter summarizes the concept of executive functioning, which includes the ability to think in advance. The chapter began by defining executive functioning in terms of self-regulatory and control functions that direct and organize behavior. Many therapists feel that executive skills are especially difficult to train because they were poorly developed before the client's injury. We have found that clients can learn executive skills, and the chapter presents specific techniques that have proven effective over the years.

To begin, the therapist should question family members and friends regarding the client's premorbid levels of executive skills. Retraining executive skills involves teaching the client to self-monitor. Along these lines, techniques such as behavioral charting, predicting consequences, and videotaping are helpful. A method for teaching goal setting along with a mnemonic that summarized the goal-setting process was presented. Specific games for training the ability to think in advance were described, including "What Would Happen If" and "Scenario Generation." We also discussed the importance of grooming and dress, listening skills, and clarity of verbal expression. The chapter ended with a discussion of techniques for training time management, including identifying peak performance times, external aids, time marking, and planning in advance.

REFERENCES

Anderson-Parenté, J. (1994). A comparison of metacognitive ratings of persons with traumatic brain injury and their families. *NeuroRehabilitation, 4*(3), 168–173.

Baddeley, A.D. (1986). *Working memory.* New York: Basic Books.

Baddeley, A.D. (1990). *Human memory: Theory and practice.* New York: Allyn & Bacon.

Brown, A.L. (1978). Knowing when, where, and how to remember: A problem of metacognition. *Advances in Instructional Psychology, 1,* 77–165.

Case, R. (1992). The role of frontal lobes in the regulation of cognitive development. *Brain and Cognition, 20,* 51–73.

Cicerone, K.D., & Wood, T.R.S. (1987). Planning disorder after closed head injury. *Archives of Physical Medicine and Rehabilitation, 68,* 127–132.

Diller, L., & Ben-Yishay, Y. (1987). Outcomes and evidence in neuropsychological rehabilitation in closed-head injury. In H.S. Levin, J. Grafman, & H.M. Eisenberg (Eds.), *Neurobehavioral recovery from head injury*. New York: Oxford University Press.

Duncan, J. (1986). Disorganization of behavior after frontal lobe damage. *Cognitive Neuropsychology, 3*, 279–297.

Janowski, J.S., Shimamura, A.P., Kritchevsky, M., & Squire, L.R. (1989). Cognitive impairment following frontal lobe damage and its relevance to human amnesia. *Behavioral Neuroscience, 103*, 548–560.

Lezak, M. (1993). New contributions to the neuropsychological assessment of executive functions. *Journal of Head Trauma Rehabilitation, 8*, 24–31.

McCarthy, R.A., & Warrington, E.K. (1990). *Cognitive neuropsychology: A clinical introduction*. San Diego: Academic Press.

McGlynn, S.M., & Schacter, D.L. (1989). Unawareness of deficits in neuropsychological syndromes. *Journal of*

Clinical and Experimental Neuropsychology, 11, 143–205.

Miller, G.A., Galanter, E., & Pribram, K.H. (1960). *Plans and the structure of behavior*. New York: Holt, Rinehart & Winston.

Pease, A. (1981). *Signals*. Toronto, Canada: Bantam.

Pollens, R., McBratnie, B., & Burton, P. (1988). Beyond cognition: Executive functions in closed head injury. *Cognitive Rehabilitation, 6*(5), 26–33.

Sternberg, R.J. (1985). General intellectual ability. In R.J. Sternberg (Ed.), *Human abilities: An information processing approach*. New York: W.H. Freeman.

Welsh, M.C., & Pennington, B.F. (1988). Assessing frontal lobe functioning in children: Views from developmental psychology. *Developmental Neuropsychology, 4*, 199–230.

Ylvisaker, M. (1995, January). *Executive functions and communication following traumatic brain injury*. Paper presented at the annual meeting of the Society for Cognitive Rehabilitation, Albuquerque, NM.

Chapter 20

Effect of Physical Condition on Cognition

A client's physical condition can have a major impact on his or her ability to perform everyday activities such as remembering someone's name or figuring out how much money must be spent at a store (Tariot & Weingartner, 1986) as well as his or her overall cognitive performance (Davies & Thomson, 1988; Herrmann & Searleman, 1990; Risko, Alvarez, & Fairbanks, 1991). Indeed physical condition is probably the single most important factor that affects how clients perform incidental and intentional cognitive tasks. An increase in physical fitness, general health, sleep, and relaxation typically improves most aspects of cognition. Furthermore, certain times in the day are better for remembering and thinking. For example, most people describe themselves as either morning or evening people. Changes in a client's routine that disrupt patterns of rest, activity, and food intake can interfere with attention and memory.

As we discussed in Chapters 4 and 9, attention is a key element of cognition. Poor condition lessens thinking skill because it restricts the client's ability to pay attention (Schneider & Shiffrin, 1977). As physical deficiencies or impairments lessen attention, the rate with which the client can process information decreases. Several known deficiencies may interfere with

attention and mental effort, the ability to retrieve information later on, or the association of information with an appropriate response. Poor physical condition may impair memory processes by lessening the ability of the central processor to rehearse and to attend to the contents of working memory. Therefore, no idea or image in working memory is likely to receive adequate attention, produce a salient trace in working memory, or effectively cue retrieval from long-term memory. Also, the sensory and working memory's physiological receptivity and readiness for processing are reduced (Herrmann & Searleman, 1990). The person may only attend and remember when there is a large incentive to do so (Parenté, 1994).

CORRECTION OF PHYSICAL DEFICIENCIES

In some cases, a client's physical deficiency may be beyond correction. However, the prescriptions that follow address mainly physical concerns that most adults can correct. Common sense combined with a few innovative manipulations can rectify most physical problems, at least enough to improve the client's thinking skills.

Physical Fitness

Exercise helps the client maintain strength, stamina, and cardiovascular condition (Blumenthal & Madden, 1988). It therefore creates the potential for vigilance in most cognitive tasks. It also helps relieve the client of the "blues," lessens stress, improves sleep, and enhances digestion, all of which help cognition. Clearly, it reduces anxiety and tension, and it may also improve attention and short-term memory. The client need not engage in strenuous exercise to improve cognition. A 20-minute walk each day is probably sufficient if a person has not been exercising previously.

Energy Cycles

Head injury survivors often have less strength to meet the challenges of the day. Moreover, what strength they do have is cyclical. There are certain times in the day and days in the week when thinking is most lucid. For most of us, the best time to perform cognitive tasks is between 11 a.m. and 4 p.m. This peak in cognitive performance probably occurs for several reasons. First, people get more involved with their activities by midday. Second, they gradually lose their sharpness later in the day as general fatigue sets in. Third, their attentiveness varies with daily biological cycles such as those in body temperature, respiration rate, and pulse rate (Wyon, Andersen, & Lundquist, 1979). Cognitive ability also tends to be at its best on Fridays and Saturdays. A peak in cognitive performance occurs on these days, probably because the anticipation of the weekend lifts a person's mood (Folkard & Monk, 1978). These peak times are applicable to clients who are employed, in training, or receiving therapy on a regular schedule. Different peak times may apply for clients who are unemployed, retired, or have sleep disorders. A therapist can assess a client's peak performance times simply by paying attention to when the client is most alert and most able to think clearly.

A client's routine time for waking and sleeping also affects his or her daily peaks for mental clarity. If the client is a morning person, who goes to bed early and rises early, then he or she will learn more efficiently earlier in the day. If the client is an evening person, then the evening is the best time to learn new things. Clients can make the best use of their strength by performing cognitive tasks during their peak times.

Most clients should schedule meetings on Thursday or Friday. The client and family should try to minimize or at least decrease the number of cognitive tasks the client must carry out when there are anticipated disruptions of daily and weekly cycles. When life does not allow the client to schedule an event at an optimal time, he or she can at least attempt to be more alert when the event does occur.

Any disruptions to the client's cycle can diminish his or her cognitive capacity. For example, a client may not get regular sleep after a family dispute, when attempting new employment, or when beginning formal training. Therefore, when there is a shift in the client's cycle, there should also be extra time to recuperate before taking on major intellectual tasks.

Sleep

Proper sleep obviously makes a person strong and alert for cognitive tasks (Idzikowski, 1984; Tilley & Statham, 1989). Getting sufficient sleep before an exam or an interview is essential for remembering quickly and accurately. We all can recall occasions when we were forced to stay awake much longer than usual. The next day, we fumbled for our words and struggled to remember answers that normally we would have remembered easily. The client can ensure getting a good night's sleep if he or she avoids eating and drinking late in the evening, avoids thinking about personal troubles prior to bedtime, and goes to bed at approximately the same time every night.

Eating Habits

Poor nutrition places added burdens on cognition. A balanced diet supplies sufficient vitamin levels to guard against deficiencies that produce cognitive deficits. Certain foods or a vitamin supplement must be included in everyone's diet to prevent cognitive deficiencies. Vitamins may help cognition because they enhance brain chemistry. This remains to be proven, largely because too little research has been done on the effects of vitamins on the chemistry of the normal brain. Nevertheless, the foods and vegetables that experts recommend as "cognitively nutritious" include beef, pork, kidneys, liver, fish, shellfish, milk, eggs, cheese, vegetables, kelp, and onions. Recently, it has been reported that drinking lemonade immediately after studying facilitates later recall, apparently because sugar aids the absorption of information into long-term memory (Gold, 1987). Whatever the client eats, moderate amounts are recommended before a period of intense concentration (Smith, 1988). Large amounts of food make anyone sleepy and unable to pay attention. "Cognitively nutritious" vitamins and minerals include choline, B-complex vitamins (especially B1, B6, and B12), iodine, manganese, folic acid, zinc, and L-tyrosine. Irregular eating habits may cause a mild vitamin deficiency. If this is the case, the client should take a supplement. There is no need, however, to take large quantities of vitamins daily. A simple daily supplement will suffice because most of the supplement is excreted the next day anyway.

Sensory Difficulties

Poor eyesight or hearing can prevent a person from thinking and remembering well (Cutler & Grams, 1988). Sensory difficulties slow the initial registration of information and make it harder to notice cues that help one to remember. Sensory difficulties also may lead others to conclude that a person has cognitive deficiencies. This erroneous conclusion stems from the assumption that cognitive failures occur only because of poor cognition or laziness. Unfortunately, when a person with a sensory deficiency explains frankly that a cognitive failure was due to a sensory deficiency, others may regard the explanation as an excuse. If the therapist suspects a sensory deficit, a medical examination is in order. If the deficit is confirmed, the client will probably be advised to use occasionally some device

to correct for his or her problem, such as magnifying or prism glasses or hearing aids. Although these devices may impose some inconvenience, the improved performance they enable more than compensates.

Illnesses and Prescription Drugs

Illnesses, major and minor, may interfere with cognitive performance because discomfort diminishes attention (Herrmann, 1995). When our ability to pay attention is lessened, we do not register or remember as well as when we are healthy. Similarly, we do not think or solve problems as readily. Even a minor illness can impair cognitive performance. The impairment due to major illnesses will even be worse. Exhibit 20–1 presents a list of various illness conditions that are known to affect cognition adversely.

Taking steps to reduce discomfort and control symptoms will improve cognitive performance during an illness. Also, if the client has a chronic illness, the therapist should check whether the side effects of the client's treatment or medication influence cognition. Medicines are rarely identified explicitly as interfering with cognition per se (Polster, 1993). Occasionally, a medicine's effect of diminishing the client's capacity to pay attention is noted on the box and label.

Any medicine that lowers the client's attentive powers will reduce how much he or she registers and remembers. If a prescription medicine lessens the client's ability to pay attention, the client or the client's caregiver should discuss the problem with a physician. Many physicians are unaware of the cognitive contraindications of prescribed and over-the-counter medicines. Therefore, if a client is taking any medication or multiple medications, it is often worthwhile to investigate the cognitive impact of medicines. Some medicines that are known to impair cognition are amphetamines, analgesics, antipsychotics, anxiolytic cardiovascular medications, antibiotics, anticonvulsants, corticosteroids, antidepressants, glaucoma eye drops, antihistamines, lithium, antihypertensives, pulmonary antiemetics (with medications like scopola-

Exhibit 20–1 Illness Conditions That Impair Cognition

- Cancer, especially brain tumors
- Heart attack/heart condition, mini/major strokes, hypertension
- AIDS
- Pneumonia, tuberculosis
- Encephalitis
- Meningitis
- Hepatitis
- Polio
- Syphilis, gonorrhea
- Hemophilia
- Sickle-cell anemia
- Multiple sclerosis
- Epilepsy
- Parkinson's disease
- Huntington's disease
- Pick's disease
- Addison's disease
- Hyperthyroidism, hypothyroidism

- Dementia: Alzheimer's disease, Korsakoff's disease
- Age-related memory impairment
- Environmental illness/toxic exposure
- Chronic fatigue syndrome
- Nutritional diseases: anemia, beriberi, Kwashkiorkor, pellagra, scurvy, hypoglycemia
- Protozoan diseases: malaria, African sleeping sickness, amebic dysentery, intestinal infection
- Worms in the blood, intestines, liver, or lungs
- Anoxia (e.g., from COPD)
- Chronic pain
- Arthritis
- Headaches, especially migraines
- Allergies
- Colds, flus
- Learning disabilities (e.g., attention deficit, dyslexia)
- Emotional/mental illness: anxiety disorders, depression, manic depression, schizophrenia, dissociative disorders, post-traumatic stress disorder

mine), and sedatives. All electroconvulsive shock also impairs cognition.

Numerous illness conditions impair cognition directly. These include Alzheimer's disease and related diseases, Korsakoff's (alcoholic) syndrome, brain tumors, mini/major strokes, multiple sclerosis, and low blood pressure (Khan, 1986; Mayes, 1988; Wilson, 1987). Very low blood pressure, a life-threatening condition, reduces one's ability to register and remember. Apparently, low blood pressure impairs memory and thinking because it lessens a person's ability to pay attention. Fortunately, the medicines that are used to treat low blood pressure often restore attentive powers and alleviate the cognitive problems that go along with the condition. If the client has both a head injury and one of these cognitive illnesses, the need for specialized treatment is obviously increased (Zasler, 1991).

Alcohol and Illicit Drugs

Several substances impair cognitive performance. Perhaps the best known is alcohol, sometimes called the "amnesia food" (Polster, 1993).

Marijuana has effects on cognition that are similar to those produced by alcohol. Indeed, the pill form of marijuana has an effect that induces a high comparable to several drinks. People who take this pill learn a list of words more slowly than sober people, and when asked to recognize whether a digit was in a digit series presented moments before, they recognize the test digit more slowly than people not under the influence. Other illicit drugs, such as cocaine, hallucinogens, inhalants, opiates, and PCP, also disrupt cognition. The bottom line is that cognition is most efficient when a person is sober. If the client has abused certain substances before injury, it may be difficult to persuade him or her to cease the abuse. The therapist may find it necessary to refer the client for drug and alcohol counseling and even regular drug testing as a condition for further treatment.

COMMON STIMULANTS

Mild stimulants commonly found in tea, coffee, sodas, or tobacco supposedly may make the client more attentive and thus better able to perform cognitive tasks. However, the client should be made aware that even common stimulants like coffee and tea often have adverse effects on cognition (Erikson et al., 1985). Indeed, head-injured people are known to have more adverse reactions to stimulants than non-head-injured people. However, in some situations, for example, if the client sleeps excessively, a mild stimulant may help him or her stay awake and pay attention. It has sometimes been assumed that nicotine facilitates memory, presumably because it may make a person alert while performing a cognitive task (Peeke & Peeke, 1984; Wittenborn, 1988). However, recent research indicates very clearly that nicotine can impair memory considerably, as much as a few alcoholic drinks (Spilich, June, & Renner, 1992). Nonsmokers are quicker than smokers at remembering lists of digits. Moreover, nonsmokers score higher on tests of memory for a written passage, digit span, reproduction of a visual pattern, and learning pairs of words. We recommend that if the client smokes, he or she should not do so before a cognitive task. Although there are exceptions to the general rule, our review of the literature indicates that a client is usually better off not using stimulants. Stimulants may come in handy for fighting fatigue, but may also exact a cost.

CONCLUSION

Clearly, good physical condition is one of the necessary ingredients for good cognitive performance. To avoid lowering his or her performance level, the client should follow some common-sense guidelines:

1. *Remove discomfort due to minor illnesses.* Discomfort limits attention and concentration.
2. *Eliminate noxious substances.* Drugs and alcohol, including caffeine and nicotine, impair the ability to pay attention and can upset emotional balance.
3. *Create a well-balanced diet.* Do not over-eat before cognitive tasks. Moderate eating prevents the sleepiness that comes with overeating.
4. *Get enough sleep,* and adhere to consistent cycles of wakefulness and sleep. Sufficient sleep and consistent sleep cycles are essential for effective thinking and memory.
5. *Take account of energy peaks.* Determine whether you are a morning or an evening person, and perform the most difficult tasks at that time.
6. *Stay in shape.* Physical fitness predisposes good cognition. Good physical condition also creates self-esteem.

REFERENCES

Blumenthal, J.A., & Madden, D.J. (1988). Effects of aerobic exercise training, age, and physical fitness on memory-search performance. *Psychology and Aging, 3,* 280–285.

Cutler, S.J., & Grams, A.E. (1988). Correlates of self-reported everyday memory problems. *Journal of Gerontology, 43,* 582–590.

Davies, G.M., & Thomson, D.M. (1988). *Memory in context: Context in memory.* New York: John Wiley.

Erikson, G.C., Hager, L.B., Houseworth, C., Dugan, J., Petros, T., & Beckwith, B.E. (1985). The effects of caffeine on memory for word lists. *Physiology and Behavior, 35,* 47–51.

Folkard, S., & Monk, R. (1978). Time of day effects in immediate and delayed memory. In M. Gruneberg, P.E. Morris, & R.N. Sykes (Eds.), *Practical aspects of memory.* London: Academic Press.

Gold, P.E. (1987). Sweet memories. *American Scientist, 75,* 151–155.

Herrmann, D.J. (1995). *Illness and cognition: Report prepared for the associate director for research and methodology of the National Center for Health Statistics.* Hyattsville, MD: National Center for Health Statistics.

Herrmann, D.J., & Searleman, A. (1990). A multi-modal approach to memory improvement. In G.H. Bower (Ed.), *Advances in learning and motivation* (pp. 175–205). New York: Academic Press.

Idzikowski, C. (1984). Sleep and memory. *British Journal of Psychology, 75,* 439–449.

Khan, A.U. (1986). *Clinical disorders of memory.* New York: Plenum.

Mayes, A.R. (1988). *Human organic memory disorders.* New York: Cambridge University Press.

Parenté, R. (1994). Transfer and generalization of cognitive skill after traumatic brain injury. *NeuroRehabilitation, 4,* 25–35.

Peeke, S.C., & Peeke, H.V. (1984). Attention, memory, and cigarette smoking. *Psychopharmacology, 84,* 205–216.

Polster, M. (1993). Drug-induced amnesia. Implications for neuropsychological investigations of memory. *Psychological Bulletin, 114*, 477–493.

Risko, V.J., Alvarez, M.C., & Fairbanks, M.M. (1991). External factors that influence study. In R.F. Flippo & D.C. Caverly (Eds.), *Teaching reading and study strategies at the college level.* Newark, DE: International Reading Association.

Schneider, W., & Shiffrin, R.M. (1977). Controlled and automatic human information processing: I. Detection, search, and attention. *Psychological Review, 84*, 1–66.

Smith, A. (1988). Effects of meals on memory and attention. In M.M. Gruneberg, P.E. Morris, & R.N. Sykes (Eds.), *Practical aspects of memory.* New York: John Wiley.

Spilich, G., June, L., & Renner, J. (1992). Cigarette smoking and cognitive performance. *British Journal of Addiction, 87*, 1313–1326.

Tariot, P., & Weingartner, H. (1986). A psychobiological analysis of cognitive failures. *Archives of General Psychiatry, 43*, 1183–1188.

Tilley, A., & Statham, D. (1989). The effect of prior sleep on retrieval. *Acta Psychologica, 70*, 199–203.

Wilson, B.A. (1987). *The rehabilitation of memory.* New York: Guilford.

Wittenborn, J.R. (1988). Assessment of the effects of drugs on memory. *Psychopharmacology, 6*, 67–78.

Wyon, D.P., Andersen, B., & Lundquist, G.R. (1979). The effects of moderate heat stress on mental performance. *Scandinavian Journal of Work Environment and Health, 5*, 352–361.

Zasler, N.D. (1991). Pharmacological aspects of cognitive function following traumatic brain injury. In J.S. Kreutzer & P.H. Wehman (Eds.), *Cognitive rehabilitation for persons with traumatic brain injury* (pp. 87–94). Baltimore: Paul H. Brookes.

Chapter 21

Emotional Issues

Emotional discord affects virtually every aspect of the cognitive system. Because emotions affect attention, they may reduce the client's ability to absorb and to retain new information (Watts, MacLeod, & Morris, 1988; Wells & Mathews, 1994). Therefore, anything that helps to repair the client's emotional state will improve concentration, memory, and the ability to control and to allocate thinking and processing (Baum, Cohen, & Hall, 1993; Hertel, 1994). In situations in which the person is in a great deal of emotional distress, it may be necessary to refer the client to a psychotherapist or to begin a medication trial. In many cases, the problems can be addressed via group and individual therapy.

NEGATIVE EMOTIONAL FACTORS

Disorientation

A hectic and harried lifestyle can create a certain amount of disorientation (Reason, 1988). Whatever its origin, confusion hampers performance. It lowers the level of attention to one's immediate surroundings and one's ability to focus attention. Alternatively, a very predictable and routinized lifestyle can also lower attention and ability to concentrate. Sometimes a person can become so relaxed and adept at a task that proficiency slackens. Experience and practice with most tasks create a skill that becomes so automatic that we cease to pay full attention to the task at hand. As our attention wanes or wanders, errors increase. These errors can have drastic consequences. For example, airplane accidents are sometimes caused by experienced pilots who inadvertently throw a switch in the wrong direction (Reason & MyCielska, 1983). We can all recall times when we started to drive off in our car and realized that the safety brake was still on. Concentration is affected by how well the environment allows the client to pay attention to the task at hand. There are optimum levels of noise and physical comfort for performing cognitive tasks. Total silence and maximum comfort are probably not the best conditions for cognition. Neither are tight-fitting clothes, uncomfortable furniture, or extremely loud noises.

In general, slight discomfort will make a person more alert than will coziness. Slight discomfort ensures that your client will not be drowsy. Coziness gives a feeling of safety, but it may lead the client to fall asleep. It is therefore reasonable to suggest that environments and modes of dress that are not too comfortable ensure that the client will pay better attention.

Depression and Mood Swings

Head injury survivors typically experience a wide range of moods that may fluctuate hourly or daily. Because moods and emotional states have such a pronounced effect on memory and cognition, it is important for the therapist to assess the extent of the client's mood swings before attempting treatment. In most cases, severe depression or mood swings impair memory and thinking.

Depressive states, whatever their intensity, impair cognitive performance (Hertel, 1994; Williams, Watts, MacLeod & Mathews, 1988). The slightly negative mood we feel after someone insults us diminishes our ability to pay attention. Normal depression weakens cognitive performance because of a preoccupation with unhappy thoughts that lowers the client's level of attention and reduces his or her capacity to focus attention (Hertel, 1992, 1994; Yesavage & Sheikh, 1988). Depression may also decrease attention powers because it can alter brain chemistry in a way that slows absorption of novel information and lowers the ability to retrieve stored information.

Depression weakens cognition so much that some doctors regard cognitive failure as a major indicator of clinical depression. Besides stress, most head injury victims experience depression periodically, if not continuously, during recovery. Thus, depression slows the cognitive rehabilitation process and can put a limit on the degree of recovery. Treatments that relieve depression, such as antidepressant drugs or psychotherapy, can restore cognitive abilities and improve overall cognitive functioning (Watts, 1988).

Stress

Stress has known adverse effects on thinking and memory. For example, nurses who work in high-stress situations, such as intensive care wards, manifest more cognitive failures than those who work on routine wards (Broadbent, Cooper, Fitzgerald, & Parks, 1982). Women scheduled to have mastectomies manifest a greater number of cognitive and absent-minded errors than usual in the period just prior to surgery (Reason, 1988; Reason & Lucas, 1984). Although stress can be debilitating, people need an optimal level of it to survive (Spielberger, Gonzales, & Fletcher, 1979). Likewise, most victims of head injury experience enormous stress while undergoing rehabilitation. High levels of stress and emotional problems at home greatly slow the therapy process and can put a limit on the degree of recovery. Clearly, the therapist must take whatever steps necessary to reduce the client's stress levels. However, a certain low level of stress can facilitate therapy. The trick is to maintain an optimal level of stress that is motivating but not overwhelming.

Relaxation relieves stress. It also decreases the distractibility that interferes with cognitive performance. The client will obviously benefit from incorporating into his or her daily routine a variety of ways to relax, such as naps, reminiscing with a friend, listening to music, and watching TV. Exercise may reduce stress and improve a client's mood. Relaxation techniques have generally been found to facilitate thinking and memory with the elderly (Yesavage, Rose, & Spiegel, 1982; Yesavage & Sheikh, 1988). More research is needed to explore and validate all the various claims of Hatha Yoga for improving cognition. To the extent that these exercises help the client relax, they can certainly provide some benefit. The client need not spend a great deal of money on exercise machines or membership in a health spa. Simple activities like stretching are just as effective.

Attitudes

A critical factor in a head-injured person's stability is his or her attitude toward recovery. Part of the rehabilitation process is developing accurate self-perceptions about postinjury cognitive functioning. Developing a positive attitude is especially difficult because the efficiency of thinking skills varies from day to day and month to month with physiological factors and retraining. Also, the head injury survivor must develop a new self-concept with respect to others and must learn a different side of acquaintances and friends. All of these factors force the person through an often unbearable attitude adjustment.

Attitudes about cognition are typically deep rooted. They usually stem from the client's memory of his or her ability to do certain tasks in the past. Attitudes do not change easily, but they can be changed. Herrmann (1990) described a variety of attitudes that affect cognitive performance. These are discussed in detail below.

A client's attitudes about the content of a cognitive task may or may not be appropriate. Certain kinds of task content are especially difficult to register and remember. Certain kinds of problems are more difficult to solve. Each kind of task requires a special approach so that the attitude can be altered to facilitate cognition. Problems with task content usually stem from information that is uninteresting or emotionally stressful.

Lack of Interest

Great achievements involve considerable stress, and those who triumph do so in part because they are motivated. Successful recovery from a head injury is a great achievement. For head injury survivors to succeed as they hope, they must first develop motivation to succeed.

One way to motivate clients to perform is to pay them to do so (Parenté, 1994). Give a person money to remember something, and he or she will recall more when compared to one who is not paid or otherwise compensated. Money, however, is extrinsically rewarding, and there is no guarantee that it has lasting effects. The ultimate goal of therapy is to change the person's behavior so that it is motivated by personal values or intrinsically rewarding goals. If the client cannot attain an intrinsic state of reward, then the therapist must extrinsically reward good performance. If the rewards are not apparent, then some effort is necessary to identify them.

Boring information is obviously hard to register and remember. People will often forget something that someone said or something that they were to do because they were uninterested. Pointing out the usefulness of the information and how it can help the client in some way can

override the boring aspects of the information. The client should therefore ask questions such as "How is this information useful to me?" or "How will this make my daily activities easier?" If the client cannot answer such questions, he or she and the therapist should rethink whether the client should learn the task or the material at all.

Suppression, Repression, and Denial

Horrible memories such as the details of the client's accident are usually repressed but may surface unpredictably. In fact, they are often so easily remembered that they intrude into a person's consciousness without warning and cause embarrassment. For example, we can recall several clients who would begin crying during a session for no apparent reason. When questioned, they stated that some aspect of the session triggered the image of their accident and caused the uncontrolled crying.

Memories connected with only moderately negative emotions may be more difficult to recall. The emotion can lead the client to suppress the cognition. Suppression is a common reaction to negative feelings. There are at least two ways for the clients to protect themselves against suppression.

First, if the client takes deliberate steps to face up to the negative cognition, then suppression will be less likely to occur. A focus on the positive makes this task easier. For example, many clients say that their accident was really a wake-up call that averted an early death due to drugs and alcohol. Obviously, it is not always possible or appropriate to focus on the positive. However, it is important for the client to realize that something good arises out of every negative circumstance. The therapist should therefore point out any positive aspect of a negative event.

When using this manipulation, the therapist should bear in mind that even if clients can focus on some of the good aspects of a basically negative experience, negative feelings will remain. Thus, although adopting a positive view may diminish the likelihood of suppression, it is still possible for suppression to occur.

Second, one can set up back-up systems so that if suppression does occur, one can reduce its negative consequences. Often suppression of something unpleasant leads to even greater problems. For example, one client had a meeting with the IRS for an audit of his unpaid taxes since the time of the accident. He suppressed the meeting because it was going to be unpleasant. However, missing the meeting because he suppressed the time created new problems.

Some negative memories are so threatening that they are *repressed* rather than suppressed (Erdelyi & Goldberg, 1979). Although suppressed memories can be remembered with effort, repressed memories usually cannot be remembered at will. Repression removes any awareness of the information, blocking it from our normal means of remembering. The classic example of repression is the soap opera character who, after some traumatic experience, becomes unable to remember the experience at all. Some psychologists believe that everyone represses some memories; others believe that repression occurs less commonly and that it may indicate a serious adjustment problem.

Access to repressed memories comes only after recalling many related memories. If the therapist suspects that the client is repressing part or all of an important memory, the services of a clinical psychologist with some experience working with head injury survivors may be necessary. Because of the possibility of a violent reaction to the recovery of a repressed cognition, this is an aspect of treatment the therapist cannot expect to handle alone.

Disturbing information that is not suppressed may be distorted or simply denied. The distortion may occur either during an initial experience or later, during retention. The function of distortion or denial is to make the cognition consistent with our self-image, goals, or fears (Greenwald, 1980, 1981). Distortions are difficult to assess because they protect our view of ourselves. Some distortion in cognition is normal, but an excessive amount can lead to maladjustment. Distortion and denial, as well as repression, are indications of an unacceptable state. The extent of denial is an index of emotional fragility. It is difficult to challenge these mechanisms because the therapist risks an emotional upheaval with unpredictable consequences.

The first step is to determine if the person has suppressed or repressed a memory or is in a state of denial. Usually, repressed memories are difficult to work with because of their potential emotional impact. For example, we dealt with one man who, to describe his accident, stated, "They told me I was driving a car." With further questioning, he stated, "They told me everyone was killed." After several sessions, he experienced an emotional breakdown as he recalled the details of his accident. He had repressed the fact that he was driving drunk and had hit a woman and her child who were crossing the street. He experienced a near-psychotic break when he recalled the vivid impression of the look on the woman's and the child's face just before the car made impact.

Suppressed memories will typically come out more freely once the client comes to trust the therapist. If the client is part of a group, suppression lessens when other group members share their experiences freely. These are usually things the person is not proud of or that are embarrassing. For example, one client was assaulted in a park and recalled that he attempted to fight off his attackers before receiving the blow on the head that caused his head injury. He had some training in the martial arts; however, when he tried to use a well-practiced kick, he slipped and sprained his ankle. Another client recalled that just before his auto accident he was intimately engaged with his girlfriend and that this had led to a temporary inattention to his driving.

Denial is the most common defense mechanism the therapist will encounter. It can be quite persistent. When a client is in a state of denial, the therapist can ask the group members to offer their opinions concerning the client's state of denial. These opinions are usually better accepted than those offered by the therapist. The purpose is to provide the client with consistent observations from his or her peers.

Denial may be persistent and lasting. For example, we have videotaped several clients who have not performed well on various tasks. When shown the videotape, their denial was so pronounced that they said, "That's not me." It is important for the therapist to realize that denial is a defense mechanism that signals emotional fragility. If the client persists in denying the problem or the denial does not lessen substantially with time, this should be a signal to the therapist that the client is not yet ready to deal with the issues that are raised.

MOODS AND MEMORY

The effect of emotional mood state on memory has been well researched. To some extent, the mood state can serve as a cue to facilitate recall (Leight & Ellis, 1981), and therefore, it is useful to consider mood as a context that can be used to help the head-injured person retrieve information. This is because memory retrieval is known to depend on returning to the state of mind in which the information was originally perceived (Bower, 1981). Several authors have proposed *network theories* of memory that include emotional components (Anderson & Bower, 1973; Collins & Loftus, 1975; Schneider & Shiffrin, 1977). These are discussed in detail in Chapter 14. As they apply to memory, the models assume that memories are stored as nodes in a network and that the nodes are connected via association. Activating any node initiates a memory. Activation spreads from node to node via an associative network. Ideas are literally the collections of nodes and their associations.

Bower (1981) suggested that emotional nodes are also part of our network of ideas. Emotional experiences are stored along with semantic and procedural information, and similar emotional experiences later evoke the same memories. Accordingly, if a head-injured person is depressed, most of the information he or she learns is stored in a depressing context. Consequently, the information may come to mind if the person becomes depressed again. It may not be available if the person is not depressed because the original context is not present. If the therapist can reinstate the original mood, a client may be able to retrieve information that would otherwise be un-

available. The client may also be able to recall information by first asking, "What mood was I in when I learned this?" The client should also assess his or her mood while learning novel information so that it can be used as a potential cue for recall later.

The client's emotions and moods can also affect the quality of learning. In general, learning is easier when the material fits the client's mood. For example, depressed persons will have a relatively easy time learning material presented in a negative context and a relatively difficult time with information presented in a positive light. This is probably because they pay more attention to materials that are congruent with their mood (Bower, 1981; Bower, Monteiro, & Gilligan, 1978; Plutchik, 1990).

Hertel (1994) provided an eloquent summary of the research on mood and cognition with special emphasis on extrapolation from theories developed with uninjured populations for head injury rehabilitation. She concluded that improving mood is likely to lead to improved attention and concentration, especially when the task is unstructured. Therefore, the therapist should ask first whether the treatment is even feasible before attempting to repair the client's mood.

Hertel's (1994) review concluded that depression limits memory most when the task requires a conscious effort. In these situations, some form of self-questioning procedure, environmental manipulation, or prosthetic device may be necessary to improve recall. For example, a sophisticated medication reminder may be necessary to alert a severely depressed client to specific medications he or she needs to take at certain times of day.

Finally, memory may be quite good in situations that do not require a conscious or deliberate effort. The therapist should therefore train the client to relax and not to make memory an issue. In these situations, the client should simply trust his or her memory because it is probably accurate. For example, if the client is depressed and wants to call a friend but cannot immediately recall the friend's phone number, his or her first recollection of the phone number may be accurate.

SELF-ASSESSMENT OF PERFORMANCE

Most people feel they can assess their performance accurately. They feel as confident about their ability to think and to remember as they do about other abilities, such as vision or hearing. However, as we discussed in Chapter 2, the truth is that most of us do not have an entirely accurate view of how well we perform different cognitive tasks (Herrmann, 1990). When people are asked how well they perform cognitive tasks in everyday life and in the laboratory, their answers do not generally agree with objective measures of performance in either realm. This finding is also apparent with head injury survivors (Anderson-Parenté, 1994).

Sometimes people maintain an incorrect assessment of their skills out of denial. Sometimes their attitudes stem from another's observation about their cognition that was incorrect. Regardless of the underlying cause, clients' attitudes about the difficulty of different cognitive tasks are often flawed, and their decisions about which tasks they should take on or avoid are often wrong. The focus of treatment is first to acquaint the client with the demands of the task and then to provide an assessment of how well the client can physically or mentally measure up to those demands.

Anderson-Parenté (1994) studied these phenomena with head-injured clients and their families. She gave 40 head injury survivors and their family members alternative forms of a learning disability questionnaire that measured cognitive attributes such as attention, memory, and reasoning. Each of the family members rated the client on the various items, and the clients also rated themselves on the same items independently. She also tested each client with an extensive neuropsychological battery. This provided an objective measure of cognitive performance to which she correlated the subscales of the questionnaires collected from the family members and the clients. The results indicated that head injury survivors generally underestimated their deficits relative to the family members' ratings. The family members' ratings were significantly correlated with a wider range of neuropsychological

measures than were the clients' ratings. The clients' and family members' ratings on the questionnaire were correlated with different types of neuropsychological measures.

With respect to the first finding, although the general pattern of ratings was similar for the clients and the family members, the tendency for the clients to underestimate their deficits was apparent across a variety of ratings. Anderson-Parenté (1994) suggested that therapists should therefore interview family members whenever possible to form an accurate assessment of the client's skills.

Family members' ratings produced about twice as many significant correlations with the neuropsychological variables as did the clients'. This finding suggested that family members are a valuable source of information. It is also important to note that the clients' ratings yielded more significant correlations than had been previously reported in the literature. Clients may therefore provide useful ratings on certain aspects of their skills and behaviors.

Family members' ratings of abstract behavioral qualities such as reasoning, memory, and attention were generally correlated with the neuropsychological test scores. The clients' ratings of these same qualities were generally uncorrelated with the test scores. However, the clients' ratings of the more concrete skills were generally correlated with the test scores.

Anderson-Parenté (1994) suggested that therapists can use these findings in several ways with their clients. It is important for therapists to accept that clients' perceptions of their performance on concrete tasks such as writing or math can be quite accurate. It may be necessary, however, to correct their attitudes about their ability to assess accurately the less concrete and visible aspects of their behavior. Family members are a better source for estimating clients' more abstract reasoning skills. Generally, clients underestimate the severity of their disorders, although they may correctly assess overall patterns of strengths and weaknesses. The difference between clients' and family members' ratings can be a useful index of the degree of the client's denial. Therapists should get family member ratings wherever possible because these provide useful information about behavior in an everyday context that the one-shot neuropsychological evaluation cannot capture.

EMOTIONAL CONDITION CHECKLIST

The information reviewed above makes it clear that a good emotional condition is necessary for good cognitive performance. The following is a checklist that summarizes most of these issues. We recommend that the therapist use the checklist to ensure that the various qualities of the client's lifestyle are working to his or her advantage.

1. *Maintain an optimum level of activity.* Avoid a hectic lifestyle, and avoid getting in a rut. Too little or too much activity lessens the client's capacity to pay attention.
2. *Keep stress at a manageable level.* A little stress keeps the client alert, but too much is distracting.
3. *Engage in recreational activities,* such as hobbies, sports, and socializing. Activity relieves stress.
4. *Take time to relax* daily, on weekends, and on annual vacations. This will reduce stress and renew the client's strength.
5. *Get enough rest* by maintaining a regular sleep schedule. It may help to take a short nap just before a period of intense cognitive effort.
6. *Exercise regularly and within limits.* The client will be less stressed and feel stronger immediately, and the feeling will remain for several hours afterward.
7. *Try innovative ways of relaxing* such as yoga exercise and yoga meditation.
8. *Talk out problems* with therapists, family members, or friends.
9. *Study in a balanced environment* where there is low-level background noise such as low-volume classical music and where furniture is not overly comfortable. Don't be too comfortable.
10. *Establish a useful attitude about a task* by asking how the task is relevant or useful.

CONCLUSION

Learning ways to manage one's emotions, attitudes, and motivation is crucial for mastering cognitive tasks. Learning and thinking are best accomplished when a client is calm, cool, and collected. Therefore, preparing oneself to think and remember is especially important after a traumatic brain injury. Time spent engaging in calming behaviors such as stretching or resting before trying to learn something is time well spent. Knowing not to engage in complex memory or thinking tasks when emotionally upset or stressed is also important.

Depression has dramatic negative effects on memory and thinking. If the client is depressed, individual psychotherapy and/or medication may be warranted. Indeed, it may be necessary before the person can focus well enough to benefit from cognitive rehabilitation therapy.

Mood and emotion can also have some beneficial value as memory aids. If the client experiences a strong emotion when learning something new, he or she can attend to the emotion and use it as a cue to recall the information later on. Simply asking how he or she felt at the time of the incident is often sufficient to produce recall of the information. To use emotion as a cue, the client must flag the event with the emotion at the time when the two occur together.

REFERENCES

Anderson-Parenté, J. (1994). A comparison of metacognitive ratings of persons with traumatic brain injury and their families. *NeuroRehabilitation,4*(3), 168–173.

Anderson, J., & Bower, G. (1973). *Human associative memory*. Washington, DC: Holt, Rinehart & Winston.

Baum, A., Cohen, L., & Hall, M. (1993). Control and intrusive memories as possible determinants of chronic stress. *Psychosomatic Medicine, 55,* 274–286.

Bower, G.H. (1981). Mood and memory. *American Psychologist, 36,* 129–148.

Bower, G.H., Monteiro, K.P., & Gilligan, S.G. (1978). Emotional mood as a context for learning and recall. *Journal of Verbal Learning and Verbal Behavior, 17,* 573–578.

Broadbent, D.E., Cooper, P.F., Fitzgerald, P., & Parks, K.R. (1982). The Cognitive Failures Questionnaire (CFQ) and its correlates. *British Journal of Psychology, 21,* 1–16.

Collins, A.M., & Loftus, E.F. (1975). A spreading activation theory of sematic memory processing. *Psychological Review, 82*, 407–428.

Erdelyi, M.H., & Goldberg, B. (1979). Let's not sweep repression under the rug: Toward a cognitive psychology of repression. In J.F. Kihlstrom & F.J. Evans (Eds.), *Functional disorders of memory* (pp. 335–402). Hillsdale, NJ: Lawrence Erlbaum.

Greenwald, A.G. (1980). The totalitarian ego. *American Psychologist, 35*, 603–618.

Greenwald, A.G. (1981). Self and memory. In G.H. Bower (Ed.), *The psychology of learning and motivation* (Vol. 15, pp. 201–236). New York: Academic Press.

Herrmann, D.J. (1990). *SuperMemory*. Emmaus, PA: Rodale.

Hertel, P. (1992). Mood and improving memory. In D. Herrmann, H. Weingartner, A. Searleman, & C. McEnvoy (Eds.), *Memory improvement: Implications for memory theory*. New York: Springer-Verlag.

Hertel, P. (1994). Depressive deficits in memory: Implications for memory improvement following traumatic brain injury. *NeuroRehabilitation, 4*(3), 143–150.

Leight, K.A., & Ellis, H.C. (1981). Emotional mood states, strategies, and state dependency in memory. *Journal of Verbal Learning and Verbal Behavior, 20*, 251–266.

Parenté, R. (1994). Effects of monetary incentives on performance after traumatic brain injury. *NeuroRehabilitation, 4*, 198–203.

Plutchik, R. (1990). *Emotion: A psychoevolutionary synthesis*. New York: Harper & Row.

Reason, J.T. (1988). Stress and cognitive failure. In S. Fisher & J.T. Reason (Eds.), *Handbook of life stress, cognition, and health* (pp. 405–421). New York: John Wiley.

Reason, J.T., & Lucas, D. (1984). Using cognitive diaries to investigate naturally occurring memory blocks. In J. Harris & P. Morris (Eds.), *Everyday memory, actions, and absentmindedness* (pp. 57–70). London: Academic Press.

Reason, J.T., & MyCielska, M. (1983). *Absentmindedness*. Englewood Cliffs, NJ: Prentice Hall.

Schneider, W., & Shiffrin, R.M. (1977). Controlled and automatic human information processing: I. Detection, search, and attention. *Psychological Review, 84*, 1–66.

Spielberger, C.D., Gonzales, H.P., & Fletcher, T. (1979). Test anxiety reduction, learning strategies, and academic performance. In H.F. O'Neill & C.D. Spielberger (Eds.), *Cognitive and affective learning strategies*. New York: Academic Press.

Watts, F.N. (1988). Memory deficit in depression. In M.M. Gruneberg, P.E. Morris, & R.N. Sykes (Eds.), *Practical aspects of memory*. New York: John Wiley.

Watts, F.N., MacLeod, A.K., & Morris, L. (1988). A remedial strategy for memory and concentration problems in depressed patients. *Cognitive Therapy and Research, 12*, 185–193.

Wells, A., & Mathews, G. (1994). *Attention and emotion: A clinical perspective*. Hillsdale, NJ: Lawrence Erlbaum.

Williams, J.M.G., Watts, F.N., MacLeod, C., & Mathews, A. (1988). *Cognitive psychology and emotional disorders*. New York: John Wiley.

Yesavage, J.A., Rose, T.L., & Spiegel, D. (1982). Relaxation training and memory improvement in elderly normals: Correlations of anxiety ratings and recall improvement. *Experimental Aging Research, 8*, 198.

Yesavage, J.A., & Sheikh, J.I. (1988). Nonpharmacologic treatment of age-associated memory impairment. *Comprehensive Therapy, 14*, 44–46.

Chapter 22

Cognitive-Enhancing Nutrients and Drugs

Good nutrition is essential for high-level cognitive functioning. Indeed, most people would experience a substantial improvement in thinking and memory simply by changing their diet. Attempts to develop a "smart pill," however, have met with mixed success. Clearly, this type of substance would be the most expedient means for improving cognition after traumatic brain injury. But this type of research effort is in its infancy, and it is perhaps too early to determine whether the quest will be successful. Therefore, the goal of this chapter is simply to summarize the current state of research on the topic of nutrition, drugs, and cognition.

Comprehensive discussions of nutrition effects on cognition have not been widely published in the cognitive rehabilitation literature. The search for drugs that improve thinking has intensified in recent years, and there are now a few published summaries plus a variety of popular books on the topic (Dean & Morganthaler, 1990; Dean, Morganthaler, & Fowkes, 1993; Hock, 1987; Pelton, 1989). There seems to be no shortage of articles dealing with the use of drugs for treating behavioral problems after head injury. O'Shanick and Zasler (1990) provided an excellent review of this literature. Zasler (1990) also documented evidence that certain drugs may be useful for treating cognitive dysfunction, although there is no generally accepted treatment

protocol and most of the substances have not been widely discussed or their effects clearly documented.

This chapter limits discussion to those drugs and nutrients whose cognitive-enhancing effects have been documented in published scientific papers. Even with this criterion, there is a great deal of variability in the experimental findings. There is also considerable variability between the results reported with animal versus human trials. Generally speaking, there seems to be no clearly documented drug or nutrient effect that occurs consistently in published studies of groups. However, many head-injured clients may individually experience improvement of their thinking skills with certain drug or nutritional interventions. Whether to begin a drug or nutrient trial is therefore an individual matter.

The therapist's role when discussing nutrients and drugs with the client is only to acquaint the person with the variety of substances available. The therapy may also provide the client's physician with materials that describe the effects of various substances on cognition so that the client and his or her physician can make an informed decision about the usefulness of any of these substances. Most head-injured clients will want to try these substances and may experience some improvement if properly guided. However, most of the nutrients discussed below are available without prescription, and some clients may self-medicate with unpredictable consequences. Consequently, *we strongly recommend that clients always consult a physician before making any changes in their diet or beginning use of any other cognitive-enhancing substances discussed in this chapter or in any of the popularly available books.*

We begin the discussion with a summary of various nutrient substances that may improve the person's thinking and memory. We then discuss some of the drugs that have been developed for the same purpose.

COGNITIVE-ENHANCING NUTRIENTS

Most of us would benefit from taking a multiple vitamin daily. Indeed, some cognitive disorders are caused by vitamin deficiencies. For example, memory loss due to chronic alcohol use results, in part, from thiamine deficiency. Perhaps some portion of the client's cognitive deficit can be attributed to poor nutrition and remedied with a multivitamin supplement. There are several concentrated vitamin compounds or "brain formulas" available that contain high levels of vitamins and minerals essential for cognitive functioning. We have noticed a number of these compounds with brand names like Brain Pep, Brain II Formula, IQ Plus, MemorAid, and Nutrimental. These are usually available in health food stores at exorbitant prices. Although the formulas certainly contain a specific collection of nutrients that are necessary for thinking and memory, there is no documented evidence that any particular brand is superior to another. Moreover, there is little evidence that any one of them improves thinking and memory relative to simply taking a multivitamin supplement.

Most of these substances contain a variety of amino acids, such as cystine, glutamine, methionine, phenylalanine, and tyrosine. They may also include ascorbic acid, biotin, chromium, cobalamine, folic acid, germanium, inositol, manganese, phosphatidylserine, potassium, ribonucleic acid, riboflavin, taurine, thiamine, and zinc. All of these nutrients have been shown to be essen-

tial for the brain to function normally. There is little evidence, however, that massive doses produce rapid or significant improvement in cognitive skill. There is some evidence that thinking skills are improved with regular use of beta carotene, vitamin E, and ascorbic acid (Lesser, 1980). The effects are gradual and may take months to notice. This is because most of the nutrients are excreted the following day and it may take several weeks before there is a sufficient blood level to produce a noticeable improvement. Consequently, much of the evidence of cognitive enhancement with megavitamin therapy is anecdotal.

COGNITIVE-ENHANCING DRUGS

A variety of drugs have been investigated as potential "smart pills" (Dean & Morganthaler, 1990). These are prescription substances that generally fall into four categories (Moos, Davis, & Gamzu, 1990). The first category includes *vasodilators and various metabolic enhancers.* These are thought to treat narrowing cerebral vessels that are assumed to be responsible for various forms of dementia. Hydergine was one of the first drugs to be widely used for this purpose. Hydergine is composed of various ergot alkaloids (Exton-Smith, 1983; Hindmarch, 1979). Over the years, it has been used for treating memory and cognitive deficits secondary to senile dementia (Hughes, 1976; Yoshikawa, 1983). In addition to its vasodilation properties, it may increase the amount of certain neurotransmitters in the brain (Copeland, 1981; Enmenegger & Meier-Ruge, 1968) and increase oxygen use and circulation (Rao & Norris, 1971; Weil, 1978). Nandy and Schneider (1978) suggested that hydergine also stimulates axon and dendrite growth.

Vinpocetine is another metabolic enhancer that is thought to improve microcirculation and increase glucose and oxygen use in the brain. The drug is derived from Vincamine, which is extracted from periwinkle. Vinpocetine was shown to improve memory in a majority of patients who suffered a variety of neurological disorders (Otomo, 1985; Subhan & Hindmarch, 1985).

The second class of drugs includes the *nootropics* (Poschel, 1988), which are thought to affect higher cognitive functions and have been used with some success for treatment of dyslexia (Wilsher, 1987). The nootropic substances are some of the most interesting of the cognitive-enhancing drugs. The word *nootropic* is a Greek term that literally means "acting on the mind." Various types of nootropic substances have been used with humans, but with less success than is typically found in animal studies. For example, piracetam was shown to improve learning and memory in both animal and human trials (Chase, 1984; Conners, 1984; Diamond & Browers, 1976; Dilanni, 1985; Giurgea, 1973; Giurgea & Salama, 1977; Mindus, 1976). The actual mechanism of action is unclear, although the drug may enhance communication between the cerebral hemispheres via the corpus callosum (Buresova & Bures, 1976) or stimulate production of the neurotransmitter adenosine triphosphate (Nickerson & Wolthuis, 1976). The effects of piracetam may be augmented by choline, and the combination has been shown to improve memory and cognitive functioning in persons with senile dementia (Bartus, 1981; Ferris, 1982). One of the major advantages of this type of drug is that it does not cause stimulation or sedation or have any analgesic effects. It generally has minimal side effects (Dejong, 1987).

Several other nootropic substances are chemically quite similar to piracetam and have similar effects (DeNoble, 1986). Aniracetam, for example, has been found to improve cognitive functions in animal studies (Cumin, 1982), and it may affect a wider range of skills than does piracetam (Vincent, 1985). Murry and Fibiger (1986) reported that pramiracetam enhanced rate of learning and electrical activity in certain areas of the limbic system. Oxiracetam also improves memory in animal studies (Mondadori, 1986) and is more potent than piracetam (Itil, 1986). Ferrero (1984) reported improvement of memory and cognitive skills with humans who took oxiracetam. Ammassari-Teule (1986) reported that the offspring of female rats given oxiracetam while pregnant were superior on tests of learning and retention to those offspring of control rats.

The third class includes the *psychostimulants* (Coper & Herrmann, 1988; Evans & Gualtieri, 1987), which affect the person's attention/concentration. Although these have been used with some success for treating attention deficit disorder in childhood and adolescence, they are probably not very useful for treating memory and cognitive impairments after head injury.

The fourth and largest class of drugs are *mechanism based*. These include a variety of substances with very different drug actions. One group of mechanism-based drugs is known as cholinergic agonists (Goldberg, Gerstman, & Mattis, 1982). These substances affect the synthesis of acetylcholine in the brain. They generally produce some improvement in memory if the dosage is customized for the individual client. Treatments that combine a choline-rich substance such as lecithin with another substance that blocks the production of choline inhibitors in the brain (e.g., Physostigmine) generally show the greatest effect. Other drugs, such as ondansetron and zatosetron, have been found to block the inhibition of acetylcholine. The drugs thus increase the release of this neurotransmitter, thereby improving cognitive performance.

The adrenergic system is also partially responsible for the storage and retrieval of memory. Drugs such as epinephrine, which affect this system, have been found to facilitate memory. Neuropeptides such as vasopressin have also been shown to improve memory (Greidanus, van Wimersma, & Wied, 1985; Zagler & Black, 1985).

Vasopressin deserves special attention because it consistently improves memory and attention. It is released by the pituitary gland, and its production is enhanced by stimulant drugs and retarded by other substances such as alcohol and marijuana. Vasopressin causes a general improvement of long-term and short-term memory, concentration, recall of novel information, and retention (Gold, 1979; Legros, 1978). Reversal of amnesic effects with vasopressin use has also been reported (Oliveros, 1978), along with significant recovery of function after head injury and diseases such as diabetes insipidus (Laczi et al., 1982).

Reducing fatty deposits in the nerve cells of the brain and central nervous system is another mechanistic approach to improving cognitive functioning. Centrophenoxine is one such drug that has been used for this purpose (Guili, 1980; Nandy & Bourne, 1966; Nandy & Schneider, 1978; Riga & Riga, 1974), although it has not been widely used with head-injured persons.

Several other drugs have been reportedly used for treatment of various dementia conditions after head injury and degenerative diseases. Many of these substances have been found to be effective in human trials. They are difficult to classify according to the above schema, although they are certainly worthy of mention as potential treatments for cognitive deficits.

Deprinyl

Trade-named Eldepryl, deprinyl is a form of monoamine oxidase inhibitor responsible for the breaking down of neurotransmitters. It was originally researched in the 1950s and has been used for treatment of Parkinson's disease and, more recently, Alzheimer's disease. Although it has not been widely studied as a treatment for cognitive dysfunction after head injury, it certainly has the potential for that type of application.

DHEA and Pregnenolone

The steroid dehydroepiandrosterone (DHEA) is produced naturally in the adrenal gland. DHEA levels typically decrease with age. Pregnenolone is a substance that is converted into a variety of steroid substances, including DHEA. This substance also naturally decreases with age. Both have been used for treatment of age-related cognitive deficits. However, there has been no systematic research reported with these two substances for treatment of cognitive deficits after head injury.

OTHER SUBSTANCES

A variety of other substances have been used to improve cognitive functioning. Ginseng, an oriental herb, has been used to improve circulation and mental functioning (Petkov, 1987; Quiroga & Imbriano, 1979). These authors suggest that ginseng improves cognition by increasing production of various neurotransmitters, by stimulating the adrenal cortex, by increasing the supply of blood to the brain, or by increasing blood flow and general metabolism via its effect on areas of the brain such as the hypothalamus and pituitary glands. Regardless of the cause, ginseng has been generally found to improve fine motor coordination, to improve attention, and to shorten reaction time. Simon (1977) reported improved memory and concentration in animal studies and with the elderly after ginseng was administered.

Ginseng comes in a variety of forms, but they all contain the same basic active ingredients. These are glycosides with vitamins A, E, B1, B2, and B12, along with folic acid, biotin, and ascorbic acid. Ginseng compounds may also contain minerals including calcium, copper, cobalt, iron, magnesium, manganese, phosphorous, potassium, sulfur, and sodium. There are several varieties of ginseng, although the most common is Siberian ginseng, which comes from Russia, and Panax ginseng, which comes from Asian countries such as China, South Korea, and Russia.

Ginkgo (actually *Ginkgo biloba*) is another herb that has cognitive-enhancing properties. Several authors report subjects' increased attention and concentration after using ginkgo (Allard, 1986; Hindmarch, 1986). Schaffler and Reeh (1985) reported improved respiration resulting from ginkgo. A variety of other effects have also been reported, including improved short-term memory (Hindmarch, 1986) and lessened deterioration due to aging and degenerative disease (Allard, 1986; Warburton, 1986). It is unclear how ginkgo effects these changes, although it is possible that it increases blood flow in the brain by relaxing the microcapillaries.

Dimethylaminoethanol (DMAE) is a form of cortical stimulant and mood elevator (Hochschild, 1973; Pfeiffer, 1957). Small amounts of DMAE are produced by the body and are thought to increase the synthesis of the neurotransmitter acetylcholine in the brain (Ceder, 1978) by raising the choline levels in the blood. The effect of DMAE is unlike that of stimulants. There is no reported jitteriness, only a mild stimulation that is more like a heightened state of awareness or alertness. There is no reported withdrawal or depression when it is discontinued. For these reasons, it has been suggested as an alternative treatment for hyperactivity and attention deficit disorder and for treating learning and behavioral disorders (Oettinger, 1958; Pfieffer, 1959).

Deanol is a prescription drug that is similar to DMAE and has a similar effect. It was originally marketed for treatment of learning problems and attention deficit. Murphree (1960) suggested that it increases attention/concentration, and Hochschild (1973) reported that it increases life span in rats.

Although there are other cognitive-enhancing nutrients, we focus on these because they have been the most widely investigated and because there is considerable evidence that they produce some positive effects. However, many have not been used with head-injured clients, and it is questionable how much affect they will have with this population.

CONCLUSION

Many head-injured clients will want to try nutrient and drug treatments to improve their thinking skills. These substances are especially attractive because of the promise that by simply taking a pill, the client may improve his or her cognitive functions overnight. It is important to inform the client that, with the exception of hydergine, few drugs are routinely prescribed for treating cognitive dysfunction. This chapter illustrates that a variety of potential candidates could be used, but physicians are usually unaware of these drugs, their proper dosage or course, and their potential side effects. It is therefore reasonable to assume that most physicians will be reluctant to prescribe them. Moreover, although many nonprescription nutrients have been found to improve cognitive functioning, their effects may take months to appear. Megadoses of nutrients will probably have little effect be-

cause the client will excrete most of the dose within days.

We would like to reemphasize that self-medication using drugs or nutrients may be dangerous. The therapist should therefore warn the client that drugs or nutrients should be taken only under medical supervision. In addition, expensive brain formulas are probably no more effective than a multivitamin. Although many of the drugs mentioned in this chapter can be ordered by mail, the client is specifically warned against this practice.

What can the client do to improve his or her cognition using cognitive-enhancing nutrients and drugs? First, he or she can consult a nutritionist to determine an appropriate diet, perhaps with a multivitamin supplement. Second, the client should consult a physician to determine if any of the substances discussed in this chapter would be appropriate for his or her specific situation.

REFERENCES

Allard, M. (1986). Treatment of old age disorders with *Ginkgo Biloba* extract. *La Presse Medicale, 15*(31), 1540.

Ammassari-Teule, M. (1986). Avoidance facilitation in adult mice by prenatal administration of nootropic drug oxiracetam. *Pharmacological Research Communications, 18*, 1169–1178.

Bartus, R. (1981, March). Profound effects of combining choline and piracetam on memory enhancement and cholinergic function in aged rats. *Neurobiology of Aging*, 105–111.

Buresova, O., & Bures, J. (1976). Piracetam induced facilitation of interhemispheric transfer of visual information in rats. *Psychopharmacologia, 46*, 93–102.

Cedar, G. (1978). Effects of 2-dimethylaminoethanol (deanol) on the metabolism of choline in plasma. *Journal of Neurochemistry, 30*, 1293–1296.

Chase, C. (1984). A new chemotherapeutic investigation: Piracetam effects on dyslexia. *Annals of Dyslexia, 34*, 272–278.

Conners, C. (1984). Piracetam and event related potentials in dyslexic children. *Psychopharmacology Bulletin, 20*, 667–673.

Copeland, R.L. (1981). Behavioral and neurocortical effects of hydergine in rats. *Archives of International Pharmacodynamics, 252*, 113–123.

Coper, H., & Herrmann, W.M. (1988). Psychostimulants, analeptics, nootropics: An attempt to differentiate and assess drugs designed for the treatment of impaired brain functions. *Pharmacopsychiatry, 21*, 211–217.

Cumin, R. (1982). Effects of the novel compound aniracetam upon impaired learning and memory in rodents. *Psychopharmacology, 78*, 104–111.

Dean, W., & Morganthaler, J. (1990). *Smart drugs.* Menlo Park, CA: Health and Freedom.

Dean, W., Morgenthaler, J., & Fowkes, S.W.M. (1993). *Smart drugs II.* Menlo Park, CA: Health and Freedom.

Dejong, P. (1987). Safety of pramiracetam. *Current Therapeutic Research, 41*, 254–257.

DeNoble, V. (1986). Vinpocetine: Nootropic effects on scopolamine-induced and hypoxia-induced retrieval deficits in step through passive avoidance response in rats. *Pharmacology, Biochemistry and Behavior, 24*, 1123–1128.

Diamond, S.J., & Browers, E.Y.M. (1976). Increase in the power of human memory in normal man through the use of drugs. *Psychopharmacology, 49*, 307–309.

Dilanni, M. (1985). The effects of piracetam in children with dyslexia. *Journal of Clinical Psychopharmacology, 5*, 272–278.

Enmenegger, H., & Meier-Ruge, W. (1968). The actions of hydergine on the brain. *Pharmacology, 1*, 65–78.

Evans, P.W., & Gualtieri, C.T. (1987). Treatment of chronic closed head injury with psychostimulant drugs: A controlled case study and an appropriate evaluation procedure. *Journal of Nervous and Mental Disease, 175*, 104–110.

Exton-Smith, A.N. (1983). Clinical experience with ergot alkaloids. *Aging, 23*, 323.

Ferrero, E. (1984). Controlled clinical trial of oxiracetam in the treatment of chronic cerebrovascular insufficiency in the elderly. *Current Therapeutic Research, 36*, 298–308.

Ferris, S.H. (1982). Combination of choline/piracetam in the treatment of senile dementia. *Psychopharmacology Bulletin, 18*, 94–98.

Giurgea, C.E. (1973). The nootropic approach to the pharmacology of integrative activity in the brain. *Conditioned Reflex, 8*, 108–115.

Giurgea, C.E., & Salama, M. (1977). Nootropic drugs. *Progress in Neuropsychopharmacology, 1*, 235–247.

Gold, P. (1979, November). Effects of 1-desamo-8-arginine vasopressin on behavior and cognition in primary affective disorders. *Lancet*, 992–994.

Goldberg, I., Gerstman, L.J., & Mattis, S. (1982). Effect of cholinergic treatment on post-traumatic anterograde amnesia. *Archives of Neurology, 38*, 581.

Greidanus, T., van Wimersma, B., & Wied, D. (1985). Hypothalamic neuropeptides and memory. *Acta Neurochirurgica, 75*, 99–105.

Guili, D. (1980). Morphometric studies of synapses of the cerebellar glomerulus: The effect of centrophenoxine treatment in old rats. *Mechanisms of Aging and Development, 14*, 265–271.

Hindmarch, I. (1979, November/December). The effects of an ergot alkaloid derivative (hydergine) on aspects of psychomotor performance, arousal and cognitive processing ability. *Journal of Clinical Pharmacology*, 726–731.

Hindmarch, I. (1986). Activity of *Ginkgo Biloba* extract on short-term memory. *La Presse Medicale, 15*(31), 1592.

Hochschild, R. (1973). Effect of dimethylaminoethyl p-cholorophenoxy-acetate on the lifespan of male Swiss Webster albino mice. *Experimental Gerontology, 8*, 177–183.

Hock, F.J. (1987). Drug influences on learning and memory in aged animals and humans. *Neuropsychobiology, 17*, 145–160.

Hughes, J.P. (1976). An ergot alkaloid preparation (hydergine) in the treatment of dementia: A critical review of the clinical literature. *Journal of the American Geriatrics Society, 24*, 490–497.

Itil, P.M. (1986). CNS pharmacology and clinical therapeutic effects of oxiracetam. *Clinical Neuropharmacology, 9* (Suppl. 3), 570–578.

Laczi, F., Valkusz, Z., Laszlo, F.A., Wagner, A., Jardentrazy, T., Saasz, A., Ezilard, J., & Telegdy, G. (1982). Effects of lycine vasopressin on memory in healthy individuals with diabetes insipidus patients. *Psychoneuroendocrinology, 7*, 185–191.

Legros, J.J. (1978, January). Influence of vasopressin on learning and memory. *Lancet*, 41–42.

Lesser, M. (1980). *Nutrition and vitamin therapy.* New York: Bantam.

Mindus, P. (1976). Piracetam-induced improvement of mental performance: A controlled study on normally aging individuals. *Acta Psychiatrica Scandinavica, 54*, 150–160.

Mondadori, C. (1986). Effects of oxiracetam on learning and memory in animals: Comparison with piracetam. *Clinical Neuropharmacology, 9* (Suppl. 13), 527–537.

Moos, W.H., Davis, R.E., & Gamzu, E.R. (1990). Pharmacological "prospectives." In L.J. Thal, W.H. Moos, & E.R. Gamzu (Eds.), *Cognitive disorder: Pathophysiology and treatment* (pp. 309–328). New York: Marcel Dekker.

Murphree, H.B. (1960). The stimulant effect of 2-dimethylamino-ethanol (deanol) in human volunteer subjects. *Clinical Pharmacology and Therapeutics, 1*, 303–310.

Murry, C.L., & Fibiger, H.C. (1986). The effect of pramiracetam (CI-879) on the acquisition of a radial arm maze task. *Psychopharmacology, 89*, 378–381.

Nandy, K., & Bourne, G.H. (1966). Effects of centrophenoxine on the lipofuscin pigments of the neurons of senile guinea pigs. *Nature, 210*, 313–317.

Nandy, K., & Schneider, F. (1978). Effects of dihydroergotoxine mesylate on aging neurons in vitro. *Gerontology, 24*, 66–70.

Nickerson, V.J., & Wolthuis, O.L. (1976). Effect of the acquisition-enhancing drug piracetam on rat cerebral energy metabolism in comparison with methamphetamine. *Biochemical Pharmacology, 25,* 2241–2244.

Oettinger, L. (1958). The use of deanol in the treatment of disorders of behavior in children. *Journal of Pediatrics, 3,* 571–575.

Oliveros, J.C. (1978). Vasopressin in amnesia. *Lancet,* 42.

O'Shanick, G.J., & Zasler, N.D. (1990). Neuropsychopharmacological approaches to traumatic brain injury. In J. Kreutzer & P. Wehman (Eds.), *Community integration following traumatic brain injury* (pp. 15–28). Baltimore: Paul H. Brookes.

Otomo, E. (1985). Comparison of vinpocetine with ifenprodil tartrate and dihydroergotoxine mesylate treatment and results of long-term treatment with vinpocetine. *Current Therapeutic Research, 37,* 811–821.

Pelton, D. (1989). *Mind, food and smart pills.* New York: Doubleday.

Petkov, V. (1987). Effects of standardized ginseng extract on learning, memory, and physical capabilities. *American Journal of Chinese Medicine, 15*(1), 19–29.

Pfeiffer, C. (1957). Stimulant effect of 2-dimethylaminoethanol: Possible precursor to brain acetylcholine. *Science, 126,* 610–611.

Pfeiffer, C. (1959). Parasympathetic neurohormones: Possible precursors and effects on behavior. *International Review of Neurobiology, 10,* 195–224.

Poschel, B.P.H. (1988). New pharmacologic perspectives on nootropic drugs. *Handbook of psychopharmacology,* 11–18.

Quiroga, F., & Imbriano, A.E. (1979). The effect of Panax ginseng extract on cerebrovascular deficits. *Orientacion Medica, 28,* 86–87.

Rao, D., & Norris, J. (1971). A double blind investigation of hydergine in the treatment of cerebrovascular insufficiency in the elderly. *Johns Hopkins Medical Journal, 130,* 317.

Riga, S., & Riga, D. (1974). Effects of centrophenoxine on the lipofuscin pigments of the nervous system of old rats. *Brain Research, 72,* 265–275.

Schaffler, K., & Reeh, P. (1985). Long-term drug administration effects of *Ginkgo biloba* on the performance of healthy subjects exposed to hypoxia. In J. Angoli (Ed.), *Effects of Ginkgo biloba extracts on organic cerebral impairment* (pp. 77–84). Amsterdam: Eurotext.

Simon, W.C.M. (1977, February). *Efficiency control of a gero-therapeutic containing ginseng by means of Kraepelin's working test.* Proceedings of the International Gerontological Symposium, Singapore, 199–206.

Subhan, Z., & Hindmarch, I. (1985). Psychopharmacological effects of vinpocetine in normal healthy volunteers. *European Journal of Clinical Pharmacology, 28,* 367–571.

Vincent, G. (1985). The effects of aniracetam (RO-13-5057) on the enhancement or protection of memory. *Annals of the New York Academy of Sciences, 244,* 489–491.

Warburton, D.M. (1986). Clinical psychopharmacology of *Ginkgo Biloba* extract. *La Presse Medicale, 15*(31), 1595.

Weil, C. (1978). Pharmacology and clinical pharmacology of hydergine. In C. Weil (Ed.), *Handbook of experimental pharmacology.* New York: Springer-Verlag.

Wilsher, C.R. (1987). Piracetam and dyslexia: Effects on reading tests. *Journal of Clinical Pharmacology, 7,* 230–237.

Yoshikawa, M. (1983). A dose-response study with dihydroergotoxine mesylate in cerebrovascular disturbances. *Journal of the American Geriatrics Society, 31,* 1–7.

Zagler, E.L., & Black, P.M. (1985). Neuropeptides in human memory and learning processes. *Neurosurgery, 17,* 355–369.

Zasler, N. (1990, September). Pharmacologic approaches to cognitive and behavioral dysfunction after traumatic brain injury: Selected bibliography. In *Proceedings: Cognitive rehabilitation and community integration* (pp. 23–40). Richmond, VA.

Chapter 23

Incentive Motivators and Cognitive Rehabilitation

Getting the client to comply with treatment goals and to use strategies spontaneously is perhaps one of the most difficult aspects of the cognitive rehabilitation process. Damage to one or more areas of the brain may destroy critical brain structures that mediate or control the client's motivation to comply with therapy. Many therapists notice that a client makes marked improvement when there is a tangible goal, as when return to work is within reach. Although it is generally assumed that the success or failure of therapy reduces to a question of motivation, there has been a general dearth of research that has determined what motivates clients in therapy and the extent to which incentives facilitate cognitive rehabilitation after head injury (Parenté, 1994).

The major purpose of this chapter is to make practical suggestions that therapists can use to improve their treatment effectiveness and their clients' compliance with treatment. The chapter begins with a brief historical overview of the incentive concept along with a discussion of reward, punishment, and motivation as they apply to the rehabilitation process. We next present and

evaluate an incentive-based model of cognitive rehabilitation. The model assumes that thinking and memory will improve immediately and dramatically if there is a relevant incentive to perform. We discuss the results of several experiments that test this assumption and expand on it. The results of these experiments indicate that poor recall after a head injury can be substantially improved with an appropriate incentive. The implications of the model for rehabilitation treatment planning are presented in detail, along with specific suggestions that therapists can implement into their practice.

WHAT IS INCENTIVE?

An incentive is something a person values and would like to obtain. The fact that humans will work for what they perceive to be valuable is nothing new. However, during the mid-1940s, Clark Hull (1943), an American psychologist, formally theorized that human behavior and cognitive skill could be systematically manipulated with incentives. He described a theory of incentive-based learning in his book *Principles of Behavior* and integrated the concept into his larger theory of behavior. Students of this behavioral theory such as Logan (1960, 1968) were quick to refine and elaborate the incentive portion of Hull's theory. The incentive notion was

This chapter is adapted from *NeuroRehabilitation*, Vol. 4, No. 3, R. Parenté, Effects of Monetary Incentives on Performance After Traumatic Brain Injury, pp. 198–203, © 1994, with permission from Elsevier Science Ireland, Ltd., Bay 15K, Shannon Industrial Estate, Co. Clare, Ireland.

not systematically applied within the head injury field until the later part of this century (Parenté, 1994).

According to the early incentive theorists, the things that a person knows how to do are called *habits*. Those things that have value to a person are called *incentive motivators*. Incentive theorists assume that combinations of incentives such as money and motivating physiological drives such as hunger or thirst are responsible for energizing habits into actions. Basically, we all learn habits over the years because of some physiological need to do so, such as the need to eat, drink, and have a comfortable place to live. However, another learning process occurs in addition to habit learning. This is incentive learning, or learning that all behavior has consequences. These two types of learning can occur separately. For example, many people are aware of the incentives associated with certain professions although they never become doctors, lawyers, or businesspeople. Likewise, many college students learn a complex skill or content major while in school but never receive the rewards associated with using this knowledge because they switch to an unrelated profession after they graduate.

The early incentive theorists documented several principles of incentive-based learning. First, performance was faster and more accurate when the reward was larger than when it was smaller. These theorists also noticed that the amount of reward was not the only factor that controlled behavior. Other things such as the quality of the reward or how much time intervened between the behavior and the reward were also factors. For example, most people will work harder and longer when the reward is an expensive dinner at a four-star restaurant than when it is a hamburger and french fries at a fast food restaurant. They will also be less inclined to work if the anticipated dinner is to occur at some distant and unspecified time in the future.

The early incentive theorists also noticed that the incentive value of a reward depended upon the type of reward the person was accustomed to receiving. A shift from working for a large reward to working for a smaller reward initially resulted in lowered performance. The reverse was

also true: A shift from working for a small reward to working for a larger reward improved performance markedly. For example, it may be difficult to give a full effort in a job that pays $20,000 a year after being laid off from a job that pays $40,000 a year. Likewise, many employees experience a dramatic improvement in their work performance when they move from a low-paying position to one that provides a marked increase in salary.

Clark Hull and his students were not the only psychologists to discuss the concept of incentive. Mowrer (1956, 1960) also discussed the topic from a slightly different perspective. He felt that learning resulted from an association of behavior with one of four conditions: the presence of something pleasurable, the presence of something unpleasant or noxious, the removal of something pleasant (e.g., the removal of a warm and nurturing tone from the therapist's voice), and the removal of something noxious (e.g., a break in a particularly stressful or difficult therapy session).

According to Mowrer, when a person's behavior results in a reward, some aspect of the situation comes to elicit *hope*. When behaviors result in an unpleasant outcome, the situation becomes associated with *avoidance*. Individuals learn *disappointment* when their behavior results in the failure to achieve something or the removal of something they cherish. They learn *relief* when some event signals the removal of an unpleasant state.

Mowrer's model (1956, 1960) of behavior defined *incentive* as the anticipation of a positive, pleasurable, or rewarding state. This definition is similar to his definition of hope because both involve the anticipation of something pleasurable or rewarding. Hope and incentive are not identical, however. For example, a million dollars has incentive value although one may have little hope of becoming a millionaire. Although his description of the process differed from Hull's (1943), both models assumed that humans use the feedback from their gains and losses to modify their behavior. In Mowrer's system, the feedback from one's interaction with the environment determined one's current state of hope, disappointment, relief, or avoidance.

Other theorists such as Skinner (1969) and Ferster and Skinner (1957) developed the notion of schedules of reward and discussed how these could be used to explain the incentive notion. Briefly, they noted that the quality and amount of a person's behavior could be predicted by the pattern of rewards he or she received. The notion of incentive learning was actually quite similar to Skinner's concept of reward in his model of behavior. Logan (1968) produced the most comprehensive incentive theory. Both he and Skinner asserted that behavior was affected not only by the amount of reward but also by incentive motivators such as the delay and the quality of reward, along with drives such as hunger and other physiological needs.

We are not concerned with which of these theories is correct. There are similarities between them that have clear implications for rehabilitation after head injury. Perhaps the most important commonality is the assumption that there are at least two types of learning—*habit learning,* which lays down the blueprints of our behaviors, and *incentive learning,* the knowledge of possible gains that certain behaviors are likely to produce—and that both types of learning were necessary for behavior to take place. Although habit and incentive learning coexist, they can also occur independently. Both are necessary for some learned behavior to occur spontaneously. Habits are the action plans that gradually develop through experience with the world. However, we also learn the incentive value of the various action plans, which is the realization that a specific behavior always has a consequence. Without habit learning, there would be no action plans to follow. Without incentive learning, there would be no way of directing behavior.

This incentive learning process is typically disrupted after traumatic brain injury. That is, it seems that persons with traumatic brain injury either have a difficult time learning incentives or cannot retain the incentive relationships that they do learn. It is therefore reasonable to suggest that they may be able to learn habits but may not be able to implement them because they cannot effectively pair the incentive relationship to direct the habit.

Incentive Versus Motivation

There is no clear distinction between incentive and motivation. It may be useful, however, to think of motivation and incentive as a push-and-pull mechanism. Motivators are "sticks" that push a person to act, and incentives are "carrots" that attract a person toward a goal. In most situations, not acting on a motivation threatens a negative consequence, and incentives encourage a positive consequence. As applied to the field of head injury rehabilitation, the distinction implies that the therapist can use at least two methods to change a client's behavior. Unfortunately, most therapists feel that their only recourse is to push or prod the client to adopt a more efficient or more socially appropriate behavior. Often the therapist can unwittingly assume the role of a police officer or parent figure. However, the therapist can foster a far more productive therapy environment by simply creating an attractive incentive to perform (Atkinson & Wickens, 1971). In our experience, the most effective therapists spend a great deal of time creating incentives for good performance and compliance with treatment goals (Parenté, 1994). Clients typically work hardest in therapy when encouraged by possible positive consequences of their behavior. The "gun-to-the-head" approach, in which they perform because they feel that some negative consequence will occur if they do not, is less useful.

Rewards and Punishments

It is tempting to think of incentives as rewards and punishments as motivators. This is not the case, however, and it is important for the therapist to realize the differences between these terms and their implications for work with clients after traumatic brain injury. We have already discussed incentives and motivators. With respect to rewards and punishments, it is important first to define the terms specifically. Rewards are used to increase a desired behavior. Punishments are designed to decrease an unwanted behavior (Wolpe, 1958). For example, the therapist may reward the client for using a memory strategy spontaneously or punish the same client in some way when he or she behaves in an obnoxious manner. In our experience, rewards are effective for modifying clients' behaviors. Punishments generally are not effective for this purpose.

Rewards and punishments can also be positive and negative. The term *positive* refers to the application or giving of something, whereas the term *negative* refers to taking something away. A positive reward is therefore something the client receives that increases the likelihood that he or she will respond the same way in the future (Kleinsmith & Kaplan, 1963). For example, giving the client verbal praise after each correct response in a therapy session is an example of positive reward. Positive rewards are typically effective and, in most cases, easy to use. A negative reward is the removal of something unpleasant as a means of increasing some behavior of the client. This type of reward does not work well in most situations because the therapist first has to put the client into a noxious state in order to remove it later.

A positive punishment is the infliction of something the client does not like each time an unwanted behavior occurs. We do not recommend using positive punishments because they usually lead to aggressive behavior and can have unpredictable consequences. Negative punishment means taking something away from the client each time an undesirable behavior occurs. For example, if the client smokes, the smoking break could be eliminated. Negative punishments can produce hostility and aggression and should be used sparingly; that is, they should be used only when the therapist feels that the punishment will not produce a response that is more undesirable than the response he or she was trying to eliminate in the first place.

AN INCENTIVE-BASED MODEL OF COGNITIVE REHABILITATION

Therapists will often begin treatment with the assumption that the client's thinking and memory processes are damaged. Parenté and Anderson-Parenté (1991) referred to this assumption as the "broken-brain" model of cognitive rehabilitation.

The treatment goals of this approach are therefore to teach the person compensatory strategies that get around the problem, to strengthen the damaged process via stimulation therapy, or to train the person to use some compensatory device that obviates the problem. Unfortunately, many therapists do not give much thought to the incentive value of their treatment. The primary goal is to teach clients new cognitive skills, and the therapist assumes that clients will use these skills when the need arises (Levy, 1977; Levy & Loftus, 1984). However, clients often learn the skill but never actually apply them spontaneously. Parenté (1994) outlined an incentive-based model of cognitive rehabilitation that predicts this phenomenon. We discuss this model below, along with its implications for treatment intervention.

The incentive-based model of cognitive rehabilitation is consistent with all of the theories outlined above. It is, however, most closely aligned with Logan's (1960, 1968) concept of incentive motivation. As applied to head injury rehabilitation, the model has two basic assumptions. First, at least two types of learning go on in cognitive rehabilitation, *strategy learning* and *incentive learning*. Strategies are memory techniques, or cognitive skills that the client learns in order to perform some type of task. Ideally, the therapist teaches the client strategies that will carry over into the client's activities of daily living. However, the client also learns the incentive value of the new behaviors—that is, the realization that use of the strategy produces a reward or otherwise results in some desired state of affairs. These two types of learning coexist in most situations, although they can also occur independently. The second assumption is that both types of learning must occur before the client will spontaneously use the learned strategies. Incentive learning occurs through real-world experience. Without incentive learning, the client may learn compensatory strategies but will not necessarily use them.

The incentive-based model of cognitive rehabilitation differs from the broken-brain model in that it asserts that the cognitive system is still basically intact and can function quite well under certain conditions. The broken-brain assumption denies the client's ability to think and remember effectively under most conditions, and the goal is to compensate for its malfunction. The incentive model assumes that cognitive deficits can be dramatically improved with incentive learning. Accordingly, the primary goal of therapy is to create an environment in which there is an appropriate incentive, one that is sufficient to ensure adequate levels of cognitive performance, and in which the client can associate the newly learned strategies with some reward.

It may be difficult for many therapists to lessen their reliance on the broken-brain model. Clearly brain injury produces tissue damage, which definitely affects the client's thinking skills. Most clients reportedly had adequate thinking skills before their injury, and there is a clear decrease in these skills after the head injury. It therefore seems obvious that the damage to the brain that resulted from the head injury has affected the client's ability to think and to remember. We do not entirely reject this assumption. We do, however, question its value as an effective model of head injury rehabilitation. It is necessary to consider other factors that may affect the recovery process and determine the course of treatment.

The multimodal model discussed in Chapter 2 identified several other factors that can produce cognitive deficits. Diet, drug use, and premorbid educational level are just a few of these factors. The depression and elation of rapid mood swings have known effects on thinking. Both mood states restrict the ability to organize information because they keep the client from attending and processing (Bower, 1981; Hertel, 1994). Moreover, in many cases, the client cannot think and remember effectively because he or she does not see any reason to do so. The lack of incentive learning in most therapy situations leads many clients to question the value of the treatment because they do not see its relevance.

Evaluation

The incentive-based model of cognitive rehabilitation assumes that memory and cognitive deficits that accompany head injury can be ameliorated with appropriate incentive learning. Therapists can teach clients strategies that will improve their performance in certain situations; however, clients will usually not use them unless they also learn the incentive relationship that elicits the strategy spontaneously. Teaching strategies creates the potential for the client to engage in new behaviors; teaching incentive enables the client to initiate the behavior spontaneously. Without incentive learning, clients may learn new strategies but may never use them on their own.

Tests of the Incentive-Based Model

Parenté (1994) provided preliminary tests of the incentive-based model in a series of experiments. These experiments have continued, and the results have remained stable. In each experiment, the model predicted that clients could remember quite well if there was a reason to do so. It was therefore reasonable to assume that manipulations of incentive could produce rapid and dramatic improvements in thinking skills. This prediction stood in sharp contrast to the broken-brain assumption, which predicted that thinking skill would improve slowly as the person gradually learned effective compensatory strategies.

Three experiments were performed that addressed this issue. The overall conclusion was that cognitive skills can improve immediately and dramatically after head injury, often to average levels, if the therapist creates a relevant incentive to activate the client's performance. An abbreviated discussion of these experiments is presented below. The reader is referred to Parenté (1994) for an in-depth treatment of these results.

Initially, 24 clients participated in these experiments. Since the time these results were first reported, we have run over 100 subjects in similar experiments with the same result. The complete results for 30 of these subjects are presented below. Each of these clients was receiving cognitive rehabilitation after a traumatic brain injury. The clients' ages varied between 18 and 50. Their IQs generally fell in the low-average range (mean = 85), and tests of memory indicated a general decline (mean MQ = 80). Each client was considered mildly to moderately impaired according to criteria adopted by Maryland's Division of Rehabilitation Services.

Although the therapeutic goal of each of these experiments was to show the client that his or her thinking and memory could change markedly with the appropriate incentives, the treatment also provided experimental evidence in favor of the incentive-based model of cognitive rehabilitation.

In this experiment, the clients played the first card game discussed in Chapter 10. The number of correctly and incorrectly identified cards was used as a measure of performance. Ten clients participated in this experiment, and each repeated this card game four times, each time under a different incentive condition. In the first game, a baseline condition, no incentive was provided. In the second game, the therapist provided a $100 incentive. No incentive was provided in the third game. In the fourth game, the therapist again provided a $100 incentive, but now a $100 bill was actually placed in front of the client so that he or she could see it while playing the game. In both the second and fourth conditions, the therapist told the client that getting the $100 was contingent on perfect performance.

Again, the therapeutic purpose of the experiment was to demonstrate for the client that his or her thinking processes could improve rapidly when there was a reason to perform. Clearly, the entire experiment occurred over a period of less than an hour, and it would have been unreasonable to conclude that improvement was due to some long-term organic change.

Twenty additional traumatically brain-injured clients were asked to play the game once. Another group of 20 college students also played the game. These subjects played the game with no incentive, and their group performances served as a basis for comparison.

The 20 head-injured survivors in this study performed initially about as well as one would expect from a sample of head injury survivors. With no incentive, their performance in the first and third conditions was within the range of the 20 survivors who had done the experiment once with no incentive. However, when a $100 bill was placed in front of them, their performance increased immediately and fell in the lower end of the range expected of college students. Removal of the incentive had the effect of lowering

their performance to a level within the range of the survivors who had done the task once. Reinstating the incentive had the effect of increasing their performance to the level of the college students.

The results of the first experiment showed that a monetary incentive was sufficient to improve performance in a card game task that measured attention and immediate memory. In the second experiment, we replicated this result but used a different task to extend the generalizability of the incentive effect. Ten head injury survivors were tested, five with a digit span task and five with a letter span task. The digit span group was asked to recall random number strings that were presented on a computer screen. The strings increased by one digit with each presentation, and the test continued until the subject could no longer recall the string on three successive attempts. The client's digit span was the largest digit string he or she could recall during the session. The letter span subjects received a similar test, although these subjects recalled consonants rather than random digits. The subject's letter span was the longest string of consonants he or she could recall during the session.

The experimental design was identical to the one used in Experiment 1. There was no incentive in the first and third condition, whereas a $100 incentive was available in the second and fourth conditions. The clients were told that they would receive the incentive if they correctly recalled a nine-digit and nine-letter string correctly on two successive trials. We measured digit and letter spans for 20 college students and 20 head injury survivors for comparison purposes.

The results of this experiment were quite similar to those of the first. There was significant improvement of performance when an incentive was provided. Although these subjects generally performed at a level comparable to most head injury survivors when there was no incentive, their performance improved to levels comparable to college students' when an incentive was provided.

The first two experiments indicated that monetary incentives were sufficient to improve performance on tests of attention and immediate memory. The third examined the effect of incentive on other, more subtle aspects of memory. Specifically, the third experiment assessed the effect of incentive on information storage, the transfer of information between immediate and long-term memory, and long-term retention.

The third experiment evaluated the effects of monetary incentive on performance in a word-learning experiment that used the Buschke Selective Reminding Procedure (Buschke, 1973). We chose the Buschke procedure because it measures several different memory processes simultaneously. These include short-term memory, specifically, the client's dependence on short-term memory; long-term storage, or the ability to transfer information from short- to long-term memory; long-term retrieval, or the ability to retrieve information from long-term memory; consistent long-term retrieval, or the ability to retrieve information repeatedly from long-term memory; and organization, or the ability to recognize and use the built-in semantic organization of the word list.

Ten head injury survivors participated in this experiment. We read a 12-item list of common nouns that could be organized into six semantic categories. The actual words used were dog, cat, table, chair, red, green, north, west, Mars, Venus, gun, and knife. The words were read in a random order on the first trial. The client then recalled as many of the words as he or she could remember in any desired order. When the client could not recall any more of the words, the therapist repeated only those the client had been unable to recall. The client attempted to recall the entire list again, and when his or her recall failed, the therapist restated those that were not recalled on that trial. This type of learning procedure is called *selective reminding* because the therapist reminds the client only of the items that he or she failed to recall on a given trial. The procedure continued until the client could recall all 12 words on two successive trials. The task was administered until the clients could recall the words perfectly on two successive trials. This was the baseline condition in which no incentive was provided.

In the incentive condition, the same clients learned a second list: paper, pen, hand, foot, moon, sun, wall, floor, day, night, yellow, blue. The cli-

ents were offered $100 for two perfect consecutive recalls of the word list within six trials. Five of the clients learned the first list and then the second; five learned the lists in the reverse ordering. This procedure was necessary to protect the results from bias due to the possibility that one list might have been easier to learn than the other.

The results were also consistent with those of the first two experiments. Incentive affected most of the measures of memory. The largest difference occurred with the long-term storage, consistent long-term retrieval, and organization measures. The results were less striking for the overall recall, long-term retrieval, and the short-term retrieval measures. Incentive improved certain measures of the client's ability to retrieve information from long-term memory and to perceive the built-in semantic organization. Because this effect occurred within minutes, it could not have been the result of a gradual improvement of cognitive functions.

FROM THEORY TO PRACTICE

The broken-brain model assumes that cognitive dysfunction after head injury is due to a damaged neural mechanism. We have not abandoned that model, but we feel that the mechanisms of memory and cognition may not be as damaged as was once thought. Our thesis is that the client has not learned the appropriate incentive motivators that are responsible for initiating effortful processing. Although the therapist can certainly teach the client habits and strategies, creating incentives is perhaps the only way to ensure compliance with treatment goals, attention and concentration during treatment sessions, and spontaneous use of strategies (see also Eysenck & Eysenck, 1980; Meacham & Singer, 1977).

The incentive-based model of cognitive rehabilitation provides clear directions for treatment that are quite different from those derived from the broken-brain model. Accordingly, therapy interventions should focus on identifying incentives that are uniquely relevant to the client—specifically, those that the person will work to achieve. Without these incentives, therapy efforts will be overly time consuming and will produce only marginal improvement.

Monetary incentives are not the only effective rewards (Dolan & Norto, 1977). Clients also value social praise, companionship, and interesting games and stimulation (Maslow, 1970). On the other hand, computer software for cognitive rehabilitation may be useful only if it engages the client's interest. Once the novelty of the program wears off, the computer may sit unused. On the other hand, many clients will play computer games for a much longer period of time. We have found that computer software for cognitive rehabilitation usually produces gains in attention/concentration alone, and it is possible that more interesting computer games would produce even greater gains. There are currently a great many different computer games that not only are challenging but also require logic, foresight, and reasoning. Moreover, with the advent of virtual reality systems, the incentive value of the software is likely to increase markedly.

Current Needs and Interests

Therapists are well advised to monitor the client carefully to determine what he or she needs and what types of activities he or she finds interesting. Some clients find that certain rewards are not adequate to engage their interest. For example, one client who was financially independent did not see much value in a $10 reward. Social stimulation was a better incentive for him. Another client was a merchant marine before his head injury. We tried to get the client to play the children's game called "Memory" that trains visual spatial retention. Many therapists are familiar with this game. Briefly, several pairs of pictures are placed face down in an array on the table, and the client must turn over two cards at a time and remember the location of the pair. This particular client found the game boring and childish until he replaced the original cards with two decks of playing cards that each had identical nude women on the flip side of the cards. Using his own cards, the client played for hours

at a time. We do not advocate using pornography or sex as therapy facilitators. Indeed, this client's technique was never used with any other client. This is, however, an example of how a simple manipulation of an often-used memory training game can produce a level of incentive that greatly facilitates compliance.

Premorbid Interests

The therapist should interview family and friends to assess the client's premorbid interests and should try to construct therapy materials that accord with these interests. For example, one client was interested in motorcycles. We determined that he had severe reading problems. Reading comprehension training therefore used motorcycle magazines for training. The client was also asked to disassemble and to reassemble a motorcycle engine, a task that required reading an entire engine repair manual.

Social Relationships

The client's relationships with family, friends, and other clients can have a powerful incentive value. The incentive is especially strong when the client becomes romantically involved or finds an accepting friend. The incentive may involve a sexual character, but more often it is based on acceptance, companionship, and a sense of inclusion within a social network. We have noticed that many clients will make a special effort in treatment simply because they want to be accepted by their family or their friends. For this reason, we encourage social relationships and remind the client that the respect that others give will largely depend upon the effort the client makes to be accepted.

Positive Reinforcement System

We encourage family members to establish a positive reinforcement system in the home. The client's progress toward goals should be clearly charted, and the rewards for certain goals should be obvious. Rewards can be anything—for example, dinner at the client's favorite restaurant. One family promised their son a Caribbean cruise if he obtained a certain GPA in college after he returned from his convalescence.

Direct Payment

If the client agrees, the family can allocate payment of Social Security and disability benefits on an allowance basis. These monies are then paid to the client contingent on a certain level of performance. The client's job then becomes his or her therapy. This type of situation is purely voluntary, however, and the client must agree to it first.

Another form of direct payment involves building a monetary incentive system directly into computer games and software for cognitive rehabilitation. That is, the reward occurs when the client achieves a certain level of performance on the task or on some transfer task. For example, we modified many computer training exercises so that a random number and letter code would appear on the screen once the client reached a certain level of performance. The code remained on the screen for about 10 seconds, and the client had to memorize it and report it to the therapist to receive a monetary reward. The codes were relatively easy to remember for the lower levels of performance. For example, a code such as X5ZP7 yielded a $10 reward when the client achieved 70% performance on a reading comprehension program. Remembering larger strings such as L4B4ZX earned $20 once the client achieved 80% performance on the same task. In each case, the client had to remember the code long enough, without writing it down, to report it correctly to the therapist who would delegate the reward.

Continuous Availability of Incentives

The therapist should make incentives available even when the client is not in the therapy ses-

sion. For example, in the first experiment, the clients were encouraged to practice these card games at home. They were told that the reward would still be available any time they could demonstrate perfect performance on the task. Daily practice was perhaps the best way to achieve the reward. Before the therapist made the incentive continuously available, the clients would not practice the tasks on their own. After the incentive was made available, most clients reported practicing the card games every day. The fact that most clients will continue to perform on their own for the chance to earn a reward later is perhaps the most efficient aspect of the incentive-based model.

Believability of Incentives

The value of the incentive will depend upon the client's belief that he or she will eventually receive it. Disbelief can occur for several reasons. Some clients may not believe that the therapist will actually give them the reward once they achieve the specified performance level. Others may not believe that they can perform well enough to achieve the incentive. Usually, however, the clients will give the task a try once they see another client try and succeed.

Feasibility of Incentives

It may seem to the reader that arranging social incentives or giving monetary rewards is either too difficult or too expensive to be practical. Social activity can be fun and novel, and the therapist can usually arrange with the family to provide this type of incentive. With respect to monetary rewards, we have found that most clients never quite reach the required performance criteria to achieve the reward, although they still make the effort. The monetary rewards are therefore quite efficient. For example, only two clients ever received the $100 rewards offered in the experiments reported above. Moreover, many clients will work quite hard for a far smaller reward. In general, the use of incentives is likely to be an exceptionally inexpensive treatment compliance technique.

REFERENCES

Atkinson, R.C., & Wickens, T.D. (1971). Human memory and the concept of reinforcement. In R. Glaser (Ed.), *The nature of reinforcement*. London: Academic Press.

Bower, G.H. (1981). Mood and memory. *American Psychologist, 36*, 129–148.

Buschke, H. (1973). Selective reminding for analyses of memory and learning. *Journal of Verbal Learning and Verbal Behavior, 12*, 543–549.

Dolan, M., & Norto, J. (1977). A programmed training technique that uses reinforcement to facilitate acquisition and retention in brain-damaged patients. *Journal of Clinical Psychology, 33*, 496–501.

Eysenck, M.W., & Eysenck, M.C. (1980). Effects of monetary incentives on rehearsal and on cued recall. *Bulletin of the Pschonomics Society, 15*, 245–247.

Ferster, C.S., & Skinner, B.F. (1957). *Schedules of reinforcement*. New York: Appleton-Century-Crofts.

Hertel, P. (1994). Depressive deficits in memory: Implications for memory improvement following traumatic brain injury. *NeuroRehabilitation, 4*(3), 143–150.

Hull, C. (1943). *Principles of behavior*. New York: Macmillan.

Kleinsmith, L.J., & Kaplan, S. (1963). Paired associate learning as a function of arousal interpellated interval. *Journal of Experimental Psychology, 66*, 190–196.

Levy, R.L. (1977). Relationship of overt commitment to task compliance in behavior therapy. *Journal of Behavior Therapy and Experimental Psychology, 8*, 25–29.

Levy, R.L., & Loftus, G.R. (1984). Compliance and memory. In J.E. Harris & P.E. Morris (Eds.), *Everyday memory, actions, and absentmindedness*. London: Academic Press.

Logan, F.A. (1960). *Incentive: How the conditions of reinforcement affect the performance of rats*. New Haven, CT: Yale University Press.

Logan, F.A. (1968). Incentive theory and changes in reward. In. J. Spence & G. Bower (Eds.), *The psychology of learning and motivation* (Vol. 2, pp. 1–30). New York: Academic Press.

Maslow, A.H. (1970). Motivation and personality (2nd ed.). New York: Harper & Row.

Meacham, J.A., & Singer, J. (1977). Incentive effects in prospective remembering. *Journal of Psychology, 97*, 191–197.

Mowrer, O.H. (1956). Two factor learning theory reconsidered, with special reference to secondary reinforcement and the concept of habit. *Psychological Review, 63*, 114–128.

Mowrer, O.H. (1960). *Learning theory and behavior*. New York: John Wiley.

Parenté, R. (1994). Effects of monetary incentives on performance after traumatic brain injury. *NeuroRehabilitation, 4*, 198–203.

Parenté, R., & Anderson-Parenté, J. (1991). *Retraining memory: Techniques and applications*. Houston, TX: CSY.

Skinner, B.F. (1969). *Science and human behavior*. New York: Macmillan.

Wolpe, J. (1958). *Psychotherapy of reciprocal inhibition*. Stanford, CA: Stanford University.

Chapter 24

Social and Environmental Issues

The social environment can have an enormous impact on the client's thinking skills (Belmont, 1989). It can be an especially supportive context that improves the client's overall cognitive status. In some social situations, for example, the client must demonstrate that he or she knows who others are and what they do. Everyone must make and keep appointments. Everyone must recall what monies or social favors they owe to others, respond appropriately in social situations, and do chores that others depend on them to do. Clients' performance in these situations largely determines how others judge them and treat them thereafter (Ostrom, 1989). Failure to remember things like a relative's birthday or a wedding anniversary can damage the social fabric of the family or friendships. Friends and family members may take offense at the client's apparent social indiscretions even when they know that the client has sustained a head injury. Brothers and sisters of younger clients may act as if they are embarrassed by the client in social situations. Indeed, the loss of social grace is perhaps the most devastating thing that clients can face after head injury. Clearly, part of the loss involves poor memory. When a client forgets someone's name, has word retrieval problems during a social exchange, or has obvious problems carrying on conversations, there is an immeasurable loss of self-esteem that damages the recovery process.

Alternatively, when a client successfully recalls another's name and information about the person, understands the point of a conversation and successfully contributes to it, or recalls important events and facts quickly and accurately, his or her social skills and relationships are reaffirmed.

This chapter explains how various aspects of social situations affect a client's memory and thinking skills. The therapist's goal is to get the client to monitor his or her cognitive performance in relation to others' social expectations. We also present various techniques for using the social environment as a memory and cognitive aid.

FACTORS THAT AFFECT SOCIAL COGNITION

Feedback

Sometimes people comment about how well or how poorly a client performed a thinking task. However, this "cognitive feedback" cannot be taken at face value. People sometimes inaccurately say that someone's thinking is better or worse than it really is. Their comments may be intended to show a kindness toward a client. Regardless of the intention, it is important to distinguish contrived feedback from accurate feedback. To get an idea of the types of responses to their disability that head-injured clients dislike, we asked 20 head-injured clients to list three such responses that were especially annoying. Exhibit 24–1 is a rank-ordered list of the most commonly mentioned items.

The clients were unanimous in their assertion that it was better to receive accurate feedback than the responses in Exhibit 24–1. In some cases, negative feedback may cause distress, but it may also increase the client's motivation to improve. False feedback simply has no value whatsoever. Indeed, false positive feedback will give the client an unrealistic sense of well-being or failure. It is therefore useful to acquaint family members with the more common forms of contrived feedback and to warn them of its negative effect on the therapy process. In general, it is wise to focus on the positive but not to ignore the negative aspects of the client's behavior and cognition.

Influence of the Social Context

Most people find it especially difficult to hold a lone dissenting view among well-respected friends or authorities (Ash, 1956). For example, if the client is reminiscing about a previous good time that was shared by several others who did not have the same experience, then the accuracy of his or her recall will come into question. This type of situation could lead the client to change his or her account to accord with the group consensus. Indeed, most clients face an enormous skepticism from others about the accuracy of

---

Exhibit 24–1 Common Responses to Head-Injury-Related Disability that Clients Dislike

- Minimizing or failing to recognize deficits
- Unwarranted praise
- Unwarranted excuses for cognitive failure
- Unwarranted reassignment of responsibility
- Overallowance of time to complete a task
- Smothering: telling clients they require help with every task

---

what they recall (DeBono & Hamish, 1988). They often sense this skepticism. However, it is important to bear in mind that a client's memory may be right when others say it is wrong. The therapist should therefore train the client to monitor the accuracy of his or her recall in order to learn when it is likely to be inaccurate. Taking notes and keeping a diary is one way of monitoring recall. Regularly rehearsing shared events with others is another. Keeping photo albums and watching home videos of shared experiences are also ways of improving the accuracy of the client's recollections (Markus, 1980; Rogers, 1977; Rogers, Kuiper, & Kirker, 1977).

Current Status of Relationships

Often the most important factor in others' trust of the client's thinking skills is how he or she gets along with them. If the client reflects, intentionally or unintentionally, a lack of regard for other individuals, those other people will generally discount the client. They will also be less inclined to help the client in social situations or to facilitate his or her social adjustment.

State of Home Life

Cognition is helped by a harmonious living environment. If a client's home life is full of arguments and disputes, these issues will compete for the limited cognitive effort and will limit processing of other important issues. Most head injuries place enormous pressure on the family. Aside from the injury itself, domestic distress is probably the biggest single factor underlying a client's poor cognitive functioning. For cognitive training to be effective, it is essential that the therapist do everything possible to help the family maintain some degree of normalcy and civility in their daily encounters.

For most clients, the majority of cognitive processing is carried out in response to others. This type of social skills training begins in the supportive atmosphere of the home. If it does not, the client is forced to relearn these skills in the less accepting social environment outside of the home. However, the school of hard knocks involves exposure to many potentially embarrassing and dangerous situations. For example, one client frequented a local bar to escape an intolerable home situation. Although he did not drink while he was at the bar, he had occasion to say something that offended another patron. A fight ensued, and the client suffered another head injury.

Social Information

Social information affects cognition in three ways. First, social customs determine which cognitive tasks a person chooses to perform (Cole & Scribner, 1974; Roberts, 1985). Second, success or failure affects the client's motivation to attempt another social encounter (Lord, Saenz, & Godfrey, 1987). Third, the quality of the feedback determines the quality of the client's memories of success or failure (Lord & Saenz, 1985; Meacham, 1988).

REQUISITE SOCIAL RESPONSES

Many social situations require a conventional response. For example, etiquette and social convention require a variety of complex cognitive skills, including memory for social events and rituals, knowledge of preexisting intimate relationships, and prior obligations. To train this skill, we refer to books on social and business etiquette to make lists of common social situations and the appropriate responses. The client literally memorizes these responses with drill and practice.

Clients often need simply to recognize the social demands that they face in unique social situations. This is especially relevant in complex social or cultural ethnical situations. For example, the therapist may have to teach clients specific social customs within their culture that will reduce the likelihood of an offensive statement or action (Shotter & Guald, 1981). This can often

be accomplished by creating checklists of reminders of what the client will need to know before attending parties, meeting relatives, or attending social events. For example, one client immersed in a complex family environment made a 3 × 5 card for each person in his extended family. The card listed the person's work, immediate family members, interests, dislikes, and other specific characteristics. The therapists quizzed the client on these facts until he had relearned them. He then reviewed each card prior to meeting the family members in social gatherings. This procedure helped the client to regain his family's acceptance.

Posted cue cards are also helpful to ensure that the client does not fall prey to other social difficulties. For example, computer software or even a large wall-hanging calendar can remind the client of important social events such as birthdays, anniversaries, and other events the person might share with friends. Forgetting these can have devastating social consequences. Some conventional memory tasks must be performed on precise days or dates. For instance, failing to pay taxes on time can create distrust of the client's competence. In every culture, people honor certain holidays or religious days. Observance of these days is considered by some as an index of the person's commitment to the cultural or religious group. Forgetting to recognize the day or event publicly can sometimes lead to social rejection by others.

Finally, cultures establish ways to behave that indicate appropriate attitudes and ways to behave that indicate antisocial modes of behavior (Rothbart, 1981). In some cases, the prosocial behaviors are taught explicitly ("always say please," "don't interrupt"). In other cases, it is expected that the person will adopt the behaviors by watching elders or other people in power. If a person manifests antisocial behavior, even if unintentionally, others may describe him or her as "forgetting his or her place." Thus, identifying the client's awareness of social factors can be an important part of his or her treatment plan. Moreover, training the client to behave in a socially appropriate manner is perhaps one of the greatest services the therapist can provide.

Formal Social Cognition

Cocktail parties, meetings, reunions, and even informal get-togethers require people to remember and commit to memory a variety of names, topics, and protocols (Wyer, 1989; Wyer & Srull, 1986). Although these situations may be extremely difficult for the client to handle, some prior preparation can help him or her through the event. Consider the process of remembering the names of several people whom the client will meet at a party (Bond & Brockett, 1987). A simple social set can smooth the flow of conversation during almost any introduction. Training the client to ask a few select questions, such as what the person does for a living, whether the person has children, how old the children are, and whether the person has any special interests, is usually all that is necessary (Edwards & Middleton, 1987; Keenan, MacWhinney, & Mayhew, 1977). Typically, the client can spend most of his or her time listening. Indeed, the LISTEN mnemonic outlined in Chapter 11 is good prior training for this type of social activity.

Before the client leaves the party, he or she will want to remember to thank the host. Such customary memory tasks constitute what are often called *cognitive rituals*. They are usually easy to train, and most clients can perform them without difficulty (Goldsmith & Pillemer, 1988).

Casual Conversation

Like organized social events, polite conversation also requires a person to attempt one or more cognitive tasks. For example, if the client takes a walk and encounters a neighbor, he or she may be expected to recall his or her hobbies, how this person's children are doing in school, and perhaps the latest headlines or sports scores (Holtgraves, Srull, & Socall, 1989).

Cognitive Obligations

Daily life requires people to make and meet appointments, repay favors, and do chores that others depend on them to do. Some of these tasks may be for friends or family; other tasks are necessary for one's job or are simply part of daily living, such as remembering to change one's engine oil every 5,000 miles. The client's failure to perform these cognitive tasks can lead family, friends, and acquaintances to make negative judgments about his or her caring, sensitivity, manners, or even intelligence. This is especially true when others experience some negative consequence resulting from his or her cognitive failure. Obligations require a person to remember spontaneously when to perform them. The spontaneous remembering depends on several factors, such as the obligation's importance or its proximity, how many other obligations must be remembered, and how many distractions occur at the time the obligation must be met (Doerner, 1986; Kimble, Hirt, & Arnold, 1985; Kimble & Zehr, 1982).

Personal Relationship Management

Success or failure at certain cognitive tasks may be construed by others as an index of the client's personal regard for them. One such task is the recall of personal information about the other person in a relationship. Although symbolic tasks may seem relatively trivial when they arise, their importance to other people can be crucial to continuing a close relationship. Exhibit 24–2 lists several cognitive tasks that are symbolic of respect or affection. There are many such tasks that may convey affection, respect, and love to others in a relationship. We suggest that therapists use this list as a starting point for training recognition of these social signals.

Cognitive Pacts

People form pacts with others about how to share in the learning and remembering of certain kinds of information. Pacts are especially common between people who live together because they often need to divide up chores ("you remember to take out the trash, and I will remember to pick up some milk on the way home").

Exhibit 24–2 Cognitive Tasks Symbolic of Respect or Affection

- Remembering the person's name
- Remembering the person's title
- Remembering the person's professional successes
- Remembering the person's areas of expertise
- Remembering to give the person the floor when topics of his or her expertise arise
- Remembering details of the person's career history
- Remembering having made promises to the person and whether one has kept them
- Remembering an event shared with the person
- Remembering the person's likes, dislikes, pet causes, hobbies, projects at work
- Remembering appointments made with the person
- Remembering special acts to be performed for the person (such as a greeting or parting kiss, holding a door, serving breakfast in bed, or buying flowers or candy)
- Remembering special occasions to be honored (including birthdays and anniversaries, as well as other traditionally special days, like Valentine's Day, Mother's Day, Father's Day, Secretary's Week)
- Remembering tasks the person expects one to do and considers important
- Remembering mannerisms of the person that signal a change in his or her needs or moods

Pacts are also common between coworkers, who may similarly divide responsibilities.

Implicit pacts are agreements that were never formally arranged. These are potentially dangerous to people with memory problems because they may well forget or fail to register their part of the bargain ("I thought that you were going to pay the phone bill"). Most people cannot recall their cognitive pacts at will, but they can recognize them as they occur, especially when they are broken. Cognitive pacts can, if forgotten, lead to arguments. As a head-injured client recovers, it is helpful to review the nature of pacts and expectations. It is also important to write them down and place them in plain view, preferably in the form of a checklist. This will ensure that others perceive that the client is living up to his or her social bargains.

DISPOSITION TO PERFORM COGNITIVE TASKS

Group Identification

The accuracy of a person's cognitions can be affected by the influences of groups to which he or she belongs or identifies. Matters that are consistent with our religious, political, and social beliefs are learned and retained better than matters inconsistent with those beliefs (Goethals & Reckman, 1973). For example, after reading a balanced passage that discusses the pros and cons of a political issue, most people remember more facts about the side they favor and fewer facts about the side they oppose. In addition, when tested again later, people retain more accurately the facts about the side they favor and less accurately the facts about the side they oppose. This phenomenon has come to be known as *selective recall* (Read & Rosson, 1982).

A person's group identification can be based on a stereotype (e.g., pertaining to race, religion, gender, or age). A stereotype can affect selective encoding of information in the same manner as described for group identification (Bodenhausen, 1988; Hamilton & Trolier, 1986). For example, it is well accepted that racism (Dovidio & Gaertner, 1986; Van Dijk, 1987) may affect encoding. Cognitions may be biased by sexism as well. For example, males and females tend to remember better when to terminate an event if the event is consistent with their gender. Males time the charging of a battery better than the baking of cookies, whereas females time baking better than battery charging (Ceci & Bronfenbrenner, 1985). College-age women and men learned the very same ambiguous passage of directions differently depending on whether the passage was given a "feminine" title or a "masculine" title. Specifically, women remembered more ideas from the passage than men when the passage was labeled "Repairing a Shirt," whereas another group of men remembered more ideas from the same passage than another group of women when the passage was labeled "Repairing a Workbench" (Herrmann, Crawford, & Holdsworth, 1992). Similarly, elderly people tend to learn less readily because of beliefs that learning ability decreases with age (Hamlett, Best, & Davis, 1985). One or more of these standard stereotypes (race, gender, age) may undermine the client's performance. Also, defusing of a preexisting stereotype can facilitate training efforts.

Probably one of the most powerful stereotypes is that of head injury itself (Rothbart, 1981). The client was exposed prior to his or her injury to a variety of media stories about head-injured people and their cognitive deficits. The movies are full of stories involving head-injured characters. Films like *Frankenstein* and *Donovan's Brain* convey a dismal, frightening picture of a person with limited cognitive skill. Thus, clients should be informed that others may perceive them as unpredictable or dangerous. A client cannot know to what degree someone will be influenced by these stereotypes (DeBono & Hamish, 1988).

Cognitive Reputation

In any circle of acquaintances or coworkers, the client will have a reputation for how often he or she succeeded or failed at cognitive tasks in the past (DeBono & Hamish, 1988; Hovland & Weiss, 1951). Clients are typically sensitive to the fact that their reputation has changed as a result of the injury. For example, one client who worked as a heavy equipment mechanic stated that his biggest problem when he returned to work was his reputation. He had been known as

the expert, the person everyone else came to for consultation and advice, the person who could solve mechanical problems better and faster than anyone else in the shop. After his head injury, however, his coworkers' opinions changed dramatically. They ranged from "Well, he can still do the job" to "He ain't right in the head." It was therefore necessary to discuss with the client a new criterion for success. In his case, the criterion was to simply remain employed but not necessarily to live up to his former expectations.

THE DYNAMICS OF SOCIAL COGNITION

Ironically, cognition is more likely to fail when one is with others than when one is alone. Interaction dynamics and conversational manipulations determine the persuasiveness of what the client says (DeBono & Hamish, 1988). Thus, a client's cognition can fail in social contexts in at least two ways. First, cognition fails because various aspects of conversations make it too distracting to attend and concentrate effectively. Second, even when clients can attend to the conversation, they may still fail to communicate their thoughts clearly and accurately (Allport & Postman, 1947; Kimble, Hirt, & Arnold, 1985; Kimble & Zehr, 1982).

Clients benefit from training to manipulate conversations (Edwards & Middleton, 1987; Goldsmith & Pillemer, 1988). For example, a client can avoid forgetting if he or she can get others to reiterate what was just said. Such a strategy helps a person encode who said what and also delays the input of new information. For example, we train clients who have just been introduced to a stranger to confuse the pronunciation of the person's name. Asking questions and trying to summarize points for verification are similar strategies that usually get the other person to repeat information. Conversational ploys buy time for retrieval of hard-to-remember information because they slow a conversation or restrict it to just one or two topics (Holtgraves et al., 1989).

CREDIBILITY OF COGNITIVE PERFORMANCE

Good cognition is useless if others do not trust the person's thinking skills. Sometimes a loss of confidence in a person's cognitive skills can be crucial. Even if the client has successfully recalled something in a social context, others may not find the information credible. There are, however, several ways to bolster credibility.

Expression

Confidence in his or her recall is likely to increase the client's credibility. Considerable research has demonstrated that witnesses in court will be regarded as remembering the truth if they sit up and speak confidently. For example, John Dean, of Watergate fame, was regarded as having excellent cognition because he conveyed his recall of the events of Nixon's presidency in a convincing fashion. However, later investigation showed that his recall was full of inaccuracies (Neisser, 1988; Synder & Uranowitz, 1978).

Content

To be convincing, a person's cognitive claim should be internally consistent. Major contradictions between facts make a report appear illogical and indicate that the underlying cognition is distorted. The therapist should also discuss with the client several other issues that affect the credibility of his or her statements. People with whom the client interacts will invariably discount what he or she says if the statement contains obvious inconsistencies. The client's statements will tend to be better accepted if they have a corroborating source, such as newspaper reports, books, or another person who can back up what he or she says.

Nonverbal Communication

People convey the state of their cognitive processing not only by appropriate verbal communi- cation but by effective use of nonverbal signals. We have discussed this topic in detail in other chapters, so we will only mention the gist of the information here. In essence, many nonverbal signals are virtually universal. We suggest that the therapist use the signals listed in Exhibit 24–3 as a starting point for training nonverbal communication. Videotaping a client in conversation and pointing out the nonverbal signals in Exhibit 24–3 is an excellent way to train the client to recognize these social signals in themselves and others. It is especially effective if the therapist turns down the sound so that the client is forced to recognize the signals without any language cues.

Editing Recall

Screening and monitoring of recall are important to ensure that the client does not "blurt out" something offensive. Answers that come quickly and seem very familiar are sometimes incorrect. Some errors are simply strong habits that we cannot disinhibit. For example, one client who was a military officer before his head injury was used to telling subordinates to be quiet until he

---

Exhibit 24–3 Nonverbal Signals

Indications of Confusion
  Blank stare: eyes wide and unblinking
  Look of surprise: eyes wide, eyebrows raised
  Look of guilt: eyes wide, head lowered, shoulders raised
  Facial grimace
  Mouth open
Indications of Trying To Remember
  Thinker's pose: hand to chin or finger to temple
  Faraway stare: gaze slightly upward to one side
  Downward stare, pensive look
  Head scratching
  Palm hitting
  Furrowing of brow
Indications of the Tip-of-the-Tongue State
  Snapping one's fingers
  Shaking one's fist
  Repeated "oh's"

had finished speaking. This ingrained habit was unacceptable in the civilian environment. Perhaps the best way to avoid this problem is to train the client always to say a sentence mentally before actually saying it out loud. Another rule of thumb is that if there is *any* doubt about the appropriateness of a statement, the client is better off inhibiting it.

CONCLUSION

This chapter covered the social factors that can affect clients' cognitive performance and disposition to perform cognitive tasks, social responses that will be required of clients, ways in which clients can maximize their cognitive performance in social contexts, and ways in which clients can bolster their credibility.

REFERENCES

Allport, G.W., & Postman, L.J. (1947). *The psychology of rumor.* New York: Holt, Rinehart & Winston.

Ash, S.E. (1956). Studies of independence and conformity: I. A minority of one against unanimous majority. *Psychological Monographs, 70*(9; whole no. 416).

Belmont, J.M. (1989). Cognitive strategies and strategic learning: The socio-instructional approach. *American Psychologist, 44,* 1442–1448.

Bodenhausen, G.V. (1988). Stereotypic biases in social decision making and cognition: Testing process models of stereotypes. *Journal of Personality and Social Psychology, 55,* 726–737.

Bond, C.F., Jr., & Brockett, D.R. (1987). A social context-personality index theory of cognition for acquaintances. *Journal of Personality and Social Psychology, 52,* 1110–1121.

Ceci, S.J., & Bronfenbrenner, U. (1985). Don't forget to take the cupcakes out of the oven: Prospective cognition, strategic time-monitoring, and context. *Child Development, 56,* 152–164.

Cole, M., & Scribner, S. (1974). *Culture and thought: A psychological introduction.* New York: John Wiley.

DeBono, K.G., & Hamish, R.J. (1988). Source expertise, source attractiveness, and the processing of persuasive information: A functional approach. *Journal of Personality and Social Psychology, 56,* 541–546.

Doerner, D. (1986). Intention memory and intention regulation. In F. Klix & H. Hagendorf (Eds.), *Cognition and cognitive capabilities: Mechanisms and performances.* Amsterdam: North Holland.

Dovidio, J., & Gaertner, S. (1986). *Prejudice, discrimination and racism.* New York: Academic Press.

Edwards, D., & Middleton, D. (1987). Conversation and remembering: Bartlett revisited. *Applied Cognitive Psychology, 1,* 77–92.

Goethals, G.R., & Reckman, R.F. (1973). The perception of consistency in attitudes. *Journal of Experimental Social Psychology, 9,* 491–501.

Goldsmith, L.R., & Pillemer, D.B. (1988). Memories of statements spoken in everyday context. *Applied Cognitive Psychology, 2,* 273–286.

Hamilton, D.L., & Trolier, T.K. (1986). Stereotypes and stereotyping: An overview of the cognitive approach. In J. Dovidio & S. Gaertner (Eds.), *Prejudice, discrimination, and racism.* New York: Academic Press.

Hamlett, K.W., Best, D.L., & Davis, S.W. (1985). *Modification of cognitive complaint and cognitive performance in elderly adults.* Unpublished manuscript, Catholic University of America, Washington, DC.

Herrmann, D., Crawford, M., & Holdsworth, M. (1992). Gender linked differences in everyday memory performance. *British Journal of Psychology, 83,* 221–231.

Holtgraves, T., Srull, T.K., & Socall, D. (1989). Conversation cognition: The effect of speaker status on cognition for the assertiveness of conversation remarks. *Journal of Personality and Social Psychology, 56,* 149–160.

Hovland, C.I., & Weiss, R. (1951). The influence of source credibility on communication effectiveness. *Public Opinion Quarterly, 15,* 635–650.

Keenan, J.M., MacWhinney, B., & Mayhew, D. (1977). Pragmatics in cognition: A study of natural conversation. *Journal of Verbal Learning and Verbal Behavior, 16,* 549–560.

Kimble, C.E., Hirt, E.R., & Arnold, E.M. (1985). Self-consciousness, public and private self-awareness, and cognition in a social setting. *Journal of Psychology, 119,* 59–69.

Kimble, C.E., & Zehr, H.D. (1982). Self-consciousness, information load, self-presentation, and cognition in a social situation. *Journal of Social Psychology, 118,* 39–46.

Lord, C.G., & Saenz, D.S. (1985). Cognitive deficits and cognitive deficits: Differential cognitive consequences of tokenism for tokens and observers. *Journal of Personality and Social Psychology, 49,* 918–926.

Lord, C.G., Saenz, D.S., & Godfrey, D.K. (1987). Effects of perceived scrutiny on participant cognition for social interactions. *Journal of Experimental Social Psychology, 23,* 498–517.

Markus, H. (1980). The self in thought and cognition. In D.M. Wagner & R.R. Vallacher (Eds.), *The self in social psychology.* New York: Oxford University Press.

Meacham, J.A. (1988). Interpersonal relations and prospective remembering. In M. Gruneberg, P. Morris, & R. Sykes (Eds.), *Practical aspects of cognition: Current research and issues* (Vol. 2). New York: John Wiley.

Neisser, U. (1988). Time present and time past. In M.Gruneberg, P.E. Morris, & R.N. Sykes (Eds.), *Practical aspects of cognition: Current research and issues* (Vol. 2). New York: John Wiley.

Ostrom, T.M. (1989). Three catechisms for social cognition. In P.R. Solomon, G.R. Goethals, C.M. Kelley, & B.R. Stephens (Eds.), *Cognition: Interdisciplinary approaches*. New York: Springer-Verlag.

Read, S.J., & Rosson, M.B. (1982). Rewriting history: The biasing effects of attitudes on cognition. *Social Cognition, 1,* 240–255.

Roberts, J. (1985). The attitude-memory relationship after 40 years. *Basic and Applied Social Psychology, 6,* 221–241.

Rogers, T.B. (1977). Self-reference in cognition: Recognition of personality items. *Journal of Research in Personality, 11,* 295–305.

Rogers, T.B., Kuiper, N.A., & Kirker, W.S. (1977). Self-reference and the encoding of personal information. *Journal of Personality and Social Psychology, 35,* 677–688.

Rothbart, M. (1981). Cognitive processes and social beliefs. In D.L. Hamilton (Ed.), *Cognitive processes in stereotyping and intergroup behavior*. Hillsdale, NJ: Lawrence Erlbaum.

Shotter, J., & Guald, A. (1981). *Cognition as a social institution*. British Psychological Society, Plymouth Polytechnic.

Synder, M., & Uranowitz, S.W. (1978). Reconstructing the past: Some cognitive consequences of personal perception. *Journal of Personality and Social Psychology, 36,* 941–951.

Van Dijk, T. (1987). *Communicating racism*. Newbury Park, CA: Sage.

Wyer, R.S. (1989). Social cognition and social judgement. In P.R. Solomon, G.R. Goethals, C.M. Kelley, & B.R. Stephens (Eds.), *Cognition: Interdisciplinary Approaches*. New York: Springer-Verlag.

Wyer, R.S., & Srull, T.K. (1986). Human cognition in its social context. *Psychological Review, 93,* 322–359.

Chapter 25

External Aids to Cognition

Many cognitive problems after head injury can be solved by training the client to use a device that obviates the problem by enhancing or replacing poorly functioning cognitive skills (Baddeley, 1982, 1984). Intons-Peterson and Fournier (1986) found that people generally prefer to use noncommercial memory aids over internal aids such as mnemonic strategies. It has been claimed that external aids are the primary way people cope with memory problems (Graumann, 1985; Harris, 1978, 1984; Hertel, 1988; Intons-Peterson & Fournier, 1986; Jackson, Bogers, & Kersholt, 1988; Wilson & Moffat, 1984). The goal of this chapter is to acquaint therapists with a wide range of cognitive aids available today and the considerations that must be made when recommending them to clients.

HISTORICAL PERSPECTIVES

Until recently, there were almost no discussions of prosthetic aids in the literature on memory retraining. However, several authors have recently begun to emphasize their value as therapy aids (Herrmann & Parenté, 1994). Indeed, many therapists report using prosthetic aids (Park, Smith, & Cavanaugh, 1986). Kirsh, Levine, Fallon-Krueger, and Juros (1989) were the first to use the term *cognitive orthosis*. They referred to cognitive orthotic devices as guidance systems that would help a client to perform a well-defined task. Chute, Conn, Dipasquale, and Hoag (1988) described "prosthesisware," or software specifically designed for the cognitively impaired, and Egert (1988) also emphasized the importance of the design of software for prosthetic applications with head-injured clients. Cole, Dehdashti, and Petti (1994) described a model of computer and human interaction that they had used to develop a prosthetic computer system specifically for cognitively impaired clients. These authors' computer-based cognitive prosthetic model emphasized ongoing assessment of the client's abilities and disabilities in order to fit hardware and software to the client's special needs.

The use of phone and mail reminding systems has also been discussed in the prosthetics literature. Levy and Loftus (1984) reviewed the medical literature on the effects of phone and mail reminders on patients' compliance with appointments. Reminders increase compliance by 10% to 20% over that for people not given reminders. Because reminding services often involve some social interaction over a telephone, it is unclear how much the service aids memory and how much it increases a person's motivation to make appointments that he or she already remembers.

The use of cognitive prosthetics is not without its critics. Plato (circa 3 B.C.) suggested that the use of external memory aids would lead people to avoid developing their natural memories. There is, however, little evidence for this assertion. Many math teachers have claimed that use of pocket calculators has lowered students' abilities to do arithmetic problems in their heads because, for example, students need no longer memorize multiplication tables. But the reverse trend may hold in certain contexts. For example, Hertel (1988) found that the most productive research scholars (the ones who publish the most on a topic) tended to maintain the most extensive external memory files in their offices.

Hersh and Treadgold (1994) pointed out that state-of-the-art cognitive prosthetics are usually too difficult for many clients to use. Clients also require a certain degree of sophistication with electronic devices and the ability to maintain a device and to protect it from harm. Often, what devices gain in terms of portability they lose in terms of functionality. Nonelectronic devices such as notebooks and journals are perhaps the most readily accepted of the devices. They are also bulky and quite limited. Moreover, even those clients who can learn to use these devices will often forget them or simply not use them. Attempts to use human social interaction as a cuing aid may be more successful, but they require a willing human therapist or family member who is reliable.

KINDS OF COGNITIVE AIDS

Herrmann and Petro (1990) developed a rough taxonomy of cognitive aids that is presented in Exhibit 25–1. As the exhibit indicates, there are several kinds of external cognitive aids. Many of the devices discussed in this chapter have overlapping functions and are therefore difficult to classify into only one of the categories of the above taxonomy. Nevertheless, there are clear examples of each category. *Behavioral prosthetics* are changes in behavior that are specifically designed to remind the person to do something (Jones & Adam, 1979). For example, a person may tie a string on his or her finger as a reminder. *Cognitive prosthetics* refer to a general class of devices that take over some memory process. For

Exhibit 25–1 Types of External Aids

Behavioral prosthetics: behaviors that remind
Cognitive prosthetics: obviate memory and cognitive problems
Cognitive robots: carry out a routine cognitive task for an individual
Cognitive correctors: find and correct errors
Cognitive assessors: evaluate a client's cognitive capability
Cognitive trainers: provide stimulation therapy, instruction, and performance feedback
Cognitive sources: maintain or supplement knowledge
Cognitive art: visual memory and problem-solving summaries
Cognitive superstitious possessions: e.g., "my lucky test-taking pencil"

example, a tape recorder can serve as a person's prosthetic memory. *Cognitive robots* carry out a repetitive task for an individual. For example, a calculator will perform routine algorithms such as division and multiplication that otherwise must be done mentally. Some automatic coffee makers will prepare coffee at the designated time without the user's actually remembering to make coffee. *Cognitive correctors* will check and remember something forgotten or figure something out that has been either overlooked or ignored. For example, a spell checker or a grammar/punctuation/style checker on a computer will detect words that have been incorrectly spelled or grammatical statements that are incorrect. *Cognitive assessors* evaluate a client's memory capability. For example, some clients report using their scores on various hand-held electronic games to monitor their cognitive skills. *Cognitive trainers* present a person with the opportunity to learn new skills and to practice them. For example, computer-assisted rehabilitation software packages are designed to provide specific stimulation training exercises. Academic remediation software and software tutorials provide a wealth of self-paced learning experience. *Cognitive sources* maintain knowledge and records of past experience so that the user does not have to store and retain this information in his or her memory. Computerized encyclopedias hold a vast amount of information that supplements a client's memory. These sources also provide a simplified retrieval system. *Cognitive art* presents visual displays that facilitate cognitive processing. For example, a chart with nutritional information can provide information to plan one's food intake across the day. A simple floor plan can help orient a person in a hospital setting. Finally, *superstitious possessions,* such as a "lucky test-taking pencil," help give the client confidence when performing cognitive tasks.

The rest of this chapter will provide several examples of each kind of aid and describe how they may be used to assist the head-injured client. We begin with a discussion of behavioral prosthetic aids, progress to nonelectronic and simple electronic prosthetic devices for cuing memory or for organizing the environment, and then discuss several complex electronic devices that are primarily useful with higher functioning clients.

Behavioral Prosthetics

Many people perform some novel physical action that helps them to remember. Exhibit 25–2 presents examples of various behaviors that clients have reported over the years that have helped them to remember. This list is not exhaustive,

but it does provide examples of techniques clients actually use. Most are self-explanatory, so we will not discuss them further.

These behaviors are simple methods for recalling things a person has to do during the day. Often, these behaviors are all a client must do to remember individual events, objects, or activities (Myake, 1986). More sophisticated methods are necessary when the task becomes more complex.

Cognitive Prosthetics

Nonelectronic Devices

Other external aids are not based on the client's behavior. Most are simple devices that can be purchased at an office supply store. Exhibit 25–3 presents a listing of devices that we have found especially useful over the years. We detail the use of some of these devices below.

Checklists. Head-injured persons commonly leave home and forget something they were supposed to do before leaving or something they were supposed to have brought with them. They will often forget to turn off an appliance, such as the stove or iron. Not only is this dangerous, but the fear of the consequence often leads to obsessive behavior. Sometimes head-injured clients will return home two or three times to lock a door or to turn something off.

Exhibit 25–2 Examples of Behavioral Memory Aids

Ask someone to remind you.
Put something in a special place.
Wear a colored rubber band on your wrist as a reminder.
Write a note on your hand.
Switch the pocket of your wallet, your watch hand, or your ring finger as a reminder.
Wear unusual clothing.
Maintain a diary.
Put everything back where it belongs.
Put something to be taken in an unusual or a conspicuous place.
Create an automatic bill payment system with the bank.
Place momentos and souvenirs on display.

Exhibit 25–3 Nonelectronic Cognitive Aids

Checklists
Colored key jackets
Medication organizers
Notepads and post-it notes
Possession organizers
Possession tags
Photo albums and collages
Appointment calendars and diaries
Lists and signs
Large wall-hanging calendar
Cue cards posted in critical places
Whistling teapot

The problem can be solved by creating stick-on note pads with printed listings of "things to do before leaving the house." The therapist can train the client to go through the complete checklist before leaving home. The family can post more than one copy of the checklist for a day so that the head-injured person can tear off the list and take it along as a reminder that the various activities were completed. For example, a checklist may be as follows:

1. Turn off the stove, TV, and lights.
2. Lock all of the doors.
3. Turn off the faucets.
4. Check to see if you are completely dressed.

The client may then paste the checklist not only by the front and back door but also on the dashboard, wallet, or purse or in some other place where it can be easily seen. The client must learn to keep the most recent checklist in plain view to ensure that he or she remembers completing the activities.

Checklists are useful for managing a daily routine and in any situation in which the person has to repeat a routine activity. The checklist ensures consistency, completeness, and accuracy of the procedure. For example, when a client returns to work, checklists ensure that job functions are complete and correct. They can be used to remind a client to take medications. Finally, they also serve as a record of the behaviors that the client does and does not perform. Such a record is obviously useful when planning subsequent therapy.

Colored Key Jackets. Head-injured persons can become especially frustrated trying to discriminate among their keys. This difficulty can be avoided by coloring the keys with colored jackets. These jackets can be purchased at most lock-and-key stores. Once the keys are marked with different colors, the therapist can begin paired-associate training for the proper key/color associations.

Medication Organizers. Clients frequently forget to take medications. Some people make notes to remind them, others lay out the full daily number of pills in a dish each morning, then check the number left at each medication time. Others make use of devices that remind them to take their medication. The simplest reminder consists of several compartments of a box that is about the size of a client's hand. These boxes may be labeled for the days of the week or the time of day. Seeing the box passively reminds the client to take his or her medication. Plastic medication organizers are available at most pharmacies and supermarkets.

Park and Kidder (1996) reviewed the literature on methods for improving medication adherence. They noted that medication adherence is primarily time based, although some medication is event based because it is taken only after symptoms arise. For medication taking that is time based, the use of timing devices such as alarm clocks, pill cap alarms, and reminding services is recommended because memory for time is generally poor. Both time- and event-based medication taking benefit from use of pill organizers because these make it visually apparent when a pill was not taken.

Notepads and Post-It Notes. Blank notepads are very useful for listing things that need to be done. They are also useful for storing permanent records of phone numbers, addresses, and names. The therapist should train the client to carry a notepad and to write down information rather than attempting to remember it. Stick-on notepads come in a variety of sizes, and the smaller variety is recommended for affixing important messages to car dashboards, appointment calendars, refrigerators, doors, and other places where the person is likely to notice them during the day.

The value of the post-it note cannot be overemphasized. These notes, with stickum on the back, can be put anywhere the client will encounter them. The ability to create portable labels, signs, or directions immediately with these notes makes it more likely that the client will perform desired acts.

Possession Organizers. Possession organizers serve to collect and organize a client's possessions in different settings (Merrill & Baird, 1987). They facilitate memory because a person need only search the organizer to find whatever is desired (Malone, 1983). Organizers are help-ful on a desk, in a closet, or in kitchen utensil drawers. For example, tackle boxes are useful for organizing a variety of objects. Office desk or-ganizers sort devices such as pencils, pens, scis-sors, and tape. Closet organizers hold ties, belts, or shoes. File boxes are well suited for keeping personal and financial records. Stackable trays are useful for sorting papers on a desk. If pos-sible, any organizational device should be color coded to ensure easy visual scanning from a distance.

Possession Tags. To avoid clients' misplac-ing their possessions, the family should mark them in a conspicuous manner. This is best done with brightly colored labels. For example, bright-colored embroidery or DayGlo tags are especially noticeable.

Photo Albums and Collages. Everyone likes photos, but a photo album can be especially help-ful to a client who cannot recall the past or the connection between the present and the past. Specially prepared collections of photos provide a visual record of names and faces of family and friends. Periodic photos made after the injury can help the client regain a sense of the present. Photo collages are pictures pasted to a large piece of cardboard and displayed in a conspicuous place. Photo collages are especially useful in the early stages of recovery. For example, when the client is placed in a hospital room, the therapist can train him or her to recognize relatives and friends.

Appointment Calendars and Diaries. We in-clude these in one grouping because, ideally, the appointment calendar and the diary can be one book. Many therapists recommend that clients keep a memory book or some form of daily record of events and information they need. The act of keeping a daily record facilitates cogni-tion in three ways. It relieves memory of having to retain all of the details of the day. But it also fosters a better memory for the events because the process of making a record prompts addi-tional review of what happened during the day. Finally, at a later point in time, the personal notes will enhance understanding of life's events.

We recommend training the client to use an appointment calendar that can also serve as a diary. The calendar should have individual sheets of paper for each day of the month. Each sheet should have half-hour intervals so the client can circle the time and write the appointment next to the appropriate time. The calendar should also have a separate piece of blank lined paper for each day. This is used to write down directions, instructions, phone messages, and so forth next to the associated day. We also recommend that the client save approximately half of the blank page to make a diary entry at the end of the day. He or she should review the day's activities in the evening and try to summarize the events on the blank page for that day. This activity greatly improves memory for the events in the long term.

Miscellaneous Devices. The remaining items in Exhibit 25–3 require little explanation. However, some examples of their use may be helpful. Making lists of things to do is especial-ly important to ensure that the client remem-bers all the items. For example, although many therapists recommend using mnemonic devices for remembering a shopping list, we have found that most clients prefer a written list that they can take with them to the store. A large wall-hanging calendar is best placed in full view so the client cannot avoid seeing it every day. The family should write important messages in the appropriate boxes on the calendar so the cli-ent can review this information as a matter of course every time he or she passes by it. Cue cards are useful to alert the client to a sequence of actions necessary to operate a device or of things to do in an emergency situation. For example, most microwave machines require three steps to operate. The family can make a cue card to remind the client of these steps and tape it next to the microwave. In most cases, the cue card will be all the client requires to operate the machine. Cue cards for emergency phone numbers are best placed next to various tele-phones in the home. Other devices cue the client to perform some action. For example, a whis-tling teapot reminds the client that the water is boiling.

Simple Electronic Devices

Calculators. Clients with dyscalculia are helped by being trained to carry a small calculator. Inexpensive calculators (less than $5) are generally available and can fit into a wallet or purse. Ideally, a client's calculator should have a long-life battery or solar power feature. Elaborate calculators are not necessary; the four basic functions (addition, subtraction, multiplication, and division) are sufficient. Most clients will never need functions such as percentage, square root, and so forth, although some may find a memory useful. Training should emphasize using the calculator in common situations. For example, a therapist may create simulations in which the person adds up restaurant check totals, estimates the total grocery bill in a store, or computes the correct change from a purchase.

Electronic Checkbooks. Financial transactions and banking may be very difficult for persons with traumatic brain injury. For example, balancing a checkbook may be a formidable task. Several companies produce electronic checkbooks that combine the calculator and checkbook-balancing features. The Radio Shack checkbook calculator (approximately $12) is especially useful because it is simple to operate and keeps an accurate record of a checking account. It also keeps track of two charge accounts at the same time. The client enters the amount of a deposit, payment, charge, or check with a single keystroke. The device keeps an accurate account balance as well as a grand total across all accounts. It also has a permanent memory feature that keeps the information active between uses.

Personal Data Storage Devices. Several personal data storage systems can be purchased. These devices are useful for storing a variety of types of information, such as phone numbers, a Social Security number, addresses, blood type, and so forth. Many companies make these devices. For example, Rolodex, Texas Instruments, and Casio all make inexpensive electronic storage devices that cost less than $20. These may be especially useful in emergency situations when rapid retrieval of names, dates, addresses,

and phone numbers may be called for. Many electronic devices have built-in autodialing features. For example, the electronic Rolodex allows the client to access any phone number simply by twisting the dial on the side. When the desired number appears on the screen, the client can press the dial button to make the call. These devices are helpful when placed in a kitchen or on a desktop in an office.

Dialing Telephones. This kind of telephone provides for single-button dialing. Dialing phones allow the user to store several phone numbers that can later be dialed automatically by pressing a single button that corresponds to a person's name. These phones can help a client to cope with an emergency situation. A therapist should program into the phone emergency numbers such as those for the police and fire department. Each emergency number should be written on a chart that is placed on the wall above the phone. For example, the police may be listed first, the fire department second, and the local ambulance service third. To call any of these numbers in an emergency, the client needs only to pick up the receiver and push a number: one, two, or three. The phone then dials the police, fire department, or ambulance quickly and accurately.

Voice-Activated Telephones. These devices store 100 or more phone numbers and respond to voice commands. The client merely says, "Call the fire department," and the phone dials the number. This type of phone is ideal for clients with severe motor coordination problems.

Speaker Phones. Speaker phones allow the client to use the phone without holding it in his or her hand. They have sensitive microphones installed so the person can speak in a normal voice in a room and the phone will pick up the voice. The phones are ideal for paraplegics or others who cannot lift the receiver conveniently to their ear.

Tape Recorders. Cassette or dictation recorders can serve the same purpose as a notepad. Indeed, tape recorders are far better than notepads because clients can speak much more rapidly than they can write. They also pick up the nuances of conversation and other forms of discourse that are carried in voice inflections. However, many clients do not readily accept the recorders. Instead, they prefer to write new information down. They may find it embarrassing to talk into a machine, especially in public places or in front of their friends. Regardless, it is usually worthwhile to encourage clients to use a recorder by simply pointing out its advantages.

Microcassette recorder tapes are recommended over the larger cassette recorders because they are small and fit conveniently in a shirt pocket or purse. Tape recorders do not replace handwritten notes in all situations. For example, recorders may be less useful than notes for remembering prospective events over several days because the client must rewind a long tape to review them or to find a specific event. However, clients may also inadvertently overwrite older messages with newer ones. The therapist should therefore train clients to write down important messages or to act on them immediately after reviewing them.

Telememo Watches. Head injury survivors often forget phone numbers and appointments. In recent years, several telememo watches have been developed and widely sold by companies such as Seiko and Casio. These wristwatches typically can store up to 50 phone numbers, names, dates, and times of appointments, along with brief reminder messages. The watches store the phone numbers alphabetically by the person's first or last name. The client can search the list forward or backward, ensuring quick and accurate retrieval. Initially, the therapist or family member should program the appointments and alarms and also enter telephone numbers. After the client learns to use the watch, he or she can learn to insert appointments and phone numbers. Although these watches have been criticized as difficult for head-injured people to use (Naugle, Prevey, Naugle, & Delaney, 1988), we have found that most clients can learn to use the watches and that many come to depend on them.

Casio Corporation makes one notable variation on this theme. It is called the Autodialer. This watch not only stores phone numbers and messages but also dials the phone numbers for the client. One simply accesses any of the phone numbers, then holds the telephone receiver over

the watch. After one presses a button on the side, the watch dials the phone number.

An additional advantage of telememo watches is that they can be set to beep on the hour. These beeps provide the client with a consistent reminder of the temporal flow of the day. They can remind the client to review the remaining schedule for the day, thereby increasing the likelihood that the client will comply with the planned activities presented by the watch. The watch can also be set to signal that medications need to be taken.

One drawback to these watches is that none of the models are specifically made for women. Many women are reluctant to wear watches that are large and unattractive and appear to be designed specifically for men. The Data Bank-20 in the Casio series is the smallest version and may be most attractive to women.

Electronic Appointment Calendars. Just as beeping watches may cue the client to the time of an appointment, electronic reminder calendars can tell the person what he or she is supposed to do. These hand-held calendars typically are much easier to use than reminder watches. Reminder calendars display the times of an appointment and provide lengthy messages. Most of the electronic organizers have reminder features. For example, the Sharp organizer, the Casio Boss, or any of several less expensive models provide this feature.

The Voice Organizer is an especially useful electronic calendar that currently sells for about $150. The client says the appointment in his or her own words into the device, which digitizes the voice message. The client then says the time and date, and the device digitizes this information and stores it along with the message. At the time of the appointment, the device begins to beep like a pager, and the client presses the play button to hear the reminder message in his or her own voice. The voice organizer can hold hundreds of messages. It is also quite small and convenient to carry. Clients usually learn to use it in about 1 hour.

Other reminder calendars are capable of holding more information than reminder watches. For example, the Casio digital diary can hold thousands of messages. Timex makes a watch that connects to a personal computer so that the client's calendar appointments can be transferred to the watch's memory. Most reminder calendars also have a keyboard that is much easier to use for entering appointments than a reminder watch. Reminder calendars are usually small enough to fit into a purse, shirt pocket, or pants pocket. Nevertheless, some clients find the calendars bulky and prefer to use a reminder watch instead. We have found that the voice organizer is the most effective of any of these devices.

Generally, most head-injured persons can learn to use a calendar. Many find it useful to carry a calendar with them at all times. It may be necessary for clients to write down appointments each morning and to review their activities at least every hour. Ideally, the therapist can set the telememo watch to beep on the hour, then train the client to review the calendar each time the beep occurs. This procedure ensures that the client rehearses appointments several times daily. It also reduces the number of missed appointments as well as the accompanying frustration and embarrassment.

Interval Timers. Electrical or mechanical timers are often used when cooking to help monitor all manner of chores. They can be set for whatever interval desired. When the alarm goes off, the client either remembers what is required next or knows at least that something needs to be done.

Reminding Systems. Maxi-Aid Corporation sells an Appointment Minder that can be affixed to an appointment calendar. This device attaches to the calendar with Velcro and is easily programmed with on/off switches that are set at half-hour intervals. The person simply sets the times for a reminder, and the device begins to beep at that time. The client then reviews what is in his or her calendar for that time.

Neuropage. Hersh and Treadgold (1994) presented a Neuropage System specifically designed for use as a reminding system for head-injured clients. This is a paging system that a facility uses to remind several clients of their appointments. Each client wears a pager with a message screen. A monitor programs several clients'

schedules into a computer system, which, in turn, pages the clients and reminds each of various appointments or provides messages at the appropriate times. Hersh reported that this system virtually eliminated missed appointments with several head injury survivors.

Cognitive Robots

This class of external aid is designed to perform some repetitive task accurately, consistently, and completely. There are several types of robot, including computer software that performs complex but routine cognitive activities and electronic machines that perform some limited cognitive skill. Using these devices or software, head-injured clients can usually perform job-related skills at competitive speed.

Cycling Timers

These devices allow the user to program household lights and appliances to turn on and off at preset times. Many devices typically control up to eight lamps and appliances, although it is possible to obtain cycling timers that control more. These are usually available at appliance stores or electronic shops.

Motion-Sensitive Detectors

These electronic devices plug into any socket of the house and automatically turn the lights on and off when the devices sense motion or the lack of it. The devices ensure that the lights are turned off when the room is not in use.

Spelling Machines

Spelling machines are ideal for those who work in jobs that involve much written communication. Such communication requires high-level verbal skills. The client types in a phonetic spelling of a word, and the device returns the correct spelling. The person need not even enter the entire word.

A speller/thesaurus finds not only the correct spelling but also a synonym. The capability of generating synonyms allows the therapist to provide paired-associate and word identification practice. The client can use the device to practice word retrieval by recalling a word and attempting recall of the synonyms before checking the accuracy of his or her recall by pushing the retrieval button. The device provides the client with immediate reinforcement or correction. Some spellers also have built-in electronic dictionaries. The Seiko SII model has all three functions: speller, thesaurus, and dictionary. These are generally available at office supply stores. We specifically recommend the Seiko SII model, which sells for approximately $40.

Expert System Shells

Expert system shells are artificially intelligent computer programs that are designed to solve problems the way an expert would. This type of software was originally developed to solve problems for business and industry. For example, picture a company that has to hire an expert each time it has to solve a technical problem. Experts may charge several thousands of dollars per visit. To avoid such an expense, corporations often purchase computer programs that eliminate the need for experts. Employees consult the expert system whenever answers are needed to some technical problem. The advice provided by expert systems is about as accurate as that of experts.

Expert systems have also been used in traumatic brain rehabilitation. For example, a client may be unable to recall the details of complex procedures or make appropriate decisions. If a client has a personal computer, a therapist can program an expert system to do the same job and then train the client to operate the program. An example of this type of application is provided in the case studies below.

Multifunction Orthotic Systems

Cole et al. (1994) described a computer system that takes over many of the reminding functions outlined above. A laptop computer hooked into a central terminal reminds the client of a variety of daily tasks as well as serving as a message center. The client can call into the central terminal via modem for specific advice.

Cognitive Correctors

This class of device is designed to correct cognitive errors.

Grammar Checkers

Several computer packages such as Word Perfect have built-in grammar checkers that advise the client how to revise sentences to improve their clarity. They check the documents for literally thousands of rules of grammar and mark each mistake. These programs are generally available for the IBM series of computer or its clones. Grammatik is bundled with Word Perfect. It is especially good for checking grammatical content and sentence structure and for globally assessing the style of an entire document. These software packages are ideal for students who have trouble with various rules of grammar. Along with a word processor and spelling checker, these programs are sufficient to improve a client's academic performance in college or high school courses. They are also used for training correct writing style.

The use of these grammar software packages requires that the client have some insight into his or her difficulties with creating language. Typically, these packages provide general advice about defects in wording, the use of complex sentences, and so forth. Correcting problems the program identifies is still up to the individual. Nevertheless, grammar software packages make a good adjunct to therapy when the goal is to retrain language composition skills.

Car Finders

All of us have had the experience of not knowing where we parked our car in the large parking lot of a shopping mall. This problem is worse when one is searching for the car at night. For a head-injured person, this situation can be frustrating or even dangerous.

An electronic solution to this problem is a device that blinks the car's lights and honks its horn when activated by a device affixed to the client's keychain. The device activates a receiver that has been situated under the hood of the car and connected to the battery. When activated, the lights and horn go on, signaling the car's position in the parking lot. Virtually any auto security system has this feature, and the client can get one installed for less than $200.

Key Finders

Another persistent problem for head-injured persons in misplacement of common objects such as keys. Fortunately, the solution is simple. A variety of devices that can be attached to keychains and other objects make an audible alarm when the device receives a certain signal. For some devices, the signal is the sound made by clapping one's hands. Another device is triggered by whistling. Each of these devices quickly leads the user to the misplaced object. A disadvantage of the whistle- and sound-activated devices is that they may often be set off by noises that were not produced by the finder—for example, children's voices, dishwasher noises, or anything that is relatively high pitched. These false alarms can be an annoyance, but they also can provide random reminders of the location of the article. The hand-clap devices get around the problem because there are fewer frequencies that sound like four equally spaced hand claps. Head-injured clients, however, may have trouble learning to clap their hands in that particular rhythm, especially if there is motor impairment.

Our best solution for the problem of misplaced keys is to attach a pager to the client's keychain. When the client misplaces the keys, he or she can simply dial the pager and listen for the beeper. This technique also has the advantage of allowing others to get in touch with the client quickly. Many paging companies will provide the service along with the pager for less than $60 per year.

Iron with a Memory

For memory-impaired clients, ironing can be as much a hazard as it is a necessity. If the iron is put face down and then the person gets distracted and goes somewhere else, there is real danger of a fire. Some brands of irons now come with a safety shutoff switch that is activated when the iron remains flat and motionless for 30 seconds. These are sold by most department stores.

Cognitive Trainers

These devices provide a person with instruction and/or practice with functional cognitive tasks. For example, we have already mentioned spelling machines with multiple features like a thesaurus and a dictionary. Many of these also have preprogrammed word games like Hangman that the client can play. A variety of other devices and software provide more elaborate cognitive training.

Teaching machines have been around since at least the 1930s (Benjamin, 1988). Today, microcomputer stores stock shelf after shelf with self-instructional programs on a wide variety of topics, including learning how to use microcomputers. These devices are intended to facilitate and supplement learning. Modern multimedia variants of the teaching machines involve devices that actually simulate tasks the person is trying to learn (Herrmann & Palmisano, 1992). Literally any personal computer can be used as a teaching machine.

Cognitive Sources

These are devices that store knowledge and facts. Head-injured persons often experience a loss of knowledge or at least a reduced accessibility to what they previously knew. One solution to this problem is to collect objects and devices that maintain knowledge and/or records. Ideally, the client keeps these sources in one room or in proximity to where certain tasks are performed. These knowledge sources may include encyclopedias, dictionaries, thesauri, books on hobbies and games, consumer guides, the Guinness Book of Records, the Farmer's Almanac, maps, and especially computer compact disc databases such as dictionaries.

A short-term knowledge source consists of collections of recent notes or phone messages. Memo pads, shopping pads, memo stickers, and other notes are essential for the head-injured person. Repositories of these notes serve as a kind of external memory for recent episodic information. Every record represents information that needs to be retained, filed away, or be immediately accessible. Memory sources also include notes from meetings, readings, and lectures.

Cognitive Art

These are objects and devices that present visual displays that either guide a client's use of memory or solve a problem via a logical sequence. Although it is perhaps the oldest external aid to memory, the use of art to aid memory is not well known today. Since the 14th, 15th, and 16th centuries, artists have drawn or painted the floor plans of houses, cathedrals, amphitheaters, and other buildings so that people could locate and remember spatial information. Complex flowcharts are useful for structuring the decision-making process or for showing different types of organizations. Airplane magazines typically show the layout of each airport they service to orient customers upon arrival. Posted floor plans of the client's home or of the hospital can also provide a valuable reference. Training the client to use pictures such as floorplans, airport terminal layouts, or decision-making schematics is especially valuable.

Superstitious Cognitive Aids

For many people there are objects that facilitate their cognition because they believe that these objects affect cognitive processes when actually they do not. There are various explanations for why people might superstitiously come to believe that an object has some magical influence over cognition. Sometimes people use certain objects to aid their memory externally because of an unfounded belief that these objects have a power to influence memory. Usually, they justify their belief on the grounds that the object led them to perform well in the past. For example, some students use a "lucky pen" when taking examinations because they did especially well when they used it in the past. It has yet to be established whether "lucky" objects actually do affect cognitive performance. Nevertheless, if a client believes that some talisman im-

proves cognition, the therapist should encourage its use.

EVALUATION

Parenté and Elliott (1994) studied the use of external memory aids with 20 brain-injured clients. Twenty clients were asked to rate the usefulness of various prosthetic devices that could be used for improving memory and thinking skills. The clients rated slides of the devices on a scale of 0 = *not useful at all* to 10 = *very useful for people with disabilities like mine*. The clients also indicated whether they actually used the devices. Finally, they were asked to indicate whether they knew the device existed and where they could purchase it.

The clients' ratings were evaluated in three ways. We first tabulated the average rating of usefulness for the various devices. Figure 25–1 shows the size of the average rating for each device. Items that were not rated with an average of 2 or more were not included. The numbers of clients who reported using these same devices are presented in Figure 25–2. Finally, Figure 25–3 presents the numbers of clients who were aware that each device existed.

Parenté and Elliott (1994) concluded that head injury survivors perceive a variety of devices to be potentially useful for themselves and for others with similar disabilities. Appointment calendars, microrecorders, answering machines, hanging calendars, beeping watches, calculators, and checklists were highly rated for perceived usefulness, frequency of use, and availability. "Low-tech" items were generally preferred over "high-tech" items. Clients were generally unaware of many of the more complex electronic devices. Finally, less than half of the sample reported using any device at all to improve their thinking skills.

CASE STUDIES

The following are several case studies that illustrated how the various external aids outlined in this chapter were used to help three traumatically brain-injured persons return to work.

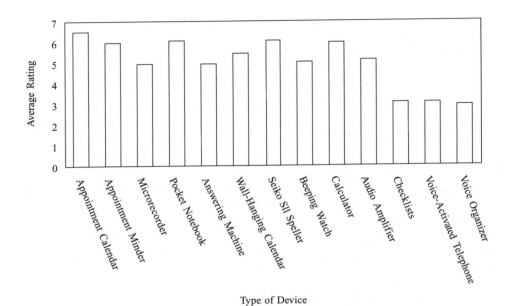

Figure 25–1 Clients' Average Rating of Perceived Usefulness of Prosthetic Devices

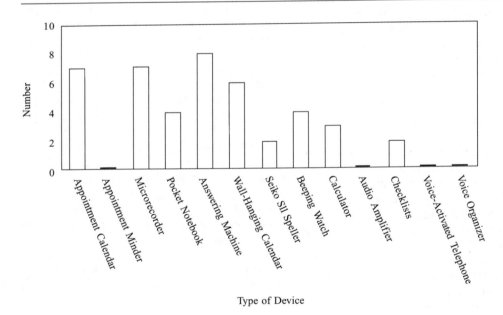

Figure 25–2 Numbers of Clients Reporting Use of Prosthetic Devices

These case examples particularly illustrate the value of prosthetic devices and cognitive robots. Each case shows how a client was able to return to work with the device but could not return without it. Moreover, the time taken to train the clients to use the devices to the point where they could return to work was always less than the time needed to return to work using conventional

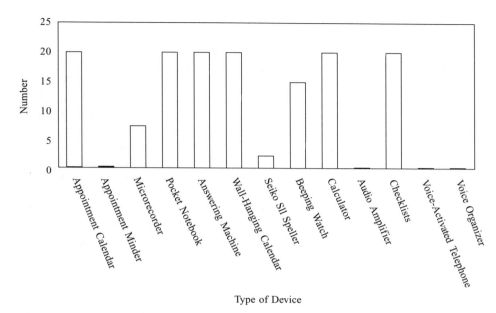

Figure 25–3 Numbers of Clients Aware That the Prosthetic Devices Existed

therapy. These devices are cost-effective and cover a wide range of applications.

Case 1

Joan was an intensive care nurse who suffered a head injury in an automobile accident. She began a program of conventional cognitive rehabilitation therapy using a computer and software designed to improve her attention and concentration. However, even after several months of therapy, she found that work was still too demanding. She could not recall necessary medications or services the patients required. She misplaced instruments and her keys, and could not find her car in the parking garage.

The client was provided with a checklist of daily tasks for the intensive care unit. The list was refined to a point where it contained all of the activities she had to complete each day. The checklist was sufficient to allow the client to perform her job because it eliminated needless repetition and rechecking.

The client also could not recall physician instructions and physicians became annoyed with

her poor memory. She was also embarrassed to use the checklist. We therefore constructed a special clipboard for Joan with a slot for a tape recorder under the clipboard. She could then carry her checklist inconspicuously and record her conversations for future review. Joan also had an automatic alarm installed on her car so that she could activate the horn with a device on her key chain. All of these devices cost less than $200.

Case 2

Lois was a 35-year-old woman who before her stroke was employed as a dispatcher for a trucking firm. She was a consultant who advised clients on delivery schedules, price rates, and the fastest way to ship freight. Fortunately, her job could be reduced to a set of rules, which allowed us to use an expert system shell as a cognitive aid.

The therapists worked with Lois to produce about 100 rules that dictated the type of advice she might give to a client. These were input into an expert system shell. Lois used the expert system to think of the most appropriate shipping advice based on various questions she posed to the client and to the system. She asked customers a sequence of questions that had been presented by the computer, then input the responses into the system, and gave the customer the advice the expert system displayed on the screen. She took a laptop computer to work each day and set it up on her desk next to the phone. Using the expert system, she eventually returned to full-time employment after a year.

Case 3

Ted was a school teacher before his serious head injury. He tried unsuccessfully to return to teaching, and then he was fired from several other jobs because of his inability to work quickly. He eventually began work at a sheltered workshop. He was able to do the job but had difficulty with certain aspects that involved counting the number of pieces of work his clients produced every day. This task required sorting and counting by category.

We provided Ted with a simple computer program that counted and sorted the pieces as they were finished. It also produced a report at the end of the day that was exactly like the one that he had to turn into his supervisor. He was therefore able to do most of the accounting work during the day, but if he didn't finish it, he could take it home and finish the data entry in the evening.

CONCLUSION

Advantages of External Cognitive Aids

This chapter presented numerous examples of external cognitive aids. The advantage of such aids is that they allow head-injured persons to function independently. They also reduce obsessive behavior associated with poor memory. Although they do not make the internal cognitive functions more efficient, they clearly help a client deal with day-to-day problems. They also increase the client's independence. They add

structure to the person's life, improve time sense, and reduce the risk of injury or embarrassment.

Sometimes external aids can improve the client's internal cognitive function. For example, the use of scheduling devices and medicine reminders sometimes allows the client to learn a medication regimen or medical routine. Although external aids certainly do not replace or obviate a good program of cognitive rehabilitation therapy, they are invaluable adjuncts to a total memory retraining program. Perhaps their biggest advantage is that they solve immediate problems and bolster the client's spirits by demonstrating that immediate and effective interventions are possible.

Limitations of External Cognitive Aids

There are several disadvantages to using many of these aids. For example, many devices are expensive, and some require extensive training time. Some clients may resist using them because they fear becoming dependent on them. Some devices create as many problems as they solve. For example, several clients have told us that beeping key chains often begin beeping with random sounds, making it necessary to take them out and turn them off. Alarm watches have been criticized for being too difficult for head-injured clients to use easily (Naugle et al., 1988; Wilson, 1987).

It is commonly held that active reminders are better than passive reminders (Harris, 1980), but there is no clear idea about the optimum number of active remindings that can be handled in a day. If buzzers are going off frequently, clients may eventually view them as an annoyance and simply turn them off without doing whatever the buzzer was supposed to remind them to do.

Complex devices intimidate clients. Many clients fear that their mental skills may never improve if they become dependent on the devices. The only way to convince them that the devices will not hurt these skills is to persuade them to use the devices temporarily while they are learning other memory strategies. Often a little experience with these devices convinces clients of their worth.

It has been suggested that use of external aids might reduce the cognitive skills that are being aided because the aid would relieve the user of experience needed to develop such skills (Estes, 1980; Herrmann & Chaffin, 1988). For example, using a calculator exclusively to do math computations means that the client does not have to do math problems with paper and pencil.

Considerations in Recommending External Aids

There are several considerations a therapist must make before recommending that a client buy an external aid. In general, the goal is to create a "cognition-friendly" environment for the client. The extent to which the environment aids cognition depends largely on the client's perception that the device will solve more problems than it creates. For example, an orderly predictable desk is "memory friendly" because it provides an easy view of cues to remember and what is needed for tasks at hand (Hertel, 1988; Malone, 1983). Cognition-friendly devices are usually automatic, attractive, and simple to operate. For example, many cars today come with several buzzers to remind the driver to perform chores required by law, such as buckling up or turning off the headlights when the car is turned off. Automatic coffee makers typically allow the client to simply add water and coffee; then the maker brews a pot at a predetermined time.

Clients use different internal memory strategies and external aids for different tasks (Chase & Ericcson, 1982; Craik & McDowd, 1987). Intons-Peterson and Fournier (1986) found that the preferences for the use of external aids differed with the kind of memory task. For example, external aids were preferred for remembering intentions to do things, and internal aids were preferred for learning new information.

Finally, external aids will not be uniformly useful with all people. For example, there appear to be clear age differences in the kinds of external aids people prefer (Cavanaugh, Grady, & Perlmutter, 1983; Jackson et al., 1988; Petro, Herrmann, Burrows, & Moore, 1991). These preferences appear to have more to do with the

life stage of individuals than any decline in memory ability with age (Harris, 1980). Of course, such differences can also be influenced by the fact that older people are generally less familiar or comfortable with technology and less likely to use it (Rybash, Hoyer, & Roodin, 1986).

Where To Find External Aids

Several mail order companies sell various kinds of cognitive aids. For example, The Sharper Image, Markline, Sporting Edge, Exeters, DAK Inc., Damark International, Selectronics, Skymall, and Maxi-Aids are some of our most frequented mail order sources. Because these companies change their listings frequently, we recommend that therapists call 1-800-555-1212 (800 information) and ask for a recent listing of any of the above companies. Perhaps the best single source for prosthetic aids is Virginia Assistive Technology Services. Therapists can call into this service via modem and search several databases with virtually thousands of devices. Counselors are also available to help the therapist find specific aids in the databases. This service will help the therapist to find the latest CD ROMS that have the ABLE-DATA and CoNet assistive technology databases so that the therapist can do his or her own searches. The toll-free number is 800-435-8490.

REFERENCES

Baddeley, A.D. (1982). *Your memory: A users's guide*. Harmondsworth, UK: Penguin.

Baddeley, A.D. (1984). Memory theory and memory therapy. In B.A. Wilson & N. Moffat (Eds.), *Clinical management of memory problems* (pp. 5–27). Gaithersburg, MD: Aspen.

Benjamin, L. (1988). The history of teaching machines. *American Psychologist, 43*, 713–720.

Cavanaugh, J.C., Grady, J.G., & Perlmutter, M. (1983). Forgetting and use of memory aids in 20- to 70-year olds' everyday life. *International Journal of Aging and Human Development, 17*, 113–122.

Chase, W.G., & Ericcson, K.A. (1982). Skill and working memory. In G.H. Bower (Ed.), *The psychology of learning and motivation* (pp. 141–189). New York: Academic Press.

Chute, D., Conn, G., Dipasquale, M., & Hoag, M. (1988). Prosthesisware: A new class of software supporting activities of daily living. *Neuropsychology, 2*, 41–57.

Cole, E., Dehdashti, P., & Petti, L. (1994). Design and outcomes of computer-based cognitive prosthetics for brain injury: A field study of three subjects. *NeuroRehabilitation, 4*, 174–186.

Craik, F.M., & McDowd, J.M. (1987). Age differences in recall and recognition. *Journal of Experimental Psychology: Learning, Memory, and Cognition, 13*, 474–479.

Egert, R. (1988). Human computer interface issues in rehabilitation medicine. *Archives of Physical Medicine and Rehabilitation, 69*, 778.

Estes, W.K. (1980). Is human memory obsolete? *American Scientist, 68*, 62–68.

Graumann, C.F. (1985). Memorabilia, mementos, memoranda: Towards an ecology of memory. In F. Klex (Ed.), *In memoriam Hermann Ebbinghaus* (pp. 63–69). Amsterdam: North Holland.

Harris, J.E. (1978). External memory aids. In M.M. Gruneberg, P.E. Morris, & P. Sykes (Eds.), *Practical aspects of memory* (pp. 172–179). New York: Academic Press.

Harris, J.E. (1980). Memory aids people use: Two interview studies. *Cognition, 8*, 31–38.

Harris, J.E. (1984). Methods of improving memory. In B.A. Wilson & N. Moffat (Eds.), *Clinical management of memory problems* (pp. 71–92). Gaithersburg, MD: Aspen.

Herrmann, D., and Chaffin, R. (1988). *Memory in historical perspectives: The literature on memory before Ebbinghaus.* New York: Springer-Verlag.

Herrmann, D., & Palmisano, M. (1992). The facilitation of memory. In M. Gruneberg & P. Morris (Eds.). *Aspects of Memory* (Vol. 1, 2nd ed., pp. 147–167). London: Routledge.

Herrmann, D., & Parenté, R. (1994). A multi-modal approach to cognitive rehabilitation. *NeuroRehabilitation, 4*, 133–142.

Herrmann, D., & Petro, S. (1990). Commercial memory aids. *Applied Cognitive Psychology, 3*, 23–45.

Hersh, N., & Treadgold, L. (1994). Neuropage: The rehabilitation of memory dysfunction by prosthetic memory and cueing. *NeuroRehabilitation, 4*, 187–197.

Hertel, P.T. (1988). Monitoring external memory. In M. Gruneberg, P.E. Morris, & R.N. Sykes (Eds.), *Practical aspects of memory* (pp. 221–226). London: Academic Press.

Intons-Peterson, M.J., & Fournier, J. (1986). External and internal memory. *Journal of Experimental Psychology: General, 115*, 267–280.

Jackson, J., Bogers, H., & Kerstholt, J. (1988). Do memory aids aid the elderly in their day to day remembering? In M.Gruneberg, P. Morris, & R. Sykes (Eds.). *Practical aspects of memory: Current research and issues* (pp. 137–142). New York: John Wiley.

Jones, G., & Adam, J. (1979). Toward a prosthetic memory. *Bulletin of British Psychology, 32*, 165–167.

Kirsh, N.L., Levine, J.P., Fallon-Krueger, M., & Juros, L.A. (1989). Microcomputer as an orthotic device for patients with cognitive defects. *Journal of Head Trauma Rehabilitation, 2*(4), 77–85.

Levy, R., & Loftus, G. (1984). Compliance and memory. In J. Harris and P. Morris (Eds.), *Everyday memory, actions, and absentmindedness* (pp. 93–112). London: Academic Press.

Malone, T.W. (1983). How do people organize their desks: Implications for designing office automation systems. *ACM Transactions on Office Automation Systems, 1*, 99–112.

Merrill, A.A., & Baird, J.C. (1987). Semantic and spatial factors in environmental memory. *Memory and Cognition, 15*, 101–108.

Myake, N. (1986). Constructive interaction. *Cognitive Science, 10*, 151–177.

Naugle, R., Prevey, M., Naugle, C., & Delaney, R. (1988). New digital watch as a compensatory device for memory dysfunction. *Cognitive Rehabilitation, 6*, 22–23.

Parenté, R., & Elliott, A. (1994, August). *Usefulness and use of prosthetic devices after head injury.* Poster session presented at the Practical Aspects of Memory Conference, College Park, Maryland.

Park, D., & Kidder, D. (1996). Prospective memory and medication adherence. In M. Brandimonte, G. Einstein, & McDaniel (Eds.), *Prospective memory: Theory and applications.* Hillsdale, NJ: Lawrence Erlbaum.

Park, D., Smith, A., & Cavanaugh, J. (1986). Metamemories of memory researchers. *Memory & Cognition, 18*, 321–327.

Petro, S., Herrmann, D., Burrows, D., & Moore, C. (1991). Usefulness of commercial memory aids as a function of age. *International Journal of Aging and Human Development, 33*, 295–309.

Rybash, J., Hoyer, W., & Roodin, P. (1986). *Adult cognition and aging.* New York: Pergamon.

Wilson, B.A. (1987). *Rehabilitation of memory.* New York: Guilford.

Wilson, B.A., & Moffat, N. (1984). *Clinical management of memory problems.* Gaithersburg, MD: Aspen.

Appendix A

Multimodal Interview Assessment

This survey instrument is designed to evaluate the various aspects of the multimodal model presented in Chapter 2. Appendix B presents several performance tests of cognitive functioning that can be used by most therapists to get an idea of the client's functional levels. However, some of the passive features of the model can only be evaluated with an interview instrument such as the one presented below. The multimodal interview therefore measures the day-to-day behaviors of the client that are indicators of the client's condition of health, chemical state, emotional status, and so forth.

MULTIMODAL INVENTORY OF COGNITIVE STATUS

Name: _____

Age: _____ Sex: _____

Instructions: This inventory may be used with the client or caregiver. It concerns the client's health, living conditions, emotional status, and use of cognitive strategies. Some of the questions will require some thought. The answers will provide the basis for a complete program of treatment. It is therefore worthwhile to administer the

inventory to everyone who works with the client or who functions as a caregiver. It should also be administered in an interview format. That is, the therapist should present and explain the various questions, record the client's or caregiver's answers to them, and write any clarifications whenever needed.

1. Does the client make more memory or thinking errors when alone or with others?
   _____ More when alone
   _____ More when with others
   _____ Same when alone as when with others

2. Do people tell the client that his or her ability to think and remember is worsening?
   _____ Yes _____ No

3. If people do tell the client that his or her cognitive skill is worsening, does he or she agree?
   _____ Yes _____ No
   If not, then why? _____
   _____
   _____

4. Are there certain people with whom the client is likely to be forgetful or experience thinking errors?
   _____ Yes _____ No

5. If yes, what is their relationship to the client?
   _____ Boss   _____ Child   _____ Spouse
   _____ Friends   _____ Parent   _____ Coworker
   _____ Doctor   _____ Other

6. Is the client's thinking and memory generally poor?
_____ Yes _____ No

7. Does the client experience thinking and memory errors mostly . . .
_____ At home _____ At work
_____ School _____ In social situations
_____ Other _____
If the client's thinking or memory fails at home, then please name the types of tasks he or she has trouble with: _____
_____
_____

If the client's thinking or memory fails at work, please name the types of tasks that trigger the failure: _____
_____
_____

If the client's thinking and memory fail in certain social situations, please identify these: _____
_____
_____

If the client's thinking and memory fail in school or other training contexts, please identify the kinds of tasks that create the biggest problem: _____
_____
_____

8. Does the client think and remember in an active mode? For example, does he or she routinely rehearse new information, use mental tricks as memory aids, or think about ways of understanding or remembering new information better or faster?
_____ Yes, often _____ Sometimes
_____ No, very seldom
Please list any mental tricks the client finds effective around the home: _____
_____
_____

Please list any mental tricks or strategies the client has found effective at work: _____
_____
_____

What sort of mental activities help the client to function in social situations? _____
_____
_____

What sort of mental activities help the client to function in school or training situations? _____
_____
_____

9. Does the client have difficulty remembering what he or she is doing from one minute to the next?
_____ Yes _____ No

9a. Does the client have trouble paying attention?
_____ Yes _____ No

9b. Does the client have trouble seeing or hearing things due to poor vision? hearing?
_____ Yes _____ No

9c. Is the client easily distracted?
_____ Yes _____ No
If yes, is the client generally distractible or just lately?
_____ Generally _____ Just lately

10. Does the client often fail when trying to solve a problem?
_____ Yes _____ No

11. Do the client's thinking skills falter more at certain times of day?
_____ Yes _____ No
If so, indicate when: _____

12. How do the client's cognitive skills compare to those of other people he or she knows?
_____ Much better
_____ A little better
_____ About the same
_____ A little worse
_____ Much worse

13. How do the client's cognitive skills compare to what they were 5 years ago?
_____ Much better
_____ A little better
_____ About the same
_____ A little worse
_____ Much worse
If better or worse, what seems to account for the change? _____
_____
_____

14. Has the client had any therapy to learn how to think or remember better?
_____ Yes _____ No

15. Has the client made any effort to learn how to think or remember better?
_____ Yes _____ No

16. Has anyone given the client advice about how to think or remember better?
_____ Yes _____ No

17. How is the client's physical health?
_____ Good _____ Average _____ Poor

17a. Does the client suffer from any illnesses today? If so, please specify:
_____ Yes _____ No
_____
_____
_____

17b. Does the client suffer from any chronic diseases? If so, please specify:
_____ Yes _____ No
_____
_____
_____

18. Has the client been under heavy stress in the past few weeks?
_____ Yes _____ No
If so, please specify: _____
_____
_____

19. Is the client under stress today?
_____ Yes _____ No

20. Has the client been under prolonged stress in recent months?
_____ Yes _____ No

21. Does the client currently have a lot of worries or fears?
_____ Yes _____ No

22. Has the client experienced any emotionally traumatic or very upsetting events recently?
_____ Yes _____ No

23. Does the client have any recurring memories that are upsetting (e.g., flashbacks)?
_____ Yes _____ No

24. How would you describe the client's lifestyle?
_____ Boring _____ Relaxed
_____ Busy _____ Hectic

25. Does the client seem motivated to think and remember better?
_____ Yes _____ No

26. Does the client take any medications prescribed by a physician on a regular basis?
_____ Yes _____ No
Please list these: _____
_____
_____

26a. Does the medication make him or her sleepy?
_____ Yes _____ No

26b. Does the medication make him or her nervous?
_____ Yes _____ No

27. Does the client use mild stimulants such as coffee, tea, or sodas?
_____ Yes _____ No

If so, then how often and how much?
How often (e.g., every day): _____
How much (e.g., three cups each day): _____

28. Does the client use any mind-altering substances (e.g., alcohol, marijuana)?
_____ Often _____ Infrequently _____ Never

28a. If often or infrequently, how often:
_____ Every day _____ Each week
_____ Each month

28b. Has the client used any of these in the last 24 hours?
_____ Yes _____ No

29. Describe the client's eating habits:
_____ Light _____ Medium _____ Heavy

30. How much sleep does the client usually get?
_____ Enough _____ Too little _____ Too much
How many hours each night? _____

31. Is the client physically fit?
_____ Fit _____ Needs exercise _____ Unfit

32. Does the client smoke or chew tobacco?
_____ Never _____ Sometimes _____ Regularly

33. Does the client make good use of his or her time?
_____ Yes
_____ No (procrastinates)
_____ No (overwhelmed)
_____ No (easily distracted)

34. Does the client write things down to help remember them?
_____ Yes _____ No

35. Does the client use any other devices to remind him or her of things that need to be done?
_____ Yes _____ No
If yes, then list these: _____
_____
_____

36. Do friends and family actively help the client to solve problems, make decisions, remember things, and so forth?
_____ Yes _____ No

SCORING THE MULTIMODAL INVENTORY OF COGNITIVE STATUS

The client's answers should be scored with respect to his or her average performance or experience. Write the numeric score in the space next to the question number on the multimodal inventory. The user will observe that more questions are asked about memory than any other cognitive mode. Memory is emphasized because it is fundamental to other kinds of cognitive performance.

Active Variables

Use of Mental Tricks (circle score for each item below)

14. Has the client had any therapy to learn how to think or remember better?
    Yes = +1   No = 0

15. Has the client made an effort to learn how to think or remember better?
    Yes = +1   No = 0

16. Has anyone given the client advice about how to think or remember better?
    Yes = +1   No = 0

    Total (from 0 to +3)
    _____ **Mental Tricks Mean** (total divided by 3)

Active Processing

25. Does the client seem motivated to think and remember better?
    Yes = +3   No = –3

8. Does the client think and remember in an active mode? For example, does he or she routinely rehearse new information, use mental tricks as memory aids, or think about ways of understanding or remembering new information better or faster?
    No, very seldom = –3   Sometimes = +1
    Yes, often = +3

9a. Does the client have trouble paying attention?
    Yes = –1   No = +1
    Active processing total (–7 to +7)
    _____ **Active Processing Mean** (total divided by 3)

Cognitive Performance

6. Is the client's thinking and memory generally poor?
    Yes = –3   No = 0

7. Does the client experience thinking and memory errors mostly . . .
    At home _____   At work _____
    At school _____   In social situations _____
    Other _____
    Score –1 for each one checked.

9. Does the client have difficulty remembering what he or she is doing from one minute to the next?
    Yes = –3   No = +3

9c. Is the client easily distracted?
    Yes = –3   No = 0
    If yes, is the client generally distractible or just lately?
    Generally = –3   Just lately = 0

10. Does the client often fail when trying to solve a problem?
    Yes = –1   No = 0

12. How do the client's cognitive skills compare to those of other people he or she knows?
    +3   Much better
    +1   A little better
    0   About the same
    –1   A little worse
    –3   Much worse

13. How do the client's cognitive skills today compare to what they were 5 years ago?
    +3   Much better
    +1   A little better
    0   About the same
    –1   A little worse
    –3   Much worse

33. Does the client make good use of his or her time?
    Yes = +2   No = –1
    Total (from –25 to +11)
    _____ **Cognitive Performance Mean** (total divided by 9)

Support Variables

Social Environment

1. Does the client make more memory or thinking errors when alone or with others?
    0 = Same when alone or more when alone
    –1 = More when with others

2. Do other people tell the client that his or her ability to think and remember is worsening?
    –1 = Yes   0 = No

3. If people do tell the client that his or her cognitive skill is worsening, does he or she agree?
    –1 = Yes   0 = No

36. Do friends and family actively help the client to solve problems, make decisions, remember things, and so forth?
    +3 = Yes   0 = No

4. Are there certain people with whom the client is likely to be forgetful or experience thinking errors?
−1 = Yes   0 = No
Total (from −4 to +3)
_____ **Social Environment Mean** (total divided by 5)

Prosthetics Use

34. Does the client write things down to help remember them?
Yes = +2   No = 0

35. Does the client use any other devices to remind him or her of things that need to be done?
Yes = +1   No = 0
Total (from 0 to +3)
_____ **Prosthetic Use Mean** (total divided by 2)

Passive Variables

Conditions of Health

9b. Does the client have trouble seeing or hearing things due to poor vision/hearing?
Yes = −1   No = +1

17. How is the client's physical health?
+3 = Good   0 = Average   −3 = Poor

17a. Does the client suffer from any illnesses today?
−3 = Yes   +3 = No

17b. Does the client suffer from any chronic diseases?
−3 = Yes   +3 = No

31. Is the client physically fit?
+3 = Fit   0 = Needs exercise   −3 = Unfit
Total (from −13 to +13)
_____ **Health Mean** (total divided by 5)

Lifestyle

24. How would you describe the client's lifestyle?
Boring = −1 Relaxed = 0 Busy = −1 Hectic = −2

11. Do the client's thinking skills falter more at certain times of the day?
Yes = −1   No = 0

29. Describe the client's eating habits:
0 = Light   0 = Medium   −1 = Heavy

30. How much sleep does the client usually get?
0 = Enough   −1 = Too little   −1 = Too much
Total (from −4 to 0)
_____ **Lifestyle Mean** (total divided by 4)

Chemical State

26. Does the client take any medications prescribed by a physician on a regular basis?
Yes = +1   No = 0

26a. Does the medication make him or her sleepy?
Yes = −2   No = 0

26b. Does the medication make him or her nervous?
Yes = −2   No = 0

27. Does the client use mild stimulants such as coffee, tea, or sodas? Yes = −1   No = +1
Does the client use them more than three times a day? Yes = −1   No = 0
Does the client use a second stimulant?
Yes −1   No = 0

28. Does the client use mind-altering substances (e.g., alcohol, marijuana)?
Often = −3   Infrequently = −1   Never = 0

28a. If often or infrequently, how often?
Every day = −3   Every week = −2
Every month = −1

28b. Has the client used any of these in the last 24 hours?
Yes = −1   No = 0

32. Does the client smoke or chew tobacco?
Never = 0   Sometimes = −2   Regularly = −3
Total (from −17 to 2)
_____ **Chemical State Mean** (total divided by 10)

Emotional State

18. Has the client been under stress in the past few weeks?
Yes = −2   No = 0

19. Is the client under stress today?
Yes = −1   No = 0

20. Has the client been under prolonged stress in recent months?
Yes = −3   No = 0

21. Does the client currently have a lot of worries or fears?
Yes = −3   No = +1

22. Has the client experienced any emotionally traumatic or very upsetting events recently?
Yes = −3   No = 0

23. Does the client have any recurring memories that are emotionally upsetting (e.g., flashbacks)?
Yes = −3   No = 0
Total (from −15 to +1)
_____ **Emotional State Mean** (total divided by 6)

Scoring Summary

The client's name: _____

Name of person interviewed and relation to client: _____

_____

Date: _____

Active Variables
____ Mental tricks
____ Cognitive performance
____ Active processing
____ Overall mean

Support Variables
____ Prosthetic use
____ Social environment
____ Overall mean

Passive Variables
____ Condition of health
____ Chemical state
____ Emotional state
____ Lifestyle
____ Overall mean

Relative Performance: The multimodal interview was designed as an assessment of change. Therefore, the absolute score on the interview is less important than the change of the score over time or after treatment. In general, the closer to the positive range, the better. Mildly head-injured clients score in the single digits just below zero. Most severely head-injured clients score below the −5 range. Most college students score in the −1 to positive range. We feel that the primary value of the instrument is to determine change in any of the modes over time.

Appendix B

Performance Assessment of the Multimodal System

The following tests are designed as a screening assessment. They are not intended to replace a comprehensive neuropsychological evaluation and should not be used in that way. Their purpose is to provide the therapist with an evaluation of the multimodal system components. Should the client's performance on any of these subtests suggest that there is a problem, the therapist should suggest further evaluation with a more comprehensive test battery.

These tests were selected according to several criteria. The most obvious was that the test should index the appropriate component of the multimodal system. However, many of the tests overlap, and they have been placed to logically appropriate categories. The user should consider that some tests may also index other multimodal systems.

Scoring is not always discussed in detail in this appendix because it is detailed in sources. Therefore, the reader is referred to an appropriate source for a thorough discussion of scoring procedures. In some cases, the tests that we provide are unpublished, and the scoring norms are based on database of clients whom we have tested over the years. In other cases, the purpose of the test is to provide insight into the client's mode of processing. Therefore, there may be no specific scoring procedure, only the therapist's subjective observation of how the

client performed the task, what strategies he or she used, or what specific behaviors the therapist noticed.

Most of these tests are readily available, and the therapist requires no special credentials to acquire them. Many come from journal articles. They may therefore be used by therapists from a variety of disciplines.

SENSORY SYSTEM

Iconic Memory Task

Brief-duration iconic flashes can be simulated using a standard slide projector. We typically type words on a page, with each word separated from the next by approximately 3 inches. These words form sentences that vary in length between one and five words. The page is copied onto overhead projection plastic using a standard copier. The individual words and sentences are cut from the plastic and placed into slide binders. The slides are then placed into a carousel projector with one blank space between the slots. When the therapist holds down the advance button on the slide projector, the carousel advances to the first slide, then immediately goes on to the following blank space. The length of time the slide is projected is approximately $\frac{1}{3}$ second. The client recalls the slide, and the task continues throughout the entire sequence of slides.

We recommend approximately 40 slides, 10 for each sentence length. The sentences should be written roughly at seventh-grade reading level.

Relative Performance

The average mildly injured client can recall roughly 80% of the three-word sentences correctly. Severely impaired clients seldom recall more than half of the two-word sentences correctly and few, if any, of the three- or four-word sentences. Uninjured college students can recall approximately 75% of the four-word sentences and all of the two- and three-word sentences.

Echoic Memory

The therapist makes up an audiotape of 30 random letters, 30 random numbers, and 30 random nouns. He or she reads these into a tape recorder with a 1-second interval between each. The therapist also makes up 3 × 5 cards with the word *number, letter,* or *word* printed on each. The therapist then plays the tape and stops it at random intervals and points to one of the cards. This signals the client to recall the last instance of whichever item is on the card. The client therefore never knows what he or she will have to recall before the therapist stops the tape and points to one of the cards. The task continues until the client has recalled at least 40 items.

Relative Performance

Mildly head-injured clients recall about two thirds of the items correctly. Severely head-injured clients recall about half of the items. College students miss only one or two items.

ATTENTION/CONCENTRATION

Digit Span

The therapist makes up a list of numbers that range from two to nine digits in length, taking care not to duplicate numbers within any string. Two examples of each string length are required. The therapist reads the numbers at approximately 1 second per number to the client, who recalls them immediately after the last number of each string. The therapist continues until the client misses two strings of the same length in a row.

Backward digit span is the reverse of the forward procedure. The therapist reads digit strings forward in the same manner as in the forward task. The client repeats the string backwards. The therapist continues until the clients misses two strings of equal length in a row.

Relative Performance

Mildly head-injured clients will recall strings of about five plus or minus two digits. Severely head-injured clients will recall strings of about three plus or minus two digits. College students will recall strings of eight plus or minus two digits.

Visual Memory Span

The therapist acquires nine blocks. These are usually available at toy stores or learning resource centers. The blocks should be approximately 1 to 2-inch squares. On one side of each block, the therapist writes a number from 1 to 9. The blocks are laid out in a random array so that the numbers face the examiner and the client cannot see the numbers at all. The therapist then uses the same number strings that were used in the digit span task above. He or she touches the blocks in the order dictated by each number string. The client then copies the order. The task continues until the client misses two sequences of the same length in a row.

The backward version of this task is similar to the backward digit span task. The therapist touches the blocks according to the same digit series used in the backward digit span task above, and the client touches them in reverse order. The task continues until the client misses two strings of the same length.

Relative Performance

Severely head-injured clients can reproduce a sequence of about three plus or minus two blocks for the forward task and the same for the backward task. Mildly head-injured clients correctly reproduce five, plus or minus two for the forward task and four plus or minus two for the backward task. College students get about seven plus or minus two for the forward task and six plus or minus two for the backward task.

REHEARSAL CARD GAMES

These games are described in detail in Chapter 8. Their goal is to assess the client's ability to rehearse novel information and to determine the number of rehearsals necessary to improve recall. The reader is referred to this chapter for a thorough review of these games.

VERBAL MEMORY

Chapter 7 references the Buschke Selective Reminding Task. This is a procedure that involves repeated measurement of the client's recall of a word list. The words are simple nouns that are read at 1-second intervals. The client recalls the words, and when he or she cannot recall any more words, the therapist repeats only those words the client failed to recall. The client again recalls the entire list of words, and the therapist reminds the client of only those words that were omitted. This procedure continues until the client can recall the entire list of 12 words on two successive trials. Buschke (1973) has created an elaborate scoring procedure that measures several aspects of memory. The reader is referred to his article for a description of this procedure. The procedure is quite flexible and works with other types of items (Buschke & Fuld, 1974; Fuld, 1980).

Relative Performance

The average head-injured person takes 8 to 12 study and test trials to learn a list of 12 unrelated nouns. The average college student learns the list in 4 to 6 trials.

The therapist can evaluate certain aspects of the client's recall without elaborate scoring procedures. For example, we usually look for the number of words that are consistently recalled each trial. This is an index of what Buschke called "consistent long-term retrieval." In essence, it is an index of how much information can be readily accessed. We also look for a pattern of recall over the test sequence in which the client simply recalls the words he or she was given as reminders on the previous trial and fails to recall those words he or she correctly recalled on the previous trial. This pattern reflects a tendency to depend on short-term memory. The number of trials needed for attainment of two perfect recalls is also of interest because it indexes learning speed. Delayed recall after a half-hour interval is a measure of long-term retention.

VISUAL MEMORY

The Rey Figure Recall Task is an extension of the Rey Figure Copy Task. This procedure is discussed in detail by Lezak (1983, p. 400). More comprehensive norms are also provided by Kolb and Whishaw (1990, pp. 845–890). The client simply copies the figure; then, after half an hour, he or she attempts to recall the shape. Data for performance on the copy and recall tasks are provided for various age groups by Kolb and Whishaw (1990).

Zoo Picture Task

We have used this task with great success over the years to measure visual memory. The therapist shows the client a picture of a zoo for 15 seconds. After the study interval, the therapist removes the picture and asks the client 5 questions. The client studies the pictures for another 15-second interval, and then the therapist asks 5 more questions. A third trial is also given. After half an hour, the therapist asks the final 10 questions.

Relative Performance

Head-injured clients average two to three correct answers over the three training trials and four to six on the delayed trial. College students average three to four correct answers on the three training trials and seven to nine correct on the delayed trial.

Multiple Encoding Task

This task involves presenting the client with a list of nine words. There are three words in each of three categories: names (Susan, Mary, Jane), planets Mars, Jupiter, Sun), and animals (Shark, Monkey, Jackal). The therapist creates a 3 × 3 array of the words on the page so that there is no obvious semantic grouping. He or she can then color one of the words in each category blue, another red, and another green. A highlighter works well for this purpose. The entire array of words, then, can be encoded according to the spatial position of the words on the page, the color of the words, the first letter of the words, or the semantic grouping to which each word belongs.

The therapist presents the sheet to the client, who studies it for 30 seconds. The client then writes any remembered words on a sheet of plain white paper. The therapist instructs the client that he or she can recall the words in any fashion that makes the words easier to recall. The task is repeated over several study-test sessions until the client can recall all the words correctly. The therapist also asks the client to recall the words from memory after half an hour.

Most uninjured individuals can recall the entire list in two or three study test trials. Most head-injured persons take 5 to 10 trials. It is important to note, however, not just the number of trials the client takes to recall the sheet but the method the client uses to recall the words. For example, if the client uses a color code, this information may be helpful when training him or her to use color groupings in the future to improve recall.

COGNITIVE SKILLS

Intelligence

Several simple and useful tests of intelligence are described in other sources. For example,

Othmer and Othmer (1989, pp. 456–457) report a simple 10-question intelligence test developed by Kent (1946). The test involves asking the client 10 factual questions and scoring his or her response on a 36-point scale.

Brown, Sherbenou, and Johnson (1982) developed a culture-free Test of Nonverbal Intelligence (TONI). The test requires the client to look at a sequence of sample shapes and to find the next logical shape in the sequence. The test does not require any reading, and it is easy to administer. It provides an especially good index of nonverbal intelligence.

Verbal Reasoning

Lezak (1983) summarized Arenberg's (1968) Poison Foods Test, which is a measure of verbal reasoning. The therapist provides the client with a sheet of paper to keep track of the components of several hypothetical meals and the consequences of eating them (person lived or died). The client must listen to the sequence of foods and determine which ones, if any, are poison. Norms for the test are provide in Lezak (1983). The test is relatively simple to administer and provides a clear assessment of the client's verbal reasoning skill.

Relative Performance

The measure of performance is how many of the poison foods the client correctly identifies. We are not aware of any formal norms for this test.

Nonverbal Reasoning

Lezak (1983) described an especially elegant method for assessing nonverbal reasoning using a set of tinker toys. The therapist provides the client with a standard 50-piece tinker toy set and instructs the client to simply make an object from the tinker toys in 5 minutes.

Relative Performance

Lezak (1983) provided a scoring schema. For example, the client's performance is evaluated for characteristics such as whether he or she made a shape, how many pieces were used, number of moving parts, whether the object moved, and so forth. The total score for all the characteristics can be computed.

Concept Learning

The therapist can use a deck of playing cards as a screening test for sequential concept formation skill. The test was originally developed by Talland (1965) and discussed in Lezak (1983). Using two decks of standard playing cards, the therapist arranges the cards into 16 runs of black-black-red-black-red-red sequences. The therapist then allows the client to turn the cards over one at a time and to try to predict the next card in the sequence.

Relative Performance

The measure of performance is how many cards the client uses until he or she can correctly predict three complete runs of cards in a row. This apparently varies with age. Head injury clients, especially those with frontal lobe damage, cannot do the task at all.

Cognitive Flexibility

Getzels and Jackson (1962) described a simple test of divergent thinking skills. The therapist lists five common objects (brick, pencil, paper clip, toothpick, sheet of paper) along with two sample uses for each object. For example, a brick could be used to build a house or used as a paperweight. The client is required to write as many uses for each object as possible. Head-injured clients tend to dwell on a conventional use of the objects. For example, the client might say, "to build a house, to build a walkway, to build a fireplace," and so forth. This illustrates a difficulty with mental switching skill.

Relative Performance

There is no formal scoring procedure for this task, only the observation of the person's response consistency and his or her ability to break set and generate a variety of novel uses of the objects.

RESPONSE SYSTEM

Word Fluency

Kolb and Whishaw (1990) described one simple test of word fluency that simply requires the client to write as many words as he or she can think of in 5 minutes that begin with the letterS. Next, the client writes as many four-letter words that come to mind in 4 minutes that begin with the letter C. The total number of words generated has been shown to correlate with performance on tests of temporal/frontal functioning.

Relative Performance

Sixty words is the cutoff point for normal college students. Learning-disabled clients can generate about 45 words. Left frontal lobectomy patients can generate about 35 words.

Picture copy

Lezak (1983) describes two complex figure copy tasks that have been used for years as measures of complex praxis functions. The Rey figure is a complex shape that the client copies. A scoring scheme is available for both adults and children. Delayed recall at half an hour provides a simple test of visual retention. The Taylor Complex Shape Copy Task (as described in Lezak, 1983) is less commonly used but equally useful for assessing perceptual motor function and visual memory.

Fine Motor Control

Luria (1966) first described similar letter-writing procedures that require the client to write alphabetical letters in repetitive fashion. We propose this simple test to determine the person's ability to write rapidly. The client first writes *mn* in cursive across a piece of plain white paper for

1 minute. He or she then writes *pq* for 1 minute. Last, the client writes *bd* for 1 minutes. The total score is the average number of combinations.

Relative Performance

College students can usually write about 25 to 35 combinations for any letter dyad. Head-injured clients typically average 15 to 20.

Written Communication

We assess writing skill by allowing the client 5 minutes to write a short paragraph concerning his or her vocational interests. The client is encouraged to write as much as possible on this theme in 5 minutes and to write a paragraph in clear English.

Relative Performance

We enter the paragraph verbatim into a word processor and score it with the grammar, punctuation, and style checker. This provides an index of "readability," appropriate use of adjectives and adverbs, fluency, spelling accuracy, and punctuation errors.

REFERENCES

Arenberg, D. (1968). Concept problem solving in young and old adults. *Journal of Gerontology, 23*, 279–282.

Brown, L., Sherbenou, R.J., & Johnson, S.K. (1982). *Test of non-verbal intelligence*. Los Angeles: Western Psychological Services.

Buschke, H. (1973). Selective reminding for analysis of memory and learning. *Journal of Verbal Learning and Verbal Behavior, 12*, 543–550.

Buschke, H., & Fuld, P.A. (1974). Evaluating storage, retention, and retrieval in disordered memory and learning. *Neurology, 11*, 1019–1025.

Fuld, P.A. (1980). Guaranteed stimulus-processing in the evaluation of memory and learning. *Cortex, 16*, 255–272.

Getzels, J.W., & Jackson, P.W. (1962). *Creativity and intelligence*. New York: John Wiley.

Kent, G.H. (1946). *E-G-Y scales*. New York: Williams & Wilkins.

Lezak, M.D. (1983). *Neuropsychological assessment* (2nd ed.). New York: Oxford University Press.

Kolb, B., & Whishaw, I.Q. (1990). *Fundamentals of human neuropsychology*. New York: W.H. Freeman.

Luria, A.R. (1966). *Higher cortical functions in man*. (B. Haigh, Trans.). New York: Basic Books.

Othmer, E., & Othmer, S.C. (1989). *The clinical interview using the DSMIII–R*. Washing, DC: American Psychiatric Press.

Talland, G.A. (1965). *Deranged memory*. New York: Academic Press.

Index

measurement of transfer potential, 67–68
negative transfer, 53, 57
positive transfer, 53, 55
predicting transfer outcome, models of, 55–57
Transfer-surface, 54
Transient ischemic attacks (TIA), 28
Traumatic brain injury (TBI), causes of, 27
Trial-and-error method
concept learning, 161
problem solving training, 148
Two-buffer storage system, iconic memory, 76

U

Understanding, in problem solving, 146

V

Verbal explanation, concept learning training, 163
Verbal labels, in memory, 39
Verbal memory, assessment of, 261
Verbal reasoning, assessment of, 262
Verbal/semantic categories, 158
Verification of behavior, self-monitoring training, 188–189

Vicaration, recovery from brain injury, 48
Videotaping, self-monitoring training, 188
Vigilance
and attention, 84
and recovery from brain injury, 49
Viral encephalitis, and cognitive/memory deficits, 29
Visual Discrimination Conditioner, 86
Visual memory, assessment of, 261–262
Visual/perceptual categories, 158
Vitamins, cognitively nutritious vitamins, 197, 210
Vocabulary, training of, 126
Voice-activated telephones, 242

W

Wernicke-Korsakoff syndrome, and memory, 28
Wernicke's area, 26
Word fluency, assessment of, 263
Word mnemonics, 109–110
ANGER mnemonic, 109–110
CALM mnemonic, 110
LISTEN mnemonic, 110
SOLVE mnemonic, 109
Writing strategy, concept learning training, 163
Written communication, assessment of, 264